S amsara
C ecilia
A llesandra
L uce
D ellaricca
E dwards
D rakke

To order additional copies, please contact us.
BookSurge, LLC
www.booksurge.com
1-866-308-6235
orders@booksurge.com

Scalded
The Making and Undoing of an Extremist

Samadhi Longo-Disse Ph.D. and Teddy Charles

2006

Scalded

Contents

Acknowledgments

The authors would like to acknowledge the following people, without whose help and support this book could not have been written.

Our readers, Alison St. John, Dr. Stephen Cameron, Deborah Ruddell, Zuliya Khawaja, Peter Winn, Stuart Kallen, Norman, Maria Rappay, Adrian Frediani, Alex Sartore, Eleanor Garner, Jean Di Carlo Wagner and Birgit Huck for their wisdom and unfailing direction, Amy Ralston, for her encouragement, Paul Disse for cover design, layout and patience, Linda Di Carlo for her brilliant technical assistance and design on the cover; Mike Schultz and Paul Christopher Disse for their technical support; the spirit of Helen and Frank Longo, who along with Jorg Dauscher, kept us alive and growing, and all the many people who inspired this work, especially those who were a part of this story.

Samsara conlicted

"…I ask you humbly: what is truth? Let me see things as they are, let nothing throw dust in my eyes."
St. Therese, The Little Flower, July 21, 1897, two months before her death.

Prologue
The Scalding

To scald v.t.To burn with or as with hot liquid or steam; to subject to the action of boiling or hot liquid; to heat to a temperature just short of the boiling point; to become scalded; n, a burn caused by hot liquid or steam. The Random House College Dictionary

When I was three, an innocent event, which later led to violence, fanaticism and addiction, stamped my life for the next fifty years.

It was a warm day in early summer when I was standing in front of my family's old black stove, where Mom was cooking meat in a large frying pan filled with oil. As she briefly stepped away, I drew closer. The smells enveloped me like a warm fuzzy sweater. I just *had* to put my finger in and taste this golden bubbling liquid. I was convinced it would melt in my mouth, like thick chocolate from the cake-mixing bowl I loved to lick from my fingers.

The bubbling and hissing had its own language, calling me. As I raised my right hand to dip my finger in the oil, the pan tipped over causing the contents to splatter on the back of my hand, scalding it. I screamed, pulling my hand away.

My wails brought the emergency brigade. Mom ran into the kitchen, yelling at me to get away, quickly applying ointment as she bandaged my hand.

I never forgot the fascination, the smells, the way I was drawn into the experience, and the burning sensation of pain. It was a paradigm for repeated patterns throughout my life.

That same year I was scalded I had my first mystical experience, dooming me to pursue God and religion. At nine, I read stories of saints and martyrs. I was going to be one of them. At age eleven, the heat of my surging hormones fascinated me. In college, this heat became a thrilling and consuming obsession for men and sex.

At twenty-four, I traveled to India pursuing enlightenment. I was like an insect being incinerated by a dazzling fire, not realizing that it would burn me up in a fanaticism that led to violence. This intensity blossomed into the addiction of being a devotee, a fugitive and a high-class prostitute.

I was like any ordinary American woman, raised in a suburb, destined to be a middle class working mother. Like most girls I had dreams of doing something special with my life. This is the story of those dreams.

This is a true story. Names, except for historical figures like Rajneesh, Mother Teresa, etc., have been changed to protect anonymity.

Samsara's Ten Commandments for her First Holy Communion

#1. Suffering is holy: I'll get to heaven by doing it and get goodies along the way.

#2. Don't go against Big People's rules. If I do, I'll get punished.

#3. Look for a saviour. I'm not good enough to save myself from making messes.

#4. I can't think for myself. I must always do what others tell me to do.

#5. Live life for others. My dreams can't possibly work.

#6. Be cozy and comfortable at all costs.

#7. Be poor: poverty is a virtue.

#8. Do all things for everybody's "greater good."

#9. If I'm good I'll get my reward, which will arrive like magic when I'm Big.

#10. Above all, keep the things that make me feel good a secret. If they find out, I'll be punished and go to hell. I shouldn't tell anyone so I can think about them when I want.

Chapter 1
The Arrest

A woman is like a tea bag. You never know how strong she is until she's put in hot water – Eleanor Roosevelt

It started on September 30, 1990, in Rhodes, one of those dazzling islands you see on Greek postcards, with psychedelic colors spilling into your eyes.

It was early afternoon, and the breeze was touching my bronzed skin as I drank ouzo with Katrin on the balcony of her flat. As close friends often do, we had been reminiscing during the last two weeks about the outrageous ways we'd solved the problems of womankind over the years and how cleverly the magic of the Greek sun had thoroughly drowned out the pressures of our work. Germany, where we both lived, was blessedly still far away. We laughed to each other that having young, intense Greek lovers, who fed us sweet lamb and baklava dripping with honey for fourteen long days and nights, also helped. The air smelled of gardenias, intoxicating the memories of space, sky and sands going on forever.

On this particular day in September, my vacation was ending. As I was packing to return to Germany, there was a prickling sensation in my back, which made me jittery. Perhaps, it had to do with having to return to work and beginning the fall season, which would change into winter and long, dark, cold days. Maybe, it was something else. Did I want to go back into the rawness of that work world?

As high-class call girls, Katrin and I worked the "bars" in Germany. But unlike Katrin I was also an exotic dancer. The hooker and stripper in me were separate from my caring for all the men who came my way. Most people didn't know how much I loved it. Loved the attention, the thrill of performing, the power I had over the men who watched me and bought me. And, of course I loved money. This work was also my sacred and covert mission: to save these men from themselves and what I saw as their addictions. Yet, even loving my work, I was worn out.

In September 1985, five years earlier, I had arrived in Germany from Oregon, penniless and shattered, after departing from a religious sex commune where I had been for ten years. I felt somewhat like a nun who leaves her convent and the only world she'd known. Germany gave me a feeling of belonging somewhere and making a new beginning.

Twelve others left the commune with me. Known by the press as the "inner circle" we were four Americans, one South African, three Brits, one Thai and three children. Our leader, an Indian woman, called Sila had been the guru's loudmouth and my idol.

A few days after our departure, I discovered that our teacher Bhagwan Shree Rajneesh had called the FBI and had accused us of salmonella poisoning, wiretapping and arson. I thought Bhagwan made up the charges because he was angry with us for walking out on him, and somebody had to be blamed.

Each of us had been a leader in creating this million-member-multi-national-billion-dollar-corporate commune. Each of us watched it disintegrate. According to Bhagwan and the press, we were also responsible for everything that had gone wrong in and around Oregon.

After arriving in Europe and learning that I was among those accused of wiretapping, I decided that I would remain in Europe for however long it took me to get myself back together, mentally and emotionally and raise enough money to hire a lawyer.

Poverty, however, does not get you an American lawyer worth anything. So, by 1990, I had gotten myself a high paying job in a bar, whose only job requirement was to "be" with men. This job, for all the wonderful money it produced, also produced a lot of pressure. To find relief from the pressure, I went to Rhodes at regular intervals to heal my soul, to be in the sun and sand, to meet my lover and be surrounded by my friends.

Especially Katrin. She was a luscious red head who came from a conventional German middle class background. Her suburban Catholicism was peppered with a lust for every wild adventure as long as it was within a fifty-mile radius. (Greece excepted). We met in the bar, drawn together by our mutual love of those white beaches and men.

"Ah, Theodora," she used to call me, "at least you understand my love affair with Greece. It's not all due to the Greek men, as some of these kids here imagine. But most of it is." Then she laughed her throaty laugh that made her eyes dance. She'd been to university, done the expected office job and became bored and unsatisfied. Hearing about the bars from a friend, she tried it one night and stayed. On her first night, within two hours, she was 600 marks (about $500) richer. She had found her profession. Just like me.

So, here I was on this last day of September, feeling uneasy.

Into my mind floated the words, *I advise you to get a lawyer.*

Jesus! Those were Maya's icy words in the fall of 1989 in her last phone call to me. She was one of the ex-commune twelve and technically my co-defendant.

"I advise you to get a lawyer. I'm not going to say any more," she said abruptly ending the call.

We had been friends, I thought. Then suddenly, this.

What had I done to make her hate me?

Shocked and disturbed for days afterwards, the call continued to bother me.

As I was packing clothes into my suitcase, it was odd that I should remember this phone call. I shook myself, trying to shrug off the incident.

I'll have to save more money when I get back. No more holidays for a while. Look up lawyers and get the wiretap case settled.

I left Rhodes early the next morning.

Katrin hugged me as my boat left the harbor for Piraeus.

I'm hugging her like I'll never see her again. What's the matter with me?

Arriving in Piraeus, I took the train to Athens, and finally a plane from Athens to Germany, arriving in Frankfurt the afternoon of October 1, 1990.

As I was walking across the tarmac, I held my breath. Since I was an American traveling on an acquired British passport in the name of Margaret Bonham, I switched to my British accent and hoped once again to assimilate back into Germany, quietly continuing my life. Every time I went through German immigration however, I got a little more nervous.

Am I going to be arrested today? That's probably why I feel so jittery. But that day, I got through passport control without a problem. The immigration police looked at my passport, looked at me and, as usual remarked, "You look so young, *mein frau.*"

My passport said I was 54.

I was 39. I always tried to make myself look older when I was traveling. I smiled and, as usual, replied, "Thank you so much for the compliment," in my best British accent.

I took the train from Frankfurt to my flat in Baden-Baden, and started to walk up the hill. It was 6:00 P.M. and dark. As I walked, the foreboding returned

It must be because I have to start work tonight and Rudi'll scream at me if I'm late. I've only got four hours to get ready.

I walked in and saw Nina, a petite Filipino stripper, getting ready for work, as I should have been. I had lived with her and her German husband, Johann for the past two years.

She nervously greeted me with, "Hello, *schatzie.* Listen, something strange happened." Her large black eyes widened and her voice went up three decibels.

"We got a call last week from the German *Kriminal Polizei* asking for a Samsara Drakke..."

Suddenly cotton was in my ears and my breathing stopped. A cold current moved up my spine.

"... I told them that we didn't know a Samsara Drakke. They then said she is the American you are living with in your apartment. We told them they must be mistaken, that we had a British lady living here, you weren't due back till October 1st and that they could speak to you then."

No one knows that name but Maya and the others I left with. The FBI must have told Interpol to find me. I have to get everything in order, NOW!

I said to Nina, "Don't worry. I'll take care of the situation. I'm sure we can straighten this out. Sorry they bothered you." I tried to sound normal.

I called the bar to check if the *Polizei* had been there.

"Yes," Adele the bartender said, "last week the *Polizei* came looking for a Frau Drakke. No one at the bar recognized the name."

Why are they asking for Drakke not Bonham?

The *Polizei* were on to me. Walking quickly to my room, I opened the armoire where I hid my old, expired American passport; Samsara's ID's and my old address book in a pouch and threw it under the bed.

Move now. Think later.

Breathing became more difficult.

How could they have found me in Baden-Baden?

My hands were moving faster than my brain.

Do what's absolutely necessary. No time.

I didn't even think about putting the Margaret Bonham passport under the bed.

Should I flee? I can walk out of here and disappear.

I had to decide instantly. I could smell the police.

No. I'm not going to run. I'll deal with this. I can.

After all those years of moving from place to place, saving money, never living normally, always planning my defense, it was over.

There was loud knocking at the front door. The clock said 6:13 P.M. It had been only thirteen minutes. *They must have been waiting for me.*

I went to the door and opened it. There were two men I didn't recognize on the doorstep.

"This is the *Kriminal Polizei.* Are you Samsara Drakke?" One of the men asked me in a very neutral tone of voice.

I didn't answer. Nina and Johann were nowhere in sight. There was just me and the police and the heaviness in the air. My breathing was audible.

"Are you Samsara Drakke, also called Margaret Bonham?" The same man repeated.

Someone had betrayed me.

I answered, "Yes".

They took me in their car.

"Why are you taking me, what is this about? " I asked.

"Were you involved with Rajneesh?"

"Yes."

"Well, that's why we are taking you. We can't tell you the formal charges until tomorrow when you will be brought into Court. The Judge will tell you. We have been told to detain you."

Sitting there, in the back of the police car, my mind went dead.

They brought me to Bühl, a city not far from Baden-Baden. Booking me, they went through my pockets, took away my wallet which had 7,000 marks (about $3,000) in it and my British passport. Then a female guard led me downstairs to a holding cell. No one else was in the cell except me.

"Try and sleep because tomorrow is going to be a long day." She said kindly, locking me in.

I closed my eyes and had a vivid dream. The people I had left the U.S. with were in the dream. Each person's face was clear, as if they were in the cell with me. Diva, Belle, Sarah, Narian, Ruby, Sila, Diana and Maya were gathered around a large, wooden dining room table.

Why are we all here?

Everyone looked worried.

Other people were involved in the wiretapping, why are only these people here?

I said out loud, "Why are we all here?"

Before they had a chance to answer, I woke up and it was early morning. I got up from the cot and rinsed my mouth just as the guard was unlocking the door.

"Come for breakfast."

I ate alone, and then was taken right from breakfast to the booking station in Baden-Baden, wearing the same clothes I was arrested in. The same clothes I had slept in.

Was this how it was going to be? Was this my life now?

Two *Polizei* started fingerprinting me. Showing me the Margaret Bonham passport, they opened it to the photo on the back page, pointing to the stately looking, blond-haired Margaret.

"Is this who you really are or are you Samsara Drakke?"

"I am Samsara Drakke." Tonelessly the words fell out of my mouth.

"You didn't really look 54 anyway." Laughing, they tried to make it light, their voices not incriminating or in any way derogatory. They were actually very kind, seeing how terrified I was.

One officer was smoking a cigarette. He looked at me and asked me, "Do you want one?"

I recognized him – he had come to the bar several times, buying me a drink once in a while. Then one night he decided to go further than holding my hand. Here in this tiny, dark police station his eyes looked at me quizzically, with a touch of sadness. But he said nothing more. There was a faint memory lingering between us of how he had held me that night when he got brave enough to invite me into the rooms at the back of the bar.

A whiff of that night was coming back to me, when the other *Polizei* agent said, "Now your picture for our records. Stand over here."

When they finished booking me, I was taken to the International Court in Karlsrühe.

Outside the courtroom, while I was waiting, a young clerk said, "You need an English-speaking lawyer because all of the charges will have to be read to you in English, and you then will have your rights explained to you in English."

"*All* of the charges?" I must have screamed because the clerk jumped back and reached out to steady me. My hands went numb and my throat constricted in pure panic.

"Do you know of an English-speaking lawyer?"

"No. "

Too fast, too much. I can't deal with this. I don't know how to deal with this. Somebody please help me.

I didn't know till later that as soon as Nina told Johann that the *Polizei* had arrested me, he had been trying to find a lawyer. The only one he knew who spoke English was his tax lawyer.

Johann was from the Mother Teresa helping professionals of the world. I knew he would bodily deliver his tax lawyer, in the hope of trying anything. And there he was at the end of the hall, walking slowly, his round face turning ashen when he saw me. He started walking hurriedly over. My watery eyes focused on him, and I immediately let out a sob that shook the guards next to me. He opened his arms and took me in. I couldn't stop crying.

"Ah, Theodora, Theodora... I try so hard to find dis lawyer for you. All I find is my tax lawyer, Herr Ryder. But he speaks gut English." Johann's tax lawyer, puffing his way behind, was a tall, thin, tidy man, in his late forties, with a nervous twitch.

One of the guards took me firmly and walked me into the Court. Sniveling, but calmer, I assumed that I was going to hear a charge of wiretapping.

The Judge asked me, "What is your name? Are you Samsara Drakke?"

"Yes."

Nothing was said about Margaret Bonham.

The Judge then asked, "You are charged by the United States Government with conspiracy to murder a federal official."

This is wrong. Nobody was murdered. They have the wrong charges...wrong person.

"The second charge is interstate transport of firearms."

Firearms? Ringing started in my ears. My mouth dried up and my legs crumbled. Johann's lawyer stepped forward to support me.

"The third charge is federal wire fraud (wiretapping)."

Like a mechanical doll, I turned to Herr Ryder, mouthing the words: "I am pleading not guilty to these charges." Then my blood started boiling and with deafening hoarseness I cried out: "I did *not* murder anybody and *I have nothing to do with firearms.*"

Herr Ryder turned red. Nobody's supposed to yell in an International Court. "They are just reading you the charges. Once we leave the Court I will explain to you what the procedure is." He wanted me to be quiet and orderly. I was desperate.

All three of us sat down on a bench outside the courtroom. The guards watched me like they were watching an insane person.

The tax lawyer began.

"You will need to get a full time criminal lawyer. There are three Judges in the High Court, who will conduct an evaluation of the charges. They will consider your testimony.

They will make the decision whether or not to extradite you to the United States. It's a long way off until or if you are extradited. I am afraid I cannot help you further because I am only a tax lawyer. I don't know anything about criminal procedures. Good luck to you." I could see that he was afraid to have anything to do with me, as if he were about to drown in dangerous waters. He didn't want to say too much.

Johann was told to leave. He looked sad, bewildered and overwhelmed.

"Call me soon," was all he could say in a broken voice, about to cry.

I was taken back to the prison, where I asked for permission to phone Johann.

"Johann, thank you for your support today, and for finding Herr Ryder. He was very kind. I can't talk much now, but I must find a *criminal* lawyer."

I waited for Johann to say *something*. Finally he said sadly, "I don't know any ozer lawyer. But, I will try. I will try."

Shit… Shit. Shit. Shit. What'll I do now?

I had used up the only phone call I was allowed to make. A guard then took me to a large room with three other women, who were there on drug charges. I was a mess and didn't want to talk to anyone.

I'm a political prisoner, in a German prison, with no lawyer, hunted by my own country. And I had no cigarettes.

The day hadn't ended from the time I left Greece. Somehow it had been 48 hours. Even with a dead mind, I had to organize myself, calm down and figure out what I was going to do step by step.

First find a criminal lawyer. Second have this lawyer call my parents. I don't want to speak to them directly because I don't know how to tell them I'm in a German prison. Dad could have a stroke when he finds out the charges. Thankfully this prison doesn't allow international calls. The lawyer can do it. If Johann can find one. Right now, deal with what's next: my cell.

There was a basin and toilet in the middle of the room,

a curtain around it and five cots with thin gray blankets. A woman was snoring in bed; two others were sitting on the edge of their beds, talking. One was smoking.

I want that cigarette.

My nicotine addiction made me brave.

"Can I have one?" I gestured to the cigarette. She gave it readily, and asked me, "What are you in for?"

"Political." I said, afraid to say more.

"Like espionage?" she asked

A light went on in my brain: they think I'm a spy. Maybe they'll like me.

"Yes." I replied, "*like* espionage."

She was eager to hear more so she gave me a few more cigarettes. Exhausted, I promised to tell her more later.

I couldn't eat the rest of the day. One thought pounded my brain.

Who told them? How did this happen?

I kept ending up with the same sinking conclusion. Maya, the woman I had tried to help in England, had betrayed me. She used what she knew as a bargaining tool in her deal with the U.S. Government.

The only other person who knew my secret identity was Diana, whom I had confided in. But she had sent me a message in 1989 saying that my identity was safe. So, it must have been Maya. Thoroughly exhausted, I sank into a long, dreamless sleep.

The second morning, I was woken up early and led into the exercise yard, where I saw the rest of the prisoners for the first time. Walking down the stairs, one person's face immediately stood out.

I shouted. "DIVA!"

She turned, saw me and motioned for me to come forward in the line. Relieved to see a familiar face, adrenalin started pouring through my body.

"What's going on? Are you here for the same thing?"

"I'm here for conspiracy," she whispered. "Is that what they charged you with?"

"Yes!" I said loudly, incredulous. "But – how? What happened?"

"Well on the 14th or 15th of September, Interpol did a sweep of all of us at once. Narian and I were arrested in Karlsrühe. He was put in the men's prison. I was put here. They went after Sarah in Prague, but she managed to elude them. I think she made her way back to England, where Ruby was arrested. They got Belle in South Africa.

"When they came for you, you weren't in Baden-Baden-."

"For this to have happened," I interrupted, "it had to be somebody who knew where all of us were. The only other person who knew who and where we all were was Maya."

"I know," Diva said, "I agree. Maya must have made a deal with the government to get a lighter sentence on her wiretapping and arson charges."

Diva was a small wiry woman with bright black eyes, whose confident words made her appear larger than she was.

"The arrests were staged with precision," Diva went on. "Agents were sent to four countries and instructed to arrest each of us simultaneously so we couldn't inform each other and escape.

Then I remembered how Maya had invited Narian to her home in London, just prior to inviting me. Of course she must have gotten all the details of his whereabouts. After that, when we met she carefully noted my phone number, my address, where I worked and what I did for a living. She was eager to hear all the details of how I obtained my British identity. She confided in me that she had been considering how to obtain another identity. She asked me how she could do it. Faced with a penalty of 20 years, she probably decided that her money couldn't buy her way out despite all the expert lawyers she hired. The Feds wanted this indictment –and all of us- so badly that they must have made a helluva deal.

What I didn't know then was that, without her testimony, the Feds did not have enough evidence to charge us with conspiracy. They knew that Germany would not extradite on a mere wiretapping charge. A more serious charge was needed for extradition, like murder and transport of illegal weapons. (Sila and Diva had been extradited five years prior on murder charges, served time and released). I had heard that when Diana went back to the States a year before, not enough information was given to the Feds to bring to a Grand Jury. They needed Maya to seal the indictment.

On this second day in prison, I understood a little more but was no closer to finding a lawyer. I had diarrhea and nausea. The smell of food made me want to vomit.

Seeing Diva each morning were moments of sanity. The rest was a nightmare.

On the morning of the third day, I thought about contacting the defense and extradition lawyer Sila used when she was charged with murder and poisoning in 1985. He had even worked for me briefly in 1989 when I had some difficulties in the bar.

Why didn't I think of him right away? I must be in bad shape.

The social worker let me leave a message on his answering machine. That afternoon, I received a message back from him saying that he couldn't be my lawyer as he was still Sila's lawyer on retainer and she was one of my co-defendants. He didn't recommend anyone else.

Shit. Now what?

The next morning, I told Diva, "I still don't have a lawyer."

"Call my lawyer and ask him to recommend somebody. His name is Thomas Burger. And he speaks perfect English."

I called. Then I prayed.

The following day Thomas had a meeting with Diva and he called me into the meeting room to speak to me. Instead of the short, balding, round, jolly fellow I imagined, he turned out to be quite the opposite. Thomas Burger was about six feet tall, pencil thin and very intense, and as I found out later, very witty. At that time, I had no idea of how influential he would become in my life.

He recommended his newly acquired junior partner in the firm, Hanna Weiss.

"She speaks good English," was all he said about her. Later on, I realized why he didn't say anything more. I didn't ask him any questions either. There was only relief that I would finally have a lawyer. Months afterwards, I found out that this was her very first extradition case and possibly her first criminal case.

Hanna Weiss agreed to meet me the following day. I prepared as much as I could. I wanted to give her every last thing. She was going to prove to the world that I was innocent.

I walked into the tiny, sterile meeting room and she said, "Hello, Samsara."

She was smaller than her deep voice and a lot broader. Pale hair, cheeks and hands were what I first noticed. Her face had no lines. Her right hand shook mine.

"Let's get down to the business," she said. Friendly and brusque.

"First, call my parents." I said. I was afraid that the Feds had already contacted them.

"I want you to tell them I'm all right. Tell them where I am. *Don't* tell them the charges. Just say that I am trying to deal with some charges from the federal government. Next, I need you to freeze my bank account in Luxembourg. No one knows about this account except me. Get the money out of Luxembourg so I can pay you. The account was set up by mail under my British identity."

The police had already informed her about Margaret Bonham.

"This is a little irregular," she said, "and I will have to see how to do this. How did you earn the money in this account?" she asked.

"Working in the bars in Baden-Baden and other cities. I wired the money to Luxembourg… and, I will need you to get some of my clothes."

I had been wearing the same clothes ever since I was arrested.

"Now, what are the Germans going to do with me?" My heart was beating very fast.

"I don't know, "she said directly.

She's got to have a solution to this mess. I don't want to be extradited.

"If the Germans don't extradite you," she said as if reading my thoughts, "You will have to stay in Germany forever, never being able to leave its borders. If you were to leave, you would be out of Germany's protection."

I'll never be able to see my parents alive again. If I go back to the U.S., the Feds'll do the same thing to me as they did to Sila as soon as she stepped off the plane, immediately piling on more charges.

"Should I hire an American lawyer?"

"Wait," was all she said.

"The first thing we need to do is find out the details of these charges, and arrange a date with the High Court," Hanna said clearly.

I was worried about money because the Luxembourg account had 20,000 marks (about $10,000) and I didn't know how far that would go. I decided then to concentrate on paying Hanna's legal bills. Who knew how long the process would take in Germany?

"What chance do I have of Germany not extraditing me? I asked.

"I don't know," she said again.

"How long do I have to stay in jail?" I asked, hoping for *some* answer.

"Germany has never granted bail to non-German citizens so you are looking at staying in this jail until the case is decided," Hanna said. This was *not* the answer I wanted but better than *I don't know.*

It was very hard to try and get things done from the prison.

First of all, there was the language barrier and my

German was not great. Secondly, it was not easy to get clothes, cigarettes and English books or make phone calls. Just getting vegetarian food and finding out what I could do each day was a big deal. Then there was the question of whether or not I could even work in the prison.

How am I supposed to prepare my case? I need paper to write on and something to write with. I've got to get clear about my part in all of this. Then she interrupted my thoughts.

"In helping you prepare your case, Frau Drakke, it may be useful for you to tell me what your life was like. From the beginning." She smiled. I expected her to talk about how we were going to deal with the charges.

"It will give some perspective," was all she said.

But time had frozen on October 1st and had still not thawed out. How could I do this? She was asking me to look back.

All the way back.

Chapter 2
The Cecilia Story

How unconditional is God's love? Not very. For if people don't do what they are told, they are shipped to a place of eternal pain.
- Joel Kramer and Diana Alstad, The Guru Papers

"Hanna, this is a very ordinary story. I was born on January 14, 1948 into a very typical family in Yonkers, New York. Mom was thirty-four when she had me. I must have wanted like hell to be born because she had two miscarriages before me and only one fallopian tube left. My parents weren't unusual, drank most of their lives, like most of the neighbors and thought the suburbs were heaven.

"Dad was a passionate, emotional, Northern Italian from Hell's Kitchen, on the lower East Side." As I said this, his face appeared suddenly in front of me in sharp relief: his bald, shiny domed head, black intense eyebrows over-looking black piercing eyes. He was extraordinarily handsome.

"Mom, on the other hand was the opposite. She was cold, tight-lipped and unemotional. I don't remember her crying, laughing out loud or hugging me." The memory of mom, slender and elegantly dressed, became vivid. Her face had small features: tiny eyes, a slightly hooked nose, a perfect rosebud mouth drawn in a perpetually thin line; eyebrows plucked in a stylish arch; tapered fingers adorned with manicured red nail polish. Though she adored Dad, she idolized his father, calling him Pop in the same tone of voice she would have used for god.

Both my grandparents died before I was born, so I only had their legends. They loved each other fiercely. Grandma Luce died of influenza shortly after Dad was born and his sister was three. Grandpa died years later, a famous bootlegger.

He was my inspiration.

"Your Grandpa was a flamboyant character," Dad began the story I was to hear many times. Sunday, the only day he didn't work, was his story-telling day. He would sit in his living room chair with the Sunday newspaper spread out on his lap and a glass of wine on the small table beside him, while I sat opposite him, waiting for him to look at me, holding onto his words.

"After your Grandma died," my father would say, "Pop brought me and my sister to live with your Aunt Cecilia in Fubine. He came to Italy eleven years later to get us both, bringing us back to New York. He had started his speakeasy by then and was the first bootlegger in New York, you know."

I always liked hearing him talk about Grandpa and Grandma. Since I never met them I invented romantic fantasies about them in my imaginary world where I lived most of my days and nights.

"Why didn't you stay in Fubine?" I asked.

"For what? Fubine was a hole in the wall in those days and I grew up there because Pop couldn't raise my sister and me alone. So he had my Aunt Cecilia bring us up. But she didn't have a pot to piss in. I remember going to bed hungry, especially in the winter months. We used to sleep in the barn with the snow falling on our heads… I was so glad he came for me that day. If he hadn't, I think I would have walked back to New York."

"How old were you when he came for you?" I asked eagerly.

"Twelve, and I only spoke Italian when I first came back. They put me in the first grade till I learned English and the kids made fun of me."

I felt sorry for Dad, a little boy without a mother, alone and ridiculed.

"Pop needed my help working, so I had to quit school. I always wanted to be a doctor, you know. But I had to give up my dreams. And that's why it's so important for *you* to have a good education!"

Speaking of education, "You know, Dad, I always wanted to learn Italian. When I hear you and your friends..."

"Don't even talk like that. You are never going to speak anything but English in this house. You are never going to be made fun of, like I was, for not speaking English." he said staring straight ahead.

So, that was that. When Dad made up his mind, he couldn't be budged.

Mom, on the other hand was infinitely budgeable. Her family was East European. She grew up hating being the eldest and raising her brothers and sisters. She wanted a business career.

"Oh, how I cried to go to school," she told me. Her head was poised over the sewing machine as the fine delicate material moved along as if by magic.

"My mother and father had so little money. My father worked hard well into the night and we were so poor my Mom had to put your Aunt and me in a rich lady's house. My poor mother did all the cooking, cleaning and mending, taking care of my four brothers at home while also cleaning other people's houses. Finally, we came back home and I started taking care of your uncles. I had to help out: I had no choice. *You*, on the other hand, *will* go to school and make something of yourself."

"But you did do well in the end." I said knowing about her being the first woman manager at Woolworth's.

"Yes," she agreed, "for a few years. I wanted so badly to keep working, but…"

"But what?"

"I met your father and we got married."

"Why didn't you continue working?"

"In those days, with a child? Are you crazy? Especially you! You were not just a handful, you were an army!"

So, I was responsible for the decline and fall of my mother's empire.

"Tell me more about Dad."

I needed to know. My father was at home so rarely that it made me feel closer to him when my mother talked about him.

"Your father dreamed of being a doctor since he was little, but in the end he had to work with his Daddy. In the 30's they opened up a restaurant. They were so devoted, those two. Grandpa got sick when your father went off to the war, as he was sent to Germany instead of Italy and Germany was so dangerous. I took care of Grandpa during that whole time, while I was working at Woolworth's, and your Grandpa encouraged me to be a manager. He was all for a woman's advancement, that man!

"When your father returned, it was Christmas, 1945 and we were married three weeks later. I still had to look after your Grandpa, so I had to juggle working, taking care of him and your father, *and* that big house. Then Grandpa died and your father was heartbroken."

"Is that why you waited three years to have me?"

"No, we tried to have a baby twice and I had problems each time…"

Was that why I was an only child?

She wouldn't go into the details, but I found out later that she had one of her tubes cauterized and was told she couldn't get pregnant again. Then I came along - unplanned and medically unfeasible. From the beginning, I was determined to make myself heard. I pushed my way out, screaming, and found rejection immediately.

My mother was terrified as soon as I was born. As a wife, it was her duty to have a child but she didn't want one.

"You were an Amazon, alright, a wild terror. You often came home scratched and scraped all over, climbing trees... I could never keep you inside the house."

So, I was a tomboy.

"No matter what I did, I couldn't get you to act like a young lady at all. I tried to dress you up in such pretty clothes and you would pull off your hat, or rip your dress, or get all muddy up to your knees... oh, the things you used to do."

I remembered the frilly clothes my mother made for me, which were so uncomfortable. They were always getting in the way. I was not the "young lady" she wanted, that was for sure. I learned quickly that I added to her depression by my boyish antics. I was her burden not the cherub on the Gerber label.

"Your father was so disappointed that you were not the son that he wanted. From the first time he saw you, he was so sad..."

Oh great. Dad wanted a son and my mother didn't want me at all. Some beginning!

I started banging my head on the back of my crib when I was eight months old. This banging continued throughout my childhood causing a big lump on the back of my head. My Uncle was convinced this head banging caused the blindness in my left eye. He also told me I did it to get attention.

But I quickly found out that no matter how loud I banged, nobody came.

Dad was at work Monday through Saturday. On Sundays he drank and for most of the day generally hid in his garage, trying desperately to have time to himself. He wasn't a flaming drunk, but was foggy and distant. Mom drank in secret every day, hiding her bottles around the house.

She didn't know what to do with me, so I developed a fantasy world, immersing myself in the lives of the Saints and fairy tales of being saved by Prince Charming. I saw myself in the story of the poor girl whose mother died and she had to sell candles in the snow until she, too died of cold. That image stayed with me for many years.

My destiny was to be somewhere between sainthood and skid row. Surely, I was going to freeze to death, unwanted and alone.

Then, I turned three.

That was the year I felt hope. I was going to become someone special. In our neighborhood us kids had a game we played a lot called, 'What Animal are You?' From the first time I played this game and every time thereafter, I was a Phoenix. I don't even know how I knew of such a bird, but was convinced that I was one, rising up from those ashes.

Like the saints going up to heaven to meet Jesus...

My favorite place was the Church down the street from my house, where I went as soon as I could walk. I went there to escape my mother's alcoholic blabber and my loneliness. The Church was dark and peaceful with a kind of presence that I couldn't name or describe. Hidden in the depths of the shadows was this very big Somebody who just listened to me crying. Somebody was there for me every time I went.

I dreaded coming home to my mother who was in a fog. Drinking made her dramatic and hysterical.

"I'M GOING TO TAKE POISON! I'm going to take poison right now, you ungrateful child! If you *ever* do that again, I'm going to beat you with your father's belt! You see this knife?" She held up the large meat cleaver from the kitchen. "I'm going to kill you and myself right now!"

There I was, small and helpless, my feet glued to the floor. I wanted to disappear into the linoleum. Instead I shut my eyes and started crying. She never killed herself. She just walked away.

I went into my bedroom and slammed the door. All my terror turned to anger. I hated her.

Why can't she be the cuddly mommy on TV, with warm hugs to go with the apple pie?

Jumping on my bed, I grabbed Andy, my overstuffed panda who was bigger than me.

"I'm so scared, dear Andy," I breathed into his ear, "I'm all alone and have nobody to take care of me. Will *you* take care of me?"

I asked all my toys to take care of me. Even the piano my father gave me when I turned seven.

However, in addition to my Panda, my favorite friends were the squirrels, birds and fish in the nearby park. I talked to them as much as I talked to Mr. Big in Church. After the birds, squirrels and fish began talking back to me, Mr. Big began answering too.

When that happened, I was in a world where everything was permanently safe, warm, and secure. No fear existed in this place. My animal friends were all there with me and The Presence became my real mother and father.

Later on, in my teens, when I read about the Saints' descriptions of their mystical experiences where they felt completely loved by a being greater than themselves; I knew this was exactly what I felt in the park and in the Church.

This was real living and I wanted more of it. There was nothing better. At seven I had found the secret of life.

Hanna interrupted my story.

"You had *this* realization when you were *seven*? This wasn't just your imagination?"

"By seven I was already in Catholic grammar school and I had heard stories about St. Therese, St. Catherine, St. Frances and many others. The nuns told me Jesus lived in that Church, so I figured that He was Mr. Big."

I loved being there with him because it was comfortable like when you have your best pajamas on, and they feel all toasty like warm marshmallows.

"I don't know why you keep going to that Church all the time." Dad snarled. "Why can't you stay home and take care of your mother?"

He didn't know what was going on at home. My mother often complained to him that she was alone in the house.

"She's always drunk. I can't stay home!" I replied rebelliously.

"SHE'S NOT DRUNK! YOU STAY HOME AND TAKE CARE OF HER, IF YOU KNOW WHAT'S GOOD FOR YOU!" he yelled at the top of his lungs.

That did it. It made me even more determined to run away. And, run away I did. Straight to Church.

Hanna looked a little confused.

"Now, isn't the Church regarded as a kind of sanctuary that Catholics take refuge in, anytime they want? What was so strange about your going to Church?"

"Dad hated the Church ever since they refused to bury his mother in a Catholic cemetery years and years before. Although he disliked the Church intensely, he never tried to stop or prevent me going to Catholic grammar school because it was what my mother wanted. On the other hand, the nuns were teaching me that it was a sin not to go to Church. Therefore, Dad was a sinner. It became my job to save his soul because Mom wasn't going to do it."

Thus my mission in life started to emerge. I was going to save souls, be a doctor (because Dad wanted this so badly and I had to please him since I wasn't a boy) and of course, be a saint (to keep having those delicious mystical experiences).

At eight, my goals in life were decided and I was firmly walking on the path to salvation which included getting as far away from home as I could. Except for a couple of hours a week on Sundays, when I wanted to be close to Dad.

"Come on, go spend time with your mother," he would say, gently pushing me away and usually in the direction of the kitchen or the sewing room where my mother was.

"But, I want to be with *you*." I would resist. I could see his exhaustion showing in the lines in his face.

I'm to blame for making him work so hard. And, for making him drink. If he didn't have to provide for my mother and me he wouldn't have to push himself so much.

"I'm only doing this job to take care of you and your mother," he told me repeatedly. I didn't understand until much later after he left the restaurant, that it was his real love.

Dejectedly I went to "look after my mother" who spent most of her time in another room. It was easier for her to sneak a drink if she were alone.

She loved her sewing and didn't want anybody – especially me - to disturb her. So, out I went.

"What was your mother like during her drinking phases? Were you close to her at all?" Hanna asked.

I watched her making notes in her neat, precise script.

"They weren't drinking *phases*. She drank all the time. But there were quiet times. It wasn't all bad. In the mornings, she was sweet and gentle. I could talk to her then. She used to buy me little presents whether or not I wanted them and she had no memory of how she had been the night before. Throughout the day she would drink. Sometimes she wandered out of the house to the road, babbling to herself, unaware that she was on a public street. By the time I came home from school, she was withdrawn, moody and angry."

"Get the hell out of here. I'm not talking to you." Her speech was thick and rambling.

"You're drunk," I said, standing as far away from her as possible, so that I could quickly escape through the door if it were necessary.

"So what, I'm drunk." She looked at me blankly and continued her rambling, not registering that I knew she was drunk. She tried so hard to hide her drinking from me, as if there was nothing wrong. I knew something was wrong, but since she denied it, I learned not to trust my own perceptions.

"And how did your father react when your mother was drunk all the time?" Hanna inquired.

"Hanna, Dad denied Mom drank."

He came home late, walked into the kitchen for dinner and asked the same question every evening: 'What's the matter with you, darling?'

By that time, Dad had been drinking all day long in the restaurant.

You know good and well what's wrong. She's drunk. At least you can hide it well. She's falling all over herself.

He would then say to my mother, "In the morning you're so sweet, and at night when I come home, you're a viper and I can't talk to you." My dad tried to kiss her and she pushed him away, as she always did.

She knew *he* was drinking and this made her mad, so she drank and got madder. *He* knew *she* was drinking, so he thought he had a right to be angry with her because mothers weren't supposed to drink.

What a mess.

"What was it like for you, growing up with both parents who were alcoholics?" Hanna interjected.

"I was often afraid, walking around on eggshells. I started to live in my made-up world more and more. There was so much tension in that house, I couldn't breathe and developed whooping cough. I stayed in my room as much as possible, pretending to do my homework. When I had to come out for dinner, there were always scenes. During the week, Mom was drunk, so I would eat fast and avoid her. Sunday was different..."

I was nine, sitting at the table, Mom on my left, Dad on my right. The table was religiously set - the places the same - the soup plates filled to overflowing, Italian-style round bread in front of each plate, serving bowls placed in the middle of the table.

This was the first course.

On the stove behind the table were pots of meat, vegetables, potatoes or pasta, ready to be served. On the countertop was the salad. We always had salad as part of our second course. The dessert of cheese and fruit was in the refrigerator, waiting for the end if we ever got there. Sometimes, Dad and I would be talking so passionately that we never got to dessert. This infuriated my mother. I looked forward to these meals because it gave me the only chance to engage my father in intellectual battles, giving me the attention I craved.

It was 1958.

"Dad, we had a discussion in class today about sending more American troops back to Korea."

He cut me off in mid-sentence. This was a big deal in our family, interrupting each other.

"What the hell do you mean? We should go to war again? We just finished that goddamn war - we don't need another one. And what about all this communist propaganda terrorizing people? This is making the country go to hell." Now, he was shouting.

I knew I hit a hot button. Yippee! He's off and running.

"Dad, you didn't let me finish..."

Then came the yelling.

"THIS COUNTRY HAS ENOUGH PROBLEMS. We don't need to go bombing the hell out of somewhere else. We need to look at how we can make more jobs."

The fever pitch in his voice continued rising. I glanced over at my mother who was sitting there clearly wondering how she was going to keep the second course warm.

"Are you finished with the soup?" Mom piped up very timidly between his sentences. She whispered, trying to get her wishes in.

"Are you finished with the soup?" she asked again.

Dad's soup plate was nearly empty. He swooped it up in both hands and drank the bowl dry between pauses. That signaled the beginning of the second course.

My mother immediately sprang up: this was her part in the play. Gathering the bowls, whether I was finished or not, she moved swiftly to set out the next course, while Dad began his next diatribe.

Somewhere between the second and third courses, Mom invariably said, "Would you stop shouting" which would set Dad off shouting more on the current topic, whereupon she withdrew and went silent.

Her revenge would usually come in either burning something on the stove, dropping a plate or souring the fruit.

From this I learned forever more that men were always dominant rageaholics and that a woman's power lay in her silent revenge.

I came out of my reverie to find Hanna looking impatiently at me.

"Our kitchen was a torture chamber where many power struggles got played out." I couldn't do anything right, not intellectually battling with Dad, or doing the chores with Mom. He was an excellent cook and taught my mother. She hated cooking but she would never admit it. Dad criticized her cooking and my lack of it. She got mad. I would then offer to "help," which she regarded as an annoyance, making things worse.

"Go study" she would say. "You must have all those books to read."

That was my cue to leave.

"This must have made you feel rejected and not good enough…" The psychoanalyst in Hanna interrupted.

"Bingo, Hanna," I said rudely. *That was obvious.*

"I retreated into my own fantasy world, where I felt accepted, *wanted.* Sometimes I ran away to the neighborhood park or the vacant lot next to my backyard or the basement *or* the Church. These became MY places where *I* was a star! Here were my animals; trees to climb and "pretend" friends to play with like all those angels and saints who lived in the Church. All my animal friends looked forward to seeing me - and they were never drunk!"

"Were there any other male authority figures, besides your father?"

The way Hanna asked the question made me smile. I knew she was probing for the psychological profile of the "international criminal" so she could figure out how my childhood and my "crimes" were connected.

"Sure," I said. "My uncles influenced me and I looked up to all men then. They were demi-gods who knew better what was wrong with me. So many of them were eager to point out my weaknesses."

My family doctor, Dr. Forsythe, for example, was a dominant force in our household. Not only did he diagnose my mother's post-partum depression, but also my "sleep disorder."

"You're just not tired enough, Cecilia, you need to play more, get yourself real tired and then you'll be able to sleep." he told me in a fatherly way, unable to see beneath the surface of our apparently "normal" family.

I never told him about the "drunk scenes" or that the drinking devastated me because I felt it wouldn't have mattered to him. He was the Family Doctor and I was just a complaining kid. Whatever he said was the solution, and reinforced my belief that whatever the man says is the way it is.

So, I dutifully took the doc's advice and played more. And, slept less. The scenes got worse. The shouting increased. My parents yelled at each other or at me. I got home as late as I possibly could from school to avoid having to deal with them. I didn't know what it was I was coming home to.

I had to make a stand.

"I'm going to be a doctor." I pronounced.

"That's nice, dear," Mom answered in thickly slurred speech.

Not the response I wanted.

"And, I'm going to be a nun." *That'll get 'em.* "A medical missionary."

"A NUN??" *Jackpot!* I could tell that I hit a big nerve because of the screech.

"It sounds like your decision about the nunnery was a reaction to your own anger at your parents," Hanna interjected, "especially at your mother for her drinking. Did you ever *see* your mother drinking, and try to talk to her before she started? Did you tell someone else about it, one of your teachers? Or couldn't you tell someone in your Church and get help if she wouldn't listen to you?"

"No, but I was *compelled* to stop Mom sneaking a drink. I would be working on my homework in the living room and could see her from where I sat opposite the kitchen. She would be in the act of getting one of her jars of liquor from its hiding place in the kitchen cupboard, when I would get up from the sofa and walk towards her, so she could hear me move. She would then turn away from the "hiding place" which she didn't think I knew about, and get pissed off that I stopped her. Then, I would get mad having "caught" her in yet another attempt, proving to me she really *was* an alcoholic, a fact I kept trying to deny. It was all a long time ago, and I never thought of trying to tell anyone outside our family. I was ashamed, and of course it would have been totally disloyal. It was one of the family secrets that none of us ever faced up to. So, instead, I goaded her."

"What convent should I enter, Mom?" I would ask sweetly, knowing she absolutely hated me mentioning this subject.

"We'll talk about *that* when the time comes." She would snap back.

My not becoming an Italian breeder would be equal to being a convict. After that, my parents tiptoed around me; afraid – I think - to jar me too much lest I *really* go for the nun idea.

Besides, as far as I was concerned, I looked the part.

I was ugly.

There was a big gap in my front teeth, so I was fitted with steel wire braces. At ten I wore thick glasses, as one eye was blind and the other nearsighted. My hair was ruined by too many perms and I wore "chubette" clothes. I looked like a large square with legs and screws coming out of my head.

I was also the dreaded "only child." This was a phrase reserved for aliens in the 1950's. I was made fun of by the other kids throughout grammar school. So, I isolated myself, had only one friend, and withdrew further into my daydreams and studies.

At least I'll be smart; and Dad will be proud of me, even if he can't stand to look at me.

Someday, my Frog Prince would come and kiss me and I would be different.

I'm going to be a beautiful nun, like Audrey Hepburn in "The Nun's Story."

Of course, I just ignored the part in the story about the nun *leaving* the convent. I would be the best nun, the best doctor, and *then* they would love me. I would finally be good enough.

At eleven, I got my period and my world changed.

"What is this awful bloody mess?" I asked Mom. She hadn't warned me of what to expect. I think she was embarrassed because she handed me pads and belts and pins, told me to put them on, saying only that the pads would "mop up" the mess.

Some of the kids at school had hinted about a "period" and I thought they said, "pyramid." But whatever it was, the Thing was supposed to make you a Woman. This meant acceptance. So, I announced that I got my "pyramid" and they all laughed at me.

I gave up. My body felt like it was someone else's anyway. I couldn't please anybody *and* I was still ugly, though not totally dumb. Something deep and radical had taken place inside me and I would never be the same again. Whatever I was before was gone forever. Suddenly on fire, I was aching for something I didn't know, feeling surges of energy, which I didn't understand.

"Does this mean I'm finally a woman?" I asked my seventh grade teacher.

"Not yet," she answered vaguely avoiding my eyes, "but it does mean a lot of changes."

She was embarrassed, too, so I figured that whatever this signified, it caused a lot of people to be uncomfortable. Did this period business also happen to nuns?

From some taboo anatomy book I recalled it was supposed to mark the beginning of being a Woman Who Could Have Babies, so I announced it to all my cousins and aunts.

"What are you doing, telling people that you have your period?" Mom confronted me. "You don't go around TELLING people!" She shrilled.

I covered my ears with my hands, trying to block out the sound. Her screaming gave me a headache.

"Why not?" I wanted to know. "Why shouldn't I? I'm a woman now!" Since I thought of myself as a tomboy up to this point, I felt like I metamorphosed from a questionable gender to a factual, proven female.

The momentous step was telling Dad. When I called him there was a very long pause on the phone. He, too, was embarrassed, and muttered, quickly, "Congratulations." Then *he* laughed. My heart broke. I wanted the event –*me*- to be special to him.

Hanna frowned. "Why didn't you feel like a girl? *Most* girls grow up like this."

I remembered scenes over the years with my uncles, aunts and cousins.

"Hanna, I was surrounded by girlie-girls in my Italian-Hungarian-Russian family who wore dainty clothes and the girls in my convent school were frilly, fussy things. But *I* was nothing like them. I didn't even think I *was* a girl."

When I started high school I finally began to make a few friends because the girls were different. I latched onto two quiet ones, like me. I still hid my "unusual" experiences from everybody.

"What kind of "unusual" experiences?" Hanna asked.

"I would study for the tests as if this were the last time I would ever see this material, or pass through this grade - *ever*. I had such a clear and distinct awareness that that moment would never again repeat itself if only I would give all that I had to it."

"Oh, my." Hanna exclaimed, "When did this start?"

"In third grade, and continued all the way through college. I wish I had lived every day that way. Instead, I was always trying to please somebody, and got lost in imagining what the other person wanted of me or thinking I was ugly. I saw the world through a dirty pane of glass, and thought that the dirt was on my side."

What was I good for? Not pretty enough to be anyone's wife; I would have to be a nun. Being a nun was the sure path to being a saint. Sainthood meant acceptance by God. And God wouldn't reject me. There was my salvation.

High school showed me that I was not good enough to be an Einstein, but if I sweated enough, I *could be* that doctor! Even if my grades dipped below 90%...

"And why did your grades have to be above that? Was that some kind of defining line?" Hanna asked.

"You bet. Once my report card had an average of 89%. I was scared all day to go home. All I could think about was how disappointed my father would be with me. Dad loved me *only* for my good grades." *What else was there to love?*

"That night, he came home and was not in his usual raging state. He was withdrawn and irritable."

He must have found out about my grades. My mother must have told him, and he is so disappointed in me that he won't even look at me.

"So, that night, since Dad had come home early, which was rare, I had to kiss my father good night, which meant I had to actually *talk* to him."

I sucked my breath in, and said in a quivering voice, "Are you angry because my report card is 89?"

"What?" He looked at me like I had said he had green hair.

I repeated the question and my voice shook a little less.

Then, he said, as if he were distracted, "No, of course not. Just keep up your grades."

God had spoken. I breathed easily. Once again I was granted absolution for my failures, and it was okay to go on living. I never underestimated that my father and God were equal in their authority over my life.

Year's later I learned that my father had called my uncle, crying on the phone because someone had told my mother he was having an affair at work, which wasn't true. He begged my uncle to reason with her. Apparently, she wouldn't listen.

After that night, she was more cold and distant, but still worried about me incessantly. Years later I saw that her worry *was* her love, but at the time I felt smothered.

In contrast, Dad's absence was as forceful as his presence. During moments at dinner when he noticed me, the intensity of that acknowledgement was like a shocking beam of laser light searing through the skeleton of my emotions. I didn't know how to interpret all that energy coming at me from the void of his being away.

This confusion pushed me into the arms of a god whose love I experienced as caressing and rapturous, not at all scary. It was a turn on.

"By the end of high school, Hanna, I knew that I didn't have the kind of dedication that was necessary for a career in medicine. My interests were way too diversified. And, of course, my hormones were reminding me that sex was just around the corner..."

"Wait, wait!" Hanna broke in, putting up a hand to stop me talking further. "That's enough information for now! We'll talk more the next time we meet." She seemed a little uncertain about going further after I mentioned sex.

So, my life is on hold... same as it is here in this prison.

Chapter 3
Inside "Nuremberg"

Hot air rises. Heaven must be hotter than hell. – *Steven Wright*

I stood up as the meeting finished. Hanna looked pensive.

What's she thinking about?

"Do you need any cigarettes?" There was a nervous tremor in her voice.

"Can you get me some?" I asked gently. "I know, I've asked a lot already."

"Sure. I'll bring some packets next time. What kind?"

"Marlboro."

And she was gone.

What was that about?

I walked slowly back to my cell. *Maybe it looked like this in Nuremberg.*

The atmosphere in Bühl was like in those World War II prison movies: all dark gray stone, cold and cavernous, with echoes of former prisoners and an eerie sense of doom.

God, it feels like whole governments are against me. I have to prove my innocence. But, am I really innocent? I did consider harming him...I thought about it and decided against it. But maybe just 'thinking' about something is considered 'conspiring' when you think about it out loud with somebody else...

Sitting on the tiny cot, memories of my more recent past started coming back.

If I write them down, it'll relieve this pressure in my head.

There were poisonings, violent discussions, bombings and years of brainwashing. These images had a burning quality to them, like fingering still hot ash after a building has been burned down.

Life before the commune was like a smear in my mind, dull against the stark memories of that time, the searing, nagging embers that bore holes in my soul. They wouldn't go away. But, I wanted them to.

Then my sobbing started all over again. Dry, racking sobs.

After a few days of being in prison, my eyes were swollen and my fingernails chewed. The pacing began. Back and forth I shuffled across the ten by nine feet length of the cell, as if walking would change things.

Make a plan. Make a plan. You have to do something. You have to change your life here. DO SOMETHING. At least write it down.

The night of the arrest... the first page started...the last moments of being on the outside, being free; the sharpness of the cold wind beating on my face as I walked towards the flat in Baden-Baden that night...

Dying down, the air inside the cell replaced the wind with a heaviness that was impure and stagnant.

I might be in this prison until extradition, which could be a long time. Then, what? More prison: another German prison? An American prison?

As far as I looked, there was only prison ahead. *They* would get me, innocent or not. Could I bear it?

You know this isn't helping. Stop dwelling on being imprisoned. Collect yourself. Concentrate on freedom. If you think about being here forever, you could end up hanging yourself.

The days moved slowly. Each day had a suffocating "sameness" to it. In this uncharted place, all I knew about myself was gone. There was no longer the desirable call girl stripper who named her price. Instead there was a lonely, scared girl who didn't know exactly what to do or how to go about doing it. That girl needed a map to find her way out of the mess. And she needed to do something with the time.

Apply for work. It'll get you out of this cell.

My work assignment came a few days later. I was sent to the laundry for which I was grateful. The night before I started work, I found my first map.

There were a few English books in the library. One of them was by Winnie Mandela, about her time in prison. Her story opened my eyes to show me that no matter how unbearable the situation, no matter how many people are against you, you can rely on your own strength, deep inside yourself.

There's the first signpost: my own strength. I'll find a way to endure this.

My situation as a cult follower was parallel to her situation as a political dissident. Her actions, like mine, were done to protect and defend her people.

That book was a gift from God to me. Winnie Mandela had done exactly what I wanted to do. Finding herself in an impossible situation she managed to achieve freedom. And, she was also a woman.

She did it.

She got out.

So could I.

Three weeks passed with only Hanna's meetings to break the monotony. Each time she had less and less information for me. And she kept forgetting my cigarettes. I had to keep bumming cigarettes from other people.

By the fourth meeting she still had not told me if she called my parents.

"Did you call my parents yet? What did they say?" Irritation was in my voice.

I had asked the same question each time and she kept promising she would contact them.

"Yes. I got through to them last night."

Her tone was so empty and devoid of emotion that it made me nervous.

"How are they? What did they say?"

"They're fine. They told me to tell you not to worry." She was organizing a big pile of papers in front of her on the table, paying more attention to the papers than to me.

"That's all they *said*? How long did you talk to them?"

She rolled her eyes, as if she couldn't remember, and shrugged.

"Didn't they ask you anything about me?" I raised my voice.

"No," Hanna replied flatly.

"What the hell did you talk about?" I sounded exactly like my father.

"Money," Hanna said, "Stop shouting at me."

We were not making any progress. Damn, we couldn't even talk.

Why can't she just talk to me like one woman to another?

There was silence and she made an excuse to leave.

A week later she managed to get the money out of Luxembourg and open a bank account from which she could pay her fees. I wondered when the High Court would "make their extradition decision," like Johann's tax lawyer told me. Hanna had not said anything about it so far, so I'd have to nag her. Nagging was my specialty.

"What are these Judges like?" I asked impatiently.

"There are three. The main Judge is the moderator. He makes most of the decisions. Then there is also the German Prosecutor who is there because the government requires someone to 'stand for extradition'. They could make a decision about extradition after going over the evidence quite independently, whether or not they ever see you."

God. My fate was in the hands of four unknown bureaucrats who could make a decision about my freedom or further incarceration from a pile of papers and other people's statements.

"But you can say what you want freely to me," Hanna eagerly added, observing my worried look. "If they meet with you, it won't be like a trial. The only recorded material is made by the Judges for their own personal notes to help them make their decisions. Nothing is admissible as evidence for a trial. Relax. Everything is going to be fine."

I wasn't so sure.

By the middle of November, Hanna came into our cramped meeting room dressed in an unbecoming, mismatched brown suit and a white buttoned up shirt. She was sweating.

"I have such exciting news."

"They are not going to extradite me!" I said uncontrollably. My heart was suddenly beating very fast.

"I don't know. But the panel of High Court Judges wants to meet with you."

I started twitching.

"What am I going to say to them? When am I going to see them?"

"This is a great honor, quite unheard of. They don't usually meet with foreign nationals in this kind of case." Hanna said haughtily.

"They want to give you the opportunity to explain your case. This is so extraordinary and unusual, possibly the first time this has happened in the history of the Court."

They actually want to hear my side of the story? This might be the first positive thing that's happened so far. Maybe, this was a step towards not being extradited.

"Exactly how is the hearing going to be conducted? Will they ask me questions?"

"Yes." Hanna said.

"Will they ask me in English?"

"No, there will be an interpreter."

"So, they will ask me questions in German, the interpreter translates and then I answer in English and it will go back through an interpreter to them in German?"

"Yes." She answered in the same monotone.

"Why can't we conduct the hearing in German? I understand enough German."

I was afraid of being misinterpreted.

"By law every foreign national has to have a court appointed interpreter and the information has to be translated into the person's native tongue and they have to reply in their native tongue. This is a German legal requirement." Hanna's voice rose as if making it high pitched gave it authority.

I always have the feeling with her that what she's telling me may not be accurate. Maybe it's because of the awful way she dresses; or that she never looks me in the eye. I shouldn't be so hard on her.

"That's probably better because my German might get things botched up."

She chuckled and agreed. "Yes, your German is really not good enough to understand a legal hearing."

Actually, I was to prove her wrong.

Then, for the first time she looked straight in my eyes.

"You will need to be very serious, forthright and clear on all your details because this hearing is going be crucial. The German High Court will make a decision about extradition largely based on what they see and hear. Tomorrow I am going to have a preliminary meeting with the Judges' secretaries and some other court officials to sign the documents and releases. The signing will be an acknowledgment that you have been formally charged. Meanwhile, do you need anything else?"

"Yes, I need cigarettes. Please pick some up for me because it's really hard to get them here. You never bought them when I asked you the first time."

"Right, okay. What kind do you want?"

Doesn't this woman hear anything I say? I've asked her for Marlboros every single week. Does she even remember what my charges are?

"Hanna, it's the same brand I've asked you for every week. And if you had gotten them, I wouldn't have to still be rationing every cigarette." My voice was grinding. Her eyes narrowed, like I'd punched her.

"I'm sorry that I never seem to do enough for you," she said exhausted.

The bitch in me melted.

"Hanna, do you think there's any possibility that I will be extradited?" I asked softly.

She paused and coughed slightly, "Ah… it's really too early to tell."

She refused to look at me although she knew I was waiting for her to say more and continued to pack her papers into her briefcase in silence.

That was not very reassuring. I expected an extradition lawyer to be much more positive and confident, to give me an explanation of why things had to be this way, and at least lessen some of my fear and anxiety.

It must be my fault. I'm too demanding. I should shut up. She's trying her best.

The tight feeling in my chest didn't go away.

Well, at least I have somebody working for me, which is better than before when I didn't have anybody.

Before she left, she took a book out her briefcase.

"I've brought something for you to read."

I was intrigued. "What is it?"

"It's an American book: *Bonfire of the Vanities.* I think it will make you feel better. It's an encouraging story."

"I've never heard of it. What is it about?"

"Read it," she said. "I think you may like it. It's about a New Yorker, like you, who gets arrested due to a series of mishaps. The American police push him to his limits. It will lift your spirits."

She left in a hurry and I went back to my cell.

Maybe there's something in this book that'll give me some positive direction.

It was another three long weeks before she brought the cigarettes. That, the dread of not knowing what would happen next and reading Bonfire *pushed me to the edge of my sanity.*

My next meeting with Hanna was going to be on Thursday.

On Monday before the meeting, I asked Diva if we could talk about what our lawyers were doing. We made a "date" to sit next to each other that afternoon in arts and crafts.

Talking to Diva was not a simple thing. She looked like a little fairy princess with curly red hair and freckles, an innocent child. Yet, something made me uneasy. I had to be cautious about what I said. Five years ago, when I confided in her about some difficulties I was having with my political research, she immediately told Sila and put me in an embarrassing position. After that there were other instances. We were encouraged to "tell" on each other in the commune. But I had to know what her lawyer was doing so I could get some perspective on Hanna.

In arts and crafts, I was painting a landscape with cheap watercolors and Diva was engaged in knitting some kind of huge, shapeless garment in washed out colors of various shades of grays and browns.

"What is it?" I asked, pointing to the object in her lap, trying to start conversation.

"It's an offering for the war effort," she said lightly.

We were silent for a few moments.

"What is Thomas Burger doing for you?" I came straight to the point.

"He's setting up the format for the hearing and prepping me with questions the Judges may ask. He's giving me a lot of information about how everything works. I'm impressed. He really seems to know what he's doing."

She went on knitting.

"That's great," I replied. "That's not Hanna's style. When I ask her a question, she's vague. I'm afraid extradition is brand new for her. I'm not even sure she knows what she's doing. Is Thomas vague with you?"

"No. Definitely not! Are you worried about Hanna? Do you want me to say something to Thomas about her?

I'm not very loyal, am I? And I don't trust lawyers. I used to be such a trusting person. What's happening to me?

"Yes." I said weakly, "Just mention my concern to Thomas and leave it at that."

I knew that Thomas was the senior lawyer and Hanna was a junior partner. There had to be a big difference in expertise.

Oh, Thomas. Please take charge of this one. This is my life we're talking about.

I finished the book. Hanna didn't tell me that the Feds took the main character to the cleaners. Everything in the story escalated into his worst nightmare. The book ended in him losing the things he valued in his life like his home, job wife and family, though he did come out emotionally stronger in the end.

Why would Hanna give me such a book to read? If this man, with all his money couldn't establish the truth, what chance did I have? Did Hanna want me to fail like this guy did?

On Thursday Hanna walked in nervously in jeans and a T-shirt.

"What the hell were you thinking, giving me that book to read?"

She was used to my outbursts by now, but her face was blank as if she couldn't remember what I was talking about.

"I can't believe that you thought that book would lift my spirits." I continued. "It didn't. Is that what you want for me? Do you want me to slit my throat now in front of you or wait till tomorrow?" I didn't care what I said.

If I have to defend my own case, I'd better start working on it.

"Why Hanna? Why? I'm already without hope. You've hardly given me any information about what I'm up against; who these Judges are or what they're going to ask me. And these Judges are the ones who will be sending me to the same wolves in that book."

Then I cried. The frustration and fear closed in on me like a big flood. Here we were still dancing around each other and I was dealing with people who wanted to put me away for a long time. I had done nothing but have useless conversations with Hanna, who hadn't even discussed any defense tactics, nor asked me preparatory questions. Instead she gave me a depressing novel to read.

"I'm sorry." Hanna said flatly. "I had no idea it would affect you this way."

Poor Hanna. Poor me. What'll we do now? She hasn't been able to help me at all. I should've realized that when she couldn't even remember a simple thing like the cigarettes.

I ended the meeting, went back to my cell and continued writing my account.

Whatever they ask me, at least I'll have the details of what I did clear in my mind.

The next day I received a big basket of fresh fruit and no cigarettes.

By the end of November, my days were beginning to have a certain momentum. I got up in the morning and went to work in the basement where the laundry was. The whole bunch of us down there laughed and told jokes. The smell of fresh clean clothes and the regularity of washing and pressing restored me. There was a comforting rhythm to it. I talked with the German, Yugoslav, Romanian, French and Italian inmates in choppy very poor German. None of the women were bothered by it, as we created our own meaningful way to communicate. The best thing about prison was the camaraderie. There was little time for feeling sorry for myself, thank God.

The days were precisely structured. We got up in the morning at 6:00 A.M. Breakfast was brought to our cells forty minutes later by the food crew. There was always a drink, porridge or cereal. Then we showered and dressed. From 7:00 to 8:00 A.M., we walked around the yard, unless it was snowing hard or pouring rain. Then we weren't allowed out. By 8:15 I was at work, until 11:00 or 11:30 A.M. Then we stopped for lunch.

In the main hallway outside our cells long tables were set out for us. In one long line, we collected plates and silverware, while servers dolled out soup, salad, rice, meat and vegetables.

Being vegetarian, I was allowed extra vegetables instead of the meat. Once our bowls were filled, we sat down and we all started talking at once. I always tried to sit near Diva and the other English-speaking prisoners, Maria and Stephanie. We talked as much as possible at lunchtime, dinnertime, at crafts and music group, but we had to be careful because the guards were everywhere, listening for any bits of information.

Forty-five minutes for lunch then back to our cells for a 15-minute break. Back at work by 1:00 P.M. In the afternoons, we worked till 4:00. After work, we returned to our cells. Dinner was from 5:00 to 6:00 P.M. Then back to our cells again. There was often some activity going on in the evening, like exercise or music group. Sometimes we even saw a video.

After a month, I was given a split shift of doing laundry and cleaning floors. Since I mopped and waxed the corridors where the prisoners were locked up, I got to know who was in what cell. This gave me the opportunity to pause at Maria's cell and chat for a moment. It had to be very brief because the guards were always patrolling.

Maria was Argentinean. She was a stunning beauty who looked like Sophia Loren with a personality like Madonna. In addition to English she spoke four other languages. Her crime was that she left Argentina and promised to carry a present to some friends in Germany. She got to Hanover and was stopped by the Polizei. The present was opened and it was found to contain half a pound of cocaine. Arrested for transporting drugs, she was in prison awaiting trial. Maria had no idea what the package contained. Still devastated by the discovery, she was dealing with her fears, sense of betrayal and at the same time preparing her own defense, all in a foreign language.

That day I turned my head while leaning close to her door, looking quickly to see if any guards were around.

"Did you get any news today about your trial?" I whispered in a voice she could hear through the door.

After a rustle of papers on the other side, the door jiggled slightly. She was pressing her mouth to the cold steel to speak.

"Yes, I finally got a date set," she whispered back.

I started to ask, "When is…" as I heard the guard turn the corner, so I left quickly and continued mopping. That was the way we conversed.

My other friend, Stephanie, was in one of two cells in the basement in a section segregated from all the rest of the prisoners. These cells were specifically kept for "dangerous" criminals. As Stephanie was a member of the Red Army Faction (RAF), a powerful terrorist group in Germany, she was regarded as being dangerous even though they had only used her as a messenger.

When the Berlin wall came down, and the Stazi (the East German secret police) were in danger of being arrested themselves, they made deals with the West German authorities. They negotiated their freedom in exchange for the identities of all of the Red Army faction, whom they had previously protected. After their arrest, the RAF members were incarcerated in different prisons throughout Germany, as the Germans didn't want to house more than one in each prison for reasons of security.

Here was my terribly dangerous terrorist friend, Stephanie, who was a slip of a girl, tiny, thin, blond and very intense. Diva had introduced me to her on the morning round up and we immediately became good friends. Her brilliant smile filled me with warmth. She had kind, compassionate blue eyes and I felt safe being with her. I trusted her. She was simple and honest. She was about the same age as me and to this day, twenty years later, we are still in contact as I am with Maria. Although, I haven't seen either of them since I left the German prison.

We were a unique team. Gathering together in the yard each morning to give each other the news of the day, we regarded ourselves as political prisoners and of course, Stephanie was the "supreme" political prisoner.

Most of the other women were in for immigration and drug charges. Stephanie, Diva and me were called the "espionage" girls. We had a kind of rank within the prison, considered to be the elite by the other inmates and the guards as well. All three of us were very well educated, so we were given a little bit more respect. The prison guards always referred to me as Frau Drakke. They never once referred to any of us as a number or by our last names, the way they do in American prisons.

As I got closer to Maria and Stephanie, my relationship with Diva became increasingly uncertain.

I met Diva at the Rajneesh commune in Poona, India in 1978, when she took over my job of scheduling people for their personal growth groups, as I moved on to organize the film and video department. When the commune moved from India to Oregon in 1981, she went right up the ranks and I rarely saw her.

The commune hierarchy consisted of Sila (who was Bhagwan's secretary and confidante on commune matters); Belle who was in charge of everybody else; and Sarah who was in charge of the money. Diva was next in line after Sarah. I was a peon.

After we left the commune, Diva, Kiku (the medical unit director) and Sila, were named in the attempted murder of one of the commune's doctors, and incarcerated in an American prison in 1986. When Sila and Diva returned to Germany after they were released a year later, I lived with them, along with Sarah and her boyfriend, Narian, who was later arrested with us in Baden-Baden. They were my only friends and I needed the support of people who knew what I was going through.

Diva was Sila's shadow: wherever Sila went and whatever she did, Diva was right there with her. Diva and Narian got together a short time before she moved in and this made me uncomfortable, but I hid it. They split up several months prior to the arrests and both found new relationships. Diva's new German boyfriend became her husband.

She often snubbed me during the time we lived together in Baden-Baden and I felt hurt. We spoke very little, but I found myself trying to please her, as if I were afraid if she didn't like me I'd be thrown out of the house. It didn't work. Gradually Narian and Sarah cut off contact with me as well. Although we were living in the same house, they barely spoke to me, communicating by notes they would leave on the kitchen table. It was very painful for me, as I wanted them to be my family, and saw myself running after them, trying to cling to them, even as they rejected me.

Eventually, I discovered that they resented me for making money and not putting it towards Sila's legal fees to fight new charges added after she arrived in the U.S. They wanted to have a common bank account and I didn't. I was making money to hire my own lawyer, so I could get free of my charges. After Sila moved back in, I couldn't take the ostracizing any more. The press was as eager to photograph Sila, as she was to have them. But I couldn't risk them photographing me, as I was living there under an assumed identity. I decided to move out.

When I saw Diva unexpectedly on the second day in prison, none of the past between us mattered. I saw a human being who could help me. Survival took precedence. I became dependent on her and her lawyer. My lawyer was connected with her lawyer and the case was all connected anyway as she was one of my co-defendants.

In addition to my frantic and fragile state of mind, I was forced to be dependent on this woman around whom I felt insecure. She was the only link to my past who could testify on my behalf. But the Feds wanted to lay other charges on her. Salmonella was found in several public places in The Dalles, Oregon in 1984-5 and rumors circulated that the Feds were eager to charge us with criminal intent.

Diva had just married a German, and Germany does not

extradite its citizens. Therefore she had a very good chance of not being extradited.

I, on the other hand, was completely alone, except for Katrin and Johann, and felt that Diva really didn't want to be bothered with me, like I was some kind of burden to her.

I was much closer to Maria and Stephanie. They had no agenda with me and became my friends because we shared so much over the next few difficult months together. We had a very deep connection that none of us understood at the time.

Thinking of them brought me tender, warm feelings that helped keep me sane and somewhat balanced.

As the days went on, I came to realize that there were other people around who supported me. The guards were on my side. They, and particularly the warden took a very great interest in my case. He later wrote a long letter of recommendation to the Judges.

Christmas was approaching, and the atmosphere in the prison changed. It became warm, as the lights went up, and small decorations appeared. We began making cards in arts and crafts and little gifts to give one another, like you do in a family. The Germans wanted their prisoners to get back to their families and integrated into society as fast as possible.

By December 24th, our second floor was like a living room with a large tree and homemade food and presents, all brought by several volunteer groups from the community. They spent Christmas Eve and Christmas Day with us. I cried much of those two days, partly from overwhelm and partly from disbelief at the kindness I was being shown.

By January I was in a much better state of mind, no longer feeling the schizophrenic terror of October and knowing that I didn't want to "rat" on other people.

Extraditing me was a sticky issue. If they decided in favor of not extraditing me, I would have to remain in Germany for the rest of my life under German legal protection. Once I stepped out of Germany's borders, I would no longer be protected, and could be arrested and extradited immediately. It would mean living a life in fear. And, if I remained in Germany, I would never see my seventy year-old parents again as they were too old to travel. Even though I didn't want to be extradited, if I were not, I'd be separated from the people I loved, forever. That would be unbearable.

I can't think of that now. Focus on what the Judges will ask.

"Working" with Hanna to prepare the case was an exaggeration. I wrote and organized all details. She simply filed the paperwork.

The days dragged on. Narian, Diva and I were to have separate hearings. The Judges would then decide if and who would be allowed bail. It would take time to decide about extradition in each case. Hanna already told me that Germany had never granted a non-German bail. But plenty of people, including Sila and Diva before me had been extradited. In any case, this hearing was going to be historic.

A couple of days before my hearing, a lawyer from the Court brought the paperwork for me to sign, acknowledging my charges. He surprised me by saying how strongly he felt that the American Government was manipulating this case similar to the way it did with Sila's case in 1985. That case had caused a stir in the German press and angered both lawyers and politicians all over the country, primarily because the Americans tried to push their agenda on the German Court. They pressured the Court to extradite Sila immediately. When she was taken back to the U.S., the American prosecutors attempted to add more charges. This got the press and German government boiling with rage. The Court was primed for a fight in my case. I had a tiny hope that they might consider giving me bail as a snub to the Feds.

The American Federal prosecutor meanwhile did not want me to be out on bail as he was convinced I was going to flee. After all, they saw my departure from the commune in 1985 as "fleeing" whereas I saw it like a nun leaving her community.

The Feds argued that it would be a crime against humanity to release us on bail. My job was to convince the German High Court that I hadn't fled anything in 1985. In my mind, I had never done anything illegal. I left the commune voluntarily and traveled to Germany because I was given a free ticket there and had nowhere else to go.

On the day of the hearing I woke up with a nervous stomach and a lot of determination. Outside the window, the leaden sky mirrored the seriousness of my mood.

Getting out of the prison van, the courthouse looked like a Gothic castle. Walking into the courtroom with its dark brown wooden paneling and high, beamed ceilings, I got goose bumps. The three Judges were already seated on a platform above me. Behind them were tall windows and below, the floors were highly polished, reflecting the painting of a medieval church above.

This is like a scene from that Nuremberg movie.

Hanna was sitting in the middle of the courtroom looking nervous.

Oh, can't she look just a little more capable? Like in charge or something?

Wearing one of her many shapeless suits, of an indeterminate black and brown shade, her skin was paler than usual. Seeing me, she wiped her hands on her skirt. On her right was an interpreter trying to hide a yawn, to her left, the prosecutor, Professor Kittlemann was breathing loudly.

My first hearing. The shape of my life will change forever.

The Judge in the center chair cleared his throat.

"Frau Drakke, I am Dr. Brendt."

The main guy. I'll have to concentrate on him.

Looking like he was seven or eight feet tall behind the platform, his dark hair and penetrating eyes were lustrous. I was to discover that he was brilliant, inventive and persuasive, asking insightful questions that would dominate the Court's decisions.

"Tell me a little bit about yourself," he asked in a very non-threatening way.

My shoulders relaxed a little and I had to force myself to breathe.

"I was born and raised in New York," I began and told him a little bit about my background and family.

The Judge sitting to his right appeared stern. Lots of fine lines covered his face. Dr. Röder was conservative, as I could tell by the tie, with squinting eyes, as if he were looking through a microscope, day and night. His hands were delicate, like his facial features. I soon learned that his mannerisms belied his powerful status on the Court and in the local government, influencing public opinion and shaping international policies.

On Dr. Brendt's left was jolly Dr. Bullmann who was to ask practical, down to earth questions. A simple man from a farming family, he was non-threatening.

After I finished my introductory statement, there was a brief silence in the Court. My heart was beating so loudly I thought the prosecutor, who was not far from me, could hear it.

"How did you end up in Germany?" Dr. Brendt asked.

Try to be brief. Concise. He already knows a lot from Sila's extradition.

"I left because the commune changed completely from when I came there as part of the initial twelve in 1981. From a group of people with a spiritual vision of harmony and peace it had become a multi-million dollar business enterprise with warring factions who were vying for control and power. This was not the place I had helped to build.

"By 1985, there was such division that I knew I had to get out to keep my sanity. Fortunately, I had a very good German friend, who was also leaving and suggested I come with him. I didn't know where else to go. I didn't want to return to my parent's home because of my confusion and despair. During that last year, the strain was enormous and my health was deteriorating. I was penniless and mentally shattered."

My voice broke. But I stopped myself from crying. I needed

to be strong, look strong and show the Judges that I had a solid perspective on the entire matter. I wanted them to see an individual who had recovered from a bad experience; was certainly not a criminal and could be a fully functioning member of society whom they didn't need to send to prison.

"What I had learned about the American Government through my research for Sila," I continued, "did not make me eager to stay in America. Nor did I have any skills to get a job. When I went to India in 1975 and decided to live in the Ashram of Bhagwan Shree Rajneesh, I was in the middle of finishing my Ph.D. in comparative religion. I abandoned my studies, deciding that what I wanted was to live in the presence of a real live Master, rather than just study it. For ten years I became immersed in communal life, which was like living on another planet. When my friend offered me a ticket, I thought the time in Germany would give me the breathing space I needed, before deciding where to go, what to do and how to get the money to do it. Setting foot in Germany for the first time was a pleasant surprise. It felt like home."

Dr. Brendt was deeply affected by my words. I was hoping that he understood my predicament. Besides, it was the truth. There was no question of fleeing.

"Excuse me but mein Deutsch is nicht sehr gut," I said apologizing for not giving my testimony in German after living here for four years. Everyone laughed. At least I was making some impression.

"How did the indictments come about?" Dr. Brendt asked gently.

Heat started rising on my face.

"A commune member named Maya had invited me to London where she lived with her rich lover, Charlize."

The German translator interpreted the word "lover" into the German word freund, which means male lover. Hearing this, I interrupted the translator and corrected him.

"It's not freund, it's freundin."

There was a slight commotion. It was now clear that I understood a lot more German than was initially thought.

"You really mean freundin?" Dr. Röder asked. There was a different reaction because freundin meant a lesbian.

"Yes, I mean freundin."

They stared at me.

"When I went to see Maya in London, I found a woman who was very scared, trying to figure out how to deal with arson and wire-tapping charges.

"She asked me what to do and talked about buying another identity. She wanted to lie low for a while and figure out her best course of action.

"I told her that there was a novel which described in detail how to do this, and it had helped me stay in Europe so I could work. She had been part of my commune family. Now she was in need, confiding in me and seeking a way to handle her fears, Dr. Brendt. I mistakenly thought I was helping a friend to sort herself out. As I see it now, she carefully pried information out of me, like where I was living and under what name, and exactly what I was doing for work. She seemed to be eager for any information about conspiracy, poisonings, arson and wiretapping.

"I believe Maya was so desperate not to be separated from Charlize that she made a deal with the Americans in exchange for a lighter sentence. Part of the deal, I learned, was obtaining information on us and handing it over to the Feds."

This brought me back to the day I was arrested.

Interpol knew exactly who Margaret Bonham was and where she (I) was living. Maya was the only person who could have given them all that information. It was not until I was sitting in my jail cell in Bühl that I understood. My "friend" had invited me to London to betray me. After all, why did she need my friendship? Charlize's money could have hired top legal advice anywhere in the world.

Dr. Bullmann interrupted my thoughts.

"You said you needed the identity to stay in Germany to

work. Why did you want to stay here and what work did you do?"

"My first job was at Berlitz in 1986. I came to Berlitz initially to take a course to improve my German. One day, I met the Director and she offered me a job teaching English. At the time, I thought: what a godsend, because I could work and earn money. I heard that I might have been charged with wire-tapping, so I wrote to some friends in the U.S. who consulted a lawyer on my behalf. His opinion was for me to stay where I was, earn as much money as possible so that I could hire a lawyer to clear up the wire-tapping charge. I was advised not to return to the U.S. then because the environment in Oregon was still very hostile to the commune members and a fair trial would be nearly impossible.

"You see, Dr. Bullmann, Bhagwan stirred up a lot of negative press after we left, describing us as horrible criminals and felons, blaming us for the attempted murder of his doctor and the salmonella poisonings in Oregon. According to him, we had started the wiretapping.

"Bhagwan neglected to mention that the wiretapping operation began because the Oregon State Police advised us to monitor calls as a security measure, after our hotel in Portland was bombed, and turn our information over to the police."

"Why do you think that Rajneesh blamed you?" Dr. Brendt interrupted.

"Because he was angry," I said. "He was enraged that we left the ranch and we left him."

Dr. Brendt made some notes on a pad in front of him.

"But how did you go from Berlitz to the bars? You, with your years of education and background? How did you get started in that kind of work? And why?"

His question brought me back to my first experience as a bar escort.

Standing at the entrance, I pushed open large imposing doors, and stepped into a thick maroon velvet curtain.

Pushing aside the curtain, my nose filled with the smells of champagne, sweat, perfume and after-shave lotion. Slowly, my eyes adjusted to the darkness. Directly in front of me was a semi-circular bar with highly polished wooden bar stools and red velvet plush barstool seat covers. On the left opposite the counter was a small octagonal wooden stage with a royal blue velvet curtain behind it. Tables and chairs were in front. To the right was another luxurious thick maroon velvet curtain.

"I wasn't making enough money on my Berlitz salary to save for an American lawyer, so I knew I had to get a second job. There was an advertisement in the paper for girls to work in a Baden-Baden cabaret as bar damen. Two friends went with me to Club Diana and applied. We thought it only meant we'd sit with people and make conversation. Then we met this friendly woman, who introduced herself as Marianne. I never knew her last name."

Marianne came into my mind clearly. She looked like a female Santa Claus but had the character of a rabid dog. To her we were a rarity: three English-speaking "ladies" who wanted to work in her bar. I thought she genuinely liked us, not seeing the dollar signs in her eyes. English-speaking girls brought more revenue. She explained that all we would have to do was sit with the patrons, talk with them as they bought us drinks called piccolos. Piccolos were low in alcohol and brought us a commission. She had a lot of English speaking clientele, especially Canadians, who preferred to speak English.

"We started work the next night, after I finished at Berlitz. My first guest was a nice German man, who wanted to improve his English. Relieved that all I had to do was sit and talk, I drank three piccolos and made a hundred marks. It was a very easy way to make money. I thought we were special because we were "foreign." Naturally in the beginning I had no idea that these bars had things that were called separeés."

The Judges nodded as if they knew what this term meant.

Bars in Germany meant "strip" bars. That first night in

Club Diana, I saw strip tease for the first time. The dancer was dressed in a long, blue, feathered boa, wrapped around her torso like a Christmas tree decorated with lights. She had black fishnet stockings, blue rhinestone stiletto heels, platinum hair and a foot of makeup. As I sat down on the bar stool, she began to dance and Marianne invited us to watch. Loud, garish music started playing and the stripper stood there bending her knees, stiffly gyrating her hips. She quickly untwined the blue boa. It fell to the floor; she stiffly curtsied and ran off the stage.

This was a strip tease? I can do better than that.

"All I knew that night," I said, "was that I could do this: sell a few drinks, and make at least a hundred marks a night which I would save for my legal bills. The opportunity seemed like a miracle. I couldn't see any other way to earn the money to return to America, hire a lawyer and see my parents again."

Dr. Röder interrupted: "So, tell us what kind of values you were taught as a young girl that you could just step into a strip bar and begin working there?"

Chapter 4
Phoenix

Lord – Give me chastity but not yet. – Saint Augustine

What were my values back then?

"Until I started college, Dr. Röder, there were only two things in my world: academic work and being a good Catholic girl. You see, I had been taught by nuns. When I turned seventeen, all of a sudden, there were MEN!"

And sex.

Laughter broke the stillness and awakened in me familiar surges of excitement. I closed my eyes for a moment as the desire to be held, caressed and adored moved gently like a wave through my body, making the courtroom vanish.

I was seventeen again... Walking on the college campus, the air was dense like thick wool. The coke bottle glasses were shed for contacts. My body had sprouted smooth curves in place of bones and angles that had been there before. The new model was not quite fitting together but produced lots of raw energy.

How do I talk about these warm sensations I feel? I'm so embarrassed.

I met Mundi after registering for pre-med chemistry. I became aware of someone openly staring at me a few feet away.

He can't be looking at me. I'm a fat ugly frump.

Turning around to see if there was anyone else there, my pace slowed. I couldn't resist a quick glance at his face.

What does he want? He's teasing me...

Hot brown eyes met mine, above a full mouth and sharp angular cheekbones in a long, narrow face. His pose was casually elegant. He sauntered rather than walked, wearing a dark blue woven shirt tucked into tight, faded jeans and badly worn tennis shoes.

"Are you taking calculus with that dumb Walker fellow?"

Wow. He's pretty direct.

I was fumbling with what to reply while this terribly superior sophomore was dazzling me, just by looking at me as a woman.

In the next few weeks, he advanced quickly from questions about calculus to taking me to the homecoming football game and kissing me. While I was freezing in the football stands, hot liquid started filling the pit of my stomach.

"You taste delicious," he said into my ear. I was already clutching him hard.

This was like those ecstatic times in church, when as a child I had escaped to that place full of gentleness, peace, warmth and excitement.

Kissing him back. I didn't care who saw me, or what else was going on. Football and hundreds of people surrounded me and I only wanted to keep kissing him.

His lips were squishy - not at all like the TV kisses from lips I thought I would feel. But that didn't matter. Only, kissing and melting into that feeling mattered.

My breathing was racing. I was a little girl, again, back in the church.

So, kissing must be holy because it's just like when I was praying so hard I stopped breathing. It can't be a sin then. OK. What next?

Mundi was all for it.

Night was our friend and the research library became our hideout. Working hard on my pre-med program during the day, I met him on the second floor behind the pre-Columbian artifacts. We would make out on the rough, scratchy carpet with the smell of dust in my nose.

Everything was fine until he touched my breast.

"Hey...that's too far." It felt like being stung by a bee.

"What? Touching?" He pulled me close again and nuzzled my neck.

"You can touch my hand, my shoulder, my face... but, not below my neck."

I want him to touch me more than anything. But the nuns had told me that a woman's private parts were reserved for marriage. How can this be wrong when it feels so good, God damnit? .

Fourteen years of church rules aren't helping me one bit now when I really need it. Well, this is a new ballgame with new rules...and I better make my own soon.

Dr. Röder coughed.

"Er, you see, sir, I wanted to learn everything there was about relationships. Since my childhood was so sheltered, I hardly had any opportunity for them. My fellow students taught me more about being human and the complexity of relating and communicating than any book. The more I shared of myself with them, the deeper I *wanted* to reveal myself and explore those depths. I was like a mountain climber eager to go on to the next challenge.

"The next challenge was having sex and dealing with my church conditioning that said sex outside of marriage merited the fires of hell. But the thrills I felt while being with my boyfriend were so compelling I became willing to gamble. The everlasting fires of this so-called hell I was taught seemed a small price to pay for the exquisite glory I imagined. How could I judge a situation - any situation - if I had not tried it out first? I began to understand that the first rule to live by was to try something at least once -as long as it did not appear to cause bodily harm. That way, I would know from first hand examination if it were valuable. Then, I could make an informed decision."

Decisions. Mundi...

My first sexual experience was an experiment.

I put Mundi's hand on my breast and kissed him. He didn't let go. There was fire in my belly and all I wanted was to keep going.

That night changed me.

"Dr. Röder, The more I pursued relationships the more conflicts arose between what I had been taught, and newly discovered feelings. Perhaps the fathers of the church made their laws governing sexual conduct because these feelings were too powerful to handle, and challenged the authority of the church.

But that's getting ahead of my story."

Dr. Brendt, however, wanted to pursue this line of thought. "Was your understanding of power and authority informed by these experiences?"

"My basic approach to men, whether they were brothers, friends, priests or lovers was submissive. This is what I was taught by my family and religion."

Dad was first, family second, Mundi, third.

Mundi was a good Italian Catholic who wanted to get engaged. He figured that would give us license to go further. I was *supposed* to agree, want to get married as soon as possible and submit to my husband. This was 1967 after all and I was still a good Catholic girl.

But, I was only just getting started in my studies on men. Not only did I not want to be engaged to anyone, conflicts about being a nun burned a hole in my conscience.

"You know, Mundi, I'm going to join a convent when I graduate."

"Yeah, right! When did you decide that? You wouldn't last two minutes in one," he said.

"Schmuck!"

I hit him playfully on the arm and quickly walked away so he wouldn't see that what he'd said touched a raw nerve.

How would I ever be a celibate nun when I craved a man's body? I wanted to be dominated by a man, to submit to his arms, his embrace, his power. But how could I feel like this? Me, a modern, liberated woman, who burned her bra, declaring economic independence? Still loyal to a church that said sex was evil?

I needed a break to think things through.

"Mundi, let's try not seeing each other for a couple of days till I sort this out in my head."

Mundi knowing better not to argue with me swallowed his hurt. Since I was insistent, he was prepared to wait for the prize of my body.

Two days stretched into a week.

Then David appeared. I hadn't seen him for over a year after he split up with one of the girls in my senior class. An R.O.T.C. man in his senior year, he was very tall and muscular, who looked older than twenty-three. I ran into him as I crossed the campus on the way to my biology lab.

"I remember you," he said. "You were in the same high school class as my ex-girlfriend, Evelyn."

His blue-green eyes and thick blond lashes immediately captivated me.

"Huh, yes," my heart started pounding.

Oh, no, this can't be happening to me. Again.

Three months later, I had an A in Biology, B+ in Chemistry, Mundi was still on hold and I had been seeing David who had just invited me to his apartment.

Up to now, he had been kissing me with more enthusiasm than Mundi could possibly produce, even if he put on thirty pounds.

Shaking with anticipation and barely repressed passion, I rang the bell outside his apartment and waited for David to answer.

My feet carried me through the door and my eyes hardly

noticed the dark, narrow cluttered hallway. Gently, he took me in his arms, slowly led me to his couch and told me to watch TV and just ignore him. Then, he placed his hand on my stomach and gradually moved it downward, in small circular movements. There were no thoughts. I just obeyed. It was thrilling. There was an old romantic black and white 50's film on the screen and I knew something extraordinary was about to happen to me.

It did. Very quickly there was a throbbing in my genitals followed by a small burst, and a flood in my veins.

"What was THAT?" I whispered.

Warm waves spread through me like I'd walked out of the cold and plunged into a warm Jacuzzi.

"You had an orgasm." He laughed.

"WHAT?"

Shit. I've done it. A mortal sin. But, how could this be a sin?

David got up from the couch, walked across the room to a desk, opened the top drawer and took something out which he hid in the palm of his hand. He looked a little sheepish and unusually shy.

"My love," he said in a very sultry tone, "I feel as if I've known you forever, and I've been thinking a lot the past few weeks that you're the woman I want to be with. Will you take this ring and marry me?"

At least I'm not frigid. But, Jesus! What'll I do about this? I'm not ready to get married.

Secretly delighted that I was finally given the seal of approval as a real woman, I was also scared.

"David, this is so sudden. It's way too soon..."

"Shush, just take it and think about what I said," he pressed the ring into my hand. No one had ever given me a diamond ring before. But then, I'd never had an orgasm before either.

This time Dr. Brendt coughed.

"We are still trying to clarify what influenced you to give up your previous way of life, as a committed Catholic starting college, with good grades. There seems to be some sort of breakdown in your morality system. No?"

"No... I mean, yes. I was grappling with a new understanding of morality. The old Catholic order in which I had formed my goals had holes in it."

I don't want to lose them. I'd better talk fast and explain carefully because I'm treading on dangerous ground. Challenging morality systems when you are considered a criminal does not look good on your court resume.

"You see, Dr. Brendt, when I started college, a whole new world opened up for me. Conflicts arose between my new feelings and my traditional Catholic upbringing. As a young woman relating to men, I was confronted by the theological categories of right and wrong, which existed in my mind. However, the elation of being adored was difficult to dismiss, along with the desire to be touched and held, like a child longing for her mother to comfort her. My own childhood lacked this warmth, this comfort of knowing that another human being yearned to be with me. So, when I started to experience this warmth through my newfound intimacy with men, I was desperate to hold onto it, at any cost - even the cost of my own eternal soul. I found an oasis in the desert after wandering around thirsty and yearning for fulfillment. As soon as I felt acceptance and appreciation, my thirst was quenched. Sex became an acknowledgment of that acceptance. I felt valued for what I was: a *female.* Up till now, I'd never had this recognition of my womanhood. I did not want to give up this precious experience for anything. In fact, I longed for more."

These words sound so shallow. How could I explain this turmoil? It was then in the flower power 60's that I got hooked on sex. How could I convey this kind of splendor to German Judges here in this courtroom?

Sex dominated me.

The force of its power pulled me out of the conventional framework of classroom and model citizen activities into a world that started to answer my real questions.

Why am I here on this earth? It must be to thrill my senses into something more than the ordinary... something beyond my knowledge of myself.

And what purpose does my life have? To melt in my lover's arms, so my senses begin overflowing and I expand into everything.

And why does this fire start inside my belly when I am touched? Because I need this other person to ignite all that is waiting to be born inside of me. I am like half a magnet, radiating, pulsating till the other half engages it... it's an unbearable attraction.

Is my reaction anything more than my hormones? Am I no better than an ordinary machine with a merely mechanical response?

I didn't know. But, to *find out* became my central mission. The only map in this search was what I experienced as a child on my knees - in prayer.

"Dr. Brendt, I hope I can give you a glimpse into what it was like by describing what happened in the relationships that changed my thinking and seeing. Previously I saw the world in strict lines of black and white. As a good citizen, I followed what society and church told me were correct. After my first experiences in the highly charged social arena of university, however, I realized that morality is formed by fear of the power unleashed in people's drives, yearnings and desires..."

"Is morality formed only by fear, in your opinion? Can you give us a concrete example of what you are talking about?"

I knew that I could, but would they be able to understand it?

"I can try..."

The concrete example was Joe.

He followed David –whom I couldn't bring myself to marry- six months later. Joe introduced me to a steamier sex than I had before. Rage at his demands that I ached to fulfill and violent anger at his self-assurance, drove me into screaming fits when we didn't have sex.

The words, 'I can't before marriage' were ridiculous now. Sex salted my life: the raunchier, the better. Before Joe, intercourse outside of marriage was wrong only because the church told me it was. Now I knew that a church dominated by fear and power politics made sex wrong.

When Joe came into my life everything and everybody took on a luminescent quality. It was as if I had moved to another dimension.

The smell of his sweat started my skin burning. I looked at the black chest hairs pushing through his T-shirt and I wanted them brushing my thighs.

Medicine, convents and preparing for sainthood had never made me feel this way.

Joe and I went to Mexico on a university project, and during that time we dove into each other's skin. Standing next to him, my pulse raced and my skin shimmered in the heat of the Mexican afternoon. I was vibrating from the moment I opened my eyes before dawn until I went to bed long after dark. Sleep was uninteresting. On my breaks, I wrote poetry that poured out of my fingers. My bronzed body radiated a magnetic heat. People looked up at me when I walked into a room. You could plug a lamp into me and light up New York.

No question about it. Balance was boring.

"In one of my relationships, Dr. Brendt, I felt as though I entered a dimension of myself where the writer, the artist, the poet had all been hiding and then emerged. It was one of the most creative periods of my life."

Back in The Bronx, after Mexico, I skimmed across the sea of campus life with buoyancy that broke barriers in people's minds and dazzled my professors. My mind expanded and I tried to understand what was happening to me, scientifically, psychologically and spiritually.

I was in love.

This state was where I wanted to live. What else could there be?

Manufacturing mortal sins with every orgasm, my sorry soul visited the confessional weekly, without fail. Fear of hell still kept me Catholic.

"Bless me Father, for I have sinned."

Again? I could hear the priest's thoughts. "Do you want to stop?" he asked.

I said "yes" and meant no.

Father could have asked me if I wanted to die, it would have been the same answer.

"I went to church weekly, Dr. Brendt, in order to seek counsel about the direction my life was going. Instead of direction, I received penance of a few Hail Marys, which I tried to do sincerely. But, my penance was mechanical and gave me no sense that what I was doing with my lover was wrong. Instead, sex gave intensity and meaning to my overly scheduled life. I certainly wouldn't stop. I was coming alive in a way I had not dreamed of before. How could I land in hell, when what was happening to me was more like the mystical experiences I was familiar with from childhood which drew me *closer* to God... just not to the Church..."

And no way was I giving them up for Thomas Aquinas' theology.

Joe Glukowski was the perfect catalyst for advanced work in both sex and mysticism. Straight from the Lower East Side, he was a tall, athletic, rowing champion, in his junior year of anthropology. The right combination to pull me out of my ivory tower and into street life, he introduced me to the world of the conservative right and redneck sports.

I brought him into the leftwing liberal world of mystery and wonder.

We fit so well together... except for the fact that I kept missing my periods.

"Don't worry," he told me, "if you get pregnant, I'll pay for an abortion."

"Joe! I'm Catholic! I can't have an abortion!"

"To hell you're Catholic! You screw all day and then go to mass – how does that make you Catholic? You're a hypocrite!"

I hated to be told the plain truth but that's what he was telling me. Besides the sex, his direct honesty fascinated me. People I grew up with told half-truths.

Eventually my period came, which meant I could seduce him all over again.

It was this power to make a man vulnerable under my fingers that I began to crave. The more I seduced him, the more he wanted me, and the more power I had over him. I seduced Joe. I seduced my teachers into giving me a better grade. I even seduced my roommates into doing things for me by a look or a smile. Seduction brought me everything I wanted... everything but serenity.

The Judges were fidgeting.

"Ah-hem," I cleared my throat. "I was confronting the issues of power and control, fear and morality. Through relationship I was powerful in manipulating men into doing what I wanted. Yet, was what I wanted moral? The Church told me that anything sexual was amoral; yet, it was precisely in sex that I felt creative, responsive and compassionate. Weren't these the same traits in the great artists and thinkers of all times? Were they all immoral?

"Before this, right and wrong was based on medieval theologians' prediction of going to heaven or hell and whether or not the Church would condemn me. But, in sex I found something new, and strangely enough it was born out of the very thing the church condemned. My soul was on one path, my body on another and my conscience was stuck."

Stuck. It's like I was being buried in the sand up to my neck on a beach. I knew I had to talk about this issue of sex and sin with someone other than Joe because I couldn't think clearly around him.

"I came to a crossroads." I said to the Judges. " I couldn't keep on being the good Catholic on the outside, waiting for these experiences to pass before going into a nunnery, when on the inside I felt more like Mary Magdalene."

Back then I wasn't sure if I wanted medicine as a career. There were no answers to life and death in medicine, only techniques and pills to deal with the pain. I had to have answers to life; not spend my time memorizing fascia. And, I wanted to play, have fun, and be adored. I wanted the childhood I had missed. I was both St. Therese and Magdalene together, where before I had just been the nun.

I was on a fence: in or out of the Church?

"To help me make this decision," I continued, "I went to have a serious talk with one of the Jesuits, whom I thought would have a broader perspective of the Church as well as an understanding of human longings and desires. Jesuits were well known for these views." The Judges smiled back wryly.

"I met Carter Dellaricca, S.J. when I took sophomore philosophy and he was a philosophy graduate student, studying for the priesthood. He tutored me in Hegel and directed the music at Mass, where I played the guitar.

That year we became friends."

Fifteen months into my relationship with Joe, as the turmoil increased, Carter became my confidante.

It was a habit for us to stay behind after Mass and talk.

"Carter, I don't know how to deal with the Church's views on birth control, pre-marital sex and abortion. What about the girl who finds herself pregnant after just one moment of passion? Why should another unwanted child pay for the mishap? Or the college student who wants to express her love to her future husband, and can't afford to get married because they'll both lose their loans? Why can't birth control be permitted, which used wisely helps avoid abortions."

I'm really talking about myself, Carter, but I can't say that.

Carter pondered the moral dilemma as though he were trying to give me the best possible reply. He took the time to consider every angle. I just ran my mouth off without thinking.

"This is a big quandary, my dear. To talk about it properly we need to look at the historical context of these issues and why they became problems for the church..." he said.

I watched him unconsciously pulling at his chin covered with fine stubble. He always reminded me of Al Pacino... and he took too long to answer, which made me impatient.

"I know why they became problems - because the Church has been afraid to deal openly with sex and women!"

That stopped him.

I didn't care what they did in 1890; I wanted to do what

I wanted. I only needed theological justification, which I thought I could pressure Carter into giving me. I was like that Phoenix, the animal I identified with as a child who could be anything she wanted. Indestructible, I was a newly transformed Amazon, emerging from the ashes of my suburban heap: an ugly duckling, President of the sophomore class. I fed on the pleasure of power over people and the attention I craved.

"Now, listen," Carter began, "It's not as simple as whether or not the Church has been adequately prepared to deal with the issue of sex, or whether women should be seen in a more liberated and just position. Moral issues, such as sex before marriage, have been debated since the Council of Trent. The role of women has been discussed since St. Paul revolutionized their place in the first century. We are dealing with centuries of disagreement... "

I couldn't *not* break in.

"Carter, it's time for individuals who are mature and rational, with a more developed understanding of how people relate to each other, to decide their own boundaries. Human beings are capable of determining their own values in each situation as it arises. And this determination may supercede any code of ethical behavior laid down by celibates in the middle ages."

I knew this would get him.

"The codes of ethical standards of morality were not decided only by priests!"

"But, the Pope has always had the final say. And, he's a celibate!"

"Stop talking about celibates as if they had a disease!"

"Well, they sure are stuck on one point of view!"

Our talks were passionate, as only two Italians can be, and I discovered with Carter that passion could also exist in the heat of intellectual debate, as well as in bed...

Dr. Bullmann interrupted my thoughts.

"Well, did you come to a clear decision or not?"

Forcing myself back to the present I said, "Well, sir, in

addition to my confusion about the Church, I was facing additional pressure from my father. He made his wishes about my medical career a forceful priority. I could not separate my own views from the voices of the Church *and* my father."

My daddy…He was such a looming figure.

He wanted his daughter to be an heir-production machine with scientific genius: an Italian version of Madame Curie. He was also an atheist convinced that the Church was full of hypocrisy.

No matter where I was he was yelling in my head.

"What the hell am I paying all that god-damned tuition to that god-damned Catholic university for?" he would say. "Educating you to be stupid?"

"Well," I screamed, "*I'm* paying for all the rest, Daddy dear, see I have four jobs on top of my schedule! WHAT ELSE DO YOU WANT FROM ME?"

These discussions, continued into the start of my sophomore year, brought historic announcements.

The first bombshell was when I told my parents that I was planning to move out of the house and onto the campus. It was like the beginning of World War II all over again.

"No, you can't move out!" was my father's immediate reaction. "No daughter of mine will do this. Leave the family before you are married! Never! It's unheard of. Nobody has ever done this in my family! You will not go!"

"Try and stop me." I stormed. "*And*, I'm also changing my major out of pre-med to psychology, because medicine isn't giving me the answers I've been searching for and… "

"LEAVING MEDICINE TO BE A SHRINK!!" He cut me off in mid-sentence. "You will simply not do this! NO!" he repeated at the top of his voice, fond of screaming to get his way.

There was no "NO" in my vocabulary about this. It was a done deal.

Now, a good Italian girl never leaves her father, who had given her everything, had done everything he possibly could for her. The only way she could leave was to get married.

I owed him. He was *not* going to forgive me.

An Italian payback was forthcoming.

"GET OUT OF MY SIGHT! I NEVER WANT TO SEE YOU AGAIN!"

"FINE!" I shouted with equal volume and slammed the door.

I still had to go back and pack.

My poor mother was hiding in the next room, as she often did, when my father and I fought. Not knowing how to bring peace and quiet to this latest impasse, she just stared at me miserably as I walked past her on my way to pack.

She followed me.

"Cecilia Allesandra, please do what your father asks."

"I can't, ma, he won't even listen to my suggestions and I don't think I'm being unreasonable. I have to travel back and forth on the train all hours of the day and night, and it's unsafe. That's why I need to move on campus, where I will be right there, safe and sound. I can come home on weekends. What's so terrible about that?"

"I'll talk to him," she promised.

I left.

He declared me dead.

Eight months and a thousand phone calls later, he agreed to "see" me - not speak - just "see." I was relieved. The phone calls I had made were filtered through my mother's alcoholic fog, so I never knew what got through to him.

It was a Sunday afternoon in May 1968 when Dad and I finally met. He looked worn out. As soon as I saw him I felt both sad and guilty. I was, of course, completely responsible for his burden. For a moment, he just stood there as if he were thinking about turning around and leaving straight away.

He started speaking and I breathed more easily.

"I told you to stay home and take care of your mother and

you couldn't do that! Then you insulted me by leaving my house and abandoning your medical studies. What did I slave all those years to send you to school for?"

He loved to split infinitives, which annoyed me. But, annoyance was the quickest way for me to slide out of my guilt.

"Dad, I've done some very creative things. In addition to my psych experiments, I've developed liturgical music that is now used widely on campus, and encouraged student participation in the peace movement..."

"God, now she's a pacifist! My daughter! A hippie pacifist!"

Wincing at the sarcasm in his voice, I'd never heard him use those words.

I didn't tell him about the pot, the sex and the radical protests that swept across the campus. He would have exploded. Again.

Neither did I tell him about Carter, my Italian Jesuit who was influencing me more than I would admit to myself. Nor did I tell my roommates because talking about it would have made it more real and I didn't want to look at what was happening between Carter and me.

I was spending more time with him, now that I was on campus, looking forward to each meeting with secret anticipation, bringing him the problems I hadn't been able to share with anyone else.

"Carter, Joe is smoking pot a lot these days, and it makes me nervous... we've stopped talking. It makes me feel cut off from him and I don't know what to do."

Carter knew Joe by sight and they had talked to each other once or twice.

"Perhaps he's going through a crisis of his own and doesn't want you to know about it."

"What do you mean?" I was intrigued.

"He may be in something so deep with you, that he's afraid." He looked away from me reluctantly. That started something.

"Cart, why do the things you say touch me so deeply?"

I wanted to say, "Why can't I kiss you?"

There was no answer.

There *was* more and more that was unspoken in our meetings these days, as I sensed a growing tension between us. It was an alluring tension, filled with possibilities that neither of us acknowledged. I became excited at the sound of his voice, intrigued by his cavalier attitude as he, striding into the chapel, was geared up to change centuries of liturgical practice in that very moment, that very Mass.

So, why couldn't he change centuries of celibacy?

One morning that spring, just before Mass started, he was tuning my guitar. I got brave. Raising my head innocently... seductively I began. "Carter, why aren't you interested in women?" I liked to tease him.

"Who said I wasn't?" He fired back looking hard into my eyes

"If you want to be a priest," I plunged on, "and you really *are* interested in women, why don't you change the rule from inside the Church? Become a one-man campaign for priestly reform. Surely the Jesuits have been known to do such things! For centuries, even!"

I smiled at my own bravado and watched his reaction. Before he could reply, Mass started.

A month later, the sexual tension between us was unbearable. We were together in classes, together at Mass, together *after* Mass, together...

It was a Friday afternoon when I laid a heavy one on him, dipping into the fierce sexual undercurrent between us. It was so present yet *so* forbidden.

"As a little girl when I prayed, ecstasy often came. Orgasm is like that for me, and the two seem connected, because the same set of feelings are stirred. So, how can celibacy be peddled as the *only* way to achieve divine states?"

I was sometimes a little too direct.

"You can't just blithely equate these things!"

His frustration was obvious from the way his face turned red.

"Carter, I'm trying to make a point here. In fact, I think I've come to quite a revolutionary understanding that there is an intimate relationship between sexual ecstasy and mystical union. For example, every time I have sex, I'm saturated with a kind of bliss that I've only experienced in Church during prayer. It's like I'm touching God, this..."

He got up and forcefully started to pace. I stopped talking.

This is too much for him: two orgasm statements in one sentence. He's going to walk out right now. I said too much.

But he didn't leave. Instead he stopped his pacing right in front of me, sat down and took my right hand in his, bringing it to his face, holding it there with his other hand. He looked down to the floor. He was smitten.

Ah, success!

It took a year for the success to become visible. The day I left university to begin my graduate seminary work in Psychiatry and Religion, Carter finally touched me with passion. We were alone when he took me by my shoulders and embraced me. It went on for more than celibate time would allow.

Dr. Bullmann cleared his throat impatiently, "are you still with us, Frau Drakke?"

Since I was thinking so much about Carter, it was a shock to hear my third husband's name "Drakke."

"Yes, sorry Dr. Bullmann, I was just thinking of how to explain to the Court the way I resolved the conflicts around the issues of morality, power and the Church. When I finished university, I decided to change the Church from the inside and God called me to be the first female Roman Catholic priest. This would enable me to serve people as I had wanted to in medicine. I saw myself as a new theologian re-designing morality. I also conveniently disregarded nagging questions about how I could support myself if I didn't get ordained.

"I completed my seminary training, going on to doctoral

work, which led me to travel to India. My field was comparative spirituality and new religious movements, one of which was the movement of Bhagwan Shree Rajneesh."

Dr. Brendt broke in, "Frau Drakke, please slow down. You told us that you had these conflicts and then you came to a resolution. And *this* led you to study for the priesthood in the Catholic Church? I thought the Catholic Church did not ordain women."

"That's correct, Dr. Brendt. God spoke to me and I understood that it was my *mission* to educate the Church on the role of women. You see, the Church had for centuries regarded all females as the equivalent of the biblical Eve who gave into the serpent and became responsible for all the bad things in the world. Every woman's weakness and proneness to immorality has been blamed on Eve. A woman's salvation is to either become a nun or marry and reject sex for any other purpose than procreation. "

There was an audible groan from the Judge section, but I forged on.

"The Church teaches that human beings are born in original sin, therefore innately tainted and fundamentally unable to make their own decisions about God without the help of the (male) priesthood. Therefore, cursed women could not be ordained unless the Church changed its theological understanding. A good God *could not* create something that was not good or pure.

Since women and men are both capable of the same endeavors both could be ordained."

Dr Röder interrupted.

"I think we should concentrate, for the purposes of this hearing, on our original question. What brought you to work in the bars? How did you go from a seminary/PhD. student to a bar *damen*?"

He uttered the term bar *damen* as if it were a virus.

"My transition from seminarian to bar *damen* was quite methodical, actually. Although it may seem strange to you, when I was studying for the priesthood, both the Jesuit community and the Episcopal women who were also applying for recognition in their all male priesthood gave me great support. And, although my aim was an historical endeavor of great impact, my theological studies were simply not enough to satisfy my questions.

"I knew the answers lay somewhere *between* sex and religion. Religion is like an aspirin you take to relieve the pain of boring living, while sex is a magic potion. You are never the same again."

Dr. Bullmann broke in. "Frau Drakke, g-get to the p-point!"

I sensed that he must have spent time in the bars, himself. The tremor in his voice showed me signs that he was stirred up. Titillated, perhaps.

His voice, however, reminded me again of Dad.

"What the HELL are you going to do with a degree in theology? What kind of job are you going to get? You're going to land in the gutter with only your shirt - if you're lucky - and your useless degree... a bag lady, my daughter, who was going to be a doctor! *Testa dura!*"

He always called me names in Italian when he couldn't make sense of what I was doing, which was most of the time. It was his way of loving me and the only way he could express his exasperation at what he wanted for me, and the hole he saw me digging myself into.

I was convinced that I was going to be the first Roman Catholic woman priest.

Dad was convinced I was insane.

"Dr. Bullmann, sir, I am trying to show a connection between my intellectual work and my personal research - if you will. I began to see that a Church that had the power to control populations through birth control had the most power on earth. The Church conditioning I had received from childhood which made me believe I was fundamentally sinful, less than men and incapable of making decisions about my spirituality myself was infecting all my attitudes about myself, my relationships, my work and God. I had to look *outside myself* for the answers, the guidance the right way to do things. But each time I did, I found only another human being's opinion on how to do things. Behind every theological dictate was a man's opinion of what he thought was the truth."

"Frau Drakke," Dr. Bullmann said testily, "be brief!"

How could I be brief? This was such a big subject.

During that time I was only dimly aware of the link between sex and mysticism. As my sexual pleasure became more and more ecstatic, I felt like I was transported onto holy ground. Praying was pure rapture. Sex brought me out of the ordinary into another place. *This had to be what heaven was like.*

With Joe, sex was all melting and merging. It was a *real* union, and there was no separation. I couldn't tell where he left off and I began. Outside the bed was raw, rough life.

"When I first started seminary, Dr. Bullmann, I was working as a probation officer to finance my degree. Every day I dealt with criminals in the New York City jails."

How ironic that now I am one.

These Judges have probably only seen drug bosses and fraudulent bank presidents. How am I gonna make them believe that I was just a simple religious girl who wound up in a world of murder, arms dealings, prostitution and false identities. I'm not sure I understand it, let alone explain it to anybody else. I was stuck in the wrong place at the wrong time. Trying to figure out what to do. My old pattern.

I was the wrong person for probation work. I got too emotional. I was the wrong woman for Joe, who wanted a submissive wife, so I left him. When I briefly worked as a chaplain, it was the wrong time for a woman to be a priest. And, it was the wrong time for a sexual zealot like myself to marry a Jesuit.

"...within the first six months at seminary, I married a former Jesuit and the Church did not ordain me. Meanwhile, I thought that the sanctity of marriage would automatically make my husband into the god who would take care of all my sexual, emotional and intellectual needs. This didn't happen."

Not only didn't this happen, but I very quickly discovered that Carter and I were incompatible sexually, which wasn't either of our faults. We had lived together the year before we got married, and sex was new, strange and awkward then, which I thought was because he had been celibate and would change when we married.

It did change. It got worse.

I got desperate and tried harder. In denial because I loved him so much, I swallowed my longings, believing that love would bring us closer, ultimately. I tried to convince myself that sex was unimportant.

I didn't succeed. I started becoming attracted to others, knowing that I was hurting him, irritable for the lack of sexual fulfillment, and unable to do anything about it. I tried yoga, counseling, Tantra – ANYTHING. Nothing helped. Even though our relationship was rich intellectually and emotionally, my body felt dead to his touch. He was my closest friend, my companion... my brother. How could I make him into a husband?

For a year and a half I mourned, cried, bitched and then gave up.

"Disappointment and despair in my marriage, Dr. Bullmann, prompted me to pour myself into ministering to patients in the hospital. This work became my lover: thrilling, compelling, satisfying. The more constricted I felt with Carter, the more intently I sought out martial arts, Zen meditation, Sufi whirling - any exotic practice which would draw me away from the gloomy concern over my non-existent sexual life. My dissertation research continued in earnest, as I pursued the work of innovative theologians like Schillebeeckx and Hans Kung. I was also headed for a collapse.

"My mentor at the seminary died unexpectedly, which resulted in my doctoral work being challenged by the hierarchy as too radical. I was questioning the one true Church theory. Eastern influences were causing me to investigate the supremacy of western spiritual techniques. In one week, my position as Chaplain ended; I received final word there was to be no ordination; one of my beloved aunts died suddenly and my car was stolen."

All this, and no sex, pushed me over the edge.

There was this small hope that the God I still believed in, still prayed to, would save me from a nervous breakdown. Something *had* to happen.

It did.

It was a Thursday evening in October 1973.

Carter greeted me as I walked into our apartment.

"There's a party across the hall, and I want you to meet this new friend of mine, who's also a theology student. He's really fascinating and has traveled widely in Asia. He may have some good input for your work."

I didn't want to go. I had a hard day; my hair needed washing and the only thing I wanted was a long, hot bath and to change into my pajamas.

Carter wasn't interested in my woes. He was enthusiastic about my meeting his newfound friend.

"Come on, it'll help you get out of that rut you're in over your dissertation."

He thinks that's what the rut's about...

Reluctantly I went, hoping to be in and out quickly. I walked across the hall and stepped into the apartment, which was zen-like: large pillows on the floor, dim lights, no furniture. There were several people from the seminary including two professors I knew holding plastic glasses of wine and talking earnestly. The room vibrated with quiet, yet intense energy.

A slim girl, with long braids, was in the corner talking with a tall, slender man whose back was to me. He had reddish-gold curly hair to his shoulders, and his body was lithe, like a long-distance runner.

He turned around as Carter and I walked in.

"Peter, this is my wife, whom I told you about. She's the

one doing the comparative work in Christianity and eastern mysticism."

I saw the blue eyes first. They looked back at me, blazing like an inferno.

The rest of him was a bronzed Greek god, speaking to me, and all I could hear was the ocean. Slowly the fire waned and his eyes took the color of those deep blue seas that are on postcards.

This is dangerous.

There was no other thought.

His mouth was moving but I didn't hear the words.

"What?" I said stupidly.

"Let's meet tomorrow and talk more about your work."

Too weak to resist, he took my brief nod as a sign of assent.

I left the room, then, telling Carter I felt sick and walked back to our apartment.

I don't want this.

I don't need this.

I'm going to bed.

The next day he appeared at my door.

"You may want this reference for your chapter on Sufi mysticism. I took this course last semester…"

So innocent… yet, I hadn't felt a current this powerful since Joe. My body shivered. I kept staring at him in the doorway.

"Are you doing your degree in eastern religions?" I asked lamely.

"Partly. It's a joint degree with Columbia…"

I don't want to continue this conversation. I don't trust myself. His body is one inch from mine. I need to be in a very public place right now.

"Let's have coffee at Zabar's and talk more."

That'll be safe… out in the open.

"When?" he pursued. Electricity was coming from him too.

"How about meeting at three?"

At 2:50 P.M. I saw him there, in front of Zabar's.

It was he who opened his arms to me first.

"Why are we standing here on Broadway?" he asked in my ear. "Let's go back..."

In his small room I went directly to his bed, quickly without too much thinking.

A surge of electricity rose sharply, flooding my senses with joy.

Who was this man? Why did he immediately *have this effect on me?*

This was the effect my husband *was supposed to have...*

My body didn't *want* to resist Peter but everything in my head screamed.

This is wrong, bad, evil, adulterous.

And my heart was thudding, my blood boiling.

Scalded.

I wanted to fuck him. Hard.... long... intensely. He wanted me. Grasping my hair, he pulled my head back to kiss me...

I was the moth. This was flame. We were both incinerated. There was no choice.

Peter James Edwards, III, changed my life.

That evening I returned to the apartment before Carter came home. Shocked and angry, I yelled at God.

How could you do this to me, God? How could this happen? Peter is Carter's friend, and Carter is my husband, with whom I have pledged to spend my life. So what if ecstasy doesn't happen in sex with Carter... maybe someday it will. I can give that up... maybe this little brief encounter doesn't have to go any further. Maybe I can stop. I have to stop it. Now.

It wasn't that simple.

Time was different after Peter.

The moments I was not *with* him, I was thinking *about* him and how I was going to tell Carter, work it out with Carter, save Carter, save my marriage, still see Peter, three of us live together...

It was insanity.

Perhaps I am addicted to insanity? Perhaps I am addicted to sex? But, I don't have sex with everybody. Well, not quite everybody. These two men... And, I didn't even want to have sex with Peter. I didn't want to even know Peter! Carter set this whole thing up... It was his fault...yeah. Believe that and we're all insane.

But from the beginning the affair was not casual and Carter did not want to live with both of us.

"I didn't look for him, you introduced us!"

Guilt made me vulnerable, afraid of Carter's anger. I deserved his wrath, incapable of letting either of them go.

I suspected I was addicted to the drama.

"Well, I certainly didn't think you would screw him!"

"So, you *are* angry!"

"Well, how would *you* be if the situation were reversed? But, so what? It won't change things. It won't make Peter go away. It won't make you want *me...*"

"Carter, I married you. I didn't want this... I didn't look for it. It came..."

I sounded like T.V. Soap.

Carter was wounded. The dignity was gone. "Sure, sure. I should have known better. After everything you told me before we got married. How could you have let this happen so easily? And, whatever you say, you're not even prepared to let him go. Say no. Walk away."

"I can't," I said flatly.

"*Frau* Drakke..." Dr. Röder's voice broke into my thoughts.

"*Frau* Drakke, you said that you would be brief, but not silent!"

There was laughter and I realized I hadn't said anything for several long minutes.

"So, what happened to you after this collapse, *Frau* Drakke?" Dr. Bullmann continued, picking up my last sentence, and leaning forward as if he were touched in some way by my words.

OK. Now, be quick. Don't lose their attention.

If they sided with me, emotionally, they might be able to understand how I came to the predicament I was in, surrendering to men I made into gods, the same way I had surrendered to Sila and Bhagwan whom I had made into gods.

"I couldn't figure out why all these disasters were happening to me at once. Asking God to help me make sense of each thing as it collapsed did nothing. My work, my dissertation, the death of my aunt, the end of my marriage after only a year and a half and a new relationship I didn't know how to handle, brought only more confusion. I couldn't see a solution. What use were all my years of theological work, when I was in the midst of a serious crisis and God was silent?

I needed the answers to the same questions that had haunted me throughout my academic journey and I needed them now for my survival."

...And, the only place I found divine inspiration was in my connection with Peter. In the heat of our moments together, I was re-awakening. It's more than sex, it was...

It was the element that infused our intellectual connection with sharpness, and our emotional sharing with compassion and honesty.

We talked about things like Eastern Zen and Christian resurrection, but mostly we talked about our powerful feelings for each other.

"Peter, all my life, I worked so hard at being good. I wanted to be the saint who never sinned... and now look at me, sinning with you..."

His blue eyes showed understanding. He'd been there.

"I don't want to hurt Carter," he said gently, "but I feel so much for you..."

"And I, *you.* But I also love *him.* How can this be possible? I didn't seek you out. I didn't *look* for you! I didn't want to hurt Carter in any way. Why is this going on like this, with no resolution? How am I going to continue any kind of relationship with Carter, when I want to be more and more with you?" It sounded to my ears like some romance novel, and I was ashamed. But it was no novel. It was my life. And Peter's. And Carter's.

Peter scrunched his face, "I think we both have to ask ourselves what we want, truthfully. I'm not saying I'm superior in any way to Carter, just different. You and I have a sexual attraction that you may not have had with Carter, but I'm not sure. Only you can decide what to do for yourself. And you *must*. For your sanity and for his. You need to make a clear decision, although I know it's hard. It's hard for me, too. Whatsoever you decide, it won't break our bond with each other."

In this room, with this man, I felt alive, creative, inventive, feminine. Marriage changed everything between me and Carter. I had to get out so he'd be free to have children with someone who would cherish him as a husband - something I could never do. I never wanted to be married in the first place as I'd not seen a marriage that worked. I was simply sexual, not marriageable. Here was the bare, painful answer.

I cleared my throat to speak to the Judges,

"I was learning far more than in all the halls of academia or the Church. The answers were hidden in the arena where sex was an essential element. It was *because* of these events that I was drawn into the world of the bar *damen* - the world of the courtesan, the women who explored this dilemma the most deeply, throughout history.

"I wanted to be one of these women. They were the most educated and original women in history, and you've probably never heard of most of them. Since they understood life so thoroughly, they were the ones who *actually* made the decisions that world leaders used to shape our culture today. And since I wanted to direct the religious world, I had to be a woman who would influence the men who would shape it. Courtesans dealt with every raw feeling and situation imaginable from jealousy to greed to passion. Learning how to transform their clients using their own god-given talents, they were the first group of women to fully support themselves financially by their own earnings. These were goals I aspired to, and..."

"*Frau* Drakke", Dr. Bullmann interrupted, "we thank you for enlightening us on this subject. That's more than enough. Now let us focus on these charges ..."

Chapter 5
For My Life

Virtue is insufficient temptation. – George Bernard Shaw

I bet they really want to hear more about my life in the bar but I'm getting very uncomfortable.

"Now, about these charges," Dr. Bullmann repeated. "What I don't understand is the connection between what happened to you in Germany and how you could have been involved in these most serious accusations. The Court needs a clearer picture of this Rajneesh Commune."

"Yes, sir, of course. It started in America when we built a city in eastern Oregon…"

Rajneeshpuram. Whatever Sila told them in 1985 I'll never know. So I'd better start from the beginning.

"As I have heard it," Dr. Brendt cut in, "This commune started out in India, then moved to Oregon. Why?"

Oh well, here goes.

"Because all of us, including Bhagwan were sick and couldn't get well; not to mention that our lives were being threatened daily."

"Threatened by what?" Dr. Röder wanted to know.

"Threatened by death and people's hatred. When Bhagwan started speaking publicly in Bombay in the early '70's, he was a university professor in robust health. He was a flaming liberal speaking out against politicians and traditional religious leaders. He targeted specific people and got instant notoriety.

"Then he moved to Poona, a rich town near Bombay when a few wealthy followers of Mahatma Gandhi wanted to donate a large sum to help him start his Ashram. The donors made the mistake of asking him to speak about Gandhi. Bhagwan said that Gandhi was a criminal because he encouraged people to hold onto their attitude that poverty is a great virtue. This attitude he said, was the single thing that eventually led India into destruction and ruin. He then began to denounce Mother Teresa, whom he described as a pawn of the Pope, dragging people blindly into more and more holy poverty."

"He denounced Mother Teresa *too*? " Dr. Röder asked incredulously. "What was the reaction to a university professor denouncing people the Indians regarded as saints?"

"The donors withdrew their money and the Indian press denounced Bhagwan. But Bhagwan didn't care. In fact, he relished the negative reports. Not only did he expose poor Mother Teresa, he started picking on every single world leader, without exception, attracting the international press.

"He particularly enjoyed concentrating on Moraji Desai, the then Prime Minister of India. Sarcastically he said that Desai drank his own urine believing that it was the 'water of life.' Listening to Bhagwan, we started to believe that India was in the hands of a buffoon, following the tradition of a masochistic madman, Gandhi."

There was silence.

"You can see why we were disliked in India. These are only a few examples of how the Indians were baited. They had no choice but to become antagonistic. The more Bhagwan insulted revered leaders, the more angry the Indians became."

"Can you blame them?" Dr. Bullmann interjected.

"No, I didn't blame them at all," I said fervently. "Although at the time, I didn't really understand that the Indians could not exactly take out their hostility on a man who proclaimed to be a sadhu, a holy man. But they *could* rail against followers.

"However, I kept ignoring the looks the Indians gave us in the streets because I was too caught up in Bhagwan's *magic*. He was very charismatic. Now it's pretty clear to me that he designed his words to irritate the public. The more he said, the more fame he incurred and the more people were against him. It is as if he *wanted* to have all this negativity directed at him. What I didn't realize then was that he was putting my life, and the welfare of all of us, in jeopardy."

"Why didn't you leave, then?" Dr Röder asked.

"I was hooked. Bhagwan mesmerized and enchanted me. He was a god incarnate and I was his apostle who would suffer for my master. I came to India with a strong religious background generated from the position of believing I was unworthy and needed an authority (priest, pope, holy man) to tell me how to be healed. I sincerely believed, from the bottom of my heart and soul, that I must have guidance from a spiritually realized person who had 'arrived,' a living saint. It was what I spent all those years in university and in seminary searching for. My life's goal was to find a master who would teach me how to *become* this saint."

"And, you didn't find a spiritual method in Catholicism, the religion in which you were born?" Dr. Röder asked.

Dr. Röder must be Catholic. Maybe he had searched for something similar.

"I found a method, but saw no living example of it. Having explored Catholicism and other spiritual traditions thoroughly, it was clear to me that none of them, not even the Pope, had what I was looking for. It didn't mean that they were not good and often gifted people. Perhaps they all were. *I* was a good person.

"But, I was looking for something extraordinary. I wanted

to experience someone who had achieved a state of being that the mystics described, beyond anything I had seen before. Prior to meeting Bhagwan, I had only read about such people. They could see God. They saw people's weaknesses and transformed them. They were not afraid to point out hypocrisy while maintaining their own integrity in the face of powerful political and social pressure. The first time I looked into Bhagwan's eyes I saw all these things, and I knew I had found someone who could show me how to develop this in myself. He looked human and divine at the same time."

"*Frau* Drakke, this is most interesting, and perhaps you can expand on this a little later, but can we please come back to the development of the Commune? You were telling us that Bhagwan attracted international press attention and people's wrath. What specifically did the Indians do to express their displeasure at Rajneesh's attacks against them?" Dr. Brendt asked.

"They reacted. Violence escalated over a ten-year period starting in 1971 when Indian leaders complained in the local press. In 1979, a gunman shot at Bhagwan's car. He had a knife thrown at him one morning during the public discourse. Daily, we were ridiculed and harassed as we walked on the Poona streets. By 1980, it was no longer safe for us to go outside the Ashram. Then there were bomb threats."

Though the fear made us jittery, the truth was that some of us got high on the drama. But I don't think the Judges would understand that…

"What did Rajneesh dislike about the other world leaders?" Dr. Brendt inquired.

"Everything."

"What does that mean?" he asked.

"Politicians were automatically hypocrites to Bhagwan. He said that ordinary people were deliberately kept in poverty their whole lives, to make politicians, religious leaders, Queens, Prime Ministers, Presidents and big businessmen wealthy. World leaders cooperated with corrupt churches by forcing people to believe that poverty was a virtue, and that the individual was too ignorant to take control of his own destiny. People had to be ruled by domineering sadists who *knew better.* Crowds followed them, voted for them in rigged, money-controlled elections believing they would be saved from sin and economic destitution."

"But Rajneesh was a spiritual leader with his *own* following. Was he any better?" Dr. Bullmann asked.

"At that time I *did* think he was better. He spoke about each of us developing our own individuality, not becoming subservient, as every politician does. He described how Mother Teresa, in her way, was also a politician, captivating the world by her *service.*

"The politician was automatically beholden to whomever was paying to have him or her elected or catapulted into leadership like Mother Teresa. She was a servant of the Church's ideology that formed her conscience."

"Novel concept," Dr. Brendt said dryly.

"We became pariahs, and then for our own safety we had to leave. The U.S. was chosen because it had the best climate and health resources, and was vast enough to house our commune of several thousand people.

"Together with satellite communes around the world, there were approximately twenty thousand of us by 1981. Bhagwan called us his sannyasins. There was a vision of all sannyasins everywhere coming to live in one place..."

Dr. Röder interrupted, "Pardon me. Please explain this word, sannyasin."

"It's a traditional Indian expression for an ordinary person who renounces their *attachment* to the world. We were also known as Rajneeshees."

"And what was the political climate in the United States just before you moved there?" Dr. Röder continued.

"The year before, press reports linked us to Jonestown. The conservative religious right was strongly influencing the media. Cults like the Moonies were regarded as vermin and investigations into their activities were underway. We were considered to be the next Jonestown cult with a sex guru!"

"And how did *that* title come about?" Dr. Bullmann almost chuckled. "I thought Rajneesh was just an anti-politician. How did he acquire the "sex guru" label?"

"Bhagwan advocated freedom from oppressive relationships of any kind including marital. He encouraged Tantra groups, encounter groups and a host of others. To outsiders our open relationships looked like free love, which meant orgies.

"Gradually everything we did was interpreted as if we were attacking the moral system of the world. If sannyasins wore robes because of the heat, it was interpreted as 'unisex' and an anathema to the Indian population. If we held hands with each other on the street, we were considered prostitutes. Of course, it didn't help that Bhagwan was fond of dirty jokes and would pepper his discourses with plenty of them every day. He loved shocking people out of their sleepy, complacent existence, which they didn't generally like!"

Everybody laughed and that eased some of the tension in the room, which had intensified when I mentioned the term, "sex guru".

"So," Dr. Röder continued, "you moved to Oregon and then what?"

"We moved to 64,000 acres of desert, which had been earmarked by the government for some project, I am not sure what. We were a small group, at first. The local people told us that "nothing" could grow on this land; that it had been legally set aside for the purpose of grazing cattle. No other use of the land was permitted without going through a process of petitions and re-designation, which might take years."

"Yes, this is what the press reported. But I want to know how your small group developed a multi-million dollar enterprise?" Dr. Röder asked, impatient to get to more meaty issues.

"In 1982 we started negotiations with the State. At the

same time we began developing the land, cultivating areas for farming, irrigation, waste management, and houses. The first priority was to eat and become self-sustaining.

"Did you folks know how to farm?" Dr. Bullmann, the farmer, asked.

How do I make them understand how complex this operation became, and how much we invested ourselves into it, which ultimately caused some of us to risk our lives?

"In the beginning we knew nothing about building a city nor farming a desert. In a few months, however, a hundred people from all kinds of backgrounds came. We began building and registering permits with the State. The City had its own town hall, clinic, department store, restaurant, school, offices, and by 1983, an airport. Nothing in state law, at that time, prohibited it. And nothing like this had happened in so short a time in the U.S. before. As we grew in numbers, our influence spread."

"What was the reaction in Oregon to all this expansion? And how did Rajneesh behave? Was he still insulting people?" Judge Brendt asked.

"Well," I laughed, "Not exactly. He didn't appear publicly right away. I think he waited to see the Ranch get underway before starting his people bashing. He also wanted recognition for our growth. After we won several national and international awards for architecture, waste management and innovative farming methods, he started to give speak giving discourses again.

"By 1983, we had to have a Press Department to handle all the people who came. Since Bhagwan handpicked the most beautiful looking super-model types to greet them, the 'sex guru' image came back. It was his strategy to stir the pot. But, the pot boiled over.

"Shortly after we purchased a hotel in Portland for our business ventures, Bhagwan was shot by a sniper while driving his Rolls. At the same time, the Oregon Governor declared he wanted us 'foreigners' out of his State. Though most of us were Americans, some Oregonians expressed fears. Since apparently anyone could incorporate a city, all sorts of other cults might try to do the same thing.

"The State Planning Commission tried to pass a bill declaring the City of Rajneeshpuram, 'religious and therefore, illegal.' We reminded them that Salt Lake City, in Utah, had always been both religious and legal."

"*Frau* Drakke, while all this was going on, what were you actually doing? For example, did you have a job?" Judge Bullmann asked.

"Yes. At Sila's urging I began a Video and Film Department. My job was to supervise the filming of Bhagwan's discourses and all the events that occurred in the commune, creating inspirational films and a historical record.

"From one camera, a small cassette recorder and a single cameraman, housed in a tiny Poona office in 1979, we grew to have three state-of-the-art video machines, our own editing machine, duplicators, a sound and production laboratory, a 23 member-crew, and hundreds of archive and film tapes by 1983.

"Along with my colleague in the audio department, we also had an international production and distribution business, whose sales to centers and bookstores around the world helped support commune operations. We were even making films for Cable T.V. about Bhagwan's work in a tiny trailer on the Ranch."

"So, you were working independently, as a filmmaker, with your own ideas and projects?" Dr. Röder was interested.

"No. I was a commune member. Anything I did had to have Sila's approval. When I came up with new ideas, I had to check them out with her before proceeding. If she thought the idea was feasible, it was a go. If not, it didn't happen.

"Everyone followed this process. You reported to your boss, who then reported to their boss, usually one of Bhagwan's inner circle for approval. This was called 'surrender' and the way the commune functioned in all areas, from a multi-national business project down to cleaning the toilets. We had to go along with what the bosses decided. To challenge their decisions was to risk being asked to leave.

"After all those years living this way, the big bosses, Bhagwan and Sila, were like gods to me. I didn't question them. I believed that what they said was for everybody's welfare, even if it didn't make sense."

"If life was so harmonious, why were there security guards, police, and guns that we saw in the news? Wasn't that against the ideas of spirituality?" Dr. Brendt asked, genuinely confused.

"It was never harmonious. Even in the beginning we upset the townspeople and ranchers. By the fall of 1983, our hotel was bombed and Sila asked me and another sannyasin to find out who was responsible."

"Weren't the police and the FBI called? Why you? It sounds like a police matter." Dr. Röder asked.

"Yes, but Sila wanted *us* to investigate *also*."

"Were you specially trained in investigation?" Dr. Röder continued. "I thought you were working in the Video and Film Department?"

"Yes, I was." I laughed. "But I had no training in video and film either before I started. This was how it was in the commune: you were placed in a job because of some quality the big bosses thought you had a talent for."

"Well what happened to the investigation? Did you find out anything?" Dr. Bullmann sounded intrigued.

"Yes. This may sound incredible, but within a week, we had located the bomber cell, traced it back to the Midwest, and found another cell linked to a militant group. All from simple clues the bomber left behind.

"At the end of that week, all the evidence was turned over to the FBI, who were just getting started on the case. This was how my career in investigation began.

My partner and I became the Ranch's FBI and CIA. In

that capacity I was told to investigate U.S. Attorney, George Tork.

"It was after the bombing that we were advised by the police to start our own Security Department, called the Peace Force, who were licensed to carry weapons. That's where the guns originally came in."

"And, were *you* also carrying weapons?" Dr. Brendt asked cautiously.

"No," I smiled.

This is gonna look great: an amateur agent who couldn't even carry a gun, let alone shoot one!

"Dr. Brendt, I am blind in one eye and partially blind in the other, so I couldn't shoot a thing. I can hardly *see* for that matter. To those who knew, it was a joke: a blind woman directing a film department *and* conducting an investigation."

"*Frau* Drakke," Dr. Brendt cleared his throat, "you are charged with *conspiracy to murder* the U.S. Attorney of Oregon, not investigate him. What was the *reason* for your investigation? Did he have anything to do with affecting security operations on the Ranch after the bombing episode?"

"Sila was concerned when she heard that his office was pressuring public officials to conduct a federal investigation because of the speed of success of our businesses. About the same time, twenty-one couples had recently gotten married, all filing for a change of status at the same INS office. This came to the attention of the U.S. Attorney's Office."

"So, Sila asked you to investigate *him* before he could investigate *you*? Is that it?" Dr. Brendt continued.

"That's what I thought, initially. We had to find out as much information about him as we could to discredit him and his investigations."

Being a thorough person by nature, I dug up his whole life: where he went to school and how he got involved in politics. Following a routine that had worked before, I then attempted to interview him. To my amazement, my request was denied. I couldn't even *call* him because his number was unlisted. He was the first and *only person* in Oregon and Washington D.C., with whom I did *not* get an interview."

"So, you interviewed other people? Why?" Dr. Brendt probed.

"After we discovered that a group was involved in the bombing, I was told to look into others like the Klan, white supremacists and so on. At the same time, I was told to find out why cults like the Moonies were being harassed by the government.

"Prior to my research on Mr. Tork, I interviewed senators, congressmen, and Presidential advisors, all in an effort to discover what the government was planning to do with *us*. I gave all this information to Sila because she wanted us to be prepared for anything that might come our way after the bombing.

"We had been unprepared for a bomb attack and weren't sure if and when there might be another one. It could have come from anywhere."

"I can appreciate how you acted out of your concern for safety, *Frau* Drakke. How did you manage to *get* the interviews with these people?" Dr. Brendt asked curiously.

"By my wits. I walked right into offices most people assume they can't ever walk into. I walked into the White House, for example, for my interview with Reagan's economic policy advisor."

"But, why did you *need* to talk with them?" Dr. Bullmann asked puzzled.

"I had to get close to them, so I could get a clear picture of their personality and how they thought. This gave me a barometer of their attitudes toward cults. In those days I felt like an army general planning battle strategy, who looks from every possible angle to determine what his enemy might use for the attack."

"Did you look upon government officials as *enemies*"? Dr. Brendt interjected.

"It was never openly stated, but Bhagwan's message was that his sannyasins were special: close to enlightenment. Those who were not with us were against us. Certainly if someone bombs you they become your enemy, wouldn't you agree?"

There was a pregnant pause.

I decided to move off this enemy topic slightly because I felt some raw nerves being exposed.

"Honestly, sirs, my training in grad school was in psychology and religion, not investigation. The best I could offer was a psychological assessment of the person's character by reading their body postures, voice inflections, and analyzing their answers to my questions in the interview.

But, Mr. Tork was different from everyone else I had come across: he wasn't visible. I usually got my pictures from newspapers, but for some reason they did not photograph him. Or if they did, I didn't find the photos. It was hard to see whom we might be up against, when nothing was reported about him.

"After I found his school yearbook, giving me a clue as to his appearance, I thought I could observe him from a distance by watching the courthouse. I planned to evaluate if he was an aggressive or a passive type, for example, so I could determine how quickly and with what force he might pursue us. But I never saw him, or any member of his family."

I could see Dr. Röder had an opinion about this.

"Are we to understand that you are accused of conspiring to murder someone you never *met?* In Germany, we do not have the same understanding of "conspiracy" as you do in the U.S. We are trying to decide if this crime is extraditable. Therefore we need to know if you ever had any contact with him?"

"I never had any contact with him, nor did I know how to get in contact with him. Not in person, nor by phone or by letter. His secretary told me that he never gives interviews. I decided to wait for him outside his office, after work, the way I'd seen reporters do. I planned to walk up casually to him and ask questions. I tried this approach with one of the representatives in Washington and he invited me into his office so that we could continue the interview."

"And what was the *real* purpose behind these interviews?" Dr. Röder continued.

"To find out anything the Ranch lawyers could use to win a case against the government. It could be uncovering a conservative religious influence in a Washington representative's background. This influence could make him vote for a law restricting certain 'religious' cities. Or a federal official might have chronic pain, for example. This might provoke him to be particularly harsh towards the next thing on his desk, which might be about Rajneeshpuram.

"Sila thought Tork was dangerous and wanted to reduce his sphere of influence over our lives. At least that's what I understood. After the bombing, our survival was in jeopardy and we were afraid political investigations could close down the City and force us to leave. There was increasing government opposition to dismantle everything we had worked for and built.

"By 1984 two thousand sannyasins lived on the Ranch. The mounting opposition at the state and federal levels triggered Oregonians, already disturbed by our growth, businesses, red clothes and new religion. Then there was Bhagwan's ninety-eight Rolls Royces. We were everyone's targets. So we had to consider *every* defense strategy.

"I did what I was told to the fullest extent, because we were taught to go to any lengths to accomplish a task. I had to prove that I was the best investigator that ever existed. So, if Sila told me to find out about this man, I was going to walk on water to find out *something*. Anything, even if it was only the color of his toothbrush.

"I had to please Sila, desperately wanting to be accepted by her and her inner circle of powerful sannyasins, some of whom headed multi million dollar corporations. I wanted to be *in* this inner circle that ran the Ranch.

"And why not? Like any employee who gives the best years of her life to a company, I wanted power *in* the company: my opinions to be listened to."

"Who did you want to listen to you? Sila? Bhagwan? Why

would they listen to you when, as you described, you were expected to take orders from *them?*" Dr. Bullmann asked.

"Because I was also the one risking my life by being undercover. *This* gave me clout. I was doing what none of them *could* do because of their visibility. So when I told Sila in the end that there was nothing useful I could find on Mr. Tork, I advised her that any further research would be unproductive. I assumed from that moment on she closed the chapter on him."

"Why did you stop there?" Dr. Röder asked.

"Because Sila was beginning to have paranoid delusions and bizarre thoughts. She was no longer thinking straight. I sensed she was considering harming Tork. *This* scared me and made me think deeply about being violent to another human being.

"I discussed this with my associates on the project. Sila was the highest authority and her views couldn't just be ignored. Every idea originating from Bhagwan –or Sila- had to be examined for the good of the commune. Murder or attempted murder could be *considered* if she wanted, and if it was done to save the commune from an enemy. This line of thinking terrified me. But I had to think about it *because* my superior, my 'god' Sila, was considering it, no matter how unbalanced she might be. I was conflicted."

"But, couldn't you see that her ideas and her behavior were wrong? You've just mentioned that you questioned her sanity and her reason." Dr. Röder asked astonished. "Why would you *have* to consider such a thing?"

"Because by then, I was completely conditioned to believe that everything Bhagwan or Sila said was true and enlightened, no matter how wrong it *appeared*. Bhagwan was constantly in opposition to 'normal' morality standards. He set his own morality and he was the pope to me. If we were in medieval times I might have been a crusader killing infidels.

"Therefore, if *one* thing proved wrong in his teaching, like getting rid of an enemy of the commune for example, then all of his teaching would be questionable. Discarding my former life, friends and family to follow him, for instance, would have been wrong. Ten years of labor, suffering, illnesses, poverty and danger would have been for nothing. He had become the rock upon which I based my life.

"So, it took me some time to finally realize that maybe somebody could be a good soldier for the commune and deal with this enemy, but it was not me. I was not fit soldier material. The horror of harming another human being was too great for me. The more I thought about it, the sicker I became, until I felt compelled to tell Sila to stop everything concerning Mr. Tork. Whatever he was going to do wasn't worth it. Even though the security force talked about protecting the commune, if Sila put an end to Mr. Tork's pursuit, *they* would not touch him. And they were the ones licensed to carry and use weapons, not me. Guns make me nervous. I have always been against them. Since college I had been actively involved in peace movements."

"Yet," Dr. Bullmann said wearily, "we have here a charge against you for the interstate transport of firearms…"

"Which is absurd, because there is no evidence linking *Frau* Drakke in any way with handling weapons or transporting them! It was not her job!" Hanna burst in.

This was her first comment since the hearing started. Her voice shook with vigor as if she had been waiting for just the right moment to make a dramatic entrance.

"Furthermore", she said triumphantly, "*Frau* Drakke has clearly demonstrated that she was involved but withdrew from a conspiracy to murder Mr.Tork. Her withdrawal thus signified the end of such a conspiracy!"

If I can just be patient, maybe all this awful drama will disappear in a puff of smoke.

I was wrong.

Dr. Brendt ignored Hanna and looked straight at me. "Did you have any contact with Mr. Tork during this entire period of time we have been discussing?"

"No."

"Was he hurt or physically harmed in any way?"

"No. Not that I know of."

"Did you tell people to go and murder him?"

"No."

"Then what exactly *did* you do?" There was a hint of exasperation in his voice. "How did this *charge* come about?"

I've gone over this a thousand times and it still hurts.

"I've come to the conclusion that when my co-defendant Maya was faced with her charges, she got scared. Perhaps in her mind our discussions trying to figure out whether or not violence was a real alternative *was* an intention to kill. I'm sure she was pressured into giving something to the Feds so she could buy her way out of a long prison sentence."

"Were you afraid of Maya?" Dr. Brendt asked softly, visibly affected by what I had just said.

"Oh, yes. I was afraid of her. I was terrified of everyone in the inner circle and she was one of them. On the outside I was The Cool Agent, but on the inside I was a mass of jelly, trying to pretend. I played a role so I could be accepted."

"I gather that this attitude also led you to become involved in the wire-tapping scheme? This seems to have been a widespread activity on the Ranch. Was this project also one of the leader's 'distorted' ideas?" asked Prosecutor Kittleman.

"No," I said emphatically. "I was told that the police advised us to tap phones for our own security after the bombing. The information we gathered went to our Peace Force on the Ranch, which I believed was then fed back to the police to prevent further attacks on us.

"Sila was the owner of the Ranch. It was her private property; she wanted to protect it and authorized the wiretap. The fact that the electronic equipment and catalogued tapes were left, and not dismantled nor tampered with, illustrates that this whole operation was for security purposes and not for any illegal activity. How can an action be criminal when the police know about it?"

"*Frau* Drakke, it is not for us to make a determination about the criminal nature of an activity in America. We can only decide if the offense is serious enough to warrant extradition," Dr. Brendt said finally.

I think we are getting to the end.

"There are two more things that I would like to say." I added quickly.

They nodded.

"I strongly believe that if I am sent back to the U.S. I will not get a fair trial because the political climate in Oregon is very negative towards sannyasins. I will not make deals using someone else's life as a bargaining tool. And, I will not testify against any of my co-defendants because I don't know what their real intentions were."

Now I can breathe...

"And what is the second thing?" Dr. Brendt asked kindly.

Thank God they didn't challenge my statement about deals.

"Thank you for all you've done for me and what you've also done for Narian and Diva. It was most kind of you to want to hear our testimony."

"Thank *you, Frau* Drakke for being so candid with us," Dr. Röder said with genuine warmth.

"How do you find the prison?" he added as an afterthought.

"Wonderful!" It was the most natural thing in the world to say, they'd been so kind to me.

There was surprise and laughter.

"Is there anything you need? Is there anything we can get for you?" Dr. Bullmann asked smiling.

"Yes, please," I said quickly. "Some more English books."

They nodded and stood to leave.

Getting up my legs were rubber. A broad, uncontrollable smile came.

I DID IT! I DEFENDED MYSELF!

And I *knew* the Judges believed me.

Chapter 6
The Cult Drug

What the caterpillar calls the end of the world, the master calls a butterfly.
-Richard Bach, Illusions

It was twilight when we left the courtroom. Hanna walked beside me down the uneven stone steps, not saying a word. She knew I was mad because during the entire hearing she only said *one* statement.

Greedily inhaling the evening air, my anger quickly turned into exhilaration. I had accomplished an extraordinary feat: I stood up for myself before all these officials. I had *defended* myself.

Spontaneously reaching out to hug Hanna, she looked at me cautiously, like she wasn't sure if I was going to choke her instead.

The prison van was waiting to bring me back. The journey would mark the start of ten days of waiting for the Judges' decision. Through the windows of the van everything looked smaller than when I'd left. When we arrived at the prison, all I wanted to do was hide, to be alone with the powerful sensations of what had just happened.

I walked into the community room in a separate section of the prison to which I'd just been transferred. There was no one there, thank God. Ten cells surrounded a communal dining and kitchen area for twenty prisoners. It was an "honor" to be transferred there: it meant you were considered "non-violent" and unlikely to escape.

My new cellmate Kristina was in for murdering her husband who tried to kill her. Not speaking English, she often spoke rapidly in a dialect that was difficult for me to understand, so we didn't talk much.

The next cell was assigned to a Yugoslav lady with jet black, curly hair and a warm, bubbly personality. I'd met her in arts and crafts, but we'd not talked before.

At that moment she entered, coming right up to me and startling me with her heavily accented English.

"How was your hearing? We were all so worried about you!" she said squeezing both my hands in her own.

"It went very well," I said a little guardedly, not sure how to deal with all her intensity.

She continued as if we were long time buddies.

"You know, I had a good friend who was a sannyasin in the Rajneesh Commune in Cologne, and he tried so hard to get me to come to Poona, but I never managed it. I was so interested in what Rajneesh had to say, especially about politics! Anyway, I wanted to talk to you before this, but we never had the opportunity. When you were transferred here I thought, *great*, I get the chance now! And *then* you have this hearing, which the Court *never* grants! So there is hope for all of us!"

She paused only to gulp air, talking so fast that I felt like I'd stepped into the center of a cyclone.

Hope?

I stood there, suddenly drained and exhausted.

"Come," she said gently, "let us have a coffee together - unless you are too tired?"

I was both tired *and* reluctant to talk, yet intrigued.

What does she mean, 'hope for all of us'?
"Ah, excuse me, what is your name?"

"Oh, of course! My name is Margret. I come from Paris, though I am Yugoslav by birth. When I was in Paris, my boyfriend and I got into the habit of signing checks way over our limit. It is a very bad habit to be in, I tell you, because once you do it a few times, you are hooked. You must keep moving, so that the checks do not catch up with you! That is how we came to Germany. We made a big mistake. The *Polizei* are much more careful than the French police! So, here I am!"

"And for how much longer will you be here?"

"For another eight months. Then they will deport me back to Yugoslavia - that is, if Yugoslavia still exists by then!"

There was a civil war in Yugoslavia. It was only after I left Bühl and Margret's letters to me stopped coming that I realized she might well have died there.

"Who was your friend who tried to get you to go to Poona?"

"His name was Dan, and he offered to pay my way, even. But, alas, I was already involved with Jacques, my boyfriend in Paris, so I did not want to go. I did read the books he sent me, though. This Rajneesh was fascinating, no? And all the stories about the sex! I want to know why he was called the sex guru; even the smallest details. Will you tell me? You are the first person I meet, besides Diva, who was really *there*! What was it like and did you have sex all the time?"

I laughed. She sounded like one of those many reporters who were hungry to learn about the sex orgies, and would not leave me alone until I told her.

"It's a long, long story," I hesitated.

"Do you mind, my asking? I often wondered how it would be to live with such a man - a guru who had no limitations about sex!" Her eyes were lit with a fire I had not seen for quite a while.

My eyes were once lit the same way - with that fire. The

hearing brought back long forgotten memories that her questions made me eager to share, and would fill in this empty space of waiting.

The worry-and-waiting time was like what happened when we lined up for Bhagwan's nightly *darshan*: meeting with the master. I worried whatever I would do or say in front of him was never good enough. I saw myself like a caterpillar, with an ugly cocoon around me. Yet, he seemed to see a butterfly in there.

"Well," I began, "in the late summer of 1975 I came to India..."

God was it raining! I'd never seen monsoons before.

Everything was soaking and mildewed, including me. India - YUK. I hated it, and wanted to get away as quickly as possible. Meet this man and go right back to Bombay, on the next plane and out of here.

This is awful. Damn! Why did I leave my gorgeous home, all my friends, my practice which I loved, to come here? To stand in the rain in somebody's driveway, waiting for a signal to walk in procession to meet some Indian on his back porch?

Am I mad?

What am I doing seeing a guru, anyway?

Sitting at a guru's feet? The idea makes me sick. These gurus are all fakes. I did all those years of research to prove it, too. How did I let myself be talked into this? Jesus Christ of the Age? I'm mad. Why did I listen to a former client?

Well, just get it over with. Then I'll fly my tush out of this god-forsaken country. I never even wanted to go to India! It's worse and uglier than I imagined!

Especially the rain: worse than New York rain. Twenty-four hours after arriving, it was still raining in sheets, ten minutes at a time, stopping and starting.

Peter and I were supposed to be in sunny Chamonix, with an enlightened Sufi, but we're here in this muck instead.

The muck reminded me of when Carter left. It was pouring just like this...

At the beginning of that year, Carter left our apartment after I went to Berkeley with Peter for a three-month psychotherapy training. Before I returned to New York there were several painful phone calls.

"Cart, you sent me last month's bills. How I am supposed to deal with them, three thousand miles away?"

"If you cared enough about *our* home, *our* life, then you would come back and deal with everything. Obviously, you no longer care. You're too wrapped up in your idyllic life with your new lover." Carter said angrily.

"I'm trying to do the best I can, Cart. I'm living in two different worlds that are *both* pulling me apart, don't you see? It's *also* hard for me."

"The only thing I see," he said, even more pissed off, "is that you are gallivanting around and I'm stuck with the work and the bills! And, a broken heart."

The conversations got worse till they stopped. There was no resolution. I had finally made the decision to continue my life with Peter because I *had* to choose between them. I knew no matter how much I loved Carter; I couldn't continue the way it was. He wanted a wife I couldn't be.

When I did arrive back in New York, our apartment was cold and empty. I picked up a picture of Carter and me, which he had left behind, and sobbed.

Why did this have to happen? I love him. Why?

That was the last time I saw him for twenty-two years. Later I learned that Carter had married a wonderful woman. Meanwhile, as life with Peter began, work was demanding. And I still looked for Carter on street corners and every place we had been together. There was a hole in my heart where he had lived. Slowly I understood that I had to get out of his way to make room for the right person to come into his life.

A few months later, Samuel, one of my clients, began talking in session about a guru he had met while traveling in India. His first words were: "Let me tell you that the greatest influence in my life right now is Bhagwan Shree Rajneesh. Whatever we do in this therapy, he has to come in."

This should have been a warning sign right there. Why would he need *me* if he had found a real master? A part of me was still hoping that somewhere out there, a Jesus or a Buddha would save me.

"Samuel," I said formally, "If you want to work with me, you'll have to put this guru on the shelf for starters. After a while, we'll see."

He was not fully prepared to go along with this suggestion yet, but afraid not to because he really wanted me as his therapist.

Six months later I said, "Samuel, now that we are coming to the end of our work together and you have experienced so many changes, you can bring your guru down from the shelf and do whatever you want with him."

Samuel laughed and went off to India.

Three weeks later, I received a letter.

You have got to come to Poona!!!! I know now, I have found the Master of the Age! He is Jesus Christ and Buddha together. You owe it to yourself not to miss this opportunity. Just come and experience it for yourself. Then, if he doesn't turn you on, you can return to New York and resume your life without a pause.

Love and in great peace,
Swami Anand Buddhasam
(Formerly Samuel Isaacson)

What else could I do? *Not* experience the Master of the Age after all my years of searching for him?

That night I had a dream in which a white-robed man, seated in a white armchair, pointed his finger at me, saying, "Come."

I woke up and for several days after that I couldn't get this image out of my head. Then, Sam sent me a photo of Rajneesh. It was the man in the dream.

I immediately booked a flight to India and that night told Peter about the dream.

"Peter, guess what? I had this strange dream last week."

Cautiously, Peter asked, "What was it *this* time?"

"Peter you *know* I don't usually see *real* people in my dreams. But in this one, I saw a man, who said very clearly, 'Come'. I'd never seen this guy before. And then Sam sent me his picture. It was Rajneesh!"

Peter's blue eyes narrowed, staring at me intently.

"A *real* person? Are you sure?" He asked wryly. "And an *Indian*? What about the Sufi master in Chamonix?"

Looking embarrassed, I started playing with the tablecloth. "Maybe we have to cancel Chamonix. Peter, we *have* to check this out."

"We?"

"Yes, both of us. It's important for both of us to go."

"Cecilia, I don't want to go to India in the monsoon season."

"Oh… is August the monsoon season? Peter, we *have* to go in August. It's the only time we can both have off together."

"Cecilia, I told you, I'm not going in August. You have no idea what India is like in the monsoon!"

"We *have* to go. Otherwise, we'll always regret it. Perhaps it won't be so bad. If it's *so* awful, we can turn right around and come back to New York. I promise."

We went in August. We cancelled Chamonix. Peter's words, "You always get your way, don't you?" hammered in my head the whole way.

It was the worst monsoon in ten years.

The first night I met Bhagwan, the rain was pouring down in sheets. The pebble-stone driveway leading to his marble porch was slick. A few people were already there as I approached his dais. A young woman with long brown hair sat at the feet of an old man, who sat upright yet relaxed in a pure white upholstered armchair.

My eyes went to him immediately. His left leg crossed over his right. He wore a white tailored robe and had a pepper and salt beard. His eyes caught mine.

Exactly the same man as in my dream.

In reality, I had never seen him before. Yet there he was, looking just as I had seen him in my dream, four months earlier.

He raised his hand, pointed his finger at me, and said, "Come."

I stopped walking.

This is *not* happening to me.

I don't see things in dreams that happen later on.

My legs took over and I kept walking down the driveway. One of the seated-on-the-floor people stood up, came over to me and said, "Bhagwan wants to meet you. Come on, sit down here, in front of him."

The other two people on the floor smiled.

Why? What's so funny?

Everything around me apart from *him* was a little blurry. I concentrated on putting one foot in front of the other.

How do you speak to a dream-come-true person?

Something I've been longing for is coming true in front of me.

And I was scared to death.

"Come here, sit in front of me," he said in a soft, strongly masculine voice.

I was still frightened but felt welcomed, like I'd come home.

What do I say?

He's not like anybody *I've seen before.*

He's certainly different from the Zen Roshis, Sufis, rabbis, priests and cardinals I'd met before.

When I focused on his face, the first thing that met me were his eyes. Those eyes were definitely not like any other human eyes I'd seen before. There was no doubt, no fear, and no uncertainty. Those eyes said: I know everything there is to know, and it's all OK with me; I'm not troubled by anything. When I looked at my eyes in the mirror, there was *only* uncertainty.

He had found the way out of that uncertainty.

I want what he has and I'm not leaving till I have it.

"I knew you were coming," he said, motioning to Buddhasam, sitting to the right of his chair. I hadn't even noticed my old client, dressed in a simple orange robe.

"Buddhasam told me. So, what is going on with you, mmm?"

Although I had rehearsed what I would say ahead of time, without thinking, out of my mouth came the words. "I'm lonely."

"You have had relationships?" he asked.

"Yes."

"And the loneliness still remains?"

"No, it changes, but there is something deeper, a longing which is never satisfied..."

I looked up and got lost in those eyes, diving into a deep ocean carrying me somewhere I wanted to go.

He continued, "...touched by relationship is loneliness. That which never is, is aloneness. Loneliness is always waiting for someone or something to make things complete, and aloneness is complete,"

It was just what I needed to hear. In that moment, I fell in love with him in a way I had never fallen in love before. He had me without hello.

"Monastery comes from the root, 'monas' which means one... there, people live together... in their aloneness..."

I heard more words, but what I was really hearing was music. My heart was singing.

"...want to take sannyas, now or..."

"Now!" I said in a loud voice that shook even me. Everybody laughed.

What I had heard about this "taking sannyas" was that I would have to wear a necklace with his picture, take a religious name and dress in orange. Yesterday I wanted no part of such a gimmicky thing. Now, there was no hesitation. I had to get close to what I wanted.

"Close your eyes."

There was silence for perhaps two or three minutes. Then, suddenly a very bright light appeared.

I got *really* scared.

Maybe I died and went to heaven. Usually, I don't see bright lights with my eyes closed, so I knew that whatever was happening was not normal. I was so scared that I kept my eyes tightly shut. There was more laughter.

"You can open your eyes."

Everybody was still there and the brown-haired woman handed me a piece of white paper with something written on it. Bhagwan explained that I would now have the name Ma Prem Samsara. He went on to say that "Prem" meant love and "Samsara" was something I would figure out.

"Wear the colors of fire from now on and this mala of 108 beads with my picture on it. Now you belong to me."

Perfect! My name "Cecilia Allesandra" never seemed to fit me. This new name *was* me. I felt like Moses coming down from the mountain having spoken with the Lord, having received a new name, a new beginning, a new life and mission. *And,* I had seen the light!

Slowly, I got up and went to the back of the porch-room to sit next to Peter.

As soon as I sat down it was Peter's turn.

Bhagwan went through the same process with him, except that he talked to him a bit longer. Peter's new name was Swami Yoga Sam.

I was in a daze. I was hooked. So, was Peter —er, Sam.

The bright light that I saw behind closed eyes turned out to be a flashlight, which Bhagwan held on the person's forehead. I laughed out loud and didn't care that people glared at me for laughing. There was a relief that I hadn't see "visions" after all. It made what happened more real, somehow.

I didn't get on the next plane to go back.

Instead I stayed a month. At the end of the month, I still detested India. But, I wanted to sell everything I had in New York and come back to Poona. I wanted to stay with this man forever.

The night before I left, I told Bhagwan what I wanted to do.

He simply said, "No."

"What? But I want to stay here with you," I said feeling scared again. He didn't want me.

"Go back to New York and open a center. Don't worry, you'll come back soon, but for now go there. Sam, you help her."

I don't want to leave you!

I wanted to *be* with him and catch this state of whatever-it-was-he-was-in for myself, as if by breathing his *air* I could make it my own. However, I read somewhere that you were supposed to be *obedient* to your master, if you were to get anywhere in the spiritual world. Damnit.

Back in New York I determined to open the perfect center and prove that I could earn enough credits to stay with him the next time around. Trouble was, I hated India more each day, and the longer I stayed in New York, the more I loathed the idea of going back. But that was where he was - my new god-guru-master. I swallowed the fact that I had succumbed to being at the feet of an Indian guru, because, I rationalized, he was not just *any* guru. He was *it*. "The Master of the Age." He was Jesus and Buddha. The second coming had arrived. I could hear his words in my head talking about an "... explosion of consciousness" and that if man "... continues to wear the old clothes, which were made for children..." he's in trouble because established religions are like "...clothes made for another state of humanity when man was more childish."

He told me to grow up and do what I was meant to do: bring a new spirituality, inspired by him, into the world.

What kind of a center would be appropriate for this new spirituality? Obviously, a neon orange one. We painted the walls a shocking carrot colour. When people walked in they got dizzy; the walls were too bright for meditation. So we held weekend long "enlightenment workshops," where the dedicated sat all day long staring into each other's eyes, asking, "Who am I?"

They all raved about "the profound effects."

One night, after a particularly successful weekend, Sam said to me, "Samsara, our life here is getting better and better. I can't tell you how great I feel. This must be what bliss is like."

I still felt something was missing but hadn't said anything. Looking down into the neon orange rug, I said forlornly, "Sam, I'm not so thrilled. In fact, I think we should put this center in somebody else's hands and go back to Poona."

"Are you nuts?" An expression Sam used often with me.

"No… it's just… that…I feel like we're *missing* by not being in Poona!"

He didn't even ask me what was missing. This was how our relationship was: I decided and he agreed, so I thought. I didn't see the natural, growing resentment underneath, for nobody likes to live with a dictator.

Within two weeks, we were back on the plane to Poona.

As soon as I arrived back in India, the westerner in me was restless to get back to New York with its comforts, hygiene and good food. Yet, no sooner back in New York, the impatient longing to return to India began again. I was increasingly desperate to know whatever-it-was Bhagwan had that seemed to make him this complete human being without any insecurities.

Going back and forth to India continued twice more in 24 months. Gradually Bhagwan's mesmerizing eyes, his voice, his certainty consumed me. He described it as the seduction of the seeker. I wondered if this was how his lover, Viviananda -the brown-haired woman I had seen on my first night- had landed here.

Fragments of his words swam in my head…

"Be a ruler of the inner world…" yes, that's *what I'm meant to do…*

"There is a true kingdom inside…" *Yes, yes!*

"We all want to become kings but we go on searching in the wrong direction…" *I've been searching outside, wasting time…*

"Be a true king. And the beauty of the inner kingdom is

that there is no competition... " He gave us each our own empires.

How could I resist?

He was clearly seducing all of us but I didn't take it seriously.

He wooed us into surrendering to him so he could transform us.

How could anybody resist?

"That is my promise..."

If I stayed with him, he would be responsible for changing me because he said a disciple was absorbed into the master. I loved it. I *wanted* to be absorbed into him, delighted to be the moth to his flame. I gave myself to him, more completely than I ever did to any ordinary man, content in my cocoon, drowning in his words.

"The moment you are empty of yourself, you are full of God. Both cannot exist together, remember... It is either you or God..."

I was hooked...happily, undeniably, irrevocably; his to do with me what he wanted. I thrilled in this intense feeling where my senses were burning. This happened in his presence. Each morning at discourse, I soaked in descriptions of what I could be: a creature, not crawling on the earth, but flying to the ultimate. He changed my vision to see the god in everyone, and that existence and god are really the same thing. I was passionately reminded that we had all forgotten why we were on this earth.

Such sweet seduction. Listening to him was like being with a lover who enchants you, like being in love, my mind was in suspended animation.

Sam was as enchanted as I was, drowning in the same sea. We were closer than ever, mirror images to one another.

When Bhagwan was a university professor, he became well practiced in using his brilliant oratorical skills as a drug, drawing in the earliest disciples.

Surrounding his magnetic presence was the warm emotional envelope of the commune, an extended family built on love, devotion and absolute trust. All ages and nationalities, we were each other's brothers, sisters and lovers. There were PhD's, lawyers, doctors, Hollywood stars, farmers and a well known Tantra diva. Everyone and everything I wanted was here.

Each day from 6:00 A.M., I was busy meditating, sitting in discourse, going to the programs and therapy groups and back to meditation again. After a few weeks I got dysentery.

So it was back to New York with Sam for the next six months.

I recovered from the dysentery, ran more workshops and earned more money. When we returned to Poona, Bhagwan was giving discourses on the evils of marriage, its hypocrisy and lack of personal freedom, saying sooner or later the other person in the relationship wants space and fear arises because husbands and wives butcher love out of boredom. Marriage remains an institution because historically men have killed woman's ego. Women are used for sexual exploitation and men are used for economic exploitation. I heard him say that marriage is the *worst*, among many other "worsts," such as organized religion, the nuclear family, formal education, and of course, government leaders. I listened intently, secure in the knowledge that my relationship with Sam was unconventional.

The punishing ashram schedule made me ill. This time, I decided to talk to Bhagwan about staying on in Poona despite the dysentery.

Bhagwan had other plans.

"Go back to New York, get married and have children."

I shouldn't have been shocked, but I was.

"Oh no." I whispered.

It was the second time I had said no, after my first "no" to starting the center.

Bhagwan looked at me sternly. You did not say *no* to your guru. His look bore into me.

"No," I repeated more weakly, "I can't do that. I've been married before and I don't want to be married again."

"This is really what you've been longing for, Samsara, and you will regret it if you do not do it, especially having the child."

Guilt. He knew *exactly* the right buttons to push.

"I'll think about it." I said at last, feeling trapped, knowing that it had to happen because the master said it.

Sam and I went back to New York via Tel Aviv and Athens. I wanted to see Israel and he wanted to visit Greece. We narrowly missed being put on the Air France plane that was hijacked to Entebbe. That incident signaled things were going to get worse.

In October 1976, we got married. We found a large house and shared it with two other couples and children. I started my practice again and waited for the baby. Inwardly torn, I wanted to be with Bhagwan *and* be in New York; to have lots of lovers *and* be in a marriage; devoted to my husband who was a wonderful man, and not be afraid of pregnancy.

Months went by and no pregnancy. I felt guilty.

The following August I persuaded our housemates to come with Sam and me to Poona. Shortly after we arrived, we all did one of the Poona encounter groups. I didn't realize that orgies might be part of it. Bhagwan often said we all needed to go deeply into sex because the work of a sannyasin begins at the sex center, where there the energy "uncoils."

During the group, Sam ended up having sex with one of the women we were living with. I was devastated. No enlightenment there.

"How could you have sex with Thelma? She LIVES in our HOUSE." I screamed.

"How can you be so angry with me? *That* was the group leader's instruction? This was what we were *supposed* to do!" Sam said exasperatedly, watching me get angrier.

I was exploding with fury, hurt, humiliation.

"But why Thelma? Why not choose someone I didn't *know*? I am really, really hurt. We all have to LIVE together. Didn't you *think* about that?"

"NO." he shouted. "Of course not! I was just responding to the moment."

Out of control, I went on shouting, saying all the wrong things I could think of to blame him, blame Thelma, the group leader, Bhagwan, the commune. Everybody *else* was responsible for my hurt.

I was also pregnant and didn't know it.

Since my period had been late many times that year, I assumed that it was because of anxiety. Consulting a sannyasin Indian doctor, who told me I was *not* pregnant, I took prescribed hormone pills to normalize my cycle. Even the doc told me I was suffering from stress... maybe it was what I *wanted* to hear.

Back in New York, two weeks later, there was still no period.

I went to my New York doctor who confirmed my pregnancy; along with the prediction that the fetus was probably deformed due to the hormone pills I had taken on the advice of the Indian doctor.

Now what had I done? I had destroyed a life out of ignorance, taking pills for an easy solution, on somebody else's advice.

Sam and I had it out.

"Sam, this is a disaster. What'll we do? If it hadn't been for that encounter group, and you and Thelma, this never would have happened!"

I was great at blaming.

"Bullshit," Sam retorted. "You never wanted a baby in the first place."

"How can you *say* that?" My eyes filled with tears.

"Because it's true, Samsara. You have to face the truth and stop blaming me, Thelma and everybody else. It was all right for *you* to have that affair with Donald back in February, but not ok for me to have sex with Thelma in an encounter group. What kind of double standard is that? Can't you see that you're just blaming me and everybody else for the things you can't face in yourself?"

He was right.

I was terrified to have a child and couldn't accept that. It would have meant I was less of a woman. But, I was also afraid that my child would be deformed. And how could I raise a deformed child?

I had an abortion.

At the clinic, Sam was supportive but upset at having lost his baby. It was a difficult time for both of us.

"Oh Sam," I whined in front of the doctor and his nurse, just as they started the suctioning, "I feel like a selfish bitch… I just don't know what else to do! I *know* you hate me."

Sam turned red with embarrassment, squeezed my hand and left to wait outside.

Sobbing after the abortion, I made the doctor bring me this tiny fetus. I *felt* she was a girl and I had to say something to her. She was an angel to me, a little saint on her way to God.

Good-bye my little one. You did nothing wrong. And now you're home, with all the other little angels.

Getting off the table, I walked slowly out to the waiting room where Sam was.

He stood up as soon as he saw me. My face was contorted.

Taking me gently into his arms he said, "Samsara, we can try again… just let yourself be."

There were more tears. And punishments.

The suction procedure didn't work the first time around and had to be repeated two or three weeks later.

The doctor assured me it wouldn't be painful.

It was excruciating. My insides raw from the scraping, I was still bleeding several days after it should have stopped.

This was proof of my guilt. I deserved to be punished by God and Bhagwan.

I was bad.

I had committed a mortal sin.

I was an incomplete woman who couldn't be a mother.

I wanted my selfish life, *my* freedom. But the price was too high.

Three months later on December 12, 1977, there was a phone call from Bhagwan's secretary, instructing me to sell everything and come back to Poona.

That was it. I rebelled. Who does he think he is? Ordering me back like a pawn?

The abortion had changed me and I was resentful. Plus, I didn't want to go back. Depressed and overworked, I was angry with Bhagwan. *He* was responsible for the pain over this child because *he* told me to *have* it.

Putting the phone down, I decided I would get pregnant again, or at least *say* I was pregnant, so I wouldn't have to go back to Poona, right away. The next day, before I could say anything to anybody, I got a telegram from Poona: "no need for any pregnancy."

Wham!

How could he *know*? He'd read my mind! I'd better go before I was told to do anything else. OK, I said to myself, this is really it. Either I go on here, suffering with my guilt, shame and anger, or I go there and die in India. Some choice. At least there, I'll give it all I've got. I'll get enlightened with or without Bhagwan or die trying. I agreed with Bhagwan that life is like a nightmare: "if you are suffering in a nightmare all that you need is to put your total energy into waking up…"

In the nightmare, we sold everything we had and left.

It was not dying that I was afraid of. It was that Sam would leave me, and I'd be completely alone in India, which I *still* hated.

I wonder if we create the very things we're most terrified of: that our fears make them happen.

In Poona nothing was the same. I struggled with being angry with Bhagwan and loving him.

That spring, Sam left me. He had an affair with a voluptuous, maternal woman, who was in every way my opposite.

The night he didn't come home I cried with self-pity and fear. For three days I was absorbed in pain and jealousy.

God, Bhagwan, why is this happening to me? What do I do now? I'm all alone. How do I go on? How do I deal with this jealousy? I can taste it. It's paralyzing me.

I was dependent on Sam for my well being. Even though I had affairs throughout our relationship, I couldn't tolerate *his*. Sam was a very giving person, sensitive, warm and easily hurt. I had pushed him too far. He couldn't take my demands, fickleness and infidelity any more. I lost his generous love.

I sat with the jealousy. It was sour and metallic.

After three days and nights without sleep I felt this yellow-green like pus oozing out of my skin and brain. I tortured myself with pictures of Sam and his new lover, praying that the suffering would redeem me.

I had caused this and couldn't blame him any longer. Exhausted, I decided to look for both of them. I found them in the meditation hall, walked over and embraced them. All three of us cried.

"I can't get rid of my jealousy completely," I wailed. "But, it's stopped eating away at me. And I know Bhagwan wants us to go beyond it and move on."

Sam looked at me cautiously. The woman just looked at her feet.

Then Sam said, "Thank you Samsara. This has been a really hard time - for all of us."

From this moment, Sam and I began a new relationship.

It was still hard for me to see them together every day. Each time was a reminder that he wanted her more than me. I was not as pretty as she was. *I* was rejected and abandoned.

That was reality.

Nobody was there to take care of me any more.

At the same time an epidemic of dengue fever and hepatitis was breaking out in Bombay.

Poona was next.

One week later I woke up and couldn't get out of bed. With a violent headache, all my bones felt like rubber. As the headache increased, so did the fever. The dengue fever made me too sick to care about living. I wasn't told that it could be fatal.

Over the next twenty hours, I went in and out of consciousness, wanting to die more than live because every part of my body was burning in a raging fire. Someone forced fluids down my throat.

After a while everything became quiet. The raging stopped and the runs started. The burning became amoebic dysentery. From that day into the next I was occupied with dragging my body from the bed to the toilet.

I was sure that things could not get any worse. Dying was preferable.

The next day, there was green gunk in the toilet and my pee was bright orange. Hepatitis. By the end of the week, my skin was yellow and I could barely move. This kind of sick I had not even imagined possible. I was suspended somewhere between living and dying.

Quarantined with four others so as not to infect the rest of the commune, we were only allowed to see the ashram doctor. There was little he could do, telling us to wait it out and drink plenty of fluids.

Two weeks later, when the quarantine was lifted, I was emaciated, weak and desperate for company.

Lying in bed, listless, I heard a familiar voice.

"Hi, Samsara." It was Sam.

"Sam! You came! Can you stay? Can you get me some food? How are you?"

This was too much neediness for Sam. He recoiled.

"I just came to see how you are... can't stay... take care and be well. If you need anything..." he said going out the door.

Watching him walk out, I lay back sadly on the pillow, too sick to have my usual dramatic reaction.

No sooner had he left, three people came into the room. I pulled myself up by my elbows. The first was a striking, dark haired Indian woman. Knocking me back down on the bed with her energy, she looked like a grinning cartoon tank in a shapeless robe.

"Hi! I'm Sila and this is Belle. Yasha, you know of course because she's your roommate."

I had a roommate? I must have been so out of it.

Yasha was tall and quiet with penetrating brown eyes. In contrast to her and Sila, Belle was leggy, blonde and buxom; saying simply, "Hello," with a sing -song accent I couldn't place.

"We're just checking up, making sure everybody's taking good care of you. Are they?" Sila's eyes bored holes into me.

"Well... yes... Thank you... I'm just a bit weak still."

"Sure you are. Yasha'll be with you, now that you're better. I'll see to that!" Sila said with great authority. "Yash quit all that late night work you're doing and spend more time with Samsara. OK? Now we've got to be going. Make sure you tell Yash if you need anything."

And they were gone before I blinked.

It took a long time to get well.

Three months later, I went back to my old job, in the same tiny airless room where for twelve to fifteen hours every day, seven days a week, I counted money. Although I disliked the job given to me, it was the job *assigned* to me. I had to smile and do it. It was called surrender. A change of work was not looked upon favorably and my request for one was denied. Sometimes I asked myself why I stayed.

"Fun" was not a word I related to at that time. There was a kind of grim dedication to the commitment of getting enlightened at any cost. Even if it meant giving up my life and free will. Even if it meant nearly killing myself. But all the pain was worth it. Bhagwan often said that we would have plenty of ecstasy, along with the suffering. And with plenty of orgasms thrown in.

I repeated his words to myself: "In life you cannot get anything free... you have to earn... "No kidding. He's gonna tell me that the cost of enlightenment is high and I have to pay for it. Bloody hell, I've been paying for it!

"...And the suffering is in love... a loving orgasmic experience is the first experience of ecstasy..."

Shit.

Everything in the ashram, from music to work was designed to induce ecstasy, or union with God by being pushed beyond one's limit. This is what we were supposed to achieve. It was why we were all there in the first place.

Buddha, Jesus and Lao Tzu had all spoken about it.

But when would it happen?

I continued working every day until some weeks later I got viral conjunctivitis. This was not surprising as my immune system was already depleted from hepatitis and parasites. We westerners became infected by parasites through the water supply.

This latest illness shattered me. I wrote Bhagwan a letter.

What am I going to do?

Surrender came the answer.

What kind of sick joke was God playing on me? What kind of test was I being given?

The conjunctivitis sealed both blood-red eyes shut. Near-sighted in my right eye, I had only worn a contact lens. The left eye was blind from birth. So when the disease hit, I couldn't wear my lens.

All my life there was a deep terror of losing vision in my one good eye. Now it was badly infected and the terror was growing.

Yasha helped me find an ophthalmologist, who was in Bombay.

The first time I went to Bombay someone from the ashram accompanied me. But since I had to keep going back for treatment, there was often no one available to go with me and I had to navigate the train journey to Bombay by myself. The streets were fuzzy, so I had to memorize them, counting paces to locate the doctor's office.

I was afraid and guilty. Being sick so often, I believed I was taking something away from the community by not working.

By the spring of 1979, the conjunctivitis improved and I returned to work. It felt wonderful to be a normal functioning member of the commune again. The airless office and the boredom of counting money no longer bothered me. Maybe this was what was meant by surrender.

"Yasha," I asked, "Does surrender mean that you no longer care what you do, even if this work is so dull and boring?"

Yash didn't seem to understand that. She was the epitome of the perfect sannyasin. It was unacceptable to admit that you thought the work was boring. Work *was* the path to surrender. It was called worship. But I didn't even care what she thought of me because I was feeling better. The sky was bluer than blue, the flowers more brilliant in the hot sun, and the ashram with its lush, tropical landscape was stimulating me. Bhagwan's words were once again those of a lover telling me "…the moment you are empty of yourself, you are full of God…"

I wanted to be in love again.

It was then that Vimal, Bhagwan's cousin, came into my life.

One day, he walked into the bank where I was counting rupees. I looked up and saw Bhagwan's eyes looking at me. Vimal's gaze held mine for a long time.

I want this man.

"When can I see you?" I asked.

"After *darshan*. Tonight. I will come to Buddha Hall."

Evening music meditation had finished when he walked in. My body sort of fell into his, with a slow undulation that was trance-like. Swaying gently, we crumpled to the ground, lying there for several minutes in each other's arms, not moving.

Enchantment surrounded us and the hall dissolved.

Quickly in one motion I took his hand and we both got up walking straight ahead. He walked faster in front of me, leading me to his room.

What'll I do? He's Indian. He'll want something different. Something exotic. How'll I touch him? Does he kiss differently?

He walked into his room, turned around and said, "Good night, Samsara. I will see you tomorrow." Just like that.

Dazed, I nodded and walked out.

The next day, I cooked for him. The day after that I cleaned his room and invited him for a massage. The oil spilled generously over his body and his hands touched mine, fingers entwining. We were *gods* turned on by our own magnetism. His eyes opened partially sending an electric charge through my body, bringing me to the brink of orgasm. Then, hard and determined, he pulled me down on top of him. There was no foreplay, only an explosion.

Orgasm blew my head off. And I imagined it was the same for him, given all the yelling and screaming that went on.

He's Bhagwan's blood family. He must be enlightened.

"I know you want me, Samsara, but I cannot be possessed by any one woman," he told me one night.

I was not prepared to lose him. "I can share you, Vimal, I'm willing. I only want to be near you, to be around you. You are like an intoxicating fragrance. I want to be the kind of woman you can come to – always."

There I go again: the chemistry had me in its power.

Time changed. There was no more monotony. Counting rupees in the bank, one by one became a new adventure. He introduced me to an India full of intimacy; the people became new, different. Indians on the street now had a sensitivity, gentleness and impressionability I hadn't seen before. I could understand how deeply they were affected *and* wounded by Bhagwan's words.

Vimal, however, went along with everything Bhagwan said, even his condemnation of India's poverty, which was unsettling to me. Within a week of being with each other, we had several heated conversations.

"Vimal, I don't understand Bhagwan's criticisms of the poor. *You're* Indian, you were brought up here, how can you be so indifferent to all the suffering around you?"

Vimal shook his head impatiently.

"It's about time people woke up to their misery and self-pity so they can start to change and bring India out of its misery. Bhagwan's right. India is so attached to being poor. She has valued it too dearly."

On this subject, he had a point. Poverty had infected everyone like a virus. Here, the earth was bleached of all nutrients; vegetables were even white instead of green. Perhaps Vimal *was* right.

It doesn't matter, anyway. He's my own little god, next to Bhagwan, my big God.

I wanted to believe that he cared for me, but once I became ill again, with another bout of conjunctivitis, he never once came to see me.

He couldn't fuck me – so what was the point?

Reality was shit.

It meant I was insignificant, a trivial thing to be thrown away. My old, deep feelings of being ugly, blind, and second best took over again. I was too worn out to be angry.

The illnesses left me with a very weak immune system and a shattered ego.

One morning, in March 1979, Bhagwan's secretary, a petite, vivacious Indian woman, summoned me to the front office. Her message from him was brief.

"Bhagwan says to get sterilized."

After all I had been through… *this* too?

To the rest of the ashram, it wasn't such an unusual suggestion. He had often mentioned in discourse that there were too many children in the world, and his sannyasins should be free to have multiple relationships, unencumbered by pregnancies. Children could be adopted, not procreated.

At the time, given my extreme emotional and physical state, it made a bizarre sense to get sterilized. Since I would be with Bhagwan until the end of my days, why not eliminate the possibility of getting pregnant? With each illness it seemed my days were numbered anyway, and I was sure that I would never make a good mother. My own mother had burned this idea into me.

Getting sterilized would be a service to mankind, I believed, although I was oblivious to the terrible emotional and physical consequences of my decision. I proceeded to make myself into a kind of eunuch.

A couple of weeks later, I walked into the local Indian surgery with all my clothes on, sat down on the operating table, lifted my robe and was given anesthesia for the first time in my life. I awoke in a narrow bed with four other Indians in the room. Another sannyasin was sitting beside my bed, dozing off. As I got up, still fully dressed, he awoke and said we should leave. A motorcycle was outside and he motioned for me to sit in back of him.

Yikes. This guy has obviously no idea of what it's like to be sterilized.

The bumpy ride caused terrible pain. My belly was sore for a week and it took me two weeks to get the anesthesia out of my system. Then, back to work.

That was the way it was.

There was not only a different concept of hygiene in India but a different concept about the value of life as well.

Life's horrible anyway; so don't bring any more kids into it. Just get on with what you have to do. Why go to the trouble of sanitizing the hospitals and purifying the water system if life doesn't really matter?

Having now been sterilized and living the revolutionary ideas of Bhagwan's communal, enlightened life, I was now special. A eunuch in his entourage, I was destined for the highest evolution a human being could attain. I would become a "ruler of the inner world."

I walked differently. Everybody outside the ashram was less educated, less technologically advanced. We were building a new society. I felt tremendously powerful, detached from *ordinary* people. I thought I was finding the true inner me. Instead, I was losing myself.

Tensions between the ashram and the Indian population in the town grew.

The more Bhagwan criticized them for their complacency, the more the local Indians loathed us. They resented us for flaunting their holy ideals of ancient sannyas - a tradition of sacred poverty and non-materialism. Bhagwan called us the new sannyasins in his discourses. We were the new holy ones: well dressed yet unattached to wealth. He encouraged us to hold hands in public; praised the way we dressed; gave us freedom to smoke cigarettes and drink beer publicly. All the while he was saying things like Jesus probably had sex with Mary Magdalene, and that Buddha was simple minded.

Real religion was love: neither Hindu, nor Christian nor Mohammedan, not a church, a dogma or a creed but overflowing love. We were told that enlightenment could happen to each of us anytime.

And if I can become a Christ then I don't need to worship Jesus.

His words echoed 'heresies' throughout history. Words like "I am God," brought death to Christ and to Al Hallaj.

Popular resentment turned to violence. In discourse one morning, Bhagwan was physically attacked by an unknown man who threw a knife at him. Shortly after that incident, my life changed.

Sila called me into her office and told me to start a video and film department to document Bhagwan's life and work in case he was assassinated. I had no idea how to start such a thing. With no prior experience in film and half-blind, being told to do this seemed ridiculous. The ashram was a little like Alice's Wonderland: some things were upside down. An Australian sannyasin, who happened to be a cameraman, came to help me, offering his own camera and tiny cassette recorder. From then on, every word that Bhagwan spoke was recorded.

By the fall, I was told to film a one-day procession to Kutch, a small village, about fifty miles away. It was a potential relocation site if things got too dangerous in Poona.

It was to be a 35mm movie production, complete with five

cameras and a 23-man crew, with equipment from a Bombay studio, where we also did the editing. Once editing was in progress, the daily videotaping of discourses continued. Bhagwan's daily routine and ashram life were covered by audio, video and film. I was directing, producing, editing and mothering my crew. They were my kids and I felt special.

In the middle of all this activity, I slipped a disc in my back but continued right on filming. All that mattered to me was that I had been given the dream work of my life, and no sacrifice was too great. Although Yasha heard my daily struggles, work became my lover, stimulating me and giving me a satisfaction, completion and artistic fulfillment that I didn't mind working right through the night. The days were not long enough.

At the end of 1980, one of my friends, a thirty year-old sannyasin, who had been German prince, died suddenly of a cerebral hemorrhage. Just prior to his death, I was told to make a film of him, a memorial to the first sannyasin that Bhagwan had declared enlightened. At that time, there were only three of us in the film studio: my cameraman, music composer and me.

For three days and nights, grief drove us. We created an extraordinary documentary; going beyond anything we had ever done before. Our beloved friend had given us a gift by his death, and the powerful reaction to the video film catapulted us into a new dimension of art. We were no longer merely recording events; we were now creating a picture of history. Sales of the video to centers around the world skyrocketed.

All my previous suffering dissolved into the exhilaration of what was being accomplished: a legacy of immense value for future generations. For the first time in history, enlightenment was on film.

Outside the ashram, however, tensions were increasing. Sila was becoming more nervous about Bhagwan's ill health and our safety.

In March 1981, I was told to pack up and move all the

equipment, film and videotapes, *and* seven non-Americans to the U.S.

Reluctantly, I did what I was told, sad to leave my dream world. Bhagwan's words echoed in my head as I packed: "drop the past as if it never existed, always start fresh, from scratch..."

I was not allowed to tell anybody – not even my own department and the people who were supposed to be coming with me, lest the press be alerted.

How do you pack up everybody without telling them?

March brought the end of fairyland.

Just when I had made my peace with India, I was told to leave it. This seemed to be a characteristic of spiritual journeys: as soon as you get to like something, it gets snatched away. Or as traditionalists would say, when you achieve detachment, you are liberated.

Or some such nonsense.

The move meant dismantling the video studio, which was located in Bhagwan's house. As his personal filmmaker, I had a close and intimate connection with him, which I craved along with the status it brought me in the community.

I also had a new love.

After being without a close relationship for four years, one of my video technicians fell in love with me. I was not eager to give any of that up. I was scared.

We had to do the move under the noses of the Indian government. Told to take nothing with us but the clothes on our backs (our equipment was our "personal" baggage), even our exit visas were taken care of quietly. How was I going to bring all these foreigners plus the equipment we had smuggled into India, into the U.S. *quietly?*

The last night in India blurred into a million details, giving me no time to feel anything much. I was scheduled to arrive in New York on Memorial Day. There would be a skeleton immigration crew at Newark airport because of the holiday.

It was a boiling hot day in May when we arrived. Sweating, I reported to immigration that we were there to film a religious festival. Miraculously they allowed me, the seven non-Americans and assorted film and sound equipment entry...

I paused, remembering the tremendous relief that I felt walking out of the airport, having done the impossible.

The dinner bell sounded, and I was back in the lifeless, airless prison world.

Margret looked at me intently, absorbed in my story. We both got up then, having to clear the table for the other inmates, who were returning from the day's work.

"*Mon dieu*, Samsara! That sounds like a *Versailles* production in a concentration camp! How could you stay in such a place? Didn't anyone care about each other? Told to go here, move there... at the drop of a hat and all that sickness and suffering. How awful!"

I knew that Margret was remembering stories of the concentration camps of her parent's time, relating some of the things I had said to what she had heard. "Margret, it's hard to give you a complete picture of the place... there *was* a lot of caring among the sannyasins, or so I thought at the time. They were like my brothers and sisters, especially since I had none of my own. I thought this was how a real family was," I said as I was getting the dishes and silverware on the table.

"It sounds like we were cold robots, but that was our idea of loving detachment: an ideal of caring for and loving people without getting lost in them. Bhagwan spoke about this as a sign of enlightenment. But, it often lead to a feeling of being elite and far above the masses."

Margret looked at me, slowly shaking her head, as the other inmates were coming in. She squeezed my hand, and we looked at each other in the way you do when you share yourself so intimately with someone, and they know you like few others in the world do. Not even my mother and father knew things I had told Margret.

We sealed a special bond that day.

The burden, which I had been carrying alone, was now shared.

Chapter 7
Release, Part One

There is a saying that the only way out is the way through –
Claudio Naranjo

Nine days later, after dinner, I got sick.

It could have been the soup I'd just eaten, or the memories that came up after talking to Margret; or just stress from continually thinking about what decision the Court was going to make. I went to bed and woke up early the next day; feeling like somebody had drained all my bodily fluids.

At 9:00 A.M. on January 10, 1991, the warden came into the dining area after the breakfast was cleared. A quiet unimposing man, I wasn't surprised to see him, as he generally walked through the prison in the morning. He came over and stood in front of me.

"*Frau* Drakke, we got the decision from the High Court this morning. The Judges have given us permission to release you on bail."

My mouth fell open. For a few seconds, time froze, and the room was silent.

They believed me! Their decision is proof I'm not a flight risk.

"This is an historic decision, Frau Drakke," the warden said smiling. "Would you like to have a piece of cake from the kitchen before you pack?"

My belly objected to the idea, but relief flooded through me.

I can leave! I can walk out of here.

"Thank you, Warden, but I'll pass on the cake."

As I looked at him I began to feel a touch of apprehension.

Here I'm taken care of – fed and housed. Outside there will be a struggle to fight the extradition, prepare my case, find an American lawyer and earn money to survive. Samsara, think of that later. Now, start to pack and say goodbye. Oh, and ask for details of the bail.

"What are the release conditions?" I asked.

"The Court asks twelve thousand marks for bail. You must report to the police station once a week and promise not to leave the country."

Free! Well…until they decide about extradition. At least they trust me.

"Eh, *Frau* Drakke, your lawyer asked us to inform you of the following which I quote, "the U.S. Federal prosecutors, are most unhappy about this decision and oppose the bail.""

"Ha! I'm not surprised, Warden."

"Well, at least you'll be able to defend yourself with more resources on the outside."

Geez, I've only got ten thousand marks left after paying Hanna. I'm two thousand marks short. Who can I ask to help me? Maybe Katrin'll be able to suggest something. I'll call and ask if she'll pick me up and we can talk about it then.

"Warden, may I use the phone to arrange transport?"

"Of course, *Frau* Drakke."

Katrin answered the phone on the second ring.

"Katrin, it's Samsara."

"Samsara, how are you? Where are you?"

"I'm fine. I'm still in the prison but they are going to release me today."

"Wow, that's great! What time?"

"Now. Can you pick me up?"

"Of course!"

"How's an hour?"

"Ok, I'll be there."

I have to pack, and say good-bye to everyone. It's been three months and ten days since the arrest, and I'm not the same person who walked in here.

I went to look for my cellmate Kristina, who was at work in the main kitchen. I couldn't go inside there to say goodbye, so I scribbled a note wishing her well in the trial. Then I went back to my cell to pack. Margret came and stood in the doorway.

"The news about you is big! I left my cleaning and came to see you right away. I'm glad you are going, but boy will I miss you! Who will tell me juicy stories, now?" she said as she hugged me. "You will promise that you write me! I think I just make a good friend, and now she goes away!"

"I will write you, Margret. You'll soon be out of here, too. How do I get letters to Yugoslavia? You'd better warn the post office." I said with sadness in my eyes, trying to be light.

"Listen, you better pray to all your commune gods that the war doesn't get worse or I'll be a dead duck," she said so despondently that there was an immediate cold pain in my heart.

It was the last time I ever saw Margret.

By the end of 1991, I had received only two letters from her, one from Germany and the other as soon as she returned to Yugoslavia. The following year the war escalated and I didn't hear from her at all. I wrote back to her three more times but there was no reply.

After she left, I finished putting things in my bag.

Next I must find Stephanie and Maria.

En route, I met one of the guards who smiled at me warmly.

"I'm so happy for you, *Frau* Drakke. You deserve to be free! I hope all goes well for you out there."

"Thank you so much! I wonder if I could be allowed to say goodbye to Stephanie and Maria?"

"Sure. Come, I'll take you to where Stephanie is working, and then we will go to Maria."

This guard, *Frau* Schmidt, was a large, kind, grandmotherly lady who told me I reminded her of her granddaughter.

Stephanie was folding sheets in the laundry. She saw us and immediately came over to me.

"I heard! I heard!" she cried. "I'm so excited that you are going! Think of what this decision means for all of us. The Court is behind you. You may not even *be* extradited. Take heart and write often! I will miss you."

"I will miss you, too, very much, and I promise that I'll write. I'll read the newspapers and follow everything about your trial. Let's see each other when this is all over... I'm coming back to Germany. That's a promise. No matter what."

I was hugging her and crying. My chest hurt and I felt like something precious was being taken from me.

"Take care of yourself," I said lamely, wanting to say something much more meaningful but there were no other words. Time was running out and I had to leave otherwise there wouldn't be a chance to say goodbye to Maria. Gathering Stephanie into me with my eyes knowing it would be a long time before I would see her again, I turned around and left.

Along the corridor, *Frau* Schmidt walked me to Maria's cell. She was not allowed to open her cell door, but Maria could slide the tiny window slot back so I could see her face, and she could see mine.

"I'm leaving here, Maria. I just got word that the Court released me on bail. I will miss you so much!"

Maria's eyes opened wide and they started filling with tears immediately.

"Oh, that's great! I'm so very happy for you! Let's write each other, yes?"

"Of course! You'll be out soon, and then we can see each other. If I'm not extradited, I will be in Germany for years..."

As soon as the words were out of my mouth, I realized that it was the wrong thing to say. Even if she were freed tomorrow, she would be deported and probably not allowed to return to Germany, which meant I'd never see her again.

"But, I don't think so," I said quickly. "I think I *will* be extradited and then *after* I get out I will come back and see you, wherever you are."

"Oh, yes!" She said with more tears. "And we can continue our talks."

Frau Schmidt signaled that we had to go. "I miss you already, my dearest Maria… I will write. Please write… "

We were both crying, now, openly sobbing. I didn't think that saying goodbye would be so hard.

I went back to my room to pick up my things and looked around for the last time. My body felt heavy as I walked down the corridor to the entrance, a place I had cleaned many times. There was a long driveway leading up to the door.

It reminds me of Bhagwan's driveway! How strange. Freedom feels a little different now. When I came to Poona I was only interested in inner freedom. Enlightenment. Then there was the arrest. I gave up the very freedom I earned by leaving the ranch and everything changed once again. Now enlightenment is nothing compared to a whiff of fresh air. Simple things are so valuable, like walking out this door.

After saying goodbye to two other guards and the warden, who agreed to write a letter of recommendation for me, I took my bag, signed some release papers, and was handed my empty wallet. All the money I had come in with had gone to Hanna.

I walked out the door alone into the steel-gray sky of that January morning.

At the end of the driveway, Katrin was waiting, leaning against the hood of her Dad's old Volkswagen. I walked into her open arms and hugged her for a very long time, holding onto her, crying and shaking from the all the powerful emotions.

"Theodora, Theodora, Theodora," was all she said, calling me by the stage name she had given me in the bar.

"Come on, sweetheart, let's get into the car. It's so cold out here."

Thank god she's so practical. Her heart is solid gold.

Her mahogany hair and large expressive brown eyes warmed me like a log fire penetrating my skin.

She's taking care of me like a sister. We are more than sisters She is with me everywhere, inside my head and my heart.

"Let's go back to your flat and have a long, long chat," she said.

Katrin had phoned Johann at work, telling him I was being released. He said he would leave work early and couldn't wait to see me.

As she drove, I babbled on, scarcely breathing. Everything looked bigger, sharper. I could taste freedom, which was sweet, like chocolate.

Pulling up to the front door, Katrin said "You know we were all worried about you in there. How are you feeling, Theodora?" She picked up my bag, opened the door with the key that was under the mat and went to the kitchen to start coffee. I didn't answer till we were in the living room.

"Ah, Katrin, it's *great* to be out." I said lighting a real cigarette that I didn't have to roll. "I thought I'd have to stay there until I was extradited to another jail. This is like some kind of miracle. I still can't believe it's happened."

She reached for my hand, squeezing it tightly.

"Now, what's your plan?"

Breathe.

"Well, I have to pay the bail money. It's twelve thousand marks. There's ten thousand left after paying Hanna. I still need two thousand…"

"Theodora," she said immediately. "I'll help you. I'll talk to the rest of the family and we'll lend it to you. When do you need it by?"

"*Katrin*… Are you *sure* you want to do this? I'll need it by the end of the week." I wasn't expecting that she'd ask her *family* for god's sake.

"Of course, sweetheart. I'll help you any way I can."

Katrin's family graciously put up the money. It was a great gift.

How do I get to be so blessed to have friends like her and Johann?

Johann was thirty-nine when I met him. He reminded me of Charlie Brown with a generous nature, curious mind and voracious appetite for food. He was so willing to help me in every way that I often wondered if he had descended from fairy godfather land.

Both Katrin and Johann had known me for three years as Margaret Bonham and only found out my real name since my arrest, and that I'd lived in a commune for ten years. Yet none of that mattered to them. They saw *me*, not the stories that I had to create to stay alive. After the arrest, I was afraid that they might shun me when the newspapers ran the whole story and they realized I had lied about my years in the commune and my assumed identity. I think they tacitly understood that the lying was not only to protect myself, but also to protect *them* from incrimination and the kind of press harassment that I had experienced when I first came to Europe in 1985.

"Katrin, I'll go back to work. That is, *if* boss man Rudi lets me work without any identification. The *Polizei* confiscated my British passport and my American passport has expired."

"Well, can't you get the *Polizei* to issue you a temporary ID?"

"Do you think they will?"

"They'd better or else we'll stop serving them in the bar!" Katrin said with a laugh.

It was easier to ask the *Polizei* for a temporary ID than to persuade Rudi, who was a tightwad and scared of complications to let me work without it. He was obsessed with identification, and had often told us stories about his many Russian, Hungarian and Nigerian "illegals" who produced false ID's. When the *Polizei* found the girls, it was Rudi who was fined.

I had no choice other than to work for him. I *had* to earn a chunk of money in a short time. I also knew that Rudi liked girls who made him wealthy. And I was definitely one of them. I was sure that my new *Mata Hari* fame, which the bartenders had vindictively circulated among my regular guests, would make even more money for him as well as for me. I would use this horrible mess to my advantage. I would become the exotic attraction men yearned for, though I knew it would arose jealousy and anger among many of the girls.

"Once I start work, I must get myself an American lawyer."

"Do you have any ideas?" Katrin asked.

"Puneet gave me three options."

"Who's Puneet?"

"He's a German friend whom I've known since 1981 from the Ranch in Oregon. We became close when he invited me to share his apartment in Karlsrühe soon after I arrived, until I could get on my feet and decide what I was going to do with my life."

"Have I ever met him? What does he look like?"

"He's a tall, thin, handsome, gay guy who recently discovered he's HIV positive. He's one of the most courageous people I know and I love him deeply. I called him a few days ago and he suggested two male lawyers and a woman."

"Well, don't take the woman, after what you've been through," Katrin counseled.

"Perhaps you're right. But, I'm very partial to having a woman defend me. I think Hanna tried her best, though she was really not up to this kind of battle. The Feds can be utterly ruthless, and I want a good strong person who will direct Hanna on this end. I think I'm going to go with the woman, because I don't trust myself with a male lawyer. I might end up trying to seduce him and forget about my case. Besides, only a woman can stand up to those bullies!"

Ah, it's good to hear the humor returning.

"Well sweetheart, you certainly need someone who knows what they're doing. You've got a tough crusade ahead."

Ten days later, after visiting the police station four times and nagging, I got my ID out of the *Polizei,* who were more than happy to give it to me just to shut me up.

Katrin met me outside the station. We went for coffee on our way to Hanna's office to call my new American attorney.

"Katrin, it feels like I've been gone for a hundred years. Everything around here *looks* the same, but feels different. I'm inside this pressure cooker and the steam is increasing. Maybe, my blood pressure is finally getting above zero."

"Theodora, just hang in there and do one thing at a time."

Johann met us at Hanna's overcrowded conference room. He wanted to check out this lawyer for himself, being skeptical of anything American and legal. I put the speakerphone on, dialing Patricia June Peterson, a criminal defense lawyer, in Seattle. Hanna sat there watching me closely. Before I could think further about Hanna's reactions the call connected.

"Hello?"

"May I speak with Ms. Peterson?"

"Who's calling, please?" an efficient voice inquired.

"Samsara Drakke from Germany."

"Just a moment, please."

I wonder how many people she has in that office?

"This is Trish Peterson."

"Ms. Peterson, this is Samsara. Narian's lawyer, George Steinmetz, recommended you, in the matter of the Rajneeshee indictments. Right now I'm on bail waiting for a decision from the High Court here on whether or not I'm going to be extradited."

"Yes, Samsara. George briefed me on the situation. Do you want to know my background and experience?" she asked.

"That's not necessary, Ms. Peterson," I said quickly. "You were highly recommended, and I know you're a woman with guts, because I can already hear it in your voice. I'm hiring you because I want to make a plea bargain."

"First, call me Trish. Second, why do you want to make a plea bargain?" she asked directly.

I liked this getting to the point right away.

"Because I won't get a fair trial in Oregon. What's the point of bringing this case to trial if I am going to be found guilty?"

"I don't believe that, Samsara. You're jumping the gun. We can ask for a change of venue, get a new location for trial. There are many things we can do when the time comes. But, first I'll need to know what the facts of the case are. For example, what was your history in the commune, your position on the Ranch and what led up to your involvement in the incidents? Can you fax me a summary in the next couple of days?

"Sure."

"I would also really like to meet with you so we could sit down and discuss all these issues. I have some other business, which is going to bring me to Europe in the next couple of weeks. I could come to Germany to meet with you."

"I would like that very much, Trish." I said nodding to everybody at the table. Katrin smiled and I could tell she liked her. Johann looked at Katrin for her reaction. He had a frown, which meant to me that he was having trouble with Trish speaking such rapid English. Hanna looked glum, as usual.

"First, I'll fax you the summary," I continued. "Then could you talk to the prosecutors and suss out what it is they want from me? You see, when I said I wanted to plea, I'm not interested in talking about anybody else. Some of my previous co-defendants apparently made deals with the prosecution in exchange for giving hearsay information. That's how the indictment on this conspiracy charge came about in the first place. I want to make it clear from the start what my stand is."

Katrin smiled broadly, while Johann nodded. I spoke slowly and deliberately so he could understand. Hanna was still looking at me, expressionless.

"That's very noble of you, Samsara," Trish replied, "but I

advise you to keep all your options open. What is the state of the extradition decision?"

"It looks like the case is very strongly in my favor. George may have mentioned that Narian, Diva and I testified separately before the High Court. They appeared to be impressed with my testimony, and I think they were on my side because they granted me bail. Hanna told me that conspiracy in German law is not the same as in American law. The Germans are much more black and white: either you've murdered someone or you didn't. Since I prevented Sila from harming George Tork, I may not even be extradited. Hanna, do you want to fill Trish in on the legal details now or later?"

"I'll fax her later," Hanna said without changing her expression.

I paused, and asked Trish the question that I had been saving for last. I was waiting until I got a sense if I liked her or not. I decided that I liked her very much.

"How much will I need to pay you to represent me?"

"I usually charge a $17,000 retainer, initially."

My blood pressure dropped.

How was I going to get the initial fee? How many hours and days would I have to work in the bar to get at least half of it?

Trish interrupted my thoughts.

"Samsara? Are you still there?"

"Yes, Trish. I was thinking how I'm going to get the retainer together. I'll call my family in Arizona and ask them to send part of it right away. Is that acceptable?"

"Of course! Thank you for being so prompt in your response, as I know this is a difficult time for you. It doesn't have to be immediate," she said softly. "Let me know what you can send when you are able. For the moment, however, the most important thing is to send me the summary, so I know what and whom I'm defending. And, thank you for choosing me. You're not alone in this anymore, Samsara. I'll be with you. And, let's talk again after you've sent me the summary. Do you have any more questions that I can help you with right now?"

"How much have you heard about the case?"

"I've read all the preliminary material including the indictments. My staff has already researched the background on the commune from newspaper reports. And there's a Rajneesh center here in Seattle we're planning to check out, quietly. I've known about the commune since it began. We have a lot of contact with Oregonians here." She laughed for the first time, and I felt this caring emotion pour through the phone.

I have a partner! And a strong one. Maybe there's really some hope.

"Thank you, Trish. I appreciate your willingness and thoroughness. I'm a little afraid, as you probably can tell, even though I like putting up a tough front. I'm glad to have you."

"Thank you, Samsara. And if you have no other questions, we can say goodbye, as I know this call is costing you."

How am I gonna to raise all that money? I don't even know how much time I have. Suppose I'm extradited tomorrow? I have to pay back Katrin's family. Then there's the rest of Hanna's fees. Now Trish's retainer. How much more? And, how am I gonna summarize all the stuff.

Katrin interrupted my thoughts. "OK, listen. First things first. Come on, Theodora; get all that worry off your face. We'll do it. You have to send her an outline, no? So, you tell me and I'll type it. I'm a very fast typist, you know. I *used* to make my living honorably," she said winking at Hanna who was still frowning.

"Oh, Katrin, that would really help. Thank you so much. Can we do it this afternoon, so we can fax it to her tonight?"

"Sure. Why not? This is better than the movies."

I looked over at Hanna, wanting to ask her if we could use the conference room and typewriter, but I had to find out about her scowl, first.

"Hanna, what's up? You know that worry lines aren't good for a young woman."

"Samsara, this is happening too fast. I know you need

this American lawyer, but why rush ahead with plea bargain decisions before you're even extradited? I think we should concentrate on preparing the extradition case first."

Meaning she wants me to prepare the case and is worried that I'll get distracted too much and she'll have to do it all.

"Hanna, don't worry. We can do both. It's good to have a back up ready in case I'm extradited suddenly. You never know."

Why do I feel so prickly? I hope that's not a portent of something.

"Let's get started. Hanna, can we use this office and the typewriter?"

Now we're one step closer to America and sorting out the mess I left behind.

Chapter 8
The Sex Guru Meets the Rednecks

If addiction is an illness, the disease is authoritarianism.
– Joel Kramer and Diana Alstad, The Guru Papers

My film department and I landed in New York in May 1981. Bhagwan's coming to America was history, and it was my job to film it. He and his entourage of personal maids, a laundress, cook, doctor and assorted companions planned to stay at an estate called The Castle in New Jersey. Although we tried to keep him away from the press once he arrived, news traveled fast. The local residents heard some rumors about a sex guru in their quiet suburban neighborhood and two weeks later, the front door of The Castle was fire bombed.

People started calling, asking us, "Is Bhagwan here?"

"No idea," was our standard reply.

How'd they get the number? We're all sworn to secrecy.

"What do you mean you have no idea? We just saw him driving down the parkway!"

I *had* to lie. *But it's not really lying, just not revealing the whole truth. No different from movie stars protecting their privacy.*

"JB, I'm getting very nervous about the archives and

equipment after the fire bombers," I said to my very proper German cameraman.

"Samsara," he said slowly and deliberately, "You haf to trust ze will of ze master, do not worry, he will stop ze archives from being blown up!"

"Now, you're being dramatic!"

"No more dramatic zan you," he shot back.

We moved the archives to a safe house.

Before any further attacks could ensue, Sila bought the ranch in Oregon on July 10th. That was the way everything was done. Fast. No hesitation. 64,000 acres at the cost of 5.75 million dollars was purchased after what seemed to me like five minutes of discussion. The money probably came from wealthy sannyasins.

We were encouraged not to ask too many questions nor look at a bigger picture. Sarah's financial department handled all the money transactions effortlessly.

In September we left for Oregon, traveling one by one, on busses so as not to attract attention. Deciding to see my parents on the way, I was nervous, as I'd not seen them for five years.

How would they interpret all the press reports, which were inflammatory and degrading?

When I arrived, the door opened slowly and Dad's expression turned from normal grump to horror.

"Ma que ta mesenport be'ng anqueti!" translated to "Jesus! What'd they do to you in that god-forsaken place?"

Mom came right behind him, tripping, "What did that guru *do* to you? Have you lost your mind, going to Oregon of all places?" *Some* greeting.

"Calm down, everybody," I said walking into the house. "Let me explain! Hello! How-are-you? *Nice to see you after all these years.* LISTEN. Dad, I don't want to hear any criticism of Bhagwan. We are just trying to live our lives and carry on his vision of peace and harmony, that's all. We want to create a space for ourselves so that we can just *live.*"

"I don't see much peace. You people are just like that weird and dangerous Jonestown cult... just like the Moonies, " he said.

"We are definitely *not* like the Jonestown people, Dad. We have no interest in politics - or killing ourselves. Anyway, Bhagwan's vision is life affirming. All we want to do is make a quiet place for ourselves, live off the land, become self-sufficient and do all those things you taught me to value as a little girl. It's the American dream."

"American dream, my ass! You're a buncha hippies who want to live in L-U-V," he said stretching out the word and putting down his glasses on the dining room table, his eyes watering slightly.

Mom was nervously rattling the dishes, getting supper ready. She rattled dishes when she was fearful that Dad and I would have a fight.

This was all in the first five minutes. What would tomorrow be like?

"You're never gonna amount to anything, Cecilia Allesandra, unless you put aside that *nonsense and wake up!*" His voice cracked when he got emotional and his hands waved all over the place.

"Waking up is what Bhagwan is trying to help us do, Daddy." I called him "Daddy" when I was exasperated and he wasn't getting it. I continued, "You've got to open your mind to new ideas and stop being a prisoner of materialism..."

"MATERIALISM," he started shouting, "is what you grew up on, young lady! I gave you everything and you wanted for nothing. You've lived in comfort from the moment you were born!"

"And now, I'm paying for it – right? You're making me pay with guilt – right? "

"I'm doing no such thing!"

It went on like that for two more days. As I was leaving he looked at me sadly.

"You're just like your mother, soft in the head."

This did not make Mom feel good. She pretended not to hear.

"Will it be cold there in the winter?" she asked. "Do you want to take some warm clothes with you... extra blankets? We've got so many we don't use. Take some."

"Ma, I can't carry blankets with me. Don't worry. Everything will be provided. You *must* come for a visit!"

"You're not going to see *me* there!" Dad said disdainfully. "I'll wait until you come home."

Home is where Bhagwan is...don't say that to him. It'll hurt him too much.

"Ok, Dad. Whatever you want."

"Call as much as you can," Mom said, afraid of losing all contact with me. There were dark circles and deeper worry lines around her eyes than I remembered.

"Of course I will!" I said quickly. My heart was thumping all of a sudden, struck by how much she cared for me. I hugged her and then turned to Dad.

"You know I love you."

"Yeah, Yeah. Yeah. If you loved us, you'd stay with us. Ah well, *pachenze!*"

Patience. This was his usual way of ending a conversation.

Then I was on the road again.

Arriving in the Great North West, the land of hippy freedom, I was now in the land where all communes lived in blissful harmony with nature and their higher beings.

Fat chance. In fact, the very thing that disliked us in New Jersey followed us to Oregon – prejudice.

Ranch life was pretty basic: miles of hills and scrubland. Nothing else. That winter, I froze my butt off sleeping in tents, ice on my pillow. We were all masochists, suffering happily for our enlightenment. We even ate outside all through the winter, snowing or not.

In November, the first trailer homes were shipped and construction started on other buildings. By spring, several small two-story houses appeared, along with a large house of beautifully landscaped grounds for Bhagwan, a cafeteria, a mall with shops and restaurants and an artificially engineered lake and dam. The construction department was headed by Ruby, a tough, determined woman. The men in her department came to be known as "Ruby's Boys." Narian, who had been arrested with me, was Ruby's key man, and Sarah's boyfriend. He was well positioned.

Clashes with the locals began when we tried to change the graze land into farmland. Our neighbors did not embrace us workaholics, especially when they began to see different colors of people arriving daily, from all over the world. Though we changed our orange robes for coveralls, cut our hair, tucked our malas inside our clothes, worked industriously and reached out to neighboring ranchers with friendly smiles – they were not convinced.

It was as if we wore signs on our heads that said "SEX GURU'S SLAVES!"

In India, the press branded Bhagwan a "sex guru," and the label followed us. The international press portrayed him as a sultan, and all of us his harem. Some Oregonians who read these reports became convinced we were sleeping with each other in orgiastic rites. A free love commune did not go down well in conservative eastern Oregon.

Our neighbors started to become alarmed as we began changing the land with bigger and better machinery. What *were* we building, anyway, an army camp?

Houses sprang up, sunflowers sprouted, where they had never grown before and a magical kingdom moved in and "took over."

The phrase, "take over" stuck to us like glue. We were doing what no one had done there before: building the city of Camelot.

"Hey, JB, Sila wants us to film the city Bhagwan's calling, Rajneeshpuram. I think we'll need Moss on the recorder, and a separate sound unit because I'll want to do interviews."

"I zought you were depressed about ze way zings were

going," he said. " We're still jammed into zis trailer with all ze archives and equipment. And now you vant to do a film! I can't work like zis, you know... *and* we've got tons of orders for videos, which I have to duplicate by hand, plus all ze editing... I can't *do* zis!"

"Yes, you can, JB, remember what you're here for."

"Drop zis drivel, Samsara. *We're* not making any progress! All ze attention is going into zose political shenanigans about Sila wanting ze city incorporated. And now we haf to have zis mayor for ze city... zat bozo zinks he's hot shit since he's been put in as mayor."

"*Elected*, JB, elected, remember?" I was getting more frustrated.

"Stop yelling at me!"

"I'm not yelling. I'm Italian remember? You should know that by now... I'm just feeling kind of alienated these days, like me and the videos don't belong – like we're an afterthought. Soon, they'll take you and Moss away from me and put you on construction."

"Zat's bullshit." JB was five feet, nearsighted and couldn't lift even the camera, let alone a shovel. " We already haf a connection with public service TV who want zese twenty-minute programs to air. Now *zat's* an accomplishment! Don't zell yourself short, Samsara."

But I did

I feel like a fish out of water. My world is reduced to this trailer with the film equipment, duplicating videos, isolated from the frenzy of building; like I'm sitting on the moon somewhere.

There was a knock on the trailer door. It was Yasha,

"Samsara, I brought you some lunch! You have to eat, you know!" I heard her say outside the door.

Thank God it's her. She'll lift me up. She always does.

I got up from my stool and went to the door.

"Yasha! How sweet of you."

"There's some here for JB too. I thought maybe we could sit outside and talk for a bit."

"Sure, Yash."

I handed JB his lunch and then went outside to eat with her. We had become very close in Poona; but on the Ranch, as Sila's secretary, her free time was limited.

I hate it that we have so little time together. She's the only one I can talk to. She doesn't push me into being a boss, which is what everybody else thinks I should be. She's looking preoccupied. What's going on?

"Samsara, I'm having a lot of trouble." When she had the chance to chat, she wasted no words.

"What kind of trouble?"

"I don't feel like I belong here."

"Why, Yash, I have those feelings, too. But *you*... you have so many important things to do and Sila depends on you. You're really needed here, my love. Don't you think it'll pass?"

"No. *This* isn't going to pass. You know I had apprehensions about what it was going to be like in America. I couldn't see us continuing the ideal way of life we had in India."

"Yash – it wasn't ideal. We had so much sickness; so much trouble with the Indians who never accepted us... here, it's different."

"I don't think so, Samsara, not with the way things are going. Sila's planning an empire for god's sake and you know Bhagwan – he'll try to smash things as soon as they're built to keep us moving. His *device* of putting up a building on a 24-hour push then tearing it down, only to rebuild it, seems to me to be a lot of spiritual hogwash. I'm not happy here. Something doesn't fit... or maybe I don't fit any more."

"I feel the same way, Yash, but I want to give it some time to see what happens. Besides, where else would we go?"

There was a brief silence. She looked away from me into the hills behind us.

"I'm going to leave Samsara."

"*What?* Have you asked Bhagwan? Have you told Sila?"

"No, not yet. I'm kind of afraid to. Afraid they'll pressure me into staying."

I was shaken. Yasha *leaving?* How *could* she?

"Where will you go?" I took her hand very gently, stroking it.

How can she go back into the world? How will she survive?

"What'll you do?" This time I was anxious.

"Don't know yet. I just wanted to tell you I'm going. I finally reached a point, Samsara, where I realized that I couldn't go on like this. My life-blood is being sucked out. I feel like somebody else's doormat. And for what?"

"I thought this is what surrender was supposed to feel like: giving up all self-interest to become enlightened."

"I just can't stand it anymore... all this *waiting to be enlightened...* for what? I'm not even sure anyone ever gets enlightened. What is it anyway? Do *you* know? Does anybody know?"

Something deep stirred in me, shaking me, disturbing me. She was the last person I ever imagined leaving - steady, unwavering Yasha: my inspiration.

How can she leave me? And, how can she question enlightenment? But, what if she's right and nobody's really enlightened? Scary thought... but what if?

"Don't you think Bhagwan's enlightened? Don't you think if it's possible for him, it's possible for us?"

"I don't know, Samsara. I just don't know any more. All I do know is that I'm tired of being stepped on and used. I'm *tired.* " She stretched the word out and her shoulders sank.

Quickly, I gathered her into my arms and held her close for a long time...

She left three days later without any fuss. One of the sannyasins drove her to the station in Madras where she took a bus to New York. I hoped she would meet up with her family there. She never wrote to me, but I saw her once, a year later, at one of the ranch festivals. She looked tanned and relaxed. I don't know why she didn't write. She never said. Her leaving left me empty and numb.

I went on filming the city's expansion but something started changing for me. I began missing something. Perhaps it was because I'd lost the intimacy with Yasha or that my current lover, the resident Harvard doctor, couldn't understand my feeling of alienation...

Every other month eye diseases stopped me working for a few days. It seemed that I'd been sick ever since I had met Bhagwan.

After my third attack, I sent a message to him.

Why am I continually getting sick? My eye is dry and sore most times and I'm afraid I might lose the sight in it.

'Try smoking,' was the answer that came back.

"Smoking?" I asked Sila, who delivered the message. "What does he mean? I should start *smoking?*"

"He recently read an article that nicotine stimulates the tear ducts in the eyes. And more moisture will help your dry eyes which could be causing your conjunctivitis."

"So, I should start smoking to make my eyes tear more?" I looked at her doubtfully.

"*Try it.*" Sila said without emotion.

She's so surrendered. No emotion; just Bhagwan's voice. How'd she get like that?

Reluctantly I tried and my eyes started watering. Now I'd just gotten addicted to cigarettes. Before I could tell if this would stave off another attack, there was a new development.

I got married.

Dr. Jim B. Drakke or Anand as he was re-named by Bhagwan came from a long line of successful doctors. His mother and father were well-known surgeons and he had franchised clinics all across New Zealand, making a fortune and ready to give a large piece of that wealth to the commune. Stunningly handsome like an actor, the commune wanted him to stay in America. To stay, he needed an American wife.

Told to meet him outside the cafeteria one night, Ruby pointed him out.

"You're Anand?" I stood looking up at this large man with a boyish grin and dark hair that fell over his Mediterranean blue eyes.

It was the eyes that locked into mine that did it: those blue eyes... like Sam's, and the familiar current. There was silence all around me except for a pulsing that started in my breast and an unexpected surge inside my genitals, like a bird jumping into the unknown.

"Yes. I'm Anand. You're Samsara?" he said very slowly and deliberately.

Nodding I walked toward him. His arm reached out and pulled me into his chest. A big ocean wave came and carried me to a calm and safe place, as if I were a dove enfolded in my father's wings. Only the feelings were definitely not those of a daughter. Many minutes passed before I could move.

"Perhaps we should talk later?" he asked.

"I'm supposed to marry you, Anand."

"I know. How wonderful."

His voice was gentle and sweet with a rhythm to it that spoke of understanding and deep emotion. Surprising - coming from such a muscular body.

"We'll talk tomorrow. Good night," was all he said

I fell in love with him from that first moment.

We went to San Francisco to be married, where I met his sister, Aimee, and her husband, Robert, who were our witnesses.

Once again being swept up in emotion, the fairy tale Prince bringing new meaning into my life.

On the wedding night, however, Prince Charming was Ice Man.

Anand kept putting off having sex with me. He had absolutely no sexual attraction to me whatsoever which I refused to accept because no one had been able resist my seduction for long.

What can I do to make you love me? How is it possible that I can fall so in love with you, and you don't feel anything at all for me? I will make it impossible for you not to love me.

Returning to the Ranch, I devised a plan, which would give us time alone, away from the commune. *Then* he would fall in love with me.

*Our videos and films need a Hollywood market for network TV.
Anand can be my helper. We'll go to Californian sannyas centers,
sell the tapes and that'll build us a larger sales base so Bhagwan can
reach more people.*

Alone, I would keep seducing him relentlessly until he
melted.

It didn't turn out the way I planned.

I didn't figure on his obsession with his younger sister.

Aimee was gorgeous, honey-haired with generous boobs
and an outrageous figure. Both Anand and Aimee had had
sporadic modeling jobs. Anand had put himself through
medical school that way and Aimee had just launched her
career as a model with a major magazine. They were devoted
to each other and Anand saw Aimee as the ideal woman. My
shape and personality were the exact opposite of Aimee's so
I couldn't compete.

When we stayed at Aimee's home in Beverly Hills, Anand
revealed matter-of-factly, "I'm in love with Aimee. Always have
been... sorry Samsara... I didn't know it would affect you so
much."

"*Affect* me! I'm not a stone, Anand."

I then went to Aimee, who acknowledged that it was true.

"Aimee, how do *you* feel about this?"

"*Awful*, Samsara. It's been a plague in our family for the
last three decades. He's had this crush on me since childhood
and I can't bear it." Aimee looked at me and the pain in her
eyes stabbed me.

I took her hand, then and said,

"What does Robert think about this?"

"My husband hates it, denies it and ignores both of us."

"*I* don't want to deny it," I said "And, I didn't know I would
also fall in love with him. I can't do anything about how he
feels for you, but I *do* want him to fall in love with *me.*

"You're the first woman who wants to take it on. He's such
a playboy with those looks of his. Do you know how many have
fallen in love with him?"

She looked at me with her big sad eyes.

"And, you married him," she said, "So he could stay in the country, right?"

"Yes, originally. I didn't know I would fall in love with him. Deep down we are so alike, so compatible. It's just I look so different from his ideal image."

Anand and I left Beverly Hills and went south to bookstores and Rajneesh centers, coming back up to Hollywood, where I met some producers. Two months went by and still no sex. He regarded me as if I were an inanimate object.

We returned to Aimee's house in Beverly Hills. That night, pressured by work and trying to please him, I accepted the cocaine he offered me.

"Try it. You'll like what it does for you."

Anand snorted coke like most people took vitamins, convinced it was good for him.

Anything. I'll try anything to get to him. Maybe this'll turn him on.

Instead, *it* got me. I began using every day, stopped eating and carried on working, thinking how great my new body was going to look. I'd look like a model, too.

Everything's going to be fine. He's even a little more affectionate when we're snorting together. And I feel so good. So on top of things! I have so much more energy now than I used to. Why are people so anti coke? I don't understand. Maybe we all don't have enough research on its benefits. Wonder if Bhagwan's tried it? It can't be harmful. Anand's a doctor, for God's sake. He wouldn't give it to me if it were really addictive.

I owned the world and could make anything happen. Power. It was *inside* me. I felt like I didn't need Anand any longer – except as my source of coke.

Anand's parents flew in from New Zealand to meet me. They were as emotionally unavailable as Anand.

Now there's mommy and daddy, who don't even relate to each other, let alone their own children. I'm living with a group of aliens.

Three doctors under one roof watched me not eat. In the

January wedding pictures I had sent his parents, I had been twenty-five pounds heavier. My clothes were now hanging off me.

"Samsara, we need to get you some new clothes! You are getting so trim – pretty soon we'll have you modeling orange-wear for Vogue!" Aimee said, ignoring the bones sticking through my ribcage.

"Here, eat some chicken and forget that vegetarian muck."

"No thanks," I said. The thought of chicken made my stomach sour. I didn't even *think* of food. There was only my new body and my drug – at least Anand and I shared *this*. It was a link into him. A few times we had even tried to make love. But each time he got an erection, down it went, and I started to get pissed off, and instead flirted with other men. I had cut my hair and got new clothes. Coke, coffee and cigarettes kept me awake for forty-eight hours at a time. I would doze and then continued working, contacting TV studios, meeting with producers, visiting bookstores and centers, often making hundreds of phone calls to promote Bhagwan's books and films.

Nothing worked. I was a mess and Anand was just as much out of my reach.

His parents left. Aimee was due to go on a modeling assignment in San Francisco and I had lost another ten pounds. By August, I couldn't eat at all. One morning, I looked at myself in the mirror while brushing my teeth. Anand and I had had the twentieth battle over his refusal to make love to me. In the eight months that we had been married, we had sex twice, both disasters.

Sunken cheeks and hollow eyes stared ghoulishly back at me.

Who is this creature? I don't even recognize this thing in the mirror and my body feels numb. Where am I? What's happening to me? What am I doing to myself?

I started crying. How long could this go on?

Then, the bathroom went suddenly black. When I woke up I was on the floor, alone and dizzy. My heart was beating wildly and I couldn't stand up.

"ANAND!" I yelled, my voice rasping, "Anand!"

It was Aimee who came. Aimee, who wasn't a doctor, said, "Samsara, you *have* to go to a hospital. You're sick. Something is *really* wrong!" Her eyes were alarmed as she leaned forward and shook me. "Get out from under his nose before you're dead."

Anand walked into the bathroom and looked coldly at me sitting on the floor. "Samsara, I think it's best for you to go. Find yourself some place to go so you can cool out for a while. All this pressure is just too much for you. You're pushing yourself way too hard."

Raising myself up on my elbows, I leaned on Aimee and tried to stand up. My body felt syrupy.

Looking at Anand, I wanted to say...

Can't you see I'm trying so hard to make you love me? Make you want me? I'm squeezing the lifeblood out of myself to make my body, my looks and my personality into the kind of woman you want!

Instead I simply said, "OK."

Leaving the next day, I took a supply of coke with me, intending to wind down and get off the stuff slowly.

Anand did not want to go back to the commune, preferring the Beverly Hills lifestyle to the boiling desert work brigades at Rajneeshpuram.

I returned alone and defeated in August 1982 to desert scrubland that had been transformed into two thousand acres of thriving agriculture surrounding a growing city.

The same afternoon, Bhagwan saw me from a distance and immediately told Sila to admit me into the clinic. He said I was dying. I resisted but in I went.

The clinic was a small trailer with a few hospital beds. I was put in a room alone, which was unusual. If you were sick and not contagious, you were in a room with other people. Was I contagious or toxic?

I'll just eat, and gain weight and become healthy again. With no Anand and no cocaine, it'll be easy. No problem.

David, the doctor assigned to me that day, marched in and announced curtly, "You're anorexic. First, you're going to start eating and stop playing games. You're going to eat three meals a day. If you don't gain one pound a day, or if you lose weight, you'll be allowed no visitors and you'll be locked in your room. If you gain one pound a day, then you can have visitors and be allowed out."

What a pompous shit. Who does he think he is?

Bhagwan had sent him, so I had to do what he said. The staff watched me carefully each time I went to the bathroom.

I'm being judged and punished for going against the rules. But which rule did I break? Is it that I got off the ranch and away from the demands of work? Free to do my thing? Free to have somebody's money, somebody's drugs, and model's clothes? Hell, I even got to go to Rodeo Drive. Sin, for sure.

But, I liked it.

I liked being part of that power-world.

And all the coke I did was not really so bad. They don't even know about it. Now, I'm back on the ranch, away from Anand, cigarettes, coffee, coke, the lifestyle. I'll be a good girl, a good sannyasin. I've lost Anand, so I have to make it work here.

Dr. David came back the next day, "Do you know about Karen Carpenter?" I shook my head. "She was a famous singer who'd just died of anorexia. I want you to read her story. Here."

The magazine article highlighted that she had stopped eating till she passed out, had a heart attack and died.

Is that what's happening to me? Anorexia?

The article explained it as a chronic eating disorder due to psychological pressures.

The pressure thing fits, but I don't have any chronic disorder, only lovesickness.

But, I was too afraid *not* to do what I was told.

"David, what'll happen to me if I *don't* gain weight?"

"You'll be asked to leave."

"Why?" I asked alarmed. "I didn't do anything wrong."

"Sila doesn't want you setting any examples. Get on the scale. Let me see. Your blood pressure's 81/56."

I had lost another pound. David was angry, looking at me accusingly.

"It's up to you. Eat, or go – *or*, die," he said flatly.

I walked back to my bed.

How could I be losing weight? I'm eating.

"I'M EATING!" I screamed. Nobody came. They were told to stay away from me.

I'm all alone now. Nobody's gonna save me... nobody's even gonna see me.

Fear started like a slow-moving snake crawling up my spine.

My body's got this order to die and it's just carrying out the program. My organs are shutting down. Not digesting, losing weight and I can't turn it off.

Night came and I tried to sleep.

Why don't I just die? Do I really want to be here? Seven years have passed and I don't see any difference: no closer to being enlightened than when I came. Bhagwan's like an unfeeling rock? I've got a sick body, a broken marriage, no money, no career, my parents can't stand me and neither can anyone else here.

Some record of achievement.

All those years I thought I was like one of Jesus's apostles but at least they had faith. My own faith has been smashed... bankrupt...meaningless. Bhagwan's clever arguments have reduced everything to shit. I can't go forward 'cos there's nothing to go to. My film career is finished because someone else was put in charge.

I'll leave. Start over. Go back to Mom and Dad since they need my help. They're the only people who'll help me. Ha! That doesn't say very much for my friendships here. Got to try it – can't stay here. I've gotta have something to stop me killing myself.

The next morning I packed my bag and got to the door.

On the porch outside, Kiku stopped me. She was a tiny woman from Thailand, head of the clinic, Sila's personal nurse, and 100% committed to her duty. She was sent to watch me.

"Where are you going?"

I didn't answer.

"Where are you going? What's the bag for?" she paused and her voice became gentle, "Come on, let me help you back to bed. You can't just walk out of here. Where will you go on foot? It's several miles to the center of the ranch and 20 miles further to the City of Antelope. You know, the people are pretty unfriendly there. Come on now, I know you don't *really* want to leave us. Not yet, anyway."

Walking just a few feet had worn me out, so I put down my bag and let her help me back to bed.

Ok, I'll wait till I'm better.

Kiku told Sila about me trying to leave and the shit hit the fan.

The next day, Sila called a mandatory commune meeting. She announced to everyone that I had become anorexic in order to draw attention to myself. When the anorexia didn't work, I tried to leave. She warned everybody not to follow my example and not to support me.

Forty-eight hours later, I found out about this meeting. The only two people who had visited me since I'd been confined, stopped coming and I got suspicious. I hadn't lost any more weight so what was the problem?

"Kiku, what's going on?" I asked her on the afternoon of the third day without any visitors.

Kiku looked down. "Nothing," she said, still looking at her feet.

"I don't believe you." Silence.

She raised her eyes and I saw she was afraid to tell me.

"Kiku, what *is* it? Tell me, please. It's better if I know."

With a big sigh, she began. "Sila had a commune meeting and spoke about you. She said nobody should support you and that everybody should feel free to leave if they want and nobody should stop them. I was wrong to have stopped you."

The news rolled off me like water on oil. *So what?*

"Kiku, forget it. You did what you did. I obviously wasn't ready to leave; besides I'm not totally well yet. Do you think that's why JB and Pia stopped coming?"

"Maybe."

I felt devastated. A day and a half later, Pia, who took over my job as head of the video and film department after I left to go on the road, came to see me.

"Pia. How great you came! So, tell me, what's been happening?"

"Hi, Samsara. Came to see how you're getting on. What happened with what?"

"The meeting?" The one where Sila said nobody should follow my example?"

"Yeah. Well, you've been pretty well ostracized. Lots of people were shocked about it. Either you did something to piss Sila off or Bhagwan is using you as an example 'cause he knows you're strong enough to take it."

"I wish I were. I feel like I got my throat cut. Nobody's been to see me for three days."

"Well, I don't care what Sila says. I plan on seeing you and so does JB. Until today, they wouldn't let us come."

"*They?* Who?"

"David and Kiku thought it would push you over the edge."

I felt like a rat in a cage. I hadn't lost but I hadn't gained *the* pound either. Three days later, after eating three meals each day, I lost another pound.

I got more scared.

I've lost everything that was valuable to me: failing in my work, failing the man I loved, failing my community, failing Bhagwan and Sila. The networks hadn't accepted the TV programs. I have no idea where Anand is.

Outside the window the dry, empty landscape stared back at me.

What am I gonna do if I can't stop this death program? Does coke do this? Does it get into the body and brain and destroy them bit-by-bit? I certainly never before experienced such utter impotence. I can't even control my own body. It's dying in front of me and there's not a damn thing I can do about it.

Goose bumps started and an idea came into my head.

Make a decision: do you want to live, or not?

The goose bumps turned into panic. My blood was on fire, and I began screaming.

YOU MOTHER FUCKER! YOU'RE NOT DOING THIS TO ME. I'M GOING TO LIVE! NOT FOR YOU BUT FOR ME!

Another thought came.

As you eat, take the calories in the food and make them stay in your body. Focus on holding onto the calories with each piece of food you put into your mouth.

At the next meal, I put the first piece of food in my mouth and concentrated on holding onto every calorie in it with all my will. The next meal, I did the same. At the end of the day, I had gained a pound.

Finally.

Something had changed. From that day on, I started gaining.

I still feel like I'm poised on a precipice. Move carefully and slowly so you don't fall back down again. Just be here, accept what you're given to do on this Ranch and carry on. Leaving's impractical anyway. Walk miles into nowhere?

By October, I was stronger and twenty pounds heavier.

Mom and Dad don't really need me. Of what use can I be to them? They have their lives. I have mine.

During the seven weeks it took me to recover I was not allowed to see Bhagwan. I started to question my devotion to him. Though it was he who had rescued me from what was almost certain death by ordering me immediately into the clinic, in the end I had saved my own life. There was now an inner reliance I hadn't had before. I finally had what I thought Bhagwan had. And I got it by reclaiming my own life.

I don't need a master to tell me what to do, anymore. Bhagwan could now simply be my friend.

Shortly after, I was allowed out of the clinic on a chilly overcast day for the first time to take a walk, unsupervised. On the road, I heard a car coming up behind me. I didn't turn around until the car was almost upon me. It was Bhagwan. I simply looked at him. No awe, no wonder, no heart stopping. He looked back at me and smiled. I walked back to the clinic feeling very ordinary and glad to be alive.

As time went on, I knew that I didn't *want* to stay on the Ranch, but decided to stick it out for a while longer. I even finished off the small amount of coke saved from my LA days. It didn't give me the same lift I craved, yet I knew if I gave into that craving, I would be its prisoner again, compelled to take more to satisfy the desire. What I desired was something more than a drug high. Something impossible, nameless, elusive.

Depression came instead. And it was winter. The little girl part of me was gone.

Winter brought added stress to the Ranch. There was so much pressure to achieve, produce and build a city in such a short time.

By December my depression was still there. Life in the commune was relentless labor; but outside looked like insanity: rats in a maze for survival.

Here, fed and housed, all I had to do was follow the will of my bosses. I even persuaded myself that Sila had acted for my own good in calling that commune meeting against me. After all, I deserved to be punished. Secretly, though, I was angry. And since there was nowhere to express the anger, I stuffed it.

My real reason for staying was because life in the commune gave each of us a "special" quality, like we were the elite of the world, which Bhagwan intimated over the last four years. All the references to "you are like kings..." certainly gave me that impression. We made our own rules, working every day, from daybreak till midnight.

At the end of the day, the laundry put our clothes neatly on our beds; our rooms were cleaned. The legal department took care of taxes. The medical department took care of our health. The only individual responsibility was to say "yes" to what we were told to do whether we liked it or not, all the while believing that we were far better off than the boring peons who trudged along in the outside world, captives to a corrupt government and bound by meaningless laws – while paying the taxes for them.

My work that winter was in the garden and my hands froze. Hating every minute of the two weeks there, I hid my hatred under smiling surrender.

Then, Belle, the head of personnel, transferred me to the Pythagoras medical clinic as a receptionist. Kiku, the clinic head, was my new boss. She had little patience for what she perceived to be middle class whiners, like me.

Since I had been a boss in my own department for so long, it was difficult watching the haphazard daily routine of the clinic, which I thought could be organized much better.

"Dr. David," I began. "Kiku has you double scheduled again. You have two lumbar patients at the same time."

"I thought *you* were in charge of scheduling!"

"Kiku keeps changing it, promising people appointments without checking the schedule book. Then the patients come to *me*, pissed off. Then *you* doctors get pissed off at me!"

"Samsara," Dr. Samarpan broke in, "I have to go to Bend Hospital because Simi has a broken leg which needs x-rays. Cancel my morning appointments. Thanks."

Then he was gone. I looked down at the book and saw that four people were scheduled for him.

"This is what I mean," I said to no one in particular. "He's got four appointments this morning. Kiku could have sent a different doctor to Bend."

Kiku's plastic smile rushed in ahead of the rest of her body. Having been with Sila all morning, she ignored me while she faced David, "Just book 'em each for twenty minutes. David, *you* see them. Just cut out your flowery talk," she said with the sugar-on-shit voice that everybody in the whole clinic hated. The woman was like a phony politician fishing for votes.

I often still thought of quitting but you didn't just *quit a* commune. Spiritual "policy" dictated you had to find a way to work through the problem. It was not ok *not* to like someone. You were supposed to figure out why you didn't like them and move through it. I decided I would learn to love this work and learn to love Kiku no matter what because I had decided to stay and now this is how I had to do it. I swallowed my revulsion.

Why am I answering phones and shuffling papers, when I have so much expertise in organization? I bloody well created a whole department from scratch.

My restlessness increased and by the spring, I'd had it. I went to see Belle. She and I had been buddies in Poona.

"Belle, I can't work in Pythagoras."

"Why? You still having trouble with Kiku?"

"No, I took care of that. I just accept her now as she is. It's easier on my blood pressure."

"Then why can't you stay there?"

"I'm going nuts, Belle. I could be doing a lot more than just filing papers."

The next day, I was put in the domestic department in Magdalena Cafeteria, chopping vegetables.

A little while into my chopping career, when I'd managed to lop off the tips of three fingers, I knew this job was not for me either.

Meantime, the commune had just purchased a hotel in Portland as a commercial front for its corporate offices. I eagerly volunteered to go as part of the domestic staff, seeing it as my chance to get off the Ranch.

I arrived in Portland at the same time the press did. Rajneeshees were making headlines. Corporate Rajneeshpuram was bursting into Oregon society, as commune businesses developed worldwide.

Belle headed Rajneesh Legal Services (RLS) and The Rajneesh Neo Sannyas International Commune, (RNSIC) a multi-national corporation, with satellite centers around the world. These corporations together with Sarah's Rajneesh Financial Institute (RFI) held meetings in Portland regularly. Sila was head of the Religion of Rajneeshism, complete with its non-profit "church" status. Ruby controlled Rajneesh Construction. The hotel was a convenient link to the world.

By 1983, several hundred thousand people across the globe were involved. Often as many as two thousand were on the Ranch at any given time. Nearly ten thousand came to the July Festival.

Portland was dynamic and, for the first time since leaving Poona, I felt at home. If I could go there from time to time, the Ranch was endurable. My first work rotation at the hotel was making beds and cleaning toilets all day. But, the atmosphere was electric with people, meetings, press and guests.

Life was organized into two-week segments: hotel-Magdalena Ranch Cafeteria-hotel. Being a manipulator, I tried to extend my time in Portland, and shorten my time on the Ranch.

When sent back to Magdalena, I spilled the entire contents of a large wok of cooked vegetables all over the floor on my first day. Nauseous from the smell, I was trying to avoid throwing up in the damn wok. Big boss Maya immediately came out and ordered me back to cutting vegetables, from which I had been transferred the last time due to badly cut fingers.

Kitchens were problematic for me from my Mom and Dad days, when they yelled at me for being in the way. They were gourmets, who told me I didn't belong. It hadn't worn off yet.

Maya bothered me from the first moment I met her. I just didn't trust her. She was a large, bright, jolly woman, in her late twenties, who seemed like she was perpetually seventeen. She had brown hair and a Charlie Brown face. She waved her hands expressively and almost never spoke to me. I tried to talk to her several times about my nausea around cooked food and each time she brushed me off with, "I'm *very* busy. Can you come back another time?" Her look made me feel like I was some insignificant complaining drone. There was *never* a convenient time.

I told people that my nausea was a lingering side effect from being sick. What I *didn't* say was that I was prepared to use any excuse to get away from the cafeteria, which I hated even more than the frozen tundra.

Diana, another profoundly surrendered peon, was my other boss. She came to Magdalena to plan and discuss menus for the two restaurants on the ranch. She ran the shifts when Maya wasn't there. But Diana, I trusted, as I'd known her from Poona days. She had a way of standing still and really listening when I talked to her.

After a particularly difficult day, I decided that I had to say something.

"Diana, I'm having so much trouble with these big pots. The smells are making me sick. Can you suggest anywhere else I might be useful?"

"Well," she said in a soft southern drawl, "Ah think we could use ya up in Portland mo'. Ah'll see what ah can do."

She knew that I loved being at the hotel because she'd spotted me there, smiling and laughing. Two things I never did on the Ranch.

Shortly after the wok incident I was sent back to Portland, and promoted to receptionist. It was the happiest time for me since Poona, with one tiny snag. Eve, the boss, scared the shit out of me and everyone else. The woman looked like a small Sherman tank, with violet eyes that bore a hole into whatever her gaze fell upon. She talked in small clipped sentences. Temperamental and unpredictable, she blew her stack all the time. Nothing anyone did was good enough. I avoided her as much as possible.

That July in Portland was unusually warm. One night at the end of an almost perfect summer day, I was standing in the lobby of the hotel after dinner. Suddenly, the whole room shook as if from an earthquake and there was a huge explosion above my head. It was so unexpected that there was no time to be scared. We each grabbed the closest person and ran out to the street. The top floor had been blown off.

"God! What happened?" The person standing next to me asked.

"Looks like someone blew off the top of the hotel," a voice said behind me.

"Like a bomb." It was hard to see clearly through the smoke and darkness.

"A bomb? Who on earth would want to bomb our hotel?"

"There's the siren. Must mean the police and fire department."

"Is anyone else inside?"

The Red Cross, police and fire department all arrived at the same time and there was chaos. Finally we were told to walk down the street to a nearby hotel, which the Red Cross had organized for us spend the rest of the night.

The next day, returning to the wreckage, we saw that the top floor was blown out and the two floors below were damaged. There was soot and water damage everywhere from the fire.

The priority was to clean up. No time to dwell on who did it.

Shortly after, one of Sila's assistants, Biriani, nicknamed Berry, called me while I was cleaning up the front office. She was a tiny, wiry woman with curly blond hair, who got right to the point.

"Sila and I have decided that we want you to go out and do some research on various subversive groups. She remembered that you researched a religious piece for the Ranch's university a year ago. She said you have an ability to dig up obscure people and find out information about them. We have a lead that the bomber is connected to one of the groups. We've heard that there's a negative attitude towards us from these groups due to the press reports of our policies of accepting everybody regardless of religious or ethnic backgrounds. Start with one of the local libraries and find out all you can and *don't dress in orange*. Dress like one of the crowd. Come upstairs to my room, I've got some regular clothes for you. You're to report back to Sila tonight."

Up I went and out I came in this ridiculous outfit. Here I was, in the middle of summer, wearing a heavy white wool pullover and wool pants. Self-consciously I went across the street to Portland's city library.

After spending the first of many afternoons in the library researching the KKK, fundamentalists, survivalists, white supremacists and others, I had a pile of solid information that fit the leads we had been given about the bomber.

That night I called Sila.

She said, "Fine. Stop everything else you're doing. You and Berry work full time on finding out everything you can about this bomber: who he's directly connected to, what's being plotted against us and bring the facts back to me so we can give it to the FBI."

The bomber who had been the only one injured, was in the hospital. Both his hands were blown off. Berry and I traced information using the numbers and addresses from the bomber's wallet, pieces of which we found in his hotel room after the blast. After several phone calls, we tracked down his house in LA, and discovered he had two accomplices who were from a cell in Chicago. In case the FBI needed it, we got descriptions of them.

The FBI was a little slow. They were just getting started on the case.

A week later, we turned over our information to them. Searching his LA house, they found some of Bhagwan's books and tapes along with manuals and paraphernalia on how to make bombs. The bomber was finally charged and convicted.

From this incident on, the state police urged us to send commune members to the Police Academy for training so that we could have our own police force on the Ranch. It became known as the Rajneeshpuram Peace Force. Berry and

I began giving information on subversive groups to the Peace force Chief, who was a small, well-built woman from East LA, named Prada.

Because of the bombing, it was recommended that we install a tape recorder at the main switchboard of the hotel. Part of my job was to record threatening phone calls, reporting them to the Chief. She in turn passed the information to the police, so I was told.

In order to gather more data on the group associated with the bomber, I compared the voices on these recorded phone calls with those of earlier calls I had discovered in my investigation of the bomber.

Putting together the evidence we had already gathered on the bomber, I managed to find associates of his all over the country along with other groups they were connected to. Whether or not the other groups were involved in our bombing incident was not certain, but the main bomber had to get money for his operation from somewhere, as he was only an unemployed baker.

Sila was delighted with what our research had turned up. Because of our success in uncovering the bomber's identity, we were assigned research full time.

"Hey, Berry, this is great stuff here. Did you know that there's a group in Idaho called The Church of Jesus Christ of the Aryan Nations with a reverend at the head and his mission is white supremacy?"

"That's old news, Samsara. We've got to find the funding behind these groups. That's where the power sources are and I'll bet you we find *their* ideologies are against ours."

"But, how could they be against us? Bhagwan's philosophy has always been tolerance for everyone – even the right-wingers. He's knocked down every group equally!"

Berry smiled ruefully, "You're so naïve. It's not that these groups per se are against us. The money *behind* them is. I think that Bhagwan has ticked everybody off by flaunting his many Rolls Royces."

"I still don't get it. Why would billionaires care? And why would they use right-wing groups to do their dirty work?"

"So the heat'll be off *them*. It makes the liberals hate the fundamentalists. Rule of thumb: use the little guy who's so busy trying to be a wanna be that he'll do anything to be accepted; or for a price."

"But this Aryan Church – this is *too* absurd. How could anyone see Jesus as being an Aryan? Frankly, I don't see why everyone doesn't recognize Bhagwan as being a master just like Jesus, or Buddha. No matter what crazy things Bhagwan has done, they all seem like masterly devices to me – indications of a wisdom beyond our ordinary day to day thinking."

"Ok, Sam, enough theology. Let's look at the Billionaires Directory and find out who's funding that Church and some of these other wacko groups."

"Sure, good idea. I love this research, Berry. I feel like an explorer in unknown territory."

Meanwhile, I thought I was helping to keep the Ranch safe. By being a *special* agent, a secret hero sleuthing around in the underworld, I was keeping the babes and little children safe from harm as *well* as assisting the police.

Even though I didn't like making up identities to cover up being a Rajneeshee, it was necessary in order to gain more information. The pretense started to give me a thrill, and eased my anxiety. I was a noble knight, a Robin Hood.

Berry was great at switching identities and I tried to be like her. Sila *adored* our antics; and I loved being wanted and needed by the power source next to Bhagwan.

We met people in restaurants, bars, on the street, in the libraries, anywhere we thought information could be found. We went to church meetings, penny socials, bake sales, barbeques. We mingled with the participants, prayed at the churches, held babies and joined in rallies. We were Miss Next-Door-Neighbor and her spinster cousin.

Sometimes I was afraid. Afraid of people discovering who we really were and afraid of what I was hearing at the meetings.

Putting on blue clothes and talking like middle class America made me feel safer. It was assumed you were a Rajneeshee if you wore any shade of red in Oregon, guaranteeing that you would be treated with contempt and suspicion.

If these nuts find out who we are, we're dead ducks. They've all got guns, and they don't care who they shoot.

In the fall, we were told to go to Washington D.C. to interview one of the Oregon senator's aides. A December 1982 INS ruling denying Bhagwan permanent resident status was supposedly connected to opposition from one of the Oregon senators. He believed that the Rajneeshees were a threat to the whole way of life in Eastern Oregon. Our PR girls had already spoken to him, and our job was to see if he told us the same things he had told them.

While in D.C. we took the opportunity to find out what other politicians were thinking of us. Our cover was that we were writers, doing a story on them. It was true. We just didn't tell them it was for Sila.

After talking to one INS official, we learned that a number of undercover agents had been sent to the Ranch to find out what was "really" going on.

Here we are infiltrating them, while they're infiltrating us. Gives me a sour feeling.

"Berry, *The Rajneesh Times* reported that the Oregon Land Conservation and Development Commission devised a set of temporary rules that are now supposed to be retroactive to August 1981, stating that a county would have to come to the Commission before incorporating a city. That affects us directly because Rajneeshpuram was incorporated in November 1981."

"Samsara," she said dismissively, "That's stale news by now because the Oregon Attorney General just issued a statement saying that the municipal status of Rajneeshpuram violates the religious establishment clause in both the state and federal constitutions. He says that the city is owned and controlled by a religion. And, on top of that, there's an injunction against any new construction whatsoever. I think we'd better investigate who and what is instigating all this legislation against us."

When we got back from D.C. in December 1983, Sila came up with an idea for Berry and I to live undercover in The Dalles. The goal was for us to live there for "a while," getting to know the people and joining groups. Eventually we were supposed to get ourselves on the Town Council. She wouldn't elaborate how long "a while" would be. I was nervous.

In January 1984 we rented a small two-room apartment in The Dalles with the kind of mismatched furniture you throw in your attic, and a dog, which the last renter left behind. Berry was getting antsy to infiltrate the locals as soon as possible.

"*You've* got to join that conservative dunking Church with Pastor Tates, who hates our guts," Berry hissed at me. She was angry and unpredictable these days and beginning to scare me. Moody from the beginning, I thought that was normal for her and I learned to take it. The pressure of living alone in this apartment with different identities, far from the commune and our friends began to grate on both of us, our nerves got more and more raw. Walking the dog, now named Socks, was my relief from all the craziness.

Because we were working long hours in scary circumstances, her instability made life difficult. Our work was secret and Sila was the only one I could talk to about her mood swings. The only thing was, Sila didn't believe me.

"You're exaggerating," Sila said one night on the phone when I was alone in the apartment. "Berry's just tired and wound up. Tell her to come back to the Ranch for some R&R for a few days."

"You tell her, Sila, she doesn't listen to me."

And indeed when Berry came in very late that night from another council meeting, she slammed the bedroom door again and went to bed.

Since I had been "baptized" (dunked) in Tates'

fundamentalist Church, I was forced to play the role of a very devoted, sweet, Christian prude.

It wasn't easy leading one kind of life on the outside and feeling the opposite inside. Living the persona of someone who was supposed to be the exact opposite to myself, and against all my theological principals, I became introverted and disoriented, often finding myself taken over by my role. *And,* there was Berry's increasing volatility.

Sitting at one Thursday night prayer meeting, I listened to Tates describe how he wanted to destroy the Rajneeshees, everything they (I) stood for and burn the place down. They (we) were witches, devils, prostitutes and Bhagwan was the anti-Christ.

I gotta get out of here.

Throughout the sermon, giant butterflies were flapping around in my stomach, so loudly I thought the congregation could hear them inside me.

Things got worse.

One night, Berry came back from a land use meeting reporting that some of the members discussed bombing the dam at Rajneeshpuram.

She'd secretly taped the meeting, and the venom in their voices chilled my spine. After that night, she started acting more and more like the personality she was pretending to be, giving me orders.

"Samsara, you're to invite Tates here, ask him directly about the Rajneesh situation and tape the conversation."

"Just like that? Are you kidding? Let him come here? He'd never go for it! Even if I hide the recorder, he'd smell something. Let's think of another way."

"Don't argue with me, just do it! You *will* do it, or I'll SEND YOU BACK TO THE RANCH!" she screamed at the top of her lungs. I knew the landlady heard her because there was a rumble below us. Berry's face was red and her eyes bulged, as did the veins in her neck.

I gotta talk to Sila again and make her understand before something dangerous happens.

Although Berry was my immediate boss, she was becoming increasingly dangerous. Part of me wanted to cover up what was occurring because I understood the pressure on her to succeed. I also did *not* want to go back to the Ranch. Covering up won over survival.

Later that week, when we returned to the Ranch to give reports, she put on her devoted sannyasin act, which fooled everybody. I was stuck between wanting to do my job perfectly, blowing the lid on Berry's behavior and surrendering to my boss because I was afraid she'd can me.

But my boss was going crazy and I was the only one who knew it.

Back in The Dalles, Berry started disappearing for two days at a time, leaving me alone. She'd return unexpectedly, not saying a word to me, ignoring my questions.

I started having headaches and severe back pain, which I later realized was because I was denying what was right in front of my eyes. Acting out my "role" as convincingly as I could and hiding my fears about Berry, I felt increasingly nervous and took risks.

I was pleased that I got evidence on Tates, recording him saying that he would do anything to get rid of the Rajneeshees evil influence, But, there was proof of increasing violence aimed our way, which I was powerless to stop – just as I was unable to stop what was happening to Berry

In the chaos, the one source of sanity was Socks, who would wag his tail and look at me with pure love. Since I was never far away from tears, he would jump up on to my bed, curl up beside me and lick my fingers, trying to console me.

Something was going to happen.

March 6, 1984 the phone rang.

"Hello," I said.

"Are you a Rajneeshee?"

"Who *is this*?" My pulse jumped.

Get calm, find out who's calling, and get him off the phone.

"This is John Sharkey from The Dalles Radio. I had your

license plate traced and it came up as registered to RNSIC. I want to know: are you a Rajneeshee?"

Damn!

"How bizarre. That car was bought used. How should I know who owned it before? And, how dare you question me!"

"Perfectly good question, ma'am. But you still haven't answered me: are you a Rajneeshee?"

"Of course, not!" I tried to sound convincing, trying to convince myself that in my current role I was *not* one.

"I don't believe you."

"That's your prerogative and misfortune. Good day." I hung up.

We have to get out of here immediately. And quietly so they don't track us. Berry's gone so I'll have to organize this myself... After yesterday, when she grabbed my hair and threatened to throw me out of the car, she crossed the line over into insanity. Where is she?? Get yourself together. Stop wasting time thinking. Call Sila.

Ruby answered the phone.

"Ruby, we've been found out. A radio news man traced the car plates and accused me of being a Rajneeshee."

"What did you say to him?"

"No, of course! But I think the gig's up and we should leave. Thing is, I don't know where Berry is..."

"Well, start packing. Think up a story to tell the landlady and we'll get you out of there."

When Berry came home late that night, she went to her room and locked the door. I tried talking to her, speaking gently from the outside, but she didn't respond. I couldn't sleep all night.

Before dawn, I took Socks for his walk, and when I came back, the door was double-bolted from inside. I called to Berry through the door, quietly, not wanting to make a scene. There was no response. I walked to a phone booth and called the Ranch. Belle answered this time and I told her what was happening.

"Ruby told me about it yesterday. What do you need, Samsara?"

"I need you to send somebody who can pry a lock and talk to Berry, so we can get out of here."

"You got it."

I sat down outside Berry's window on the side of the house, praying she wouldn't burn the house down.

To hell with her being pressured. I've been pressured, too. How could she abandon me like this? And, what was she planning? Maybe she's selling us out? Calm down. Breathe...

Pia arrived within two hours, forcing the lock open with a pair of pliers. I went inside first and Berry came out of the bedroom. When she saw me she screamed, "YOU BITCH! What the fuck did you bring somebody here for? Why did you call the fucking Ranch?" She grabbed the phone, pulled it out of its socket and threw it at me. It missed my head but hit my arm.

"YEEEKS!!!" Berry's hands went up to her hair, which she started pulling at brutally. Then just as suddenly, she stopped and went limp.

Pia took Berry's hands firmly and led her to the car, saying, "Berry, Sila wants you to come home now. Come with me. Do you want to take something for your nerves? You've been under such enormous strain. Here, take this Valium. It'll relax you. Here..."

Berry took it and started sobbing in Pia's arms.

"I'm sorry. I'm so sorry... I'm so sorry."

While Pia consoled Berry, helping her into the car, she signaled that I should stay put for a few minutes.

Badly shaken, I couldn't do much else.

When Berry nodded off and started snoring in the back seat, Pia signaled me to come out to the car.

"Lock up the place and sit in the front seat with me."

As soon as we got back to the Ranch, I reported to Sila.

She was mad that her plan had not been carried out.

"Go back to the apartment after you rest. Tell the landlady

a story, pack up and leave. I'll have a van organized for you. Bring the dog back if you want. "

Later that day I went back. The place was hot, and Socks was bewildered.

Come, my little Socks, I just want to hold you close to me.

Tears started pouring down my face.

I failed you, Sila, Berry, the project. I was supposed to keep it together. Oh, Socks, my little one. I failed.

Socks just licked my face, loving me no matter what.

I wish I could take you with me... I want to so much. But, how can I take care of you? I can't even seem to take care of myself... you, the only one who loves me just as I am- even as a failure. I hope when I leave some really good person will find you and give you the home I can't.

But his heart would be broken, just as mine was.

The next morning, seeing him running down the street after the van, snapped something in me. I cried all the way back to the Ranch. Another part of my heart deadened to what was going on in the commune.

The day after I left, the story broke in the local newspapers.

Only the PR department read newspapers and they didn't know what Berry and I had been doing. We were all conditioned not to ask questions about one another's work, since the work or "worship" as we called it, was a spiritual inner development between each of us and Bhagwan. Nobody had any idea what I'd been through.

I didn't see Berry for a few weeks, but Belle told me she was improving. I was sure that I'd never be sent off the Ranch again.

But three weeks later, on the eve of local elections, I was told to go back to The Dalles and campaign for Berry for Town Council.

"*That's* crazy," I said flatly.

Ignoring me, Sila said, "Try again."

"I'm *not* going back there, and *especially* with Berry. What if she throws the phone at me again or does something worse? I'm afraid of her, Sila *and* afraid of what she might do in public. Besides, it won't work."

Sila was determined; her face coldly expressionless. *"Just try again."*

I was really scared.

What'll Berry do next? I don't want to see her at all.

It was she who came to me, wearing a flowery dress, smiling sweetly and speaking like a little girl.

"Samsara, love, Silee said that we should try to go back to the friends that we made in The Dalles and see if they'll help us to start this campaign again." Her voice had a singsong quality, syrupy and apologetic. Wary of her but glad to get away from the Ranch, I went reluctantly.

The whole trip was a big failure. When we knocked on doors; people were hostile, threw things at us and shouted obscenities. *The Oregonian* printed a long article accusing us of voter fraud. Berry had voted twice, once in The Dalles under her legal name and once at Rajneeshpuram under her sannyas name. We left after three days.

On the Ranch there was a campaign to get more voters registered to increase our voter base in the state. Street people were bussed in from all parts of the country under the guise of a "restorative social program."

There were rumors of people being "sent" to The Dalles for "infiltration" – only I wasn't told what they were infiltrating. This made me uncomfortable.

Who are these other people and what were they doing? Would they gum up my own network?

I could do nothing but go on with my little research project on subversive groups until I was told to do otherwise.

Berry was finally transferred to another department and out of undercover work. I was forbidden to set foot in The Dalles, for which I was grateful. I never went back there again. One month later, I learned there was a salmonella outbreak, in which hundreds of people were poisoned.

Did we do it? Or were we set up to get the blame? Both are possible, now that other people are in on the act. What's gonna happen next?

I didn't have long to wait. Sila called another mandatory commune meeting. This time it was to announce that sannyasins would be saved from AIDS through safe sex, requiring all of us to change our "free-to-jump-into-any-bed habits, attend demonstrations on safe sex and the use of rubber gloves and disinfectants and line up for mandatory testing.

While this reorganization was going on, the security staff began to appear at commune gatherings with semi-automatic weapons.

The beginning of our own personal war.

I was directed to focus my research on the history of religious cities, a parallel of which existed in Salt Lake City with the Church of Jesus Christ of the Latter-Day Saints (LDS). The LDS or Mormons started their city in a similar way to Rajneeshpuram. The Mormons in Salt Lake led me to Mormons in D.C.

As an "independent" researcher, I interviewed them for an article I was planning to submit to *Sunstone* magazine, comparing Rajneeshees and Mormons. I contacted the magazine with my proposal, and told them I would send the finished manuscript. The focus of my interviews was how Mormons, who experienced so much prejudice in their day, rose in the U.S. governmental system.

Over the next few months as part of my research I met the Republican National Chairman; the Assistant Director of the Joint Economic Committee; the Assistant Secretary of the Interior, a former NASA Director; both Utah Senators; the Chief of Staff to the Chief Justice; the Deputy Assistant to the President for Policy Development; the Assistant Secretary for Water and Science; several U.S. Representatives; the Director for the Center of Strategic Economic Policy; the SEC Director; the Senior V.P. of the Marriott Corporation and the President's lawyer; the Solicitor General.

All Mormons.

From Salt Lake to D.C. and back to the Ranch, I interviewed, wrote articles and continued monitoring the phones in our monitoring room, uncovering drug and extortion plots. The more I traveled, the more I disliked American society. The commune, for all its hardship and manipulations was still preferable.

By January 1985, Sila decided to bug Bhagwan's rooms, choosing a handful of us to listen in and record. We sat in a small room in the rear of Sila's house hidden from the staff. The two houses were connected by wires laid in conduits much like underground cables. Bhagwan had started taking nitrous oxide and Valium regularly and there was a general concern that he might try and commit suicide with the help of his doctor. As legal owner of the Ranch, Sila could do whatever she wished to secure her property and, in her mind, the bugging was for the "good of the commune." If Bhagwan was threatening to abandon his own commune, it was her duty to protect it and my duty to do what I was told. Since I was still living there, I was committed to the commune's survival.

I was becoming increasingly worried about what was happening everywhere on the Ranch. Puneet, a very quiet and solemn German man, had become a close friend by then. He coordinated the monitoring system for the Peace Force.

"You know Puneet," I told him one day after a particularly disturbing incident, "I heard Viviananda and Bhagwan this morning. He was yelling at her. She said, 'you love Rose more than me... even though *I'm* the one who takes care of you. *She* only does your laundry.' After which he said, 'stop it Viviananda.' Then there was a loud whack and she shouted 'aah.' Sounded to me like he slapped her. Then he said, 'your jealousy is beyond control now! I have given you more love than I gave to anyone. More I cannot give.'

What'll I do with this information? This is our enlightened master of masters who sounds just like an ordinary angry man."

Not a god after all.

"Give the tape to me. I'll give it to Sila. Don't worry, we'll sort it out."

The tape was played for several of us, gathered in Sila's room that night. No one wanted to believe that this was going on, but the proof was on the tape, shocking everyone.

I'm getting heebe jeebies, but it's no crazier than everything else.

By then I was pretty numb.

Sila said, "Can you imagine what would happen to the entire organization if we released this? Sannyasins round the world would go into shock, confusion and denial. There would be a split, and everything we've worked for would fall apart."

Here we were, a tiny group, no more than twenty. And, we were the pivots upon which the organization of close to a million people around the world rotated. What was decided in Sila's bedroom directed all those people's lives. Like the Pope, on a smaller scale.

Sila fancied herself as a pope and we were the College of Cardinals, each having a separate sphere of being a leader. Although I never felt powerful in terms of leading people, I felt special because of my status as undercover agent. This made me a leader – or at least a savior. People on the Ranch treated me with some kind of awe, which made me jittery because I never felt I deserved it but was secretly pleased by it.

"We have to make a decision to go on protecting Bhagwan, right now," Sila said. "We already know he's being encouraged to end his life on Master's Day, July 6th, so we need to keep the monitoring going and prevent it. Ok? Ok."

That was Sila's way of getting our opinion: telling us what to do, asking if it was ok and immediately answering her own question.

But by July, there was another element. A new group of four, came from Hollywood with lots of money and gained

Bhagwan's favor. Bhagwan seemed to like the wealth, expensive watches and glamour. A coup was brewing.

They offered a new vision of how to run the Ranch, began having private "counsel" with Bhagwan and appeared to be "taking over" as Bhagwan referred to their ideas with increasing praise. Did they instigate the suicide idea? We had no way of knowing, other than to bug their rooms too. We were trying to sift out the source of this insidious plan, so we could stop it.

I tried to deny what was going on because I still held onto the belief that religious organizations were fundamentally good and holy. Instead, the tapes revealed jealousies over who Bhagwan wanted to sleep with; little pills that "expanded the heart" – whatever that meant; diamond watches being bought and private planes going everywhere everyday. The "perfect" spiritual place was full of pus under the surface.

There was no time just sit down and talk to anyone about anything. No time even to think. I was running to catch something to eat, running to catch a plane, running from one interview to another, from D.C. to Portland to Boston to New York, back to the Ranch to monitor the phones.

In addition to phone monitoring, I was responsible for the inside information that went to the lawyers and for background on the INS officials, senators, representatives and the Justice Department. All the information I had been gathering kept pointing in one direction: the state wanted to get the commune out of Oregon and the Feds wanted Bhagwan out of the country. The INS was prepared to deport him on the grounds of false statements made in 1981, concealing his intent to remain in the U.S.

When one of the state representatives held hearings on the use of Federal land in and around the commune, some local representatives introduced bills aimed directly at Rajneeshpuram, starting a petition to repeal its city charter. The state superintendent of schools threatened to cut off aid to the commune's school because he thought the school was part of a religious organization. The Feds in D.C. were concerned about the commune's growing influence as a brainwashing cult similar to the Moonies. Meanwhile, the wiretapping uncovered threats from a flood of visitors, some of whom were undercover investigators themselves leaving their own bugs behind. Paranoia grew.

The press lived on the Ranch because it produced hotter news than Reagan or the soaps. After I was interviewed at a commune meeting, I saw the copy of what was written. My own words "said" something that was opposite to what I *actually* said. No longer trusting the press to report accurately, I also no longer trusted myself to understand what was happening. The ground was caving in under me.

By the time Sila approached me about U.S. Attorney, George Tork, I was wary of everything Sila said to me. It was rumored Tork's office was carrying out the Attorney General's orders to "clamp down on the Rajneesh". From my experience in D.C., I learned that that usually meant, "eradicate."

A team of Ranch lawyers and paralegals produced briefs to counteract mounting lawsuits and legislation. They already had information that the Attorney General's Office regarded cults as a dangerous influence and a threat to the well being of the whole nation. We were at the top of the cult list because of our wealth and apparent ability to influence thousands of people.

I was in the legal department typing up notes from a recent trip, when Sila approached me.

"Samsara, I think we should get rid of George Tork. What do you think?" Sila asked me under her breath.

"Why not? Remove him from office," I said not looking up. My first thought was that she wanted to get rid of his influence. Right after that came my second thought. What does she mean? *Kill him?*

Then I looked up at her. Black eyes sunk deep into her cheeks, stared at me with a strange metallic glint.

I'd better come up with a plan before this goes any further.

"...Something. Anything the lawyers can use..." I heard her say and interrupted her.

What's she thinking? Is she going to do something unpredictable? She just cursed out Ted Koppel on Nightline, and yesterday was asking for her 'medicine' to get through another night of work.

"I'll research him, Sila. I'll handle it."

Sila turned to Belle and said, "All right, Samsara's going to take care of Mr. Tork for us. OK? OK."

I turned and left.

The next day I went to Portland library, finding nothing I could use. Then I was refused the chance to interview him. Finding myself in an awkward position, as I'd never had problems getting interviews before, I began to feel a little desperate. I had to give Sila *something* that could be used against him legally.

Because of increasing paranoia and fear about Bhagwan and other foreign nationals being deported, *any* action from state or federal authorities would be interpreted as threatening the existence of the commune.

Sila zeroed in on Tork when I told her that I found nothing substantial, the silence thick with her anger. Her eyes clouded over, giving me a clue that she was hiding something.

I used to trust you, you know. But now...have you changed so much or have I?

Back in the tiny, cramped office in Germany, I looked up at Katrin, who had sat patiently with me through the hours of typing out my summary for Trish, and paused.

"You know there was a time I had utterly believed in her... she prompted me to go undercover in The Dalles, she *gave* me a film department to create – hell, she was the one who made me see I could go way beyond my timid little self, even to walk into the White House and interview a Presidential advisor. She *believed* in me completely and I felt honored by that belief. I was her trusted servant. If anything, *I* was the one who had let her down by my anorexia, when I thought of leaving the ranch and abandoning her. She had become a hero figure for me, closer to the kind of person I could be, which Bhagwan never was.

She was my leader and I became one of her soldiers – an operative. There was a war going on against the powers that wanted to destroy us. I had a duty to follow her orders. Everything I lived for during these years was at risk.

But I had to ask myself: can I be part of something that is shrouded in lies and intrigues? What was she planning? How far would she go? Could she have someone killed? What if she asked me to hurt somebody? Could I do that?

Finally, I came to a conclusion. To hell with duty – I was a coward. I couldn't kill anybody, or be a part of killing, no matter what the reason for it. I had to tell her to stop all research and surveillance on Tork. And with that decision came the end of my former relationship with her. I was no longer a subordinate in Sila's army.

I told her and she agreed. I felt relieved that it was ended. And now I could leave.

I wiped it out.

The whole episode never happened.

Nothing happened."

"So that's *it*?" Katrin said astonished. "Nothing *happened* to him?"

"No. At least that's all I can remember."

"God! Well, let's wrap it up then and send it to Trish. Sounds like a tempest in a teacup to me, as the Brits would say."

Chapter 9
The Last Flight: "who pissed you off?"

Obeying others because they claim to be morally superior, or to have an inside track to the truth, not only breeds corruption and lies, but removes people from personal responsibility. –Joel Kramer and Diana Alstad, The Guru Papers

"Let's call Trish right away and tell her we're finished."

"Sweetheart, it's three in the morning in America! Let the poor woman sleep!" Katrin said.

The next day I called her and sent the summary by Fed Ex. Then I called Hanna, as an afterthought. I got her voice mail and left a message saying that I'd sent Trish the material.

Since the hearing, Hanna had been upset at my reaction to her statement that "I was involved in the conspiracy." That sentence acknowledged a criminal conspiracy. She realized she'd made an error. As far as I could tell, she felt guilty for not saving me. I honestly thought she should have.

Three days later, Trish called.

"From reading your material, I would strongly suggest that you consider trial," she said firmly.

"Why? The Feds'll cream me - make me look like Mata

Hari with fangs. They hate me, Trish. They can't get Sila, so they'll crucify me to make an example. We both know there's no hard evidence of anybody being harmed. And I was following orders, just like the military. But nobody'll say that to a jury. The ones who could say that in my defense are all state witnesses. They'll say whatever the Feds tell them to."

"Samsara," she said in what was to become an all-too-familiar tone, gently bringing me back to reality, "hold the sermon for a while and get back to basics. You've got to at least consider trial because it's your *right*."

"Trish, I can't afford it. I can barely afford *you* right now. I have $15,000 for you; $5000 for Hanna; and I'm in the hole for the last $2000 I owe you. That's it: end of money. So, you see, I can't afford you and I can't afford a trial."

My point was clear. How do you argue with poverty?

Trish said, "You can have a court appointed lawyer."

"WHAT? Are *you* nuts? Look, I was a probation officer in New York. I *saw* what court appointed lawyers were like. I'll sit in jail for life, for sure." I said resolutely. "Trish, I *have* to plea bargain. Stop trying to tell me to go to trial."

"What are you going to plea bargain with?" she asked. "You already said that you're not going to give any information about anybody else. What do you have to deal *with*?"

My good looks. A sinking feeling started in my stomach.

"I'll give them information about what I did – and only what I did."

Sounds lame. She's right. What do I have that they want? I won't rat. So maybe I have to consider trial… it might be the only option…

I said good-bye to Trish, worrying about how I was going to find the money to keep going.

I have to earn as much as possible while on bail, so Rudi has to hire me back. And that'll need a small miracle, as he certainly doesn't advertise for international criminals to work in his bar. Ah, Rudi, you tightwad, afraid of everybody ripping you off.

Although Katrin had kept him informed of the details of

my disappearance, trying to make it sound exciting, he was skeptical and worried about how the guests would react to my having been in jail.

It was a reasonable concern. However, *I* knew that I could turn the scenario around to make it alluring. I was an attractive spy that men *had* to spend their money on, for an exotic time they would never forget.

I would *make* it work.

By January we had one solid wedge in the extradition proceedings: the Germans did not have a conspiracy law that corresponded exactly to the one in U.S. law. This meant that there was a loophole. They might not be *able* to extradite me.

On my birthday, January 14, Hanna called me to her office.

"Sit down," she said, "They made the decision to extradite."

So much for loopholes.

I sat down slowly, the blood draining from my face.

"Why? On what grounds?"

"There wasn't enough evidence to show that you stopped the crime."

"What about the loophole?"

"The Court made the decision on the basis of the inherent seriousness of the crime. They said there was not enough evidence to support your withdrawal from the conspiracy. In Germany, if you withdraw and it is *proven*, it is considered that you are not liable for the crime."

"Well, can we appeal?" I asked nervously, feeling the tightness in my chest like somebody just punched the daylights out of me.

I'm sure I gave enough proof of my withdrawal. After all, I explained it. What more did they need? I know they believed me.

"Hanna, I'll get additional evidence and testimony that *will* support the fact that I withdrew."

Hanna needed to be convinced that we should fight the

decision. I didn't want her to see my eyes filling with tears and my shaking hands, which I hid in my lap.

"Of course we'll appeal," she said dully. "The Court encourages this and I'll apply for the papers directly." She looked down at her feet in a gesture that was becoming habitual - hesitant and unconfident. "I'm so sorry that this happened, especially on your birthday."

I stood up and hugged her. It seemed like the thing to do. But it didn't make me feel any better.

I'm so small and powerless. My life's so flimsy.

I was starting to cry when she said. "The one good thing is that they wouldn't allow the weapons charge. They *did* believe you on that and found nothing to substantiate transporting weapons. They even expressed doubt that an actual crime took place. However, they allowed the wiretapping. Here's the official paperwork," she said pulling away from my hug as if I'd embarrassed her.

Her voice softened to a whisper, "I'm so sorry... we *will* appeal."

"Hanna, can I read the extradition decision?"

"I've only got it in German. It's being translated into English. You'll have it shortly."

Two and a half hours later, her secretary handed it to me.

From The Regional Court of Appeal
Extradition of U.S. American Citizen Samsara Drakke
From the Federal Republic of Germany to the United States
Decree of January 13, 1991.

I read through it once, stunned. Then the paragraph on page 7 hit me.

"...The accused has made use of the opportunity to make a statement within the time limit set by the Regional Court of Appeal for a hearing in the case, but explicitly did not refer to her interrogation. The indications resulting from her statements cannot, on their own, substantiate the conviction of the Regional Court of Appeal of the existence of a reason for suspension of sentence..."

What did they mean, *I did not refer to my interrogation?* I grabbed the papers and marched into Hanna's office.

"Hanna, what do they mean, 'I did not refer to my interrogation?" They had all my statements from the hearing!"

"They were not formally submitted," she looked at her feet.

"WHAT? WHY NOT?" the blood was rushing to my face as I shouted.

"I had no authority to do so, Samsara. It would have meant sending the notes from the High Court Hearing to America for the Americans to give their opinion, before submitting them back to the Germans so they could make their decision... and I simply didn't have that authority... *my* statements can't damage you in an American court, but yours *can*. The American prosecutors can use your words against you."

"But Hanna, you didn't even ASK me, or tell me! I didn't know about that. We could've done it through Trish!"

She looked down again.

"We must ask your American lawyer if we can submit them on appeal..."

Deeply shocked, I slowly realized how the Judges became legally bound to make the decision they did.

She should've told me before the hearing that only the lawyer's words are entered in the record unless I specifically asked for my statements to be considered. Since she never told me that, everything I said to the Court couldn't be used to make their decision. Those poor Judges sat through all my long explanations and had to make up their minds based on that one damning sentence of Hanna's! Doesn't she realize what she's done? She didn't even ask me. All my efforts to show how I'd withdrawn were as if they had never been made at all!

I didn't know what to say.

Narian was in an office down the hall, and had just heard that he was going to be extradited. The Court had made the decision to extradite him because the charges were basically the same but there was an extenuating circumstance that I wasn't fully aware of until later. I didn't get to see him but I heard that he was also in shock.

Diva was in the office next door, unbeknownst to me, talking to Thomas about the delay in her own extradition decision. Diva had a German husband as an extenuating circumstance and a prior conviction that the U.S. was trying to tie into her charges. These two things complicated her situation.

I was too upset to think about either of them.

I picked up the office phone and called Trish. She had heard the news already, as Hanna had told her earlier that afternoon.

We got on the speakerphone. Hanna spoke first.

"Hello, Patricia, this is Hanna, here. I want to ask Samsara in your presence, if we can formally allow her court testimony to be submitted into the appeal proceedings."

"Trish," I jumped in, "I think it's a good idea. I have nothing else to lose at this point, and after all, what I said to the Judges was the truth."

"Samsara, without seeing a transcript of what you told the Judges, I cannot give a well-informed opinion."

"The testimony was not recorded," Hanna spoke quickly, "it's a collection of the Judges' notes. These notes would be sent to America, first for the prosecutor's opinion then back to the German Judges for review."

"Then, I cannot agree that it would be in your best interest, Samsara."

"Why not?"

"It will compromise you if you go to trial in the U.S. You'll be giving your case away to the government."

"But, I *am* willing to cooperate with the government!" I interrupted her. "I'm not going to change my story."

"Yes, but if you decide to go to trial... "

"Trish, I'm NOT going to trial!" I was exasperated and still shocked from losing round one, which meant I could very well be extradited. I had to talk to Trish alone.

"Can we go off speakerphone? I'd like to go over some things with Trish alone?" I saw Hanna's face go ashen.

Hanna left the room quietly but her back spoke of resignation and defeat.

"Trish, Hanna never told me that unless my non-recorded testimony was sent to the U.S. prosecutor, the Judges couldn't use it. Right before this call she just mentioned that the Judges have doubts that a crime was even committed. But their doubt may not stop extradition. If I submit my testimony, we will have more time because we'll be waiting for the Americans to respond."

"*Samsara, that doesn't sound like a basis for rescinding the extradition order, but simply a way to buy time... *"

"Trish, unless I send the testimony, I *have no* time, and I *will* be extradited. Plus, there are two other issues. At the time of the hearing, I had no American counsel. I didn't know that what I said at the hearing might be held against me. Furthermore, Hanna told me that if she made a statement on my behalf – even though it was *her* belief and not mine - about what happened with Tork, her statement couldn't be held against me in an American court."

"That's not exactly true, Samsara. Whatever the government has in their hands regarding information related to the case can be used however they see fit."

I'm mush in their hands. One lawyer's telling me one thing and the other, the opposite.

"Samsara, do you want to talk to Fronten, the U.S. Prosecutor?" Trish asked gently. "I know this must have been a deep blow to you, but I'm sure that Hanna will work on the appeal. Now, do you want to talk to Fronten?" she repeated, "If so, I should come out there and prepare you. He's coming anyway to talk to Narian."

"I didn't know that." My heart sank. Again.

Lord! Why's Narian talking to Fronten? What kind of deal is he planning to make? First Maya, then Diana... now Narian. I don't believe it. My friends, who were like my family, have all betrayed me with hearsay. Now Narian...I feel like a Jew in Germany in the thirties, betrayed by the people they lived with, out of fear of what might happen to them.

"Is Narian selling out?"

"It seems likely, as I gathered from his attorney. His lawyer thinks he's too scared to face a trial."

"I'm scared, too, right now, Trish, but I will only talk to Fronten about myself and see what he has to offer."

"In that case, I'd better come out there. You need to know what you're dealing with. These guys don't play around. They want blood."

"How delightful." There was little else to say. Everything got more horrible each day.

Trish flew in on a Friday night, March 30, 1991. She had described herself on the phone to me as "the tallest person on the plane, thin, with black hair and a black raincoat."

I had the image of a flagpole with hair, since most Germans I knew were tall, but not thin.

Johann drove me to Frankfurt Airport to pick her up.

"Johann, thank you so much for coming with me. You really soothe me. I feel on the verge of a breakdown, so many times."

"Samsara, I'm wiz you. You know zat. I hope zis woman vill help you."

Naturally, the plane was delayed.

We have only two days to prepare. I have to meet the Feds on Monday morning... not enough time. There's so much I have to tell Trish.

I never dared say very much on the phone, because it was tapped; and faxes could be intercepted.

"Why is everything going against me?" I asked Johann.

"Vhat do you mean- all against you? I'm wiz you," he said gently.

He looked at me with puzzled, tired and sad eyes. Johann was a simple, genuine man, whom I wished that I could have fallen in love with. Fortunately my feelings for him were that of a brother. He was one of the few men I had never tried to seduce.

His big arms came around me and I had the feeling of being held by a teddy bear. He offered to go all the way to England to meet with my co-defendants, in order to find out what they knew, since I was not allowed to travel, nor speak to them directly. His care overwhelmed me. I didn't deserve it.

"Everything is going wrong. Now, Trish is delayed. Why, Johann? Why is all this happening to me?"

"Samsara, look at ze positive side," in a tone he often used with me. "At least zis lawyer comes to *help* you. Try to look at ze positive side. I hate to see you zo sad and zo vorried."

I told myself to breathe.

Finally the plane landed.

Impatiently, I scanned every face coming off the plane. Trish was even taller than the flagpole I had imagined, with fierce, penetrating eyes, and a smile like a cloudburst in a clear sky. Her manner was brisk, simple, direct and warm. She dazzled me and I at first felt intimidated.

Not knowing what exactly to say to her, I just opened my mouth, while Johann took her bag.

"You probably need a good night's sleep, Trish. Or, do you want to do some work, tonight? How was your flight? By the way, this is Johann, my landlord and a dear friend. We can talk about anything in front of him, so fire away!" I was talking too fast, trying to keep up with her big strides across the airport to the car.

She had no luggage, other than a carry on, so we were in

the car in moments and headed toward the autobahn. The car quickly gained speed and she hadn't even answered my questions. Because she was so tall, she scrunched herself into the tiny car's back seat. It was then that I really looked at her and saw the exhaustion on her face. After the eighteen-hour flight from Seattle, how could I be so selfish?

"Samsara," she said with that tone again. I suddenly realized that I had stepped on her boundaries. She continued, "I think I need a good night's rest before we do anything. Let's meet early in the morning."

"Of course, Trish. I'll bring you breakfast, and if there's anything else you need, just let me know. I stocked your fridge but I'm not sure I got everything right."

So anxious to please and not alienate her in any way, I overdid things. I wanted her on my side and desperately wanted her to like me. She was marked to be my savior, a role I tended to put people in, often to my detriment. I couldn't make any mistakes.

After a sleepless night, I took a bus to her flat, which was ironically across from Club Diana where I had worked. What a different person I was the first time I went through those doors, beginning the work that changed my life.

That was 1986. This was 1991, and I had to keep focused. When I arrived at Trish's flat the next morning, she was up, showered and ready to go. It was 8:00 A.M.

She let me in and I followed her into the living-dining area, which was large and took up most of the flat. I put the paper bag containing our breakfast on the table. She motioned to me to take one of the chairs looking at me intently.

"You know, Samsara, I don't feel good about you working in the bar to pay my salary." Our eyes met and I saw a deep concern and compassion in hers that stirred my heart. It felt like a dear and wonderful friend had come into my life, one whom I could trust.

Over the past six months, who to trust and who not to trust had become very confusing. Maya had betrayed me. Narian was making a deal which meant he would surely testify against me. And the doubts I had inside caused me to wonder what I could trust in myself. The voice that said, *make a deal, it's easy... less of a sentence...* Or the voice that said, *be courageous, don't give in, don't rat.*

With Trish I sensed a deep honesty and trustworthiness. She was direct: her eyes were clear. I knew instantly that if she didn't like me she would tell me: client or no client. I was sure that once she heard my side of things, she would believe in me. Not like those lawyers who don't know if their client is guilty or not but have to defend them anyway.

I realized that she had started speaking again.

"Actually Samsara, let's talk about the bar work later. First I want to address what you wrote me in your outline. I still don't understand how you could participate in the wiretapping not knowing it was illegal."

I sighed. *Blow number one. I explained the whole development of the Ranch wiretapping. What doesn't she understand?*

"The fact is," she continued, "you didn't have a court order."

"But, Trish, the City Judge knew we were wiretapping."

"Your City Judge would have no jurisdiction in criminal matters, Samsara. She couldn't issue a court order."

"How was I supposed to know *that*? Besides, Trish, if I thought what I was doing was illegal, why would I have *left* all the tapes *there*? Leaving all the evidence to convict me?" I asked exasperated. Within five minutes, I had gone from feeling cared for to attacked. This was no way to start.

Trish took a breath.

"I think we need some tea and I'm hungry, Samsara. Let's eat breakfast first and start from the beginning. Slowly, this time."

Ten hours later, after covering my entire sannyas career, my back was stiff, my mouth had cotton in it and I was out of cigarettes. Trish couldn't stand the smoke, which I had to blow out the window. It was already dark and we decided to take a walk.

She grilled me carefully on each detail about Tork. I was nervous, tired, and on edge; afraid I was going to say the wrong thing to Fronten and his gang, which they'd use as ammunition.

Emerging from the "interrogation" room into the spring night, the air zapped me, as if I had put my finger into an electric socket. Trish looked around her and breathed deeply. She didn't say anything but I could see her stretching her long legs and relaxing as she walked. Spring in this part of Germany was one of the many things I loved about being here. It made me feel young and alive.

The air was full of promise, hidden agendas full of new discoveries, liaisons waiting to connect. The frog prince waiting in the *strassenbahn* to take me in his arms.

As we were walking, I thought about how I would be torn away from all this, if I were extradited. The countryside, the people I loved, the sweet sounds of the German language circling around us, like a gentle staccato song – I would miss all of it.

And thinking that I would never dance again, a jolt of pain passed through me.

"You know I dance in the bar, Trish and I really love it."

"What do you love about it, Samsara?" she looked surprised.

"I'm on fire when I dance, Trish. I go to another place in my mind, and my body melts. It becomes a liquid extension of the music. I never know exactly what my dance will be like. Each time it's different… each time it's new," I said wistfully. I saw the look on her face, intense curiosity and wonder.

I continued in a subdued tone. "I know this sounds stuck up, but sometimes the guests come to the bar just to see me dance. I sense that they, too, want to be carried away, along with me to a place where they could become something special, if only for a little while. Something happens when

I start to dance that simply doesn't happen with the other dancers."

"What's that?"

"The air becomes electrified as the music begins, as if the sounds themselves weave an exotic, throbbing beat into the atmosphere. It doesn't really matter *what* the music is; expectation is created and something extraordinary begins... something they can't miss.

"Miss Theodora Duncan emerges unexpectedly and they are dazzled. The bar girl they had just been with disappears and this creature materializes in her place. I make myself into some kind of magical being. Every single performance is original, with its own mood. I create a new costume each time, adding something different. I want my dance to wrap people in ecstasy, as it does me. I am making love to everyone in the room... to the whole of Germany, even to the whole world. I am drunk with love, like the Sufi poets. The dancer in my body is no longer mine; it's a goddess. Something sacred is fashioned before everyone's eyes."

I paused to look at Trish, bringing myself back from tasting that experience again. Even thinking about it, I felt the tingling in my soul and the adrenaline in my body, aching to express what was bursting out of me...

"Trish, I cannot *bear* to think that I will never dance again when I leave here. I will never, again, be *able* to dance. I'll be too old."

"Come on, Samsara, you won't be that old! Perhaps it won't be the same, but you'll still be able to dance."

"Trish, I will be too old to dance again like *this*. Even if they give me five or ten years, I'll have lost my youth. I'm already 42."

I was mourning for what had been, afraid of losing that spark, that special gift of touching sacred fire and bringing it to earth in my dance. I mourned this loss, not knowing that this very mystical experience would be repeated in another form years later.

As we walked back to the room in silence, I was looking down at the cobblestones I loved. Glancing at the curtained windows of houses with families inside, sitting down to dinner, sharing the day's adventures, I reflected how alone I was.

I did this to myself. I made this sadness and this ending. There's no one else to blame for what I have in front of me: prison. After all those years building a dream, of dedication and hard work in the commune, I have nothing. No husband, no children... parents I might never see alive again.

I shook myself. Afraid of drowning in self-pity, I resolutely stopped my thoughts.

Monday morning came overnight. Trish drove me in her rental car to the army base where the Feds had arranged to hold the interrogation. They described it as a "meeting."

We came slowly to the curb and I sat in the car numbly while Trish got out first.

A very tall, portly man hurried to meet us as if he had been watching for our arrival. He introduced himself as Paul Tomkins, the main FBI agent assigned to my case. I didn't know at that first meeting that he had been following Rajneeshee activities since 1982. Paul dwarfed everyone in the group. With thick, black, wavy hair, he was clean-shaven and soft spoken. He reminded me of a large stuffed Panda bear. He started talking immediately, before I had even gotten out of the car.

"Did you have any trouble finding this place? It's a bit off the map..." I heard the effort in his voice to sound friendly. I shivered nonetheless. My nervousness was showing.

"We found it easily. It wasn't hard." I tried to sound sweet.

"Well, we have a nice, airy room, lots of coffee and doughnuts. You know the Germans make this great pastry! I just love it." He chatted seemingly at ease. He must have done hundreds of these "meetings".

The room was large, with sun penetrating weakly through the windows all down one side onto the shiny linoleum. Three other men were standing around a conference table as we entered, all of them, like Tomkins, were wearing somber suits and highly polished black shoes.

I immediately spotted Fronten. He was my height with brown hair, a slight moustache and small, round, empty eyes. He greeted me pleasantly, and then proceeded to make small talk with Trish.

Tim Frest, the second FBI agent, was a thin, wiry man with sandy colored hair. He frowned as I was introduced to him, and continued to frown throughout the interrogation. I had the impression that his facial muscles were glued in that position.

Fronten's assistant, Harold Tich ("Tick" like the bug) the smallest man in the group, had wire-rimmed glasses, a hooked nose and thin lips that tried to smile. It looked like he was not very good at it.

Fronten hadn't said anything to me but hello. His face was impassive and I couldn't tell where he was coming from or what kinds of questions he would ask.

"Well, Samsara," he started. There was a neutral friendliness in Fronten's voice. "Shall we begin? Please sit down here. Is there anything you need before we start?"

I shook my head.

"…Tell us a bit about your childhood."

So, I began, much the same way as I did for the German Judges. Fronten was clearly in charge, making clucking sounds as I revealed my early life and what led me to the commune.

"Now that we understand a bit about what brought you to Rajneesh, what would you say was your relationship with the Bhagwan and with Sila?"

I didn't trust him. His eyes narrowed when he looked at me, like I was an insect he wanted to probe and squash. I told him the same things I told the Judges: Sila was the power and I was a pawn. When Sila gave me an order, I did it, wanting her acceptance and approval. He began to get edgy.

"Samsara, why did you use these false identities when you did your, uh, *research*?"

"The name I used while I was interviewing in The Dalles, Salt Lake and in Washington was actually not "false". The last name 'Mathis' was an alternate spelling of my former married name, and "Teddy" was a nickname. Writers often use pen names... would you say they were false?" I asked coolly.

"More to the point" his face began to get red. "Why did *you* use it?"

"Because I thought it would be less noticeable to use an ordinary name, rather than my sannyas name, Ma Prem Samsara, especially when I was interviewing in the Senate buildings and the White House... "

"You mean you actually got into the *White House*?" Tomkins interjected incredulously.

"Yes. I had arranged to interview the Chief Economic Policy Advisor to Reagan. His office was located down the hall from the Oval Office. So, when I approached the guard booth at the entrance and showed him my library card as my ID, he called to verify that I had an appointment. It was confirmed, and he waved me through."

Tomkins looked astonished and there were several distinct groans in the room. "You mean you just walked right in?"

"Yes."

They're reacting like I committed some kind of security breech. After all, I am a terribly dangerous criminal just walking into the White House for God's sake.

The redness drained a little from Fronten's face: he went slightly pale and cleared his throat.

"Why don't we take a break before we go further?"

Trish and I went to the ladies room.

"They're going to start in on you about Tork. Are you clear about what you want to say?"

"Yes, but I'm still very nervous. It's hard for me to talk about it and Fronten makes me jittery."

"Samsara," that familiar tone again. "Just breathe deeply and talk slowly. Don't rush what you say, or they'll get the impression that you're lying."

"I'm NOT lying, Trish!" My voice was high and squeaky.

"Especially don't talk in *that* tone."

When we returned, Tomkins offered me doughnuts.

"No thanks... sugar makes me jumpy, and it's hard enough to talk about all this." I wanted to say exactly what I was feeling and not hold back. I was incensed to think that they assumed I was not telling the truth. After all, I had already gone through all this with the German High Court.

"Well, let's come back to the table," Fronten said sharply, cutting short my thoughts. He no longer sounded like his former coddling self. It was already 12:30 P.M. Three hours had gone by and he hadn't gotten his "meat."

"Did you conspire to murder George Tork?" He asked me directly as if he were jabbing me with a sharp knife.

"No." Now, *my* face reddened. I remembered suddenly that Hanna had said in her statement that I was *involved* in the conspiracy.

"Tell us what you *did* do concerning Mr. Tork."

I knew I had to dive in and just keep talking till I was finished. I was afraid he would interrupt me. If he did I might degenerate into a slobbering wimp unable to talk clearly.

I started from Sila's directive, the day she came up to me in Legal Services and first asked me if we should get rid of Tork. I talked non-stop about my research and not being able to find out any useful details on him. I continued describing how I became convinced that Sila was planning to harm him. When the discussions about murder started, I told her to stop and that I would have nothing more to do with it.

I was talking so fast, staring at the table; I didn't have time to take in their reactions. Then, I saw Trish's face. She was frowning, trying to signal me that I should slow down.

It was too late. I was on a roll, afraid of losing my control and carefully organized thoughts. I didn't want to reveal my vulnerability, or how much all this affected me. I wanted only to get the story out and be finished. I had just started explaining how my telling Sila to stop actually prevented the murder from taking place, when Fronten interrupted me.

"So, you had *discussions* about murdering him?"

This time Trish cut in. "Samsara is relating a fact that's already been well established, Mr. Fronten, which is that there were many meetings at the Rajneesh commune over a period of time, where Sila's ideas were discussed... "

"And, Samsara participated in those meetings." Fronten tried to complete Trish's statement.

"We didn't say that," Trish was quick, stopping Fronten from implying that I did.

"Mr. Fronten," I wanted to be formal with him, indicating that he should end his first name basis with me. "There was a discussion about the *ethics* of murder, and whether or not harming *any* individual, under *any* circumstance is justifiable."

I was over-emphasizing because I was so nervous and felt like a little mouse cornered by a Gila monster with fangs.

"The fact *is*, Mrs. Drakke, you *participated* in discussions about *harming* Mr. Tork." He was deliberately stressing the condemning words.

"These discussions were *theoretical*, Mr. Fronten," I said, raising my voice. Not a good thing. Trish was frowning but I had to continue. "... When I felt like the discussions were moving from *talking* about ideas to actually *doing* something, I wanted nothing more to do with it. *That* was the end of my involvement."

"That is all, Mrs. Drakke." Fronten ended the session.

I was shocked. I was just getting warmed up.

Trish retorted, "Samsara came to this meeting in good faith, gentlemen, wishing to answer all your questions. Does anyone else have any questions?"

She was so diplomatic.

I wanted to smack Fronten's smug look off his face, but had the good sense to restrain myself. He had his mind made up before he came here, I realized, and it wouldn't have mattered if I showed him a videotape of my withdrawal from the conspiracy. He'd have said I staged it. He would use anything I said against me.

There were no more questions. We sat in an uncomfortable silence for a couple of minutes.

The meeting was over.

Outside the building, on our way back to the car, I said to Trish, "I spoke too fast, didn't I?"

"Yes, you did."

"It was exactly the same things I told the Judges. I didn't change my story one bit." I wanted some kind word, an acknowledgment for at least fighting this battle.

"Samsara, you did the best you could under the circumstances." She was gentle, and I could see the tender look in her eyes, as if she understood the immensity of the strain I felt.

"Will they give me a break because I talked to them?"

"I don't know, yet. We'll have to see."

On the way back to Trish's flat, my mind floated. I didn't want to think about anything. I began to wonder if I was being persecuted for trying to figure out what to do with people who were considered enemies. Maybe I knew too much about what was going on in Washington circles at that time, and was being punished. Random thoughts arose, like what happens to people when they are suddenly faced with a fifty-foot tornado coming at them.

The face of the lawyer I interviewed in D.C. a few years ago, came into my mind. He was representing an American family whose son, having found evidence of the U.S.'s involvement in the coup in Chile, was murdered shortly after. There was nothing the lawyer could do to get retribution for the family, despite compelling evidence pointing to the U.S.'s complicity in the murder. Powerless to win their case, they were all penalized for their knowledge of how the U.S. was involved. That incident reminded me of the night the FBI had seized my diary in 1985 in their raid on our house in Haüsern, Germany. They promised to return it and didn't.

We *never* saw the search warrant they said they had. I never saw my diary again.

"How are you feeling, Samsara?" Trish's voice cut in.

"Like I lost Gettysburg, Trish."

She smiled. "Well, at least Lee stood up for his principles, which is what you did."

That night my stomach churned. Trish was leaving the next day and I had no guarantees from the prosecution, despite my willingness to talk with them.

I felt drained.

I had talked to Judges and it came to nothing. I talked to U.S. prosecutors, and this, too would probably come to nothing. Why was I being cooperative at all? Sure, we would go all out on the appeal, I'd return to work and who knows what would come of it? Might be a long haul by the time my testimony was reviewed by the Judges and sent to the U.S.

It was April 2. Trish left me with a warm and supportive hug, promising to be in touch as soon as she had some news.

I went back to the bar and my worry about the defense.

Two days later at 6:00 P.M., Trish called.

She barely said hello.

"Trish, what is it?" I was frightened.

"Samsara, start packing. I just got word from Fronten that your papers were received this morning in Washington, and the extradition date is set for April 12th."

"Trish, we're at the start of the appeal, there must be some mistake." I was trying to stay calm.

"Samsara, the papers were sent directly from Bonn to Washington. Somebody over *there* signed them and sent them to the German capital."

"That's impossible! The Court is still considering my appeal!"

"Well, you better contact Hanna right away and find out what's going on. Let me know as soon as you hear anything."

Contacting Hanna was not simple, as she had already left her office for the night. I was anxious *and* angry. When I eventually reached her, my anger was inflamed.

"What the HELL is going on," I shouted into the phone, " Trish just told me that the extradition has been signed off by the Germans. How could this happen Hanna? Didn't you file the appeal?"

"I don't know how this happened, Samsara," Hanna started nervously, "Your papers disappeared from the Court in Karlsrühe and went straight to Bonn. It seems that the state prosecutor went ahead and sent them, himself."

"Can't the Judges DO *ANYTHING*?" I was screaming. Johann came running into my room from next door. His face was concerned. "Hanna, *please* find out what they can *do*! This *can't* happen like this!

But, it did.

The Judges were mad. They issued a stinging statement to the U.S. that absolutely nothing was to be added to my charges, and the transportation of weapons charge was *verboten*. In a few days' time U.S. Federal marshals would escort me out of Germany.

It was a relief to have so little time. All my attention was concentrated on the details of ending one life and getting ready for another, an uncharted frontier that none of my codefendants had crossed. I was the first person to be extradited from Germany to the U.S. for conspiracy to murder a federal official – an official I had never met.

Narian was the second.

On April 11, the day before extradition, the dawn came with a faintly cloudy sunrise. Getting out of my warm bed, the thought that this was my last day in my beloved Deutschland hit me with a sharp smack.

I walked through the *fussgangerzone* (the pedestrian walkway) in the town square and smelled the young spring flowers, tiny buds coming out, and saying goodbye to me. Everything spoke to me, that morning.

Each building glowed, radianced by the early morning sunshine. How many mornings I had emerged from the dark world of the bar into the new fresh day embracing me with its pale, delicate light; cleansing like a brief shower.

I walked the whole day, into the dusk, remembering I was leaving my beloved Germany.

Early evening, Katrin and I shared a coffee in our favorite outdoor bistro in Baden-Baden, talking about that day, back in October 1990 when I left Rhodes for Athens, and I told her then. "One never knows when one will see a beloved again," referring to everybody and everything I was leaving behind in Rhodes.

"Sweetheart," she had said, then, "you're over-emotional." Now, she just smiled, sadly.

We were both so full of raw pain that it was impossible to get words out. We sat with a heavy silence between us.

Would I see Greece again? Will I see Germany again? The way things were going, who knows?

Music from the cafes breezed around us, and I kept trying to photograph these moments in my mind, as Johann joined us. He was carrying a parcel.

"Zis is for your plane ride, Samsara." He opened up a tiny package with one of those air pillows you blow up and put behind your neck. I was touched by his thoughtfulness - so much it hurt me, and I reacted quickly without thinking.

"I can't take this on the plane, Johann. The marshals will never allow it." Seeing his crushed face, I realized I had spoken too hastily.

"Ask zem. Ze will…" His voice was feeble, choked with pain. He was feeling the tearing – lives ripped apart.

"I will. And I will come back some day, I promise you both. When everything's all done. God knows when… it might be a long time," I said numbly.

I had learned that the charges could carry twenty, thirty years…

How do you imagine that much of your life in prison?

Night came too fast. Johann and Nina took me to dinner. Hanna joined us later. Nina cried with surprising emotion that I'd not seen before. We'd never been close although we'd lived together for nearly three years.

There was no sleep.

4:00 A.M. came. April 12.

Johann drove me to Frankfurt airport. When we arrived there he said, "Come, I vill take you to breakfast, Samsara. You haf to eat."

My fork moved the food around on my plate, and I couldn't say anything. Looking into his eyes, I saw pain. I made myself look away.

We sat beneath the airport clock. 7:50 A.M. In ten minutes, I was to meet the marshals.

Johann and I walked to the meeting area. Narian was already there with his German wife Ingrid, who I barely knew. I was apprehensive about the chains I was told I might have to wear, as well as the cuffs, because my ankles were sensitive after the varicose vein operations I'd had. My arthritic right wrist had once been broken and it arthritis would not do well in cold steel.

Just as I had left the Ranch, I carried one small bag with all my belongings from another phase in my life. This one was striped so it would stand out, I hoped, in the prison baggage.

The marshals greeted me civilly. No chains. I was grateful. There were two men for Narian and two women for me.

I couldn't say anything to Narian. All eight of us walked to the gate.

"Take care of Ingrid," I whispered into Johann's ear. "She will help you because she will be missing Narian ... I love you, Johann. You've given me so much!" I held onto him, feeling his tenderness, not wanting to leave his safe embrace.

I heard a harsh voice, "Come on!" and hands pulled me away from Johann. I was "escorted" onto the plane, turning around a couple of times to wave to him as he got smaller and smaller in the distance. He stood very still, arm raised and I felt that he was crying. He was too far away for me to see the expression on his face.

Tears spilled out and I didn't care who saw. I was crying openly. I caught sight of Narian, seated several rows in front of me, crying too.

The marshals seemed to understand my tears and at least did not try to talk to me for the first hour. We flew mostly in silence until we were over Dallas. They asked me a little about what I was charged with, and what a good American girl like me was doing in a commune. The atmosphere relaxed a little, and I was even allowed to go into the bathroom by myself.

In Dallas, we changed planes. The marshals checked our baggage through customs and we went on to Portland. I was still in a fog.

Arrival in Portland was grim. Once the marshals handed us over to the Portland police, all politeness was gone.

"Drakke! Get in here!" the police cuffed and leg ironed me more swiftly than I could blink my eyes, and I was pushed into the police wagon. As the wagon pulled away from the curbside, reporters ran over to catch us as quickly as they could before we got away. The press was deliberately not told when we were to arrive, but somebody leaked it at the last minute. Flashbulbs went off like rocket fire, but later Trish told me they only got the wagon.

I saw little out the caged window on the way to the Portland city jail, as the evening light was fading. Out of the wagon, down a long driveway into the "processing station." It was hard for me to walk with those irons. I had to hop a little so the irons wouldn't cut me. The cuffs hurt, they were so tight.

The officer at the desk in the Portland jail was reading some papers in front of him as I approached, and he let out a low whistle.

"Wow, who pissed *you* off? Conspiracy to murder, wiretapping, illegal transport of firearms... *man*! Somebody must have made *you* angry!" He smiled a bit, and I could see that he was attempting to make a heavy situation light. I could also see that he was trying to connect me with the charges, for I was well dressed and softly spoken.

"The charges are not true," was all I could say, quietly, sadly and brokenly. I was additionally shocked that the arms charge followed me from there to here, as the extradition papers expressly forbade it.

I was stripped, searched and locked into a cell.

I have nothing but the clothes I'm wearing.

There was only a padded bench in the cell and a stainless steel toilet on the floor. Nothing else.

I collapsed on the bench.

Chapter 10
Night of Tape Soup

I've done so much for so long with so little, pretty soon I'll be able to do anything with nothing at all. – Air Force proverb

God, my neck is sore. Where am I?

One eye opened first, then the other, I scanned the place. There was a bare light bulb hanging above my head. The walls were dirty yellow, thick with dirt and inscribed with graffiti. The floor was cracked concrete. A stainless steel toilet was bolted to the left of the door and a phone was stuck to the wall. Underneath me was a gray slab.

The empty stillness was thick; the only sound was the throbbing in my head. This was Portland jail.

I was still wearing the same clothes I wore when I left Germany; my white jacket draped around my shoulders.

I must have pulled it over me while I was sleeping. My watch's gone. What time is it? There's no window in here. Is it day or night?

My left hip was bruised from lying on the hard surface.

Yuk, my teeth are slimy and I can smell my own breath. My right contact is sticking. It's dry. I need to rinse it. This place is the pits.

Trish said I'd get bail. God, what I wouldn't give for any kind of coffee and a cigarette. If I bang on that door somebody has to come.

Forcing my body upright, I went to the door and started banging. And banging.

Nobody came.

I banged louder. A man's voice shouted back, "Quit that banging!" The slot in the top of the door opened and cold, black eyes looked back at me.

"I need to brush my teeth and rinse out my lens!"

"Do it when you get your shower. Hold onto your pants."

"When'll *that* be?" Not answering, he slammed the opening closed.

Man! This sucks! I gotta get outta here. These guards don't care about me. My lens... If I don't rinse it out, it'll stick to my eye and cause an abrasion. I haven't felt like this since that day I left the Ranch.

The 15th of September 1985 came back into focus clearly.

I was standing in a tiny room in Sila's house, waiting to leave the Ranch for good, with a few others. I had to brush my teeth and pee, but I was afraid that even if I went to the bathroom, the others would leave without me.

That whole day was saturated with terror. People were running around, afraid like me of being prevented from going. Bhagwan would excommunicate us, for sure. The enlightenment dream was gone. Only last week, he had publicly denounced two important commune members, Jaya and Pasha, who left in the middle of the night.

Fear and sadness organized the last days of my ten years in the commune. There were no mementos of the buildings and houses we had built, or even of my closest friends.

Wham! The cell door opened and two guards announced that I could shower.

"Can you bring me the bag I came with? It's got my contact lens solution in it and I absolutely need it to rinse my lens! One of you guys took it when you put me in here."

" You'll have to do without it."

"But I *need* it! I could develop a real problem with my eye."

"Sorry. No bag. You'll have to do without it."

God damn you, I wanted to scream, but didn't.

The shower was so good I forgot to ask what time it was.

OK, think. What did you do that day you left the Ranch?

Then, I had run out of solution the day before, and I remembered thinking that I could get it 'on the outside'.

OK. I think I can hang on till tomorrow. I'll be out of this jail by then. There were the same thoughts as on that day. But, then there were also other thoughts.

Trish said that a Portland lawyer, Bob Warner, would be representing me at the bail hearings because a local was required.

Does he even know I'm here? God, I wish Trish were here, so I wouldn't have to rely on someone I don't even know!

I looked at the phone.

OK, I don't know Warner's number, but I can call Sila's Portland lawyer, Trevor Hammond. How many times did I call the man when I was helping Sila with her case in 1986? He'll help me.

I picked up the phone and called collect. Not knowing what time it was, I took a risk. The phone rang several times before it was answered by a young slightly breathless voice.

"Hammond and Pierce" the secretary said. I could hear the operator asking if Trevor Hammond would accept a collect call from Samsara Drakke.

The call was accepted.

"Why are you calling me?" he asked gruffly, surprised.

"Trevor! I'm so glad to hear your voice!" My relief was tangible: a human voice in this impenetrable, hostile place.

"I'm here in Portland jail."

"I know."

"Can you help me?"

"Samsara, surely you must have a lawyer!"

"Trevor, all I know is his name, Bob Warner. I don't even have his number."

"Samsara, you shouldn't even be talking to me," he interrupted. "I represent your co-defendant, and the only contact you can have with me is through your lawyer. If you want Bob Warner, call 697-2430. Good luck. Good-bye." He hung up.

I repeated the number, dialing it slowly.

What if he's not there? What if the office is closed?

"You have reached Robert Warner. I'm either on the phone or away from my desk. Please leave your name and number and I'll get back to you as soon as I can." Beep.

I dialed again. I got the answering machine again and the operator would not put the collect call through.

What am I gonna do now? The guards'll have to help me get this call through. I banged on the door.

"Now, what do you want?"

"I can't get my collect call through to my lawyer. There's a message machine..."

"Sorry. Try again later."

I traced the number in the dust on the wall.

Twenty-seven times later I got through. An even-toned, nondescript masculine voice said, "Hello."

"Hello. It's Samsara. Bob? Thank God! I've been trying to reach you for hours."

"I just switched my office phone over to my home phone."

"Thank God! What time is it? What day is it? I'm here in Portland jail, and they won't even give me my contact lens solution! I need to rinse my lens because my eyes are drying out and..."

"Whoa! Whoa! Hold on for a minute! Calm down! You're talking a mile a minute! It's almost 10:30 P.M. on Friday night and I'm very tired, so please slow down. It's been a long week."

Well my week has already been several lifetimes! Hell, part of me is still in Germany!

"Bob, when can I see you? Sorry for calling you so late. I had no idea of the time. This place is a windowless hole in the ground. The last daylight I saw was when I got off the plane in Portland."

"Samsara, I know it must be awful for you there."

That was all I needed, someone who was on my side and could understand this horror. Scorching hot tears burned down my face.

"Bob, it *is* awful. When can I see you? I really need my contact lens solution. Can you bring some?"

I wanted to get the most important thing out first. The rest could wait until I saw him.

"Well, tomorrow is Saturday and they normally don't allow visitors on Saturday."

"But, don't they make exceptions for lawyers? I've traveled all the way from Germany! If I don't get solution to take care of my lens, I won't be able to even see the judge! Didn't Trish tell you that I'm blind in one eye? If a dirty lens damages the other eye, I risk blindness in that eye too! It's serious, Bob. Please see what you can do."

"I'll do my best, Samsara, but I can't promise. I'll try."

"Thank you, Bob. I'll tell you the rest when you come."

"OK Samsara, try and sleep."

"Thank you, Bob. I will." We hung up.

I breathed in the dank, tumid air of the cell.

My nerve ends were raw. Without coffee and cigarettes, even the air grated on me. My clothes were damp and smelly because I was sweating so much. I had been wearing them for more than 48 hours. My pants were stained because my period came early and the guards had delayed getting me pads.

The same thing happened that day I left the Ranch. Now I'm back in Portland for the first time in six years. Except for the graffiti and the dirt, the cell walls reminded me of Sila's bedroom: gray. Her room was a prison too, but I didn't know it, then. I was afraid of what Bhagwan would say.

He'll denounce me like he denounced Jaya and Pasha. They were big shots in the organization. Jaya had been in charge of the international banking department for overseas investments, and Pasha was chief of medical services in the medical clinic, Pythagoras. They were part of our security circle. I envied them. They were the pillars of the community until they snuck away in the middle of the night, leaving without a trace.

And boy did Bhagwan give it to them! He shred them to pieces in morning discourse, the day after. Only a week before he'd praised them. I'm next. Me and the others. We'll be confetti too.

That incident reminded me of when I tried to leave the clinic and Kiku had stopped me. Something changed for me when I heard Jaya and Pasha had left. Leaving became a real possibility... a real option.

By then I was increasingly immune to Bhagwan's ravings. I had witnessed him denouncing and praising various commune members, repeating the same neurotic pattern for years. I no longer believed in his ability to judge reality. And, as I listened to him through the bugs the security team had planted in his room, I gradually became convinced that the bugs weren't put there to protect him. They were put there to protect *us.*

He had gone mad. Was that a hazard that enlightened people encounter? I didn't know what he would do next. He had already made Sila a mindless, raving lunatic by his unreasonable demands. She used to be so solid, so steady and wise...

If I stayed, would I become a mindless peon as well? I'd invested so much of my life in him, in his dream of the commune, first in Poona and now here. His dream became my own and I had helped create it.

Now, his madness was destroying it.

He was far more human than I wanted to believe.

I found myself hoping the Feds would take Bhagwan away. Then something would *have* to change.

God! What was I saying? How could I even think such a thing? How could I walk away and live with myself? How would I live with the guilt of leaving the man I had devoted my whole life to?

Clearly, there was nothing more I could do here. The

situation was too far-gone. The power play between Sila and the new favorites, the Hollywood sannyasins, was escalating and I was afraid of them. They supported Bhagwan's nitrous oxide habit and wanted to run the Ranch with a life style that included drugs, channeling spirits, mediums, and no hard work. To me, that spelled destruction.

My choices were limited - stay and have a breakdown, or leave and take my chances. Up to now I hadn't been able to secure a vehicle and drive myself off the Ranch.

But Puneet had. Last week he told me his plan. Him, I *trusted*.

"Samsara, you know that I've been pretty disturbed about what's been going on recently, especially with the Hollywood crowd. Anyway, some of us have been discussing leaving. What are *your* thoughts?"

"Puneet, I've been thinking seriously about it, ever since Jaya and Pasha left. I just didn't know how to do it. What are you going to do?"

"Several of us are going to wind up our work and turn it over to a transition team so the Ranch can continue running as usual. Then, we'll take three vans to Portland airport."

"Vans? How many people are going?"

"Right now, there are about twenty of us."

"Twenty! That many? Yes, Puneet, I want to go."

"Good."

I'll leave! But, where am I going to go? Washington D.C.? LA? New York? And what will I do, as an ex-commune member with no skills and no money?

In this cell, I had lots of time to do nothing but think.

This mess is a lot worse than in 1985. Should I go to trial? Maybe the government will offer me a deal, since I cooperated by meeting with them in Germany? Surely they will be reasonable. They must have seen by now that the whole thing was hearsay, and I tried my best to talk Sila out of doing anything wrong. Since nothing happened and no one was ever harmed, how can they make me to do prison time? I was simply a brainwashed, cult-programmed wanna-be... ugh!

So much sacrifice for what? Endless sickness, no money, no comfortable home, family or kids and then having to leave the very place and people I had given up so much for.

That day I left I wanted the people who were staying to say to me: "You did a good job, and we are all grateful to you for doing so much, giving so much, suffering so much, so that we could turn this dream into reality." But there was no gratitude. They thanked me with betrayal instead. Perhaps that was what I deserved.

In those last few hours, security watched over me "casually," pretending to help me pack my overnight bag while acting like they were my friends. Just before we boarded the vans, they searched us as if we were criminals carrying gold.

I left behind my teddy bear. He and I had been together since 1978, through the madness of India. There were times I'd talked to him when I couldn't talk to anyone else. He had been my sole companion. But, sadly, there was no room for him. My whole life, minus one teddy bear, was in that bag.

After packing, I called Sam.

"Hello, Sam. I'm at Jesus Grove."

"Samsara… are you leaving?"

"Yes. How did you know?"

"The rumors are thick. Tell me one thing though. Are you involved with those poisonings I heard about?"

"What poisonings?"

"Rumors we heard. And the fire…"

I shivered as though bugs were crawling up my spine.

What am I being blamed for?

"No, Sam. I've come to the end of my patience with journey. I *need* to go, to move on with my life. There's nothing more for me here."

"I understand. All right. Bless you, and… remember I *do* love you. Don't be a stranger."

We hung up.

Will I ever see him again? He had become a good friend.

The clock said 1:35 P.M. Time was evaporating. We were

supposed to leave in half an hour. I also had to call Anand. He had returned to the ranch in 1983. He'd also become a friend. My love for him had changed from desperate love-sickness to a simple caring for someone who had been in my life and was no longer.

He answered the phone immediately.

"Anand?"

"Hello, Samsara."

"I'm calling to tell you that I'm leaving."

"Why?"

"I can't breathe here, any longer. All the things I once treasured, like Bhagwan's teachings and hope for my own enlightenment are gone... I don't want to say more because I'm afraid it will disturb you too much."

"No, Samsara. Nothing you could say would disturb me now. I'm just a simple man, really. I gave up all that enlightenment nonsense. All I want these days is to do my job in the carpentry shop and be well fed. Nothing more... but please keep in touch, hmm? You're still my wife you know. Let me know if you need a divorce or something."

"Yes, I'll write when I have an address."

He still feels guilty, thinking he caused my anorexia.

"And, Samsara...I want you to know...I really *did* fall in love with you, in my own way..."

I swallowed and closed my eyes.

This is too much, right now. Why couldn't he have said this before? Why now, when I may never see him again?

"Thank you, Anand." I could hardly get the words out.

Please don't let me have to talk to anybody else.

I took my bag, making my way slowly through the mass of people who had gathered in the house. I had to say something to Berry. In a choking voice, I said, "Take care."

She nodded, crying too. Lots of people were crying, sobbing. "Why are you going?" Someone yelled through the chaos. Hurrying outside, I felt like a tiny fish caught up in a tidal wave.

I got into one of the vans. Puneet was the driver. We left. The whole way to the final gate, I couldn't look back.

We didn't talk much on the drive. Everyone was in shock. After several hours of driving non-stop, we pulled up outside a tiny motel near Portland and checked into four double rooms.

Eve, Diana and I shared a room. We were all restless, not quite knowing what to do. It was surreal. Eve decided to call her sister in Portland, so Diana and I stepped outside to give her some privacy. When she finished she came outside crying.

"I don't know if I should leave and go back to my sister or stay with you all and go on… I don't know what to do."

Another burst of crying.

Her outpouring of emotion suddenly reversed our roles. I knew I wasn't going back and had to show that I was unflappable. She was not going to manipulate me ever again.

"It's OK, Eve. Do what gives you peace." Looking at her I felt more compassion than anything else. She, too, had been ostracized like the rest of us.

Her crying bothered me, however because she seemed more unstable than the rest of us. Eve had been powerful and impenetrable before. This person who used to strike fear in me was now stuttering in confusion.

Now, in jail, I'm now one of the victims of her subsequent actions: arrests, indictments and shattered lives. Trish recently told me it was Eve who instigated the investigations. She dramatized our meetings into a cult war council of which the FBI was naturally eager to hear every minute detail.

The next morning, Eve went back to the Ranch, saying she just couldn't leave Bhagwan. It gave me an eerie feeling as I didn't believe what she said nor did I trust her.

Diana, Maya, Puneet and I drove on to Portland. When we arrived, Puneet needed to talk, so we went for a walk.

"Samsara, I'd been thinking about leaving for weeks, but

now that we're here, I feel like I've jumped off a cliff. Like everything before is finished. I'd never dreamed that I'd leave the Ranch this way."

"Neither did I. If it weren't for you guys, I'd really be stuck there."

"I've been thinking, it would be better for you to come to Germany for a while, so that you can clear your head, before you decide what you want to do. Several of us, including Sila, are going there for just that reason. I have family there, and you're certainly welcome to stay with me as long as you want. Maybe we join the communities in Europe."

That made sense. Puneet sounded so practical and reassuring. *And* sane.

In Portland that afternoon, I closed down the apartment where Eve, Diana, Maya and I had surveilled Tork. Puneet went to buy our airline tickets with his own money, while Maya and Diana went shopping. We arranged to meet later at a hotel downtown.

I arrived at the apartment, dreading the encounter with the landlady. Leaving without giving a month's notice, I'd given her the excuse of a family emergency. I paid the balance of the month's rent with money Puneet had given me and left my stereo system as a contribution. I was glad to be out of there.

We left Portland for Seattle the next day.

The only tickets Puneet could buy at such short notice departed from the Seattle airport. After checking into a hotel to wait for our evening flight, I walked outside for some exercise and fresh air and decided to buy a local newspaper.

On page four, I read the headlines:

"Sila and the Gang Accused by Guru of Wiretapping and Poisonings"

Stunned and shocked, I read through the article included an interview with Bhagwan saying we had criminally tapped the phones and poisoned his supporters, namely his doctor who was still hospitalized. My heart started beating wildly. I could feel the goose bumps and a cold sweat breaking out all over my body. My thoughts raced ahead of the words.

Bhagwan's describing us as criminals? We were his beloveds just a little while ago! I trusted and loved him! Sila said she always told Bhagwan everything that happened, including the wiretap. She told him it was set up at the suggestion of the police to protect the community!

But... what if Sila hadn't told him? Oh, God...

He would have been furious. Did he use the wiretap and poisonings to turn the whole commune against us? Is this his revenge? They're bound to see that the wiretap was for everyone's good as soon as they discover that the tapes are still there. Everything will be resolved. Real criminals would have destroyed evidence.

I returned to the hotel to find Maya sitting on the bed, crying hysterically and begging us to go to Mexico for reasons she was unable to articulate. The same article I had just read was flung across her bed. Maya, who later befriended me... Maya, who followed Eve, delivering us into the hands of the Feds.

Diana was quietly crying too, muttering how she badly wanted to go back to Texas and forget this whole chapter of her life. She, too, broke down later under FBI questioning.

Puneet was the rock. He came to me and said simply, "I have to pick up our tickets, please calm them down. We have to leave in a couple of hours."

"OK," I said, "But let me walk out with you." We left the room and softly closed the door.

"What do you think about all this?" I asked him, motioning to the newspaper article I held in my hand.

"Surely you can see that all this is propaganda nonsense," he replied. "Everyone will come to their senses once Bhagwan calms down. It's nothing but a hype for publicity. That's Bhagwan's technique. So, please, take care of them. They are just emotional because we're all tired and under so much stress."

Puneet picked up the tickets and we took a cab to the

airport. We decided to walk through the terminal and board separately, concerned that as a group, we might be noticed, questioned and detained from leaving.

Once the plane landed in Zurich, we met the driver Sila sent to take us across the border to Germany, to a small inn. The fog mirrored the numbness in my mind as we drove into the village of Haüsern, in the Black Forest, where Sila and five of "the gang" had already gathered.

It was late. Kiku, trembling in the cold night air, and not looking like the Ranch medical director she was just days ago, opened the door.

It was a relief to see her. She picked up my bag and we walked together into the building. The others followed behind.

"Samsara, I've been waiting for you all for hours. How are you?"

"I'm fine, Kiku. It's great to finally stop traveling. From the Ranch we drove to a motel near Portland, then Seattle, then the flight. It's good to see you. You look so rested! What's going on here?"

"Everything's fine. Don't worry about a thing. Sila's been negotiating a contract for all of us with a very big magazine for an exclusive story. If it works out, we'll have a fresh, new beginning."

That night, I sank into a dreamless stupor. Just before closing my eyes I realized that no matter what anyone said about Bhagwan, he was giving me a test by denouncing me, condemning me and ostracizing me. It was up to *me*, now, to deal with it. I could either get very pissed off and reject *him*, or somehow turn it around to where I could see it wasn't his —or anybody's- fault.

This was the game I'd signed up for - the master-disciple game. *This* time, instead of the disciples betraying the master, it was the other way around. The master delivered us into the hands of the angry crowds, the high priests, the Feds.

I was still thinking like a devoted seminarian.

When I woke up the next morning, I was ready to be dazzled.

The reporters from *Stern* magazine were already downstairs. The attention they gave us, the feeling of being taken care of and *understood* felt great.

We'd been bashed, accused, bombed, traumatized and outcast, all in a very short time. And then transported overnight to a country where I didn't even speak the language.

Stern Magazine was the unexpected angel-of-mercy-battalion. They wanted our story. In exchange they fed, clothed and took care of us for weeks.

At first the whole thing was like a miracle: I would be part of a great story, the *truth* of what really happened on the Ranch. Instead, I began to feel like a misfit. A nobody. *Stern* hardly ever asked me about anything. Compared to Sila, who had already been on network television, or Sarah, mastermind of one of the largest financial departments, or one of the other well-known leaders, I wasn't a star. *I* was a pipsqueak.

Depression grew, along with insignificance

What'll I do? What job would I get? Without speaking German or having job skills, and with criminal charges in the air, who would hire me? I couldn't exactly put on my resume: ex-cult junkie, wanted for wiretapping, seeks employment.

Once *Stern* took over our lives, we were continuously on the move. I didn't have to *think* too much about what would happen to me and I was too exhausted to care.

Several nights later, no sooner had I fallen asleep, one of the *Stern* reporters woke me. "Go out by the back door. There's a bus waiting outside. Get on the bus and lie down with the others. There are reporters around the house. Make sure they don't see you," he whispered to me. I looked over at Diana's bed, which was already empty.

The story about the group being charged with poisonings, arson and wiretaps had broken across the U.S.

The bus left Haüsern and hours later we were told to get off and change into new, non-orange clothes. We were given food and then told to get back on the bus.

With no moon, we couldn't see anything. Hours later, the bus stopped at the northernmost coast of Germany, where we went by boat to an island. There we were informed we were to be sequestered in one of the local inns, to avoid the media so *Stern*'s exclusive wouldn't be compromised.

Thus began non-stop interviews and photos. Three days later the press discovered where we were and came after us in helicopters. Once again we were pressed to leave immediately. Huddled in horse drawn buggies we were driven to a tiny airfield where planes were waiting to fly us to Hanover. As soon as we landed, we were taken to *Stern*'s offices downtown, where it was decided we should set out within the hour to Italy by bus.

Worn out, there was no time to think about what was happening. My depression was so acrid I could smell it.

After a week in Italy, we went back to Haüsern and the original inn where we had first stayed. I didn't want to stop moving for fear my body would collapse and my mind would break into pieces.

Instead, my back gave out and I was unable to function.

When I landed at the jail in Portland, I tried to act "normal." But on the inside, I was like a zombie, barely crawling from one hurtful event to the other. Like being on the receiving end of machine gun fire, every shock felt like a bullet penetrating my soul. My spirit was disintegrating - my mind evaporating.

My thoughts seemed illogical to me and I feared that I wouldn't be capable of making the right decision about a trial or a plea. In fact, I couldn't see anything beyond the present moment, which was slowly blowing me to smithereens...

In 1985, the pieces had already been blown apart. The news reported Bhagwan had been arrested on immigration charges while attempting to flee the U.S. I had a strong sense that something similar was going to happen to all of us.

After listening to the news, at 9:00 A.M. on October 28, 1985, twelve of us gathered in the Haüsern living room to discuss Bhagwan's arrest, and the possible consequences for us.

We had just moved into a large rambling house outside the village. The house looked like something out of Hansel and Gretel. The people we met in the village were sweet and trusting, accepting us like suffering refugees – which, in fact, we were. We shared a common feeling of having gone through a war, escaping the madness by our wits.

Because of our lack of money, our survival was dependent on *Stern*. The story was coming out in weekly installments and taking longer than we had all thought. It was costing *Stern* more money than they wanted to spend and we wanted to move on.

But, something awful was about to happen.

At 6:00 P.M. that night, something did.

The first thing I saw through the large picture window was a black Mercedes; followed by two others, pulling up in front of the house. There was a loud knock on the front door. A moment later Herr Knober, the owner, opened it. I heard someone inquire, "Is there a woman called Sila staying here?" Before Herr Knober could answer, three men and women pushed their way in and proceeded to the living room, where we were gathered. No one had left the house all day.

I was sitting on the floor next to Puneet, and Sila was sitting in a large armchair at the opposite end of the room. One of the three men walked directly over to Sila and said calmly, in a strong German accent,

"Are you Ma Anand Sila?"

"Yes."

"We are *Kriminal Polizei* requested by the United States to detain you. Please gather your zings quickly and come wiz us. *Frau* Kreutzer will accompany you to your room to pack." *Frau* Kreutzer stepped forward and took Sila's arm gently but quite firmly.

Just as swiftly, the next man approached Diva, repeating the same instruction and another *Frau* was produced to accompany her. The third man simultaneously went to Kiku, his *Frau* standing directly behind him.

It all happened so fast.

All three were hustled out the living room and up the stairs, to pack a single bag.

"The rest of you will stay in zis room for the moment," one of the men said to us.

A few minutes later, when Sila, Kiku and Diva came down, we tried to hug them, scrambling to say a last word with tears pouring down our faces. They were hurried through the front door and in a flurry of arms and legs, stuffed into the waiting cars. Then they were gone.

Gone.

Just like that.

Narian was standing behind Sarah supporting her.

Sarah was in an intense conversation with Herr Knober. I heard her say, "How could this happen? How can the German police just walk in here and arrest non-Germans?" Herr Knober, deeply shocked and confused, tried his best to make sense of the situation, mopping his brow, attempting to hide his own fear.

"I don't understand, *mein frau,* but we will have to find out what is going on. You must call a lawyer or go to the Consulate immediately."

Ruby was animatedly talking to her children, "It's OK, guys, just calm down. It's probably nothing serious; Sila and the girls have gone somewhere to answer questions about us. They'll probably be back soon."

Diana and Maya were both crying, talking rapidly to each other, "We're all doomed. I knew they'd get us. We should get out of here as soon as possible. Who knows what's going to happen next? I don't want to have anything to do with the German police without having an American lawyer present."

Puneet was trying to calm them, speaking slowly and deliberately. "Stop shouting. You're scaring the children. They've probably only been taken away for questioning. We don't know why and we have no idea what's going on. It might be nothing."

Belle was terrified, standing behind Sarah, as if for protection. The same fear gripped me, like I was being choked by an octopus. I forced myself to think.

Standing by the stairs, I took in the scene in front of me, shaking myself into some kind of readiness to deal with the next event.

There has to be a follow-up. The police will come back. If I'm searched, what do I need to get rid of? The only things I have on me are my library cards and student ID's in other names, which I used in my research. The police crowd might consider these as "criminal evidence". And then what would they do to me?

No sooner had I started up the stairs, than floodlights illuminated the whole ground floor, and I thought World War III had started. My legs went rubbery on the stairwell and the front door burst open. More people I'd never seen before poured through.

I had to get to my room.

Forcing myself up the stairs, I ran into my room and yanked open the closet door, breathing shallowly, searching for the cards I couldn't leave on the Ranch.

Where are those cards? Damn it!

There was a German man's voice in the hallway outside my room. Holding my breath, I stopped looking through the bag I had just pulled out of the closet.

I have to make it look like I was just getting up from a nap so they wouldn't suspect anything.

Stuffing the bag back in the closet, I closed the door quickly and jumped into bed, pulling the comforter up to my neck so they wouldn't see I was fully dressed.

The door opened and the man came in.

"You are requested to go downstairs with your friends, please," he said in clipped Oxford English.

Requested?

I became the epitome of cooperation.

"Of course," I said, smiling.

He's watching me. I have to look away from the closet.

As I came downstairs I could see several men briskly assembling us in the living room. This time, they didn't address us as *Frau*.

I could smell the fear. The air was thick with it.

A tall man, with black wavy hair, who was obviously in charge, stood in the middle of the room, surrounded by four others. He began talking as soon as I entered the room, as if he had been waiting for me.

"My name is Paul Tomkins. This is my colleague, Tim Frest. We are with the FBI. We are here through the cooperation of the German government, whose representatives are the police you see here. We have a warrant to search these premises for anything we might consider as possible evidence concerning the charges of wiretapping and murder, for which your friends are being detained. We look forward to your cooperation. The search will be conducted quickly and quietly. You will not be allowed to go to your rooms until we call you. Then, you will be accompanied there by one of the officers, who will remain present during the search." He paused, "do you have any questions?"

Silence.

Sarah said something I couldn't hear. I was trying to figure out a way to get to my room before it was searched. I heard pots banging in the kitchen next door.

Why are they searching the kitchen? What're they looking for?

Tomkins and his buddy, Frest walked out of the room, leaving plenty of his cronies to make sure we followed orders. I didn't even think of asking to see the warrant.

Maya and Sarah were talking quietly and intently. Sarah crossed the room to talk to the German police, and then Maya came over to me.

"Do you remember that tape of Bhagwan slapping Viviananda?"

The tape was the only proof we had of what was really going on behind Bhagwan's crumbling empire. It was also proof that his room was bugged.

"Yes, but I thought it had been left at the Ranch?"

Before she could say anything else, Puneet's name was called.

"Maya, I can't talk to you now, I have to get upstairs." I thought quickly,

I'll ask one of the policemen if I can go to the bathroom. Then, I'll tell him I need to change my tampon. That might embarrass him enough to let me go to my closet to get one. Once in the closet, I'll grab my ID's. I've got to put my hands on them!

"Excuse me." I addressed one of the pale looking policemen. "I need to go to the bathroom. Can you come with me to my room?"

He reluctantly agreed, looking for approval from a colleague, who nodded. Up we went. He looked into the bathroom, then motioned me inside and closed the door, while he waited in the hallway.

I went to the toilet and made sounds like a moan and astonishment.

Opening the door, I looked sufficiently embarrassed.

"Excuse me, I have my... monthly," I pointed down and then held up my hands, palms up.

"You mean you have your mensterbation?"

Poor thing. He's confused it with masturbation. Better for me.

"Yes," I said blushing suitably. "I need to go to my closet for pads." I said pointing to my room.

"Alright, then. Be quick."

He watched me like a hawk.

Reaching inside, I found the tampon box, trying to put my hands on the small packet of cards.

Damn it! Where are they? I have to find them!

"OK, now you must go away from the closet and do your business at the toilet. Come."

God! What am I gonna do?

Back to the toilet, sitting down, I actually *had* gotten my period.

As I came down the stairs, my chaperone halted and we

were told to go back upstairs, as my room was next on the list to be searched.

Diana, my roommate, and I were to be escorted to our room by two policemen.

One German. The other's probably FBI.

"Please sit down while we search your room." He had an American accent.

Yup, FBI.

Diana was so nervous her voice was shaking, but she bravely tried to make light-hearted remarks.

"Now, ya'll try to be neat with our stuff, b'cause we don't want to pick up after ya."

"We'll try, ma'am."

On the night table was my diary. He picked it up and flicked it open. *Shit! I should've hid it. What was in it? What did I write?*

Focusing on the ID's, I had completely forgotten the diary.

"I'll have to take this, to examine it."

"Will I get it back?"

"Of course. This is your property. We're required by law to return it to you."

He was getting closer to my closet, after turning the bed upside down, stripping it, poking the walls, looking behind the clock, stomping on the floorboards...

What'd they think we were hiding? Assault weapons?

"What are these?"

He found them.

My ID cards were in a small, gray purse. He was thumbing through them, now, looking closely at each picture and the name next to it.

Cold. I'm very cold. Think fast. God, if you exist at all, help me.

"They are friends of mine." Out came the words.

He looked up at me. "Why are you carrying their identifications – library cards, shopping cards?"

Fast. Why?

"Because they asked me to, for safekeeping." My voice was weak with fear. I could hardly breathe.

He looked again at the cards, flipped through them. He stopped at one and looked carefully at my picture.

Then he put them back.

He put them back!

Without another word, he proceeded to look through the rest of the closet and the bookshelf. After what felt like a very, very long time, he said,

"That's enough. We'll bring you downstairs, now."

I saw the clock by the bed. Three minutes had passed since we came in the room.

My breaths came in small gasps, which I tried to conceal so they wouldn't notice.

He looked directly at those pictures of me, all with different names and actually believed what I said. A miracle. How could they not see it was me in every one of those pictures?

Slowly walking downstairs, we joined the others. The police continued searching the bedrooms. I went to the kitchen. A lot of chattering and clanging was going on. Diana followed me.

On the stove was a large pot. Maya was vigorously stirring something in it, while Sarah was chopping onions. Next to her, Ruby was peeling zucchini and Puneet sliced garlic. At the end of the table, Belle was mashing something, as Narian sprinkled mushrooms in Maya's pot.

Why are they cooking at a time like this?

"We need your help, Samsara. Come over here and chop some potatoes."

Sure. Why not? Are we on the moon, too? I felt giddy and disjointed.

In the far corner one of the policemen was lounging on a kitchen stool, watching us. Sarah left her onions and went over to him, asking him something about what kind of food he liked. Her back was between him and us. Maya quickly reached inside her pocket and pulled out what looked like a wad of black shiny material, and just as quickly put it inside the soup, stirring heartily.

Oh Jeez, I don't really want to be here.

"You know, Puneet, I don't feel very well. The smells are getting to me. I think I'll go back outside."

In the corridor, I walked into a barrage of cameras, lights and people.

Some reporters were animatedly talking to the police. A women reporter spotted me and immediately made her way over.

"Hi. I'm a reporter for NBC. Will you talk to me?"

"What do you want to know?"

"Would you agree to talk to me on camera?"

"Why not? I have nothing to hide from you or anybody." I sounded braver than I felt.

"All right, then" She motioned to her sound man and adjusted one of the lights. She then looked directly at me and said,

"Go. What is your name?"

"Ma Prem Samsara."

"You still use your Rajneesh name?"

"Yes."

"What's going on here? What happened tonight?"

"The police came, and took my friends for questioning, they said. It looked to me like they were arrested. After that, these people arrived. They told us they were the FBI and that the German police were with them. They started searching the house, pulling our beds apart and going through our things. One of them even took my diary."

"Were you shown any search warrant?"

"No."

"Why are you letting them do this?"

"*You* try and stop them. Anyway, we've nothing to hide. We've not done anything wrong. Look for yourselves."

"Do you know anything about the poisonings you are being accused of?"

"No. I didn't poison anybody."

"Did you wiretap people?"

"*I* didn't set up any wiretap. After our hotel was bombed, two years ago, our Security was advised by the police to monitor conversations for the purpose of screening potential threats. All of our information was turned over to the police..."

I should stop talking.

"Well, thank you very much, Samsara." Sound, lights and reporter were whisked away, into the crowd as quickly as they appeared.

Diana came out of the kitchen. She looked at me very strangely.

"We took care of the tape," she whispered.

"What tape?"

"The one of Bhagwan slapping Viviananda. Sila had kept it. We found it amongst her things and put it in the soup."

"You put it in the *soup*?" Nothing was normal anymore.

"Yes."

In my mind, that became the night of tape soup. It was as bizarre as this night is...

Well, I got out of that predicament. How am I gonna get out of this one?

Chapter 11
Damned if you do and damn I won't!

The greatest pleasure in life is doing what people say you cannot do. – Walter Bagehot

I've no idea how I'm gonna get out of this predicament. Trish said I'd be out by Sunday, and I'm still here. Bob told me that it'd be Monday. It feels like years since I've seen daylight. This damn light bulb is on all the time. I can't even sleep. Must be the middle of the night. My breath stinks. I smell so bad I want to puke. God, I'm so hungry... is it Monday yet?

Bang!

Now what?

The door slammed open and in walked two guards.

"Get up! We're moving you out. Court. NOW."

Whoa! Court? Already? Must be morning.

They put leg irons on me. Then cuffs.

"Where exactly *is* the Court? And, by the way, I have to brush my teeth."

"Forget it. You're going to the holding cell."

"Where's that?"

"Around the corner and down the hall."

Suddenly, things moved very fast.

Yikes, those irons hurt! They're clawing at my ankles. How'm I gonna walk in these things?

In the holding cell, there were seven of us, silent, nervous. One of the women chewed her nails, which were red and sore looking. The air was thick with fear and pain. Bob's voice repeated in my head what he'd said on Saturday. "No problem, you should be released in your own recognizance. You've got letters of recommendation from the prison; job and character references... even the Court in Germany says you didn't flee bail there... glowing reports to say you won't flee here. No problem," he'd said.

After what seemed like a long time, we were let out of the holding cell: a string of prisoners shuffling forward together. *Like animals, linked by our leg irons.* Stepping out into the sunlight, the marshals told us to wait. I paused, blinking against the light, like a mole emerging from the dark.

Then, there were flashes of light.

Cameras.

Lots of press with cameras. I didn't even bother to look away.

It doesn't matter. I'm so tired of all this. I don't care what they do to me. They're like leeches wanting to suck out a piece of my soul. They don't care about me or what really happened.

Then the shouting started.

"Did you kill him?"

"Are you the shooter?"

"What's the jail like?"

"How have you been treated?"

"DON'T ANSWER!" the guard shouted. "Get in the van."

Good. I'm not allowed to talk.

My reflection in the van window showed a wild woman. Not having a comb since I left Germany, I looked like I put my finger in an electrical socket. The guards told me that hair bands were not allowed, as they were potential weapons. Combs were not allowed either. *They* were potential weapons.

Prisoners must be very creative these days.

My eyes hurt since I still couldn't rinse my contact lens properly, except with my saliva, and the lens kept sticking to my eye. My clothes were dirty and wrinkled. I'd been wearing them for five days. I smelled my own urine, sweat and stink.

This was how I was going to appear in Court, trying to prove I was a responsible, upright citizen, ready to be released into society.

Getting out of the van, the guards elbowed away the press, pushing me into line with several others. We were escorted to the first row by one of the guards. On the other side of the courtroom, I saw Bob and Trish in conversation. Trish waved as soon as she noticed me and smiled. They were in the third row.

The left side must be the lawyer's section.

A couple of rows in front of them were the prosecutor and the FBI. I recognized Fronten. He was wearing the same dark suit as when I'd last seen him in Germany. Behind my row and theirs there were very sedate looking people.

Must be the public, or family. Behind them was the press.

Maybe this was what the Roman games were like. But nowadays, we're the entertainment. The lions are all around us.

The first prisoner was called as soon as the magistrate sat down. I closed my eyes.

This is gonna be a long day.

I could still see my comfortable, cozy bed in Germany... my room with my things. Safe, no one hunting me, hating me, accusing me... I kept my eyes closed.

"The United States of America vs. Samsara Drakke. Is the defendant represented by counsel?"

"Yes, your honor. Patricia June Peterson and Robert Warner for the defendant."

"For this bail hearing, I see you have supplied the Court with documents to support the request for release on recognizance." The magistrate looked over at the FBI.

"Your honor, J. Edward Blake as criminal assistant to

the U.S. Attorney, is representing the Government on the wiretapping. Anthony Fronten, IV and a special team from the Justice Department's Criminal Division in Washington has been assigned to represent the Government on the conspiracy case. We object to the defendant being released on bail due to the fact that she represents a substantial flight risk."

"Do you have evidence in support of this statement?" I could tell this magistrate was a fighter by the tone of his voice.

Panic made it difficult for me to keep track of what was being said.

I've no control over my life. I'm powerless. They have all the control.

"Yes, your honor, we call FBI agent Paul Tomkins to the stand."

Why were they calling the FBI? This was a bail hearing; for God's sake... maybe he'll put in a good word for me since I cooperated with him during that interrogation in Germany.

"...And she fled the United States in 1985, remaining a fugitive-at-large until her arrest in 1990."

I kept missing some of Tomkins' words because I was holding my breath so hard

"...That is evidence enough, your honor, to indicate that she is a very great flight risk."

"I don't see evidence that she fled in 1985, Mr. Fronten." The Judge shot back. "I *do* see substantial reports in front of me that after her arrest in Germany, she was released on bail, and for three months remained in Germany, reported to the police and surrendered to United States custody, when she could have walked across the border to France. She even voluntarily spoke to you and to the FBI. She had plenty of opportunity to flee, then..."

Fronten was squirming.

The magistrate continued. "I see a letter from her landlord that he informed her that the police were looking for her, and she did not flee, but waited for them at home. I have an offer of bail from her parents and numerous letters from her family. This all seems fine to me. Instead of releasing her in her own recognizance, I'll release her on bail to her parents. Bailiff, arrange the bail proceeding. Next."

Done.

Two guards came over to me, I stood up and they marched me out of the Court.

The press' flashbulbs are back again. By my side, the guard muttered something unintelligibly to me.

More lights and cameras waited for me outside the courthouse as I got into the wagon. This time, however, I was alone behind the wire mesh separating me from the driver.

Contact lens solution was waiting for me back in the same hole that was my cell. No sooner had I got there, when the guard who had yelled at me the last three times, opened the cell door and Announced, "Come with me."

Assuming they were taking me to be released, I grabbed the lens solution bottle like it was gold bullion and followed the guard. We went along the corridor to an elevator, got in and went up several flights. Stepping out of the elevator, I noticed two large iron and glass doors at both ends of the floor. The guard walked me toward one of them. Buzzers sounded and the doors opened electronically. There were no keys in this place, only bells, buzzers, alarms, clanging and banging.

Inside, the door opened to a large room with rows of tiers, like an amphitheatre. There was an oversized desk just inside the door that jutted out into the large open space, where several prisoners were lounging and others walking and talking in small groups.

They all look so bored.

At opposite ends of the room were two TV's. The noise ricocheted off the metal walls.

"Drakke, here." The guard said like he was dropping off a bucket of slop.

"Take her to C-17."

"I'm going to be released," I said weary of the non-communication.

"Sure you are," the female guard said in a dead voice, reminding me of Rosie the Riveter.

Saints alive! Didn't they know I was going to be released? Was this the release procedure?

On the upper tier level, C-17 had a metal slab for a door with no handle. It opened and closed electronically, like everything else, leaving me, and my bottle of contact lens solution, standing in concrete above, below and around me. A light was on but I couldn't see a switch. Not a bare bulb, like in the cell from which I had just come, but a recessed light above a concrete slab a couple of feet from the floor, that had some foam attached to it.

The bed? I sat down on it.

Opposite the slab was *another* concrete slab jutting out, a foot from where the "bed" extended. The opposite slab was like a desk. Next to this "desk" was a stainless steel toilet with no cover, like the one in my cell. There was a washbasin next to the toilet. Next to the basin was another door-slab.

The slab look.

No toilet paper, nor paper towels. I later learned that was for my own protection, so that nothing could be used as a weapon or to hang myself with.

Considerate of them. Never mind, within hours I'll be released. The magistrate said so.

Clutching my bottle, I went to the basin to rinse out the same soiled lens, which I then put back in my eye. I needed disinfectant and a container to clean and soak the lens properly. The last guard informed me that it was against policy to give me any disinfectant because I might drink it.

Am I on Mars? Drink contact lens disinfectant?

The clanging started again and the door slid open.

"Come with me."

They don't know any other phrase.

The guard walked down the stairs slightly behind me. The stairwells were wide enough for two people to walk next to each other, since the guards didn't trust prisoners to walk behind or in front of them. He buzzed open a large door, a couple of flights down. We walked through and down the corridor to another dismal room. Trish and Bob were talking as I entered.

I didn't even say hello.

"Thank God for you two! Take me out of here!"

"I wish we could, Samsara, but the government opposed your bail. They are still questioning any possible release, even to your parent's house. We have another hearing set for Wednesday, April 17." Trish talked fast.

I slumped into a chair opposite them.

"You mean I have to *stay* here? I'm a little nuts, Trish. You have to understand. I haven't been able to clean my lens properly, and I think it may be damaged, which means my one good eye is compromised. I'm having difficulty hearing you because my left ear closed up on the plane and I haven't been treated for it. I've had one shower in five days. I'm in withdrawal because there's no coffee or cigarettes. I'm really not in the best shape. I can't communicate with these goons! Everything goes through a maze of electronic doors and my cell is just a horrible hole with a bare light bulb switched on day and night. "

"Samsara," Bob cut in. "I don't think the government will continue to oppose the bail, especially since your parents *put up* their house. Try to hold on till Wednesday."

"Well," I searched for something positive to say. "The good thing about cigarette withdrawal is to do it when you are being deprived of everything else, so it becomes just another one of the many shocks you are dealing with all at once. I'll patent the idea."

"That's a great way to look at it, Samsara," Trish said.

I think she was worried by my state of mind and ready to support anything I said that was remotely positive.

"Just please urge them to allow me to use the contact lens disinfectant you brought, Bob, and tell them I'm a vegetarian. All I've had to eat since I've arrived is milk and apples."

With that, the session ended signaled by the arrival of the guard. Even the lawyers' visits were regulated.

Back in the cell, I slept... and slept. A screeching buzzer sounded. The led door slid open and out I went. I didn't know if it was lunch or dinner. There was no time anymore, only the same milk, apples, meat and cardboard paste that appeared at each meal. I ate the apples.

Somewhere between then and Wednesday I was allowed to become a vegetarian by order of the Court. That meant they took away the milk, meat and apples and left the cardboard paste.

I was afraid to ask for anything I needed or do anything out of the ordinary. In addition to their controlling everything we ate and did, the guards could issue what they called "demerits," like in grammar school. One demerit and my tenuous bail would be nullified. Now that the government was hot to keep me locked up, I didn't want to give them any more ammo by getting a demerit.

On Monday, Bob tried to argue for my release to a halfway house due to medical needs, but that was denied.

Sleep was my salvation and release.

Showers were the nearest thing to pleasure I experienced in those days of endless waiting. I felt I had done nothing but wait ever since I'd been arrested: waiting for meals, waiting for exercise, waiting to see my lawyer, waiting for it to be over.

Wednesday came along with the leg-iron-animal-train-line-up. More reporters. Court. All of it was a blur. There was only the pain of isolation, withdrawal, and uncertainty that kept me constantly aware of being alive.

"Your honor," Fronten droned, "We oppose bail for Ms. Drakke because we are convinced she is a flight risk. We would like to recall Agent Paul Tomkins to the stand and introduce further testimony."

Further testimony? What further was there?

Tomkins looked more tired and thinner than when I saw him on Monday, and I wondered what he would say.

"Mr. Tomkins," Fronten continued, "I refer you to the FBI and police reports, known as document number 302, particularly in reference to the testimony given by Ma Deva Maya concerning Ms. Drakke's illegal identity and profession. Are you familiar with this testimony?"

"Yes, sir."

"Was Ms. Drakke traveling under an illegal British identity at the time?"

"Yes, sir."

"And what was her profession, according to the testimony?"

"Ms. Drakke was working as an exotic dancer in a cabaret."

"And what was her formal status in Germany regarding this profession?"

"She was a registered prostitute."

"Your honor," Bob broke in. "Prostitution is legal in Germany. Ms. Drakke was registered as required by the law. She was actually abiding *by* the law. Furthermore, there was no evidence that she used the British identity for anything illegal. It is not uncommon for people in the entertainment profession to have another name."

Good. That'll shut Fronten up!

"Basically, the issue is whether or not she is a *flight* risk," the Judge cut in. "Her identity is not on trial here. I'm going to refer this to Judge Wallace in the Federal Court because of extenuating circumstances, since he will be the Judge overseeing the case. Next."

Out I went. Once again postponed. My life was postponed.

"Wallace is going to bring up that stuff about her Greek marriage for sure..." Trish broke off as I entered the lawyers' conference room back at the jail.

Shit, here comes the Greek mess before Margaret Bonham ever happened... back when I was trying to get any kind of European citizenship just to work and earn money to pay these guys.

"When's the next hearing?" I asked, out of patience.

"Tomorrow. This time we go in front of Judge William Wallace. He's the one who will oversee the entire proceeding, including the trial."

"And, what's he like?" I asked, ignoring the trial comment.

"He's conservative but fair," Bob said." I think we'll get a fair ruling."

"And what exactly is a *fair* ruling?" The sarcasm was obvious.

"I think he'll be level headed and unbiased. He's very even tempered. I feel positive about having him in there to balance Fronten's blood-sucking style," Bob said reassuringly.

"OK." I didn't want to hear any more.

"Are you certain that you don't want to go with cooperation?" Trish asked.

"I *have* cooperated!" I said exasperated.

"No, Samsara, you haven't. Not the way they want you to. The government considers that you have not cooperated with them at all."

"Well, fuck 'em, then! I pity them. If all they have to rely on is groveling hearsay testimony from people they have cowed into thinking that the consequences of *not* cooperating are unlivable, then I pity all of them! And, I most certainly don't want to be associated with *that* crowd! I won't talk about anybody else. DON'T ASK ME AGAIN!"

Trish looked at me so tenderly in that moment, I felt like my heart would burst from the strain of keeping everything in so tightly.

"Samsara, you know Narian's lawyer spoke to me last night. He said that Narian was cooperating, and having a terrible time remembering events, what was real and what was imagined. When he asked about you, I said you weren't cooperating. He said that I was lucky to have you as a client."

She's saying that to comfort me. Trish's so considerate.

"I am lucky to have *you*," I said, tears coming in big wracking sobs.

There was nothing more to be said. Just more hours to wait till the next day.

Waiting... There's nothing to think about except the past. The future was too uncertain, too frightening.

This place looks exactly like the criminal court building in New York, back in 1970... only cleaner.

My job then was to determine if newly arrested offenders were qualified for release in their own recognizance. I had to check their backgrounds, number of priors (previously committed offenses), their jobs, their ties to the community and their family support. If there were enough positive points in their background, no matter what the nature of the offense was, it counted as evidence to recommend release.

Here I am, from a model background, with a brilliant resume, with proof of many activities in the community and strong family ties. But, I'm branded a flight risk, forced to go through hearing after hearing to prove myself. All because of my unfortunate involvement with a guru, leaving him and resorting to the only means available to me to earn a heap of money to fight these charges.

This drawn out bail inquest really had nothing to do with being a flight risk at all. Fronten was using my assumed identity and any dirt he might resurrect on my Greek marriage to intimidate me into thinking that I had no other choice but to cooperate. He would use every negative detail of the case to keep me locked up until I relented. My bail release depended on what the prison insiders call "ratting."

Maya and Diana never went through this. Eve never even saw the inside of a jail. They were all state witnesses. Sometimes I wish I could do the same...

Thursday. This time, I was taken to a different courtroom. I was way in the back and Judge Wallace looked small from where I sat. I smiled and tried to look hopeful, sweet and compliant.

"Ms. Drakke, in front of me are several documents, letters

from your family and a long resume. Tell me about your background, particularly all the jobs you have listed here."

Great. Here's my chance! He wants to know all the good things I've done.

"Yes, sir!" I started to go down the list. "I was a business consultant to a German firm; an English language teacher in Berlitz; manager of a Bistro; a video and film producer; co-founder of Lotus Therapy Institute in New York; assistant instructor in Outward Bound; director of programs on death and dying at Center City; hospital chaplain... "

"This sounds flighty to me, like you couldn't keep one steady job," he interrupted me flatly.

Trish and I looked at each other. Speechless, our mouths fell open simultaneously. Trish immediately responded.

"Your honor, Ms. Drakke has always been a very hard worker. She worked several jobs to pay her way through college and graduate school. I think her resume speaks for the merit and the diligence of her work ethic."

"And she applied that diligence," Judge Wallace interjected, dryly, "in her work as a prostitute in Germany, I see. Ms. Peterson, there is no question that the Rajneeshees were hard workers. However, Ms. Drakke, let's leave the job market for the moment and look at your present marriage. This is your *fourth* husband, I believe?"

"Yes," I said sadly, feeling any hope I had had before the hearing extinguished. He was clearly against me.

"And your husband lives in Greece?"

"Yes."

I know where this is headed.

"Your honor," Fronten piped up predictably, "Ms. Drakke can easily flee to Greece, where she can apply for Greek citizenship, and the Greek government could protect her from extradition."

There, he made the point he was itching to make.

"Your honor," Trish broke in. "Ms. Drakke has been separated from her husband since 1988. It is unlikely she would flee to him. Furthermore, it takes several years to become a Greek citizen. It is *highly* unlikely the Greek government would have grounds not to extradite under the treaty."

Judge Wallace broke in, "I'm not sure about that, Ms. Peterson, but I *am* revoking the magistrate's decision, because it is not clear to me yet whether or not she would flee under any circumstances. However, before I make a final decision about the bail, I want letters from Ms. Drakke's family showing that she had contact with them and that she is responsible to them. I want clear documentation about the value of her parent's home, and if they are willing to put their property up as collateral, as you mentioned. *Finally,* I want to know more about the situation with her husband. Exactly what is the legal status of her marriage? My clerk will set the next hearing date."

When we stood up as the Judge was leaving, I discovered that the back of my pants were wet.

Oh, Lord, my hemorrhoids are bleeding again. The worst part of this whole drama is the fear of not knowing what they're going to do to me and with me. Since the procedure so far has been out of the ordinary, anything is possible. If they deny me bail, I'll have to stay in this rotten place till some theoretical trial date, eating cardboard paste, losing my hearing, my sight... and now, this bleeding.

Trish, Bob and I met briefly after the bail hearing.

"The next date is next Wednesday, April 24," Trish said matter-of-factly, but I could hear a tremor in her voice. Or, was I hearing things? Now I couldn't even trust what I *was* hearing.

"...And, if Wallace *should* rule in favor of bail, the government is threatening to take his ruling to the Ninth Circuit on appeal."

All I want to do is sleep...

Bang!

The door slid open.

What time is it? Dinnertime? Feels like the middle of the night. Plus I've got a bad hangover.

"Come with me."

I came quietly. I knew better than to ask questions as nobody told me anything anyway.

Why not get robots to do this escorting bit... why am I going back to the holding cell? What now?

Back to Court.

It was Friday, April 19.

In Court, Trish and Bob met me. Bob informed me I was present only to witness a discussion estimating the value of my parent's house. "The government brought in an appraiser to determine its value"

Come on. This must be some kind of surreal movie. If I'm released to my parent's house, and I flee, the government'll get the house and my 70-year-old parents'll be out on the street. How could I live with such a thing? So, the Feds are demanding a special hearing at taxpayer's expense to have some appraiser dicker over the value of retirement housing? And taxpayers wonder where their tax dollars go. What a mockery of justice: spending money uselessly to determine if I'm worth $62 or $63,000?

It was over fast, thank God.

Back to the cardboard paste and once a week exercise.

Oh how I miss German prison and the daily walk, and my friends. I'm 42 years old, in prison and missing my former prison. Is that insanity or what? The days here are filled with endless monotony except for the thoughts going round and round like a toy train.

One day, walking in the yard, all of a sudden I remembered Haüsern, and the day we left for England. It was the day after the Feds' raid. The group split up. Four of us went to Switzerland by car. Another four went to Berlin. Sarah, Narian, Ruby, Diana, Maya, Puneet, the kids and me went to London. With all the stress, my body was rebelling in severe back pain.

Since Diana and Maya were married to Irish and English men, they planned to apply for their U.K. passports. Sarah and Ruby were Brits, and Puneet was German so they could travel freely throughout Europe. My American passport was expiring.

In London we took short walks out of our dismal, basement flat. We used to go in two's and walk briskly, always hurrying back to the flat, convinced we were being hunted.

Like being in a bad war movie, we discussed where we could go so as not to be hunted. The Maldives had no extradition treaty with the U.S. Neither did Nigeria.

Nigeria?

Sarah and I were in charge of finding a place to go. But, it would have to be somewhere where we could make money and support ourselves. She came up with the idea to call her old friend the Chicago Greek banker, Nikos, whom she and Sila knew well.

"Go to Greece!" he said without hesitation. "I have friends there who will help you find work and house!"

How could Nikos in the U.S. guarantee that his friends in Athens we had never met would help us find 'work and house'?

In the end, that was the only option. We left for Athens the day after she spoke to him.

BUZZ. That signaled the end of the walk in the prison yard. We lined up and were escorted back to our cells. Daydreaming was a relief.

At lunch I discovered that the morning's newspaper contained an article about me, which one of the prisoners had seen. Overnight, I became a celebrity.

Identified as one of the "evil Rajneeshees" that Oregonians hated, Bob Warner had warned me hostile inmates might make me a hate crime victim.

Nice. Add that to the list of terrors. Funny, I was labeled a terrorist by the Feds, and yet it was me who was constantly in shock.

To my relief, the opposite happened. Some of the prisoners thought I was a hero, particularly because I hadn't ratted on anyone or made a deal with the government. This gave me instant status. That meant I was besieged with questions and had to explain myself a hundred times.

I just want to crawl in a hole and sleep till this nightmare's over.

With not much else to do but watch TV, attend fundamentalist prayer groups or read trashy novels, I asked permission to visit the legal library. That meant I had to give up one of my precious walks.

Escorted to the library room, I was locked in with a few shelves of brand new legal books, which had never been opened. I started to do some research on wiretapping figuring that it would be less ambiguous to tackle than the vague charge of conspiracy.

Reading about wiretapping cases, I recalled that January 1986 morning when we first learned that twenty of us had been indicted by the Federal Grand Jury. One of Sila's lawyers had sent a ton of legal documents to the house we rented outside Athens. Along with the legal papers was also a ton of advice.

There were verbatim testimonies, largely from Eve and some of the sannyasins involved in the security system on the ranch. They described the telephone monitoring as if it had been a massive organized crime operation. We were depicted as monsters gleefully preying on innocent lambs, licking our chops at the secrets the lambs were revealing. What was clearly *not* mentioned was that we had been advised to monitor the phones for the safety of the commune. Also missing was the fact that the information was turned over to the Peace Force, who gave it to the local police, or so we believed.

Sitting in the tiny airless prison library, I discovered Section 2511 of U.S. Federal crimes within title 18. with regard to property owners:

"It is not unlawful for a person not acting under color of law to intercept a wire communication where such person is a party to the communication... unless such communication is intercepted for the purpose of committing any criminal or tortuous act..."

Well, there it was in plain fact: what I did, intercepting potential criminal acts, was for security, under the direction of the owner of the property, in full knowledge of the city judge and the police on the Ranch.

I was innocent of the wiretapping charge.

Back in my cell, I felt the same bone-weariness that plagued me during that spring in 1986 after we had read all that legal material. Still suffering from back pain, I pushed myself to find work in Athens. We all had signed up at a Greek language school, figuring that we'd learn the language and then it'd be easy to find work. Brilliant students, none of us could speak more than three words.

Not too many jobs could be applied for when all you can say is, "Hello. How are you? I am fine. My name is Cecilia. And what is your name? I am 37 years old and my mother's name is..."

I could count to ten in Greek and identify the table and chairs in the house.

Great for a deaf and dumb house cleaner.

I became a house cleaner.

The Greek banker's friends had two children who needed an English-speaking nanny, with whom they could practice their English *and* their shenanigans. They drove me nuts, pulled me out of my self-absorption and worry. And I adored them.

No sooner was I ensconced in their home, still negotiating the terms of my employment, when Sarah told me that I had to go back to Germany to help Belle prepare Sila's legal defense. She explained that I was the most logical choice, because I had the best legal mind.

Me? Legal mind? I had nothing left of a mind, then.

But, question Sarah? *Never.* She was the bulwark of our stability, the magician who paid the bills with nothing and kept us all eating.

Once again, just as I was starting to settle down, earn my keep and feel better about myself, I was uprooted and sent to a different country.

In two days I was back in Germany. Disoriented, I was of little help to Belle, at first. It took about a month before I could get my head to function in the chilly, wet, dark-gray

German spring. But, within days of arriving back, I realized we were in serious financial trouble. I had to get a real job if I were to continue eating.

As the fuzziness and disorientation cleared, I considered how to get a job without speaking German. German requirements stated that jobs go to Germans, first. Then, if there are no Germans to fill the position, European applicants are next.

Americans were at the very bottom.

I was batting below zero.

I decided to learn German.

I walked into Berlitz, the language school around the block from the house where we were staying. A dark-haired lady with an innocuous smile greeted me, cursorily viewed my application, asking, "Why are you here?"

"To learn German." I thought the question was a little odd.

Why else would an English speaker come to a German language school?

"How would you like a job teaching English?"

A job! The woman's offering me a job!

"I've always thought how much I would love to teach! How kind of you to offer me the chance." I lied.

A miracle. I left the place singing to myself.

I have a job! And one Germans don't qualify for, because Berlitz hires only native-born speakers. Miracles can happen...

Sitting in my Portland cell, another day closer to the April 24 hearing, I had to believe that there would be another miracle.

By now, many letters had been sent to Judge Wallace from my parents, aunts, uncles and cousins, all of whom rallied to my cause. My biological family members were the ones who came forth to help me. I'm ashamed now that I kept so little contact with my real family during my commune years.

Swallowing that shame, I asked them to write letters of support. Shame would have gotten in the way of what I had to do. Time was short, and this was about saving my life at least saving my *health. The longer I stay in this jail the weaker I get, mentally and physically.* I could see what could happen to me in the faces and bodies of the inmates who had been here for longer than a few months. I needed my strength for the serious battle with the Feds when it came time for the next phase of post bail hearings.

Wallace would question me in detail about my Greek husband, and this was causing me a lot of anxiety.

Until 1987 I had been dutifully registered in Germany, and never made any attempt to hide my whereabouts. I worked there, paid taxes and could have been easily found if anyone was looking for me.

But the expiry date in my U.S. passport was March 1987.

When I called the U.S. Consulate in Stuttgart in September 1986 for the renewal forms, hoping they could just be mailed to me, I was informed that I would have to appear in person to renew my passport. The day before I was to go to the Consulate, one of the U.S. lawyers called, with the message that I would be arrested immediately if I set foot in an embassy or consulate.

When I asked what I was supposed to do, the answer came back that it might be useful to establish European citizenship.

Great. How was I supposed to do that?

Sarah reminded me that I was still married to Anand and might be able to obtain Australian citizenship. I tracked him down in Sydney.

"Hello, is this Anand?"

"Yes, who's this?"

There was that familiar singsong voice.

"Anand, it's Samsara, how are you?"

"Samsara, how are *you*?"

"I'm fine. I'm calling from Germany so I have to be brief. Forgive me for not properly catching up with you. I've called to ask you a technical question. I'd like to apply for Australian citizenship as your wife. Do you have any objection to that? And, if not, how could I do it?"

"Well, Samsara. I was going to contact you about my own situation. I want to marry Jacinta. Remember her?"

Yup. Nutty as a fruitcake. Perfect for Anand.

"Oh, yes. I remember Jacinta. Congratulations. But I still would like to apply for citizenship. Can I do that before you marry her?"

"Let me ask my lawyer and I'll phone you back."

"Thank you, so much, Anand. It would help me a lot."

"Well, Samsara, I feel like I owe you something for all you went through with me."

We hung up.

He called back the next day with the news from the lawyer that Australian citizenship would take three years to establish.

So much for that option.

We arranged to get a quick divorce.

By December 1986, three months later, I had called the consulates of thirteen countries, inquiring what their waiting period was for a spouse to apply for citizenship. Greece came up as the best gamble. If I found a husband there, I could apply for citizenship, which might be approved in "three years, perhaps right away," so I was told. And, of course, money was universal in business arrangements. I could always pay to "expedite things."

I had to find a way to keep my job in Germany, temporarily returning to Greece.

In January 1987, making up a story about a terrible, sudden tragedy concerning my family (not far from the real truth), I got a leave of absence from my job, and boarded a train to Athens.

Three nightmarish days later I arrived. Stiff and sore from the sardine can-train, I emerged into the main train station and called the only single Greek male I knew, Sarah's banker's friend, Georgos. I told him why I had come to Greece, and asked him to marry me.

He was a little surprised.

"Cecilia, why don't you come and stay with me? We'll discuss it."

I thought it made good sense: we were friends after all and this was business. He was a businessman. However, I had not calculated on the attachment a Greek male has to his mother.

He was 40 and worried about what his mother would say about his marrying an American.

"Cecilia, we have to consider things more *carefully.*" He emphasized his words slowly. "Suppose I want to *really* get married? And Mama will never go for this." Georgos was educated in America, so he liked to quote, "consider things carefully" which for a Greek male, meant "forget it in this century."

I had to find somebody else and fast, pleading with the family for whom I had recently worked as a nanny, to find me an unattached male. The best they could do was a 64-year-old widower... who wanted 10,000 German marks. "For my daughter," he said.

The daughter was my age.

Christos was six foot five and overbearing. A pleasant man, he spoke only Greek and French, no English. So, we had to communicate in my bad French. I knew from the start this was going to make for a rocky marriage.

Nevertheless, I agreed, negotiating with the help of my Greek friends. He would help me. I would help him. I told him I needed to work in Europe, and the only way I could do that was to establish European citizenship. That sounded logical to him.

We couldn't get married in the civil office because I would have to go to the American Consulate and file a form. Since I was avoiding the consulate, I suggested we marry in the Orthodox Greek Church. After many translations of my birth certificate, marriage certificates, divorce certificates and every other certificate that said I existed, the Church smiled on the "arrangement" of a 64-year-old and a 37-year-old, blessing us with crowns, incense and tradition. When the ceremony was over, we went straightaway to the registry office so that I could fill out the papers for my citizenship. I was told it would take three years and lots of paperwork.

I was undaunted. I pleaded, nagged and visited the registry every day for three weeks, nagging a different official each day.

By the end of February it was clear that nothing and nobody could hurry my citizenship along.

In one month my American passport would expire.

My plan had failed. *And,* I was married to the Greek version of Grandfather Time.

My marriage to a Greek *did* entitle me to a temporary work permit; but I could only work in Greece. That would enable me to pay off my legal bills in about twenty-five years and it was no help with my passport.

The only solution to stay in Europe came in the form of a British identity...

The story would definitely not look good on my court record. And, since Judge Wallace seemed to hate me from the start, this would certainly not endear me to him.

But, surely any compassionate person would understand the desperation, panic and despair I felt. I had never meant to break the law. A lawyer had suggested European citizenship. And, my Greek husband and I were separated because I paid for the arrangement. We never even lived together.

Fleeing to Greece was not an option because I had no one to flee to. The Greek government would not protect me because I wasn't a Greek citizen.

But, how could I avoid looking like a charlatan? I was damned and I would appear to be a liar, a cheat and a fake. But, I did it to survive.

I'm still not going to make a deal, damnit!

No matter what the Judge or anybody else thinks of me.

Chapter 12
Entering Plato's Cave... Where's the Truth?

Why has the whole thing (cosmos) been constructed in this fashion? Christians say it is because we are born in sin. Buddhists say it is because we are born to suffering through ignorance. Hindu's say it's because we are born at all
- Joel Kramer and Diana Alstad, The Guru Papers

I walked over to one of the tables in the center of the prison floor and saw *The Oregonian* newspaper lying there. Saturday, April 27, 1991. I read the headline:

RAJNEESH FOLLOWER FREED PENDING TRIAL

Defendant charged in alleged death plot released to parents under tight conditions.

My head jerked back, and I snatched the paper.

Who are they talking about? Narian was released on bail ages ago as a state witness. I read on.

A woman accused of being a member of a Rajneeshee 'hit team' that planned to kill the Oregon U.S. Attorney was ordered released Friday pending trial, but only with stringent conditions.

Ma Prem Samsara was ordered to live with her parents in Arizona. They are posting their $63,000 home to guarantee her future court appearance.

I thought Fronten was against my being released...

...opposed her release, arguing she was a flight risk because when German police arrested her last October in Germany, she was traveling under a British passport in the name of Margaret Bonham. At the time, Prem Samsara was returning to Germany from Greece where her husband resides.

A second prosecutor said, "Should she flee and adopt her husband's citizenship it would be virtually impossible to extradite her." The alleged hit team hoped The U.S. Attorney's death would derail a federal grand jury investigation.

Oh God, they're talking about a 'hit team' again.

During the detention hearing on Friday, one of Samsara's defense lawyers accused the government of coercive use of detention and the Bail Reform Act by opposing Samsara's pre-trial release after not opposing the release of her co-defendant, who pleaded guilty to plotting...

Released? It's been fifteen days since the extradition. I've had five bail hearings. And I'm still here.

One of the inmates came over to where I was and began reading the article just as a guard came over to the table and announced, "Samsara, your lawyer is here."

At least they were now talking in more complete sentences.

Escorted to the lawyer's meeting room, which was as familiar to me as my cell, I saw Bob sitting formally at the steel table, his head in his right hand. His frown emphasized the deep lines, which cut into his forehead. He was looking down but glanced up as I approached. His expression read: I'm so bloody tired of all this but he only said, "Fronten is threatening to appeal Wallace's decision all the way up to the Ninth Circuit."

I fell into the chair.

"Jesus, Bob, I can't go on with this *game*. I've no fight left."

"Come on, now, Samsara," he said, putting his hand on the table, "where are your guts? We've only just started."

"And who's gonna pay for it?" No more diplomacy, just desperation on my part. Enough already of being locked up, of mind numbing gray days and dark nights, of never feeling really clean, of having tangled hair.

And, what I wouldn't give for a real cup of coffee and a cigarette.

He didn't reply to my question.

I was slowly giving up.

Three days later at 5:00 P.M., one of the guards came to my cell door.

"Come with me."

The famous phrase.

I was escorted to the Receiving and Discharge Department, and informed that I was being discharged.

Just like that. No fanfare. No preparation. Booted out.

At the end of his visit on Saturday, Bob had said, "If you're suddenly released, go to the Portland Hotel. There's no telling what might happen as nothing is going according to plan."

I had no idea what I was supposed to do once I *got* to the hotel, so focused was I on getting *out*. Like a robot, I signed the release papers, after which I was given back my watch, hair band, wedding ring, $20.00 and told to leave.

I hadn't walked on American streets for six years. Feeling like an alien, I stepped out sharply into the spring dusk. The world looked very big with lots of noise and lights and I caught myself lingering.

Walk. Walk as fast as you can so nobody recognizes you.

I was wearing the same clothes I had worn when I was

extradited from Germany, which were given back to me in exchange for the prison jumpsuit. They had been washed, but were still stained from having been worn continuously my first week in jail. My clothes and me had been all over the news; so I wasn't too enthusiastic about wandering around, ready to be the next report by some journalist.

However, I had to go into a store for cigarettes and coffee. In a phone booth outside the store, I looked up the address of the Portland Hotel.

Thank God, it's close.

Mechanically walking there, I saw it on the corner ahead of me, a simple nondescript box with three stories. I walked through the doors, across the lobby, straight to the front desk. Assuming that Bob had already arranged for my registration and payment, I announced that I had a reservation.

The hotel clerk asked me for my name.

"Samsara Drakke," I whispered so nobody else could hear, although the lobby was empty apart from us.

"I'm sorry, ma'am. There's no reservation under that name."

"Uhm. Can I possibly use your phone?"

Don't show any reaction.

"Sure. Right over there."

"Thank you, uhm, my bag was left on the plane and it's on its way here." I mumbled.

What else could I say? That I had just been released from jail on federal charges? Hardly.

I dialed Bob's home number and to my relief he answered the phone immediately.

"Hello, Bob, I'm at the Portland Hotel, just like you told me the other day. There's no reservation for me and I only have $12.00."

I was a little irritated that he'd told me to come here and there was no reservation and no pre-payment.

"Hello, Samsara. You mean you want me to pay for the room?" He sounded annoyed.

"Bob, you can bill me for it. What *else* can I do? What else would you *suggest*? I don't even have the bag I came on the plane with. Do you know what the federal marshals did with it? I don't even have a toothbrush or comb."

I was whispering so the clerk wouldn't hear me. Just like a mechanical robot: I just had to get through this night somehow.

"I have your bag, Samsara. It's locked in my office, so you'll have to wait till tomorrow for me to bring it. I'm trying to sort out your travel arrangements to Arizona. They want you out of Portland immediately. You have to leave by bus tomorrow, first thing." He still sounded irritated.

I had no intention of hanging around.

"Come to my office around 9:00 A.M. You have to go to the Probation Office before you leave. Give the phone to the clerk and I'll get you registered. Congratulations on making bail," he added almost as an afterthought.

The first thing I did when I got to my room was to have an endlessly long hot shower, washing my hair twice with hotel shampoo. Then I sat on the bed, smoking three cigarettes one after the other. I thought about Bob.

Hadn't he had a client released from jail before? Didn't he know they had no money?

I felt numb. Something like lead had been poured into me and I was incapable of feeling anything at all.

I crawled into real sheets and a glorious dead sleep.

In the morning, Bob surprised me by coming to the hotel. I thought it was to pick me up but it was really to sign his credit card bill. He drove me to the Probation Office. The place was another nondescript gray box.

There's that guy from Probation, who I saw in Court. I think he likes me. Maybe he'll be my PO.

No such luck.

He left the room and Matthew Sims, a towering African-American with a very sour disposition, walked in.

"The minute you get off that bus in Arizona, you report

straight to the U.S. District Court, Pretrial Services. They will secure you with electronic monitoring. If you attempt to escape, your parent's home will be forfeit immediately. They will lose *everything.* Do you understand?"

"Yes."

"You may go, now." More like "get out!"

Bob stayed at the Probation Office. His goodbye had relief in it: he was glad to get rid of me. Fortunately the bus depot was within walking distance.

On my way there, I had to find a phone booth to let my parents know they would soon be seeing their convict daughter. Dad picked up the phone, which he almost never did. It must mean that Mom was drunk.

"Dad, I'll be coming in on the bus from Portland, arriving in Sun City on Friday, May 3 at 4:00 P.M. Can you pick me up?"

It was the first time we had talked since Germany. Trish had talked to them more than me in the last few weeks.

"All right. Call us when you get to the station." He hung up. He sounded gruff, unhappy and not at all pleased to have to pick me up, too. He didn't even ask me how I was.

Thirty hours later, I looked around as the bus pulled into the Sun City, Arizona depot. I was convinced that I had died and gone to hell. The streets were barren concrete enclosed by high concrete walls. This was concrete-land. Behind the walls were houses, which I assumed were also built of concrete. The sun burned down, beating the streets mercilessly. At 3:45 in the afternoon it was 102 degrees and this was only May. I shuddered to think what July might be like. Not a single car drove by; there wasn't anyone to be seen on the streets.

What have I got myself into? Would staying in jail have been better?

Off the bus, I called home.

"Hello?" There was hesitation in the thick voice.

"Mom?"

"Get one of the taxis to drive you straight to the house."

Dad said, pulling the phone away from Mom. "I'll pay the cab when you get here."

"I'll pay for it." I said abruptly, Annoyed that he hadn't come to pick me up and upset that Mom was drunk. I still had twelve dollars. At least, I could pay for my own damn taxi ride.

"You have no tits!" These were my father's first words after not seeing me for nine years since his visit to the Ranch in Oregon. I didn't reply, immediately feeling self-conscious.

"Do you want a drink?" He asked once we were inside the house.

"No. I don't drink." Since leaving the bar I was grateful not to *have* to drink. The last thing I wanted at four in the afternoon was alcohol.

"First, I have to call the Probation Office and let them know I've arrived. Then we can sit down and catch up."

I tried to sound casual after the international arrest and extradition; numerous bail hearings, with federal prosecutors challenging my case to the Ninth Circuit Court of Appeals and being targeted by the national press. It didn't work. My voice cracked, which of course they ignored.

We were standing in the living room and I noticed Mom was staring at me, glassy-eyed. Dad went into the kitchen.

"May I use the phone?" I asked with a still-cracked-voice.

"Of course!" He said gruffly. "This is your house, *too*, you know." That was a first! Since we'd had that argument after I'd left home shortly after starting college, he'd never made me feel like it was my home.

The phone rang and rang. Eventually a male voice answered.

"Probation Office, Phoenix Division."

"Hello," I said hesitantly. "This is Samsara Drakke. I've just arrived at my parent's home in Sun City. I was told by Matthew Sims, from the Portland Office, to call as soon as I arrived here."

"Just a moment, let me get your file."

After about five minutes, he came back on the line. "Says here that we are to set you up with electronic monitoring under house arrest. But it's 4:35 and since it's Friday, we'll have to make the appointment to come out to the house on Monday morning to set up the electronic equipment. You have the weekend to relax. Just remember to stay put. You are still under house arrest." The officer warned in his official voice.

How am I supposed to do this?

My hand shook as I replaced the receiver and turned around. I jumped. Mom was standing right behind me.

"Are you tired?" She said, confused, anxious, unsteady, slightly drunk and upset.

I wish she could just say that she missed me. Poor Mom. I can tell she wants to know everything that's happened to me in the last nine years.

"Are you hungry? You must be hungry! Look at you, you haven't been eating enough, you're so thin! What can I make you? What do you eat nowadays? And look at those clothes! I've made you eighty-eight skillion clothes... you never could dress properly, Cecilia Allesandra. Do you want to take a shower before we eat? Is there..."

"I think I'll unpack before dinner," I smiled weakly.

I started to walk down the hallway to the bedroom. Nothing had changed. The pictures were the same, in the same spots on the walls. All was the same as I last saw it... even the bitterness.

Death was everywhere. The house smelled like a cemetery.

"Well, it won't be long now... I don't have many more years on this earth and neither does your father." Mom began the dinner conversation.

Dad didn't want to waste time and quickly cut Mom off. "How are you going to pay for this lawyer?"

"I hope to get her court-appointed."

"And that means?"

"If you don't have any money – which I don't - an accused can petition the Court to appoint a lawyer. I'm going to ask for Trish because she's already been working on my case for the past six months."

"She's not very good," Dad said abruptly.

I was flabbergasted. "What do you mean?"

"Well, if she were *that* good she would have gotten you out on bail right away!" He exclaimed.

"Dad, it had nothing to do with Trish! She's worked her ass off! The damn prosecutor was out for glory and wanted to make me his sacrificial lamb by dragging me through all those useless hearings at the taxpayers' expense, just because I didn't want to be their stool pigeon."

I was furious, cursing more now that I was around Dad. He had that effect on me. *How could he even think that about Trish? The woman is a saint.*

"Alright! Let's not argue!" Mom interjected, fearful of a battle like the old days.

The rest of the dinner was in silence.

After dinner, I helped Mom with the dishes, just like I used to before I'd moved out, twenty year ago. Then all three of us went into the living room where Dad immediately turned on the TV. Just like the old days.

"I'm going to my room. I'm tired."

"Do you need anything?" Mom asked anxiously.

"No thanks, Mom. I don't."

She sounded more sober. Food did that to her.

As I walked down the hall towards my room, I felt the old sinking in my guts and a choking feeling in my throat, like being suffocated. *Just like the old days.*

The weekend was a repeat of my last visit nine years ago, which was a repeat of my childhood. Mom was sweet in the morning but by two in the afternoon she had started drinking. Dad was sullen and belligerent in the mornings but sickeningly sweet and gruff in the afternoons after several cocktails.

Over the weekend, a letter arrived from Trish.

May 3, 1991

Dear Samsara,

Good news today: Judge Wallace has agreed for me to
be your court-appointed lawyer. He will not appoint Bob,
however, but will allow me to pay Bob for non-duplicative legal
research. I can submit vouchers and will eventually be paid
$60 an hour to represent you. It also means that the Judge
should approve some auxiliary services such as an investigator.
So, financially we are in business, albeit something close to a
non-profit business.

Don't choke on the enclosed billing. Nancy has been
keeping track of all my hours in case the Judge required us to
pro-rate my services...

I stopped reading.

*I didn't care about the billing. God, this is the first good news I've
had. Trish is going to help me. She'll get me out of this mess. She'll
mow down those fat cats from DC like a tank. Oh, thank God! At
last something's working in my favor. She told me that it was highly
unlikely that the Judge would appoint her because she was out-of-
state. But he did! Yippee! So miracles can happen.*

This was just the first one.

Monday came with electronic monitoring plus stacks of
legal papers.

Samsara Drakke, CR-90-00146-006: Conditions of House
Arrest:

1. You must have a telephone at your residence and provide
the U.S. Probation Office (USPO) with a copy of your phone
bill. You may not have call forwarding.

2. You must allow the USPO to visit you at your residence at any time.

3. You may leave your residence during curfew hours for genuine emergencies. You will report any emergency to your USPO. You will be expected to provide documented proof of any emergency.

4. You must provide copies of your paycheck stubs and verification of medical and dental appointments.

5. You agree to pay the cost of electronic monitoring.

They expect me to pay the bloody cost of their confining me?

6. You understand that a tamper-proof, non-removable wristlet will monitor you, which will be at work 24 hours a day.

7. You understand that you will receive random telephone calls during your restricted hours and agree to respond verbally.

8. You and your family agree to limit telephone calls to 5 minutes and leave the line open for 5 minutes after each call.

9. You agree that a violation determined by the telephone monitoring equipment will be considered evidence of a probation violation and a computer printout will be used as evidence in a revocation hearing.

I was restricted to "the residence" with the exception of shopping with my parents and one-hour church services on Sundays. There was no time to even look for a job and the paycheck stubs I was supposed to show.

I signed the document.

They set up the equipment and left.

Our one phone was in the living room, which meant that when it rang at night, I had to jump out of bed and run into the room to answer it in time.

The calls started coming in: 12:35 P.M., 1:42, 4:00, 4:15, 7:00, 8:30, 10:00, 1:30 A.M., 3:00 A.M, 5:30 A.M....there was hardly time to sleep more than a few hours before the telephone rang, followed by a cold, mechanical recorded voice to "clock in" my response.

Probation told me that if the equipment failed to clock you in, the police would be notified immediately and several squad cars dispatched to "the residence."

No sooner was I hooked up to the electronic monitoring when I was called to Portland for another hearing. I had to notify the Arizona office and get permission to leave.

The hearing, set for May 10th, was supposed to be quick, officially appointing Trish as my lawyer, with all the same people present.

There must be a better way to waste money than make us all come back to Portland simply to reinstate the paperwork.

But I was glad to leave Arizona and that cemetery-telephone-madness and get back on a Greyhound bus.

The long bumpy journey, sleeping curled up in a cramped seat for 20 hours, with a bus change at 3:00 A.M. in LA's drug-infested depot, was preferable to the tormented sleeplessness in the retired desert compound-enclosed Sun City West.

That was the frying pan; I couldn't imagine that the fire would be worse.

Bzzzzzzzzzzzzzzzzzzt! The alarm in my $10 room at the Portland YMCA, shrilled at 5:30 A.M. Exhausted and wired, my night had been sleepless. The Y was around the corner from the hotel that the commune once owned.

Trish and Bob were to meet me at Bob's office at 8:00 A.M. From there we would go to the Courthouse. I wanted us to be the mighty gruesome threesome, but I felt like we were really the three Stooges, having filed enough motions to fill a law library, and getting nowhere.

The only memory of that day was when the Court logged Trish in as my counsel, and the court reporter had a fit of coughing and had to leave the room. Everything else was a blur. In the Court's hands, my life was reduced to tiny dots in the Federal Criminal Computer. There was fear all around me.

I'm a registered offender-to-be. For the rest of my life I'd have to put a "yes" in the felon slot on every job application.

I was back in the desert before I could turn around.

It was May 20,1991 and at 6:00 A.M., it was 99 degrees and another bleak, shatteringly bright day. Depression shook me awake. It was a dull gnawing sensation.

Life is over, done, finished, and no matter what you do there'll never be any more happiness. Get out of bed. Move. Don't stop. Your life is in other people's hands and they want to crush you like an insect.

I reached over to the bedside table, blinking my contact lens into focus picked up the single sheet of paper and the beginning of my letter to Stephanie, which I had placed next to the cold coffee cup.

My dearest Stephanie,

Nothing more... I had started a letter to her and couldn't write anything else. There was no inspiration left in me. Nothing positive. Only anger. Anger at everybody walking around free, while I was stuck with this mess.

Ok. Ok, Samsara, you did this to yourself. And the whole damn thing escalated way out of proportion. Why couldn't you just lead a simple, quiet, normal, uneventful life, like all these people around here, with their retirement and their golf clubs? You would probably have ended up just like them, too: angry and bitter under the surface, insulting each other like my parents, deeply ashamed with their empty lives and realizing that perhaps they really didn't like their partners after all.

The blinds moved slightly. A small breeze, like a blip, hissed through the heat. Outside the streets were empty, sterile, like a morgue. Each house looked like a plastic cutout.

It's the sameness that gets to me, dulling my edges. I'm not as sharp as I used to be... five witnesses are against me. All for shorter sentences. Why can't I do it too? It would be easier on everybody. For Mom and Dad's sake, just do it. Everybody'll understand... eventually.

I understand duress. I understand pressure. But, after all those years in spiritual practice, haven't I learned the first thing about integrity? Or honesty? OK. Get off your pulpit, Samsara. Today I'll call Trish and ask her exactly what the Feds want from me. If they get too nasty I can always hint that I'll leak all the dirt I found out in Washington, and how eager the Justice Department was to squash us, for example.

Mom met me in the kitchen.

"How'd you sleep?" she asked sweetly.

I know she really loves me, and has a hard time showing it. She's more freaked out than me.

"Fine, Ma. How're you?"

"Your lawyer called this morning, and she said to tell you that your hypnosis sessions were approved. What does that mean?"

"It means, Ma, that the Court is allowing me to be interviewed by a psychiatrist to help me remember the events of what actually happened during the conspiracy. I have big gaps in my memory."

"Well, I hope it goes well. I have to put your father's clothes out before it gets too hot."

And with that she walked out onto the patio and started hanging clothes on the line, as if I'd said that I was going shopping.

The phone rang.

"Hallo, Zamzara! How are you?" His German/English accent was so delightful.

"Johann! I am *so* happy to hear from you. How are you?"

"*Gut* Zamzara. Very *gut*. I hear zat you were released from ze jail and are home. Are you awright? Was it terrible zere? Can we talk? Is the phone watched?"

"I'm OK, except that I'm having problems with my

teeth and yes, the phone is *watched*. We can only talk for five minutes, as I have to keep the phone line open for the electronic monitoring calls. But I survived the jail. It made me appreciate German prison more."

"What's *wiz* your tees?"

"You remember Dr. Ritterman the dentist who pulled out my tooth by mistake? She didn't bother to treat the hole properly and now I have an abscess. Dental treatments have used up all money I got back from my bail in Germany."

"Ah, Zamzara, I am so sorry hearing *dis!*"

"Ah well. It's been the least of my problems although my mouth has been like that volcano in the Philippeans that was just on TV. Speaking of which, how's Nina's family? Were they affected by the volcano?"

"They are all fine and Nina too. She gives love to you."

"And how are you and Nina doing?"

"Ah yes, it is difficult. We fight all ze time now. Two days ago, she trow all ze plates from ze kitchen to me. Zey missed my head but I don't know what more I can do wiz her."

"Johann, why do you still put up with all this?"

"I still love her Zamzara. I am still such a pullover."

"You mean pushover. You're just too good and too sweet, you know."

"Ah, Zamzara, why zey can't all be like you?"

"Then all the German women would be behind bars!" I laughed.

"But we men would be happier! And zen we could *do* more for you ladies!"

That's it. He's starting to make me cry.

"My dear Johann, I must say goodbye now. Thank you so much for calling. I love you so much."

"Take care of you, my Zamzara. I call again soon! *Tschüss.*"

When I heard the familiar *tschüss,* which is how we said good-bye to each other, I really started to sob. Mom came into the living room. She stopped and stared at me.

"Are you crying? So early in the morning? You're not going to get anywhere crying you know. So stop it, Cecilia Allesandra. When are you going to grow up? Come and eat some breakfast. Your father's been waiting long enough for you to get off that phone."

The days droned on.

On May 31st, the day before I left Sun City for the June 3rd hearing in Portland, I had my first job interview. It took six hours to get to Phoenix and back, taking three busses each way, as I didn't have a driver's license.

I resolved that when I returned from the hearing, I would apply for volunteer work with a hospice or elder day care in Sun City. I knew *they* would accept me because they took *anybody*.

That night Puneet called me for the first time.

"Hello?"

"Samsara, it's Puneet. How are you?"

"Puneet! What a great surprise. I'm fine. How are you? It's been such a long time. I'm so happy to hear from you."

"Yes, we haven't talked since you were in Bühl - much too long. I *did* get your letter from the jail, and the other letter about what the prosecutor said at the hearings. But I had to call you and tell you something about what *I* think is going on."

"What's that?" I got scared and he got right to it.

"Samsara, why don't you do a deal and then the whole business will be over? Your letters sound like you're slipping into some kind of 'poor me' routine, which will get worse the longer you hold out. Why not just plead guilty, face what you have to face and get on with your life?"

"Puneet, I can't do that. I thought I made that clear..."

"Samsara, listen to me! I'm going through some heavy times with Hans these days, and frankly it's taking all my energy... I think he's cheating on me and my jealousy's driving me mad. So, I'm not in the mood to hear about *your* difficulties, especially because it just feels like self-pity. Think about someone else for a change. Why don't you think about how your principles are affecting your parents?"

"Puneet, I can't believe what you're saying. I *am* thinking of them! I think about them every day and night. How can I not? They're always reminding me of how much they're suffering because of me! I feel it keenly. But what kind of daughter would I be if I sold out my own principles? Would they be proud of a rat, selling possibilities and suppositions that will certainly hurt other people, just to get a shorter sentence? And, of *all* people, I thought *you* understood that. I'M NOT GUILTY AND I'M NOT GONNA TO SAY I AM!

As for finding the simplest way out, *I*'m responsible for whatever I decide to do and I can't live with the consequences of hurting others, just to benefit myself. How can anything anybody imagines they saw or heard become absolute fact? I'm thinking of going to trial because at least I'll be able to say what really happened. Even if they cut my head off!"

"OK, Samsara, don't get so sanctimonious. It can't be that bad."

"YOU HAVE NO IDEA. Have you ever been under house arrest? Night after night we get no sleep because the phone rings continuously checking on me. Mom and Dad bitch the whole day because they're so tired. My life is a nightmare of impossible decisions, fury, fear and unbearable loneliness.

"Furthermore, what the Feds are doing is sick and outrageous and I'm not going to stand for it. Trish calls me every other day with something new they want from me. I'm told about statement after statement by the state witnesses who are against me... that my *friends* said against me. They were *your* friends too.

"It's true that I pity myself, along with every other emotion, because I'm just human. I'm not giving in because that would make me weak. And I have to be strong to save myself, for no other good reason than I have to take care of these two old people who have no one else to look after them."

The words were like a dam breaking inside of me.

"I'm all alone in this struggle. And that's how it is. I feel your love and your support and see you in my heart, but you're not *here*. *I* have to face this alone. I don't have a boyfriend like you have, or Maya and Charlize, to hold my hand through it all.

"I'm not going to let myself be abused like I was in the commune. Looking back, I hadn't felt good there for a long time but I stayed, hoping for approval and love from people I didn't even like, because of some religious belief. Above all, I was a good soldier for God."

I stopped, wondering if I had said too much but feeling lighter for having said it. I could hear Puneet breathing heavily.

"OK, Samsara, I certainly can't say anything when you put it like that. I'm not in your shoes... I'll try to be more sensitive the next time we talk. I love you and support everything you're trying to do. It's very courageous."

"Oh, Puneet, it's not courageous. It's just the only thing I can live with! You, Trish, Maria, Steph, Johann, and Katrin are my lifeline! I couldn't keep going if I didn't have all of you! How else could someone as small as me stand up to this international horror show?"

"Someday, Samsara, you'll have to write a book, but I don't know if anyone would believe you!" He chuckled and it was so good to hear him laugh. Puneet was in the midst of his own health problems, dealing with his rapidly progressing AIDS, I felt guilty yelling at him.

"I'm so sorry that I'm edgy, Puneet. I'll be more myself when this terrible pressure is off. Please bear with me. I need you... Now, I've got to get off the damn phone, but I hate saying goodbye to you... I love you so!"

"Remember, I love you too and our love is strong. I'm holding thumbs for you, Samsara!"

I put the phone down caressing it gently, feeling the depth of love between us.

I couldn't bear never to see him again.

After the next hearing, again with the same pressures from the Feds, I took the smelly, crowded bus back to Sun City. On the journey I scrawled a letter to Johann.

Thursday, June 6th.

I'm sitting on this very bumpy bus going back to Arizona after the last Portland hearing. Please forgive the scribble. I wish I could hear your voice.

The Judge actually approved of a psychiatrist to determine whether or not I was sane.

Do you think I'm sane? The shrink's supposed to help me remember things. So, do I make him think I'm sane or do I just be me and let him decide?

I think I'll just be me. That way if he thinks I'm insane, it'll be certifiable.

We filed a motion to fund a study to show that there's still prejudice in Oregon against Rajneeshees, which was denied, as was the motion to change the trial venue. None of this surprised me. If you get the chance, let Diva know, as it might help her fight her own extradition. She should know that she's unlikely to get a fair trial in Oregon in the near future.

I'll send you a news clipping describing the coercion the government is using against me, which you can also pass on to Diva. I'm not allowed any contact with her. She could ask her lawyer to present it to the German Court to show that the government acts unfairly unless everybody does what *they* want.

I'm going to stop now because it's getting too bumpy. I'll write again soon. I miss you my dearest. Thinking of you always lifts my spirits. Give my love to Nina...

The rest of the bus ride was noisy and uncomfortable. There was little relief in being back home. Mom was in her daily fog. Dad seemed more than usually distracted.

I wish I'd stayed in jail. At least I would have gotten jail time credit. I feel so guilty because I cause them nothing but grief. They try so hard to take care of me. Mom makes my food and Dad takes me to the dentist. And, I give them nothing in return except more problems. I'm incapable of doing anything for anybody. I'm a wreck.

When I came back, there was a letter from Stephanie and a postcard from Katrin, who was again in Greece.

Stephanie's letter was short, describing the media attention around her terrorist group. She urged me not to give up under the pressure. Even though she was a million miles away she understood the challenges that were in front of me.

In fact, both Stephanie and I were little guys.

In my case, many people thought I was something more, which is why they kept trying to involve me in meetings that I knew nothing about. Some state witnesses "confirmed" me at meetings in Rajneeshpuram during the time I was actually in Washington D.C. – three thousand miles away.

I read Katrin's card before I looked at the picture on the other side. The dramatic colors of the Greek landscape, where I had made a home, brought tears because I thought I'd never see it again. She wrote simply:

My darling,

How dare they presume that you could get a fair trial when all that stuff was going on and people were spewing venom in those newspapers? I READ the reports. Well, at least you got the shrink. Don't worry; he'll do something for you. Everybody here sends their love and we're all begging the gods to cheer you up and give you strength. You'll get through this one, just like you got through everything else. Remember I love you. Write when you can. I'm fine.

She doesn't know the latest, that the government is requesting their shrink to evaluate me, and if he produces contrary results, that might cancel out what Trish's expert finds.

In the end, it's gonna be up to God. What a power play. Surely truth is the silent witness. Everybody's got a different perception of what happened.

The next day I wrote back to Katrin.

Thanks for the card. It brings me back to the times we wandered in the Butterfly Garden near the harbor. Do you remember those early mornings when we stayed up all night with our lovers and they'd finally left? Then we'd gossip till late morning watching the waves on the beach as we drank pots of Greek coffee.

I got approval for the shrink. He'll hypnotize me. That's going to be the stick of dynamite I need to blast through this fog.

It's chaotic here. Mom and Dad are restless and demanding. I'm caught up in their worries. None of us know what's going to happen. So get your Greek gods working on devouring those Feds for me.

Sweetie, I hug you. I can't write any more. Maybe later.

I hope that your Mom and Dad are doing better and that your Mom is recovering from her eye surgery. How I wish I could be there to be with you.

I wasn't being too successful in the getting-it-together department, and the next hearing was in less than one month.

Instead I was losing it. The meeting was arranged for July 3rd in Santa Fe. The shrink was coming in from Washington, D.C.

I arrived there on July 2nd feeling too many emotions to think straight. I hadn't seen Trish since the last hearing in Portland. She was calm and poised.

Nothing seems to ruffle her.

"How are you? Are you nervous?" Trish asked as we settled into the hotel room.

"Sure. I'm a mess. I'm worn out from the pressures of

trying to dig out the truth and make a decision about a trial that I feel I've already lost."

I'm pissed off already and I haven't even asked her how she is.

"Listen Samsara. For the next three days put aside all the decisions about trial and just place yourself in this man's hands. After you finish your work with him we'll have a better idea of how to proceed."

She was right. Trish had a way of being right about everything she did. There was a stubbornness and certainty that came from her east coast roots. After living in Seattle for a while, she claimed that the west had a tranquilizing influence on her life.

The sterility of Arizona seemed to only be feeding my obsessive worrying. I had to separate myself from what was making me nuts in order to concentrate on what I had come here to do. Trish could see that I didn't really want to talk.

"Go to sleep, Samsara. I've got paperwork to do. It'll be an intense day, tomorrow." She gave me the excuse I was looking for.

But sleep evaded me.

It was too quiet in the hotel room. The place was beautiful and made me feel worse – I didn't deserve it.

Excited and edgy, I couldn't eat breakfast the next day. Instead I drank two cups of strong coffee and smoked several cigarettes, which made me more edgy. Trish arranged for the shrink to come at 9:00 A.M. The meeting was going to be in the room next door.

There he is, there's the door. Mr. Punctual.

Trish and I both got up in one move and went in to meet him.

"Good morning, Samsara, Trish. My name is Dr. James Corden and I will be working with you during these next few days. Please sit down."

He doesn't even get up to greet me. The man's cool and stoic all right, just like the furniture.

I sat down in the chair opposite, while Trish stood.

"I'll leave you two and come back later," she said.

I couldn't take my eyes off him.

"First of all," he began, "I'd like to tell you a little about myself, so that you feel more comfortable in talking to me. Is that ok?"

"Yes, that's fine."

His eyebrows were drawn.

Can I trust him? Thinning, sandy hair. Those hands are really large. His blue eyes are so still.

"I completed my medical training at Harvard, interned at Mount Zion Hospital and did my psychiatric residency at Albert Einstein College of Medicine in New York. I began my studies of new religious movements while I was a research psychiatrist at the National Institute of Mental Health, concerned with the mental health consequences of people in these groups. I was asked to be the lead investigator because of my long-term familiarity with counter-cultural movements, amongst other things. Since then, I have interviewed perhaps 500 participants in some 25 different religious groups. So you see, I have talked to a lot of people." He chuckled, then. His warmth came through the chuckle and relaxed me.

"At present," he continued, "I'm a Clinical Professor in the Departments of Psychiatry, Community and Family Medicine at the Georgetown University School of Medicine in Washington, D.C. I've been using hypnosis as a therapeutic tool for ten years and teach medical hypnosis at Georgetown. I hope you will be perfectly comfortable if we decide to pursue this procedure in order to unlock these memories that Trish mentioned you were having difficulty with."

That made me feel exalted and even more afraid.

"Just one more thing, Samsara: I did extensive research on Bhagwan, in the 70's, when I spent time at meditation centers and the ashram in Poona. I interviewed Sila and Bhagwan extensively in Oregon. I also traveled to Crete, where Bhagwan went after the Ranch disbanded and spoke to him a few months before his death. Since the 80's, I've kept contact with many disciples and ex-disciples, and had the opportunity to observe how they dealt with the decline of the movement and his death.

"I wanted you to know all of this before we started, and I hope that it may help you to feel more at ease with me. I realize that you have already been through many difficult experiences. This is not going to be another interrogation, I promise you that."

Jim's manner was far from the biting, machine-gun-fire questioning I had become used to with the Feds, prosecutors, courts and guards.

"How do you feel about being here, and everything I've said so far, Samsara?" My body was stiff, like a soldier before a court martial.

"Not as afraid as I thought I would be." I said with a weak smile. "That's some background."

None of the prosecutors, not even Trish, had met Bhagwan. None of them had any idea what it was like to be zapped by a guru thus becoming someone entirely different.

"Would you like to begin by telling me where you were born and what your childhood was like?"

I could hear myself talking once again as a professional. I was in the company of a colleague. It was refreshing.

Two and a half days later, we reached the outer layer of my fog.

"What does this fog look like?" Jim asked like a dedicated researcher about to embark on a discovery.

I hesitated for a moment, trying to find the most accurate description of this vague and nebulous thing.

"It's like a gray veil. I can see shapes and outlines behind it, but I can't distinguish what they are or what's going on. I've tried to penetrate it. Nothing lifts it. I've been asking myself and God if I'm afraid to see what's in there and so far I haven't got any answers either way."

Trust now existed between us. In the past fifty hours Jim knew more about me than God. He responded kindly, and a bit sadly to this disorientated, rumpled woman in front of him. I didn't hear any judgments in his statements.

"I understand, Samsara. This disintegration is probably something many others in the commune have been going through as well. Many devotees don't even realize what they've been through and are still suffering years later, unable to stay in one place or job or relationship for long."

He shifted in his chair.

"You mentioned that you were away from the Ranch, interviewing politicians during much of 1984 and 1985, which is when the prosecution placed you at these plotting meetings. Do you have any evidence to support this?"

"We have an investigator working on it, but the information coming in is very sketchy. So far we have one date in February confirmed by a hotel registration in D.C. and one in April. I wish there was something more concrete. The only witness who could confirm that I wasn't at those meetings is Puneet, a friend of mine who lives in Germany. The problem is that he's also a fugitive charged with wiretapping. If he were to be put on the stand for the defense, the prosecution would say to the jury that this is the testimony of a *fugitive*. How credible is that?"

"Well, Samsara, that sounds no worse to me than the testimony of a bunch of turncoats." I was surprised that he used those words but I later found out that he had heard about how sannyasins had betrayed each other.

"Yeah, but the jury'll see only that the U.S. Government has dressed them all up to look like Martha Washingtons and Abe Lincoln who are all barring their souls to tell the real truth about the big, bad cult.

"Plus they're against me. That's why I agreed to do this with you. I want to know. It makes me sick, Jim, to have to say that I'm guilty of intending to kill Tork when I'm not. I know this much, but I can't see *why* I know.

"If I could see what actually happened and discover that I *am* guilty, then I can honestly go into a plea bargain. But, right now, all I feel is sorrow, confusion, pain, torment and my incapability of killing anyone. I can't go to trial like this.

If a jury finds me guilty, the maximum penalty could be life in prison."

"For conspiracy to commit murder?"

"Of a federal official, yes. And, from the way Judge Wallace handled my bail hearings, he's certainly unsympathetic to me."

"What's happening with the wiretapping charge?"

"The Feds told Trish that if I plead guilty they would drop the wiretapping charge. If I go to trial, they'll prosecute me on wiretapping as a second charge, with a second trial. And, if I bring the conspiracy to trial, first, and I'm acquitted by some miracle, then they will bring up the wiretapping and ask for imprisonment, which they haven't done for any of the other 20 people in the wiretap indictment."

"And you think they'll try?"

"Yes. They want to nail me one way or another. If they can't own me like a state witness, they want to nail me. They want to make an example of me. Since they can't get Sila, they want to say: look, this is what happens to those who won't cooperate."

"Why can't they get Sila?"

"She's somewhere in Switzerland and since she's now a citizen, Switzerland doesn't extradite its own."

"Oh, I see."

"I'm in an odd position. My German lawyer made an error when she gave her opinion during the hearing, which meant that the transcripts of the entire German Court inquest can't be used in my defense. My extradition papers were mysteriously sent to Bonn and then to Washington D.C. before my appeal was ever acted upon.

"Germany refused to allow the third charge of transporting illegal firearms, but the Feds included it anyway, defying the German Court. The Feds then fought my bail, which was granted immediately to every other defendant. Finally, they're threatening to prosecute me on two separate charges with two separate trials."

At that moment the image of Plato's cave came to me. There everything was backwards: the truth was hidden in the recesses, somewhere, inside the fog. Hypnosis seemed the only key, the final key.

"Are you ready to begin the hypnosis, now?" he asked gently.

"More than ready."

Chapter 13
Mr. Alford, if you please

A=x+y+z
If A=success
X=work
Y=play
Z=keep your mouth shut
– Albert Einstein

Finally this is it. I hope I'm doing the right thing.

"Samsara, close your eyes, sit comfortably and relax. I'm going to take you into a deep hypnotic state.

Are you willing to go back and see what really happened?"

"Yes."

"I'd like you to go back to just before that meeting with Sila in Rajneesh Legal Services where she first introduced the subject of Tork. Take your time. When you are there, raise your index finger, that's your 'know' finger."

"OK."

"Now go through what you remember of the conversation

from start to finish. Are you willing to share these events with me?"

Me: Yes. I see the desks and people in Rajneesh Legal Services. Belle's there, busy with the lawyers. Sila's on the other side of the room. She motions to me with her hand to come over. I walk over and sit down beside her. I see the fear and upset written all over her face. She's the one person who carries the primary responsibility for whatever might happen to Bhagwan and the entire community if federal and state investigations try to shut the commune down.

Sila: Samsara, I think we should get rid of George Tork. What do you think?

Me: Um-m... Why not? Get him out of office. We'll have to find out something *about* him, first and what he's planning. OK. I'll research and try to interview him, starting in Portland at the library so I'll need a driver.

Sila: OK, take Eve.

Jim: What are you feeling now?

Me: A little confused. I'm not exactly sure what she means. I want to believe she means get rid of his power over us by simply removing him from office. I've also got this feeling in my gut, though, that she's planning something harmful. She's been paranoid lately, scaring me.

Jim: What do you mean? Give me an example.

Me: The week before, Ted Koppel interviewed her on *Nightline*. Koppel threw her off the air because she started ranting, raving and swearing and wouldn't stop. She even *looked* crazy.

Jim: All right go back to the room. What else are you thinking?

Me: I'm afraid of Eve.

Jim: Why are you afraid of her?

Me: She's gonna hurt me.

Jim: How?

Me: She'll yell at me, humiliate me and make me feel stupid in front of people, like she did when she was my boss at the Portland Hotel. She often told me I never listened and it was my biggest problem.

Jim: All right. Let's move ahead to when you meet Eve.

Me: I approach and she continues writing as though I'm not there.

Eve, I have a message from Sila. She ignores me and continues writing. Eve, listen, this is important. Sila just told me she wants to get rid of Tork. *Then* she looks up.

Eve: What?

Me: *Stay calm.* First we're gonna research him by going to the Portland library, before anything... deal with him through the lawyers. Sila told me to come and ask you to be my driver.

Me: She looks at me like I'm an insect.

Eve: Sila sent *you* to tell *me* this?

Me: Yes.

Eve: Why didn't she come and tell me herself? Why did she send *you*? Why did she... I don't believe you. I'm going to ask Sila myself.

Me: Fine, ask her.

Jim: Why did you need a driver?

Me: Because I'm blind in one eye.

Jim: OK, move forward in time, till you see Eve again.

Me: That evening in Jesus Grove, where Sila and all the administrators including Eve, live. Eve comes in and I look up. She's smiling strangely at me and starts to speak.

Jim: What does she say?

Eve: Samsara, I spoke to Sila. Everything's all arranged. We leave early tomorrow morning. I'll come by your house and pick you up. I've got the car and money. I'll get food and a thermos of coffee in the morning.

Jim: What're you thinking?

Me: Why is she being so *nice* to me? Doesn't matter just keep her nice. Who knows how long it's going to last?

Jim: OK. Now, move forward in time to the point that you and Eve talk next about Tork.

Me: We're on the road, close to Portland.

Eve: How are we going to research Tork?

Me: First, we'll go to the library and dig up his background. As soon as I get enough info, I'll call his office and request an interview. That's worked with all the other officials I've researched before. I'm sure it will be a breeze with him.

Eve: OK. Let's use my apartment; it's only a few blocks from the Portland Hotel. That way we'll dress in blue and don't have to come in contact with any sannyasins.

Jim: Are you having any doubts about what you are seeing? Does it seem pretty clear?"

Me: Very clear. Belle was with Sila in the legal department when she first brought up Tork. I didn't *remember her* before.

Jim: Well, that'll happen. You'll see more and more things you didn't remember. But, of course you did see them then. Samsara, had you and Sila spoken about Tork, before you met with her in legal services?"

Me: (Shakes head).

Jim: No? OK. Had you and Sila spoken about Bhagwan's immigration case prior to that day?

Me: (Shakes head).

Jim: No? Did you know *anything* about it?

Me: (Nods).

Jim: Yes? What?

Me: I read a report about it in *The Rajneesh Times.*

Jim: Did Sila ever mention it before she brought up Tork?

Me: In 1983 she talked to the whole commune about Bhagwan's immigration and how the INS was denying his status as a religious leader.

Jim: Your memory is working very well. So the whole commune knew. Now, take a deep breath and go a little more deeply. Did you overhear any conversations that Sila might have had with other people prior to that day?

Me: No.

Jim: When were you first aware of Tork?

Me: From *The Rajneesh Times.*

Jim: Did you ever hear any conversations about enemies of the commune?

Me: No.

Jim: Did you ever hear or see this term stated?

Me: Yes. There was an article in *The Rajneesh Times* about some prominent politicians who were referred to as enemies of the commune.

Jim: OK. Did Sila use the word *kill?*

Me: No.

Jim: You're sure?

Me: Yes.

Jim: OK. What did you feel when Sila said, "get rid of Tork?"

Me: Like she was talking of getting rid of an annoying insect. I was afraid she meant to 'squash' it. That's why I told Eve.

Jim: All right. Let's leave those memories there and move forward in time to the library. What did you find?

Me: Very little. The President appoints the U.S. Attorney. There were a few articles mentioning Tork's cases. No pictures. It was strange not to find even a single picture but I knew I'd get a personality assessment of him in an interview.

Jim: What do you mean, 'personality assessment'?

Me: I learned to predict the speed and accuracy of how a person makes decisions from reading facial features, body postures and language, from my previous work as a counselor in the '70's.

Jim: So, after the library what did you do?

Me: I called Tork's office from the phone booth outside the library. His secretary answers the phone.

Secretary: Hello?

Me: Hello. I'm Theodora Mathis, a freelance writer doing a series of articles on prominent political figures. I'd like to interview Mr. Tork. When would that be possible, please?

Secretary: The U.S. Attorney does not grant interviews.

Me: Oh, why is that?

Secretary: It's just his policy. He doesn't give interviews.

Me: Do you have any information or PR that you give to reporters?

Secretary: No.

Me: May I talk to you about him and his work?

Secretary: The policy of the office is not to grant interviews.

Me: How would one find out more about him then?

Secretary: Have you checked the library?

Me: Yes, and I hardly found anything.

Secretary: I'm sorry I can't help you. Good day.

Me: She hangs up. I'm stunned. Not even the Solicitor General, the President's lawyer, for God's sake, refused me... and I have to find something, otherwise...

Jim: Otherwise what?

Me: Otherwise Sila might do something crazy.

Jim: Let's leave the feelings alone for a moment and return to you and Eve. Does Eve suggest anything?

Me: Yes.

Eve: You could go to the courthouse to look for him.

Me: And, who am I supposed to look for at the courthouse? I don't have a *clue* as to what this guy looks like. Maybe I'll call his home and ask him for an interview.

Jim: Do you call him?

Me: There's no number listed. He *really* doesn't want to be contacted. What is this man hiding from? He must have a *schoo*l picture somewhere. I'll find a yearbook picture of him.

Jim: Are you telling all this to Eve?

Me: Yes.

Jim: So what do you do next?

Me: I discover that he graduated from Brown University in Rhode Island, and locate his yearbook photo so I have something to help me recognize him at the courthouse. I'll try to interview him on the courthouse steps. Sila will accept my research and she'll use the lawyers against him. I'll get stuff on him if I have to sleep at his doorstep. I *have* to.

Jim: When do you next talk to Sila?

Me: Four days later. I walk into Sila's bedroom, where she and I usually talk. She's on the phone.

As soon as she finishes the call she looks at me.

Sila: Samsara? What do you have?

Me: An old picture of Tork. As the US Attorney he takes his instructions from the Attorney General. Don't you think we should look more closely at the AG's office in *Washington?*

Sila: What else did you find out about Tork?

Me: That he doesn't give interviews. His home phone is unlisted. Have *you* ever seen him?

Sila: No. So, what's your next plan?

Me: I'm going back to Portland. I'll see Tork, one way or another, and give you a personality profile. I'll knock on his door or talk to him outside the courthouse.

Sila: OK. And, Samsara, don't talk about this research with anybody but your helpers.

Me: Sila, you know I don't talk about my research.

Sila: I'm just reminding you.

Jim: OK. Let's take a short break, Samsara. Why don't you and Trish take a walk and get some fresh air? I'm going to bring you out now. 1-2-3-4-5... You're refreshed and ready. We'll meet back here in an hour, OK?

Boy, It's good to stretch.

"How was that?" Jim asked.

"Nice. I didn't want to come back."

"You didn't *want* to?"

"No. I wanted to stay there. I liked it."

"What did you like about it?"

"It was peaceful."

"Good."

Walking slowly out of the room, I go next door and knock. Trish answers after a moment.

"Jim says it would be good for us to go for a short walk, Trish."

"Great! Let's get a snack in the mall next to the hotel, then. I'm ready for food!"

It feels weird to walk around a mall in Santa Fe after I've just been in Sila's bedroom. Oh well, it'll do us both good.

The snack turned into shopping. Trish was sidetracked by the craft shop in the mall and her passion for jewelry.

"What do you think of these?" she asked me, trying on long thin silver loops.

I started choking as despair stuck in my throat and I couldn't answer.

I'm struggling for my life, and she's trying on earrings? Will I ever be carefree again? .

Trish sees my face and walks over to hug me briefly. "I know, Samsara, that you must feel overwhelmed right now. I wish I could take that away from you, but I can't. Do you want to go back?"

Words wouldn't come. Instead, I started crying. She took my arm and walked me back to the hotel quietly, without another word.

I want to continue. I don't want to loose this clarity. Now that I've found a way into the fog, I don't want to forget.

"How was your walk?" Jim asked.

"Let's get on with this, Jim. I'm afraid that if we don't move on quickly, I'll just lose it."

"All right, Samsara. Close your eyes and breathe deeply. Move forward in time, now and tell me where you are after you arrive in Portland."

Me: I'm in the voter registration office.

Jim: What are you doing there?

Me: Eve and I are looking for Tork's address in the public records. I only find a box number, which means it must be outside Portland, on one of the rural roads. I try to figure out how to find a house from a box number. Even if I find the mailbox, there could be several together. Only the owner would know which box is his.

Jim: How are things with Eve?

Me: Cautious. I'm still afraid of making a mistake, and of her yelling at me, maybe even hurting me the way Berry did.

Eve's stronger than Berry, and more powerful in Sila's inner circle.

Jim: Move ahead to where you find his house. Is anybody there?

Me: No. Nobody. No dog. No sign of life.

Jim: Any cars?

Me: No.

Jim: What do you do then? Do you and Eve talk about what you're going to do?

Me: Not till lunch. I say: Eve, this Tork investigation is confusing. When I investigated the bomber, and subversive groups, I didn't interview them. When I interviewed politicians, I didn't investigate them. So, I don't quite know how to put the two together. Do you think we should wait until evening and knock on Tork's door. I'll ask him for an interview, saying that I'm a freelance writer and want to do a story on him, kind of like the 'politico at home.' Eve stares at me.

Eve: Are you nuts? Go to his *house*? Just walk up there and ask him, just like that?

Me: I say to Eve. OK, so I won't go up to the front door. We'll sit here, off the road and check the cars out for anyone who looks remotely like his yearbook picture. Then we can follow the car at a distance and see if he goes into the Tork house. How about that?

Eve: OK, we'll try it.

Jim: How long do you sit there and what happens?

Me: Till dark. Nothing happens. Nobody comes. I suggest to Eve that we return early in the morning to see if any cars come out of that house. The next morning, a man drives a medium sized car down the hill from the Tork house, but neither Eve nor I see him clearly. I decide that we should return that evening to see if the same car returns to the house and perhaps get a better look at the driver. Then we can take down the license plate number.

Jim: Why would you want that?

Me: If I can't get a clear look at him, I can go to the

courthouse parking lot, identify the car and wait to see him there.

Jim: What does Eve say?

Eve: I think we have a better chance of seeing him there than we do here.

Me: Good idea. *Great. She likes that idea.*

Jim: Let's move forward. What happens the next morning?

Me: Eve has to go back to the Ranch.

Jim: Does someone else come?

Me: Yes.

Jim: Who?

Me: Maya.

Jim: How do you feel about that?

Me: Excluded, left out. I don't know why Eve is leaving and Maya's coming.

Jim: Did you and Maya talk about Sila's plans?

Me: Yes.

Maya: Sila wants to get rid of him, you know. Did she tell *you* about her other plans?

Me: What plans?

Maya: Sila will tell you if she wants to.

Me: *What's going on?* Maya says nothing more.

Jim: Ok Samsara, move forward to the next time you go the house.

Me: It's 6:00 A.M. and we're waiting in the car near the turnoff. We see a man driving.

Me: Do you think you can get a plate number from this distance?

Maya: I can try.

Jim: What do you do next?

Me: We decide to go to the courthouse parking lot to identify the car.

Jim: Move forward.

Me: Later that afternoon, Eve returns to Portland, comes to the apartment and takes Maya aside. They have a whispered conversation in the kitchen. All they tell me is that Belle's coming to Portland the day after tomorrow to give a press conference. At 7:00 P.M. there's a knock on the door and Diva arrives. Maya says she has to make a phone call and leaves. This is strange because there's a phone in the apartment. When she comes back she tells me that Diva will drive me tomorrow.

Jim: How do feel about Diva being there?

Me: OK.

Jim: Go forward to what you and Diva do next.

Me: We drive by the courthouse and see a McDonalds right opposite it. We go in McDonalds for breakfast and I notice there is this big window looking out on to the courthouse. I tell Diva that we should sit at the window and watch. If the garage entrance is there and the courthouse over there, I will be able to spot anyone who resembles Tork while we're sitting here. I show her the picture.

We sit in McDonald's for two hours. Hardly anyone walks by.

Diva: It's already nine. We've hardly seen anyone. There must be more people driving to work. Do you think that maybe there's another entrance?

Me: We leave McDonald's, see the other entrance, and while walking into the garage area, find the same car Eve and I saw earlier.

Jim: Can you read the number on the plate?

Me: Looks like Y1? 8?

Jim: Look at it again. See it as a whole.

Me: YI489.

Jim: What color is the car?

Me: Dark.

Jim: What make is it?

Me: I don't know makes of cars. It's square. Where do you see what make it is?

Jim: On the back, above the bumper. Do you see an insignia, like a Mercedes Benz?

Me: No. There's nothing on the front either.

Jim: What do you and Diva say?

Me: What's the point of hanging around here? The best time to see him is at the end of the day.

Jim: Does Diva say anything else to you?

Me: Yes.

Diva: Now is the time we have to be strong, and begin to fight back, Samsara. I learned that after I testified in a big court case recently against the commune school. They wanted to shut it down saying it was a religious school.

Jim: What are you feeling?

Me: Something's going on that she's not saying.

Jim: What do you think it is?

Me: I think she's feeling a lot of pressure. I wanted to ask her what Sila's plans are but I hesitate to bring it up.

Jim: Why? What are you afraid you're going to hear?

Me: That Sila's planning to harm Tork. On one hand I'm really curious, on the other hand I don't want to know. I don't want to deal with it.

Jim: What else were you feeling, then?

Me: That I'm not doing enough for the commune.

Jim: In what way?

Me: What *am* I doing? Nothing. I'm flying off to Washington, New York and Utah, interviewing big shots. The rest of the time, I'm sitting in the phone monitoring room at the Ranch. I'm not going out to the public and standing up for our rights and beliefs.

Jim: Is this what you think Diva means by being strong?

Me: Yes.

Jim: OK. What do you both do next?

Me: We go to our Portland Hotel to meet Belle.

Maya: Eve's going to meet Belle at the airport, and then we'll all drive out to Tork's house.

Me: Why?

Maya: To clue Belle in on what we're doing.

Me: OK. When she arrives, she's wearing a blue skirt,

which doesn't fit her, and a white blouse with sleeves past her fingers. I get into the back seat with Belle while Maya takes the driver's seat and Eve sits next to her.

Belle: I feel so uncomfortable in these clothes! They don't even fit me... let's get on the road and get this over with. So, where are you guys taking me?

Eve: We're bringing you out to the house.

Belle: House? I thought it was an apartment. Didn't you guys say you were taking me to the apartment?

Eve: No, we're taking you to Tork's house.

Belle: Well, we gotta make this fast cause I have to get back to the Hotel for the press conference. Now, what's all this about Tork and his house?

Me: I'm trying to identify him. And since he doesn't give interviews at his office, I had to go to his house.

Belle: Yeah, yeah, yeah. I know that. Come on, what else?

Me: His phone's unlisted, so I thought I'd catch him at his house and ask him for an interview there, but Eve said that was a stupid idea.

Belle: So, sounds like nothing to me. What have you come *up* with?

Me: Yesterday I found his car in the garage at the courthouse. So, if I miss him at home, I'll see him there.

Belle: Sounds like a waste of time to me.

Me: But I have to get *something* on this guy to appease Sila.

Eve: You know Sila said she wants to get rid of him.

Belle: You mean, kill him?

Eve: Yup. That's right. That's what Sila said.

Belle: THAT'S LOONEY!

Me: Yes, it *is* crazy, Belle, but I think she could be persuaded to go through the lawyers...

Eve: *But,* we've gotta consider doing this, if this is what Sila wants.

Belle: That's ridiculous! What's that gonna do?

Eve: Sila seems to think that if we kill Tork, the investigation against the commune will stop, or at least it will throw a big wrench into it.

Me: Belle, what do you think? This is really dangerous. I don't think that is a good idea at all.

Belle: No, this doesn't feel good to me either.

Jim: Are you asking her for help?

Me: Yes. I wanted her guidance to end this whole discussion once and for all.

Jim: Do you and Belle talk further about the killing idea?

Me: Yes. I ask her: how can we even consider doing such a thing? Should we even be *discussing* it?

Belle: You know, Samsara, Sila's crazy right now. She comes up with a lot of outrageous ideas. I don't know what to think any more. It's NUTS. You want my opinion? I think it's dumb. Now, take me back to the hotel.

Jim: What's Samsara thinking at this point?

Me: I don't know what I'm going to do. I hoped Sila would be satisfied with my research but now I see that it's much worse than I thought. Even Belle won't help me. I better get out of this whole thing before anything dangerous starts. What am I going to tell Eve? What am I going to tell Sila? I'm really scared of these guys. I wish the whole thing would just go away...

Jim: Then what do you do?

Me: I go back to the apartment with Eve.

Jim: What does Eve say to you?

Eve: We've got to think about taking stronger steps, you know. The whole defense of the commune is at stake.

Jim: What are you thinking?

Me: What does that mean, the "*whole defense* of the commune is at stake?" By killing *Tork?* That doesn't make sense. But Eve is much better informed about plots against the commune. Maybe these people *are* enemies. Maybe I have to *think* it over carefully. Hey, Eve, do you think we *really* should consider this?

Eve: Of course! It's just an *idea*. Nothing has to be *done*.

Bhagwan always tells us to think about all possibilities, even if they go beyond the norm. It might not be *practical.*

Me: What do you mean practical?

Eve: I don't even know if it's possible; if we could even *do* it.

Me: I've only seen it done in movies. In *real life?* I can't even... how would you do something like this?

Jim: What are you feeling right now?

Me: Nervous. Sweaty. Scared. My mind is saying: this is a movie and this is a movie script. This is not real. I have to talk it out no matter how awful or strange or dangerous it feels. The commune's at stake.

Jim: What else did you say to Eve?

Me: But, we don't even know what he *looks* like. This is *absurd.* Even to *think* about such an idea is nuts.

Eve: Maybe nothing's possible.

Me: Right. Maybe nothing's possible. Maybe if we actually went *through* a scenario in our heads we would see we couldn't do it.

Jim: Are you saying this or hoping this?

Me: Both. I'm saying the words and desperately hoping that if we just think about it we'll see that this is absurd. Nothing would be accomplished *and* that would surely be the end of this horrible idea.

Jim: How do you feel about Eve?

Me: Scared. I'm scared she'll talk me into this. Now, I'm even *considering* a scenario of killing someone, where previously I wouldn't have even thought about it. As soon as she mentioned Bhagwan, I felt *compelled* to look at killing as an option. Tork was a threat to the commune and he had to be eliminated. But, I don't want to talk about it any more with Eve. I just want to appear strong so she will leave me alone.

Jim: Let's move ahead to the next time you go on surveillance and the mention of getting rid of Tork comes up. Where are you and who are you with?

Me: The next day. I'm sitting in the car. Eve and Diva are in the front seat, Maya's in the back seat with me. Eve's driving.

Eve: Let's park the car, walk around and really think this thing through.

Jim: What are you feeling?

Me: Cold. Clammy. Frightened.

Eve: In the movies, somebody has to stop the car and then somebody else shoots the guy. Of course we'd have to use silencers.

Jim: What are you doing?

Me: Thinking. *This is surreal, happening too fast. I have to say something.*

What would happen *after* the man gets shot?

Eve: Then, um, there has to be a getaway car.

Maya: Well, Narian could drive it. He could park the car up there and wait, but that's clumsy... not practical.

Me: You know, this is like a really bad movie. What? You mean we're going to do a rehearsal?

Diva: Yeah, but that doesn't sound like it'll work. That's pretty stupid. I mean, what are we gonna do? Somebody's gonna stop this car, then somebody's gonna jump out and shoot him? Then, we're gonna get in the car and drive away? Sounds messy to me.

Jim: What are you feeling and thinking as this goes on?

Me: I don't want it to be happening. When Diva says that she thinks it won't work I feel relief.

Jim: What happened after Diva says that?

Maya: Listen you guys this sounds really nuts. What does the car look like anyway?

Me: I'm not sure. I *think* I found his car, but I'm not positive.

Maya: Well why don't we go to the garage. All of us can see what his car looks like

Me: Yes, let's get out of here. I just want all this to stop. It's *crazy.*

Jim: What about wrong?

Me: In this situation, there's no wrong or right. Bhagwan and Sila are the only right. I couldn't get to wrong.

Jim: OK. Now, leave that for the moment and go back. Did you go directly to the garage from there?

Me: Yes.

Jim: Did you find the car?

Me: Yes.

Jim: And, what did you do then? Did you say anything?

Me: Yes. This is the same car I saw before with Diva.

Jim: And what are you doing in the garage?

Me: Four of us walk toward this car. I say, OK, fellas, you saw the car, now let's go. I don't like walking around in this garage.

Maya: Wait a minute, wait a minute. Let's look at the car. Let's think about this…what could we do with this car?

Me: Berry one time had the idea of putting sugar in a carburetor.

Maya: Sugar in a *carburetor*?

Me: Yes! Berry said that if you put sugar in the carburetor, it stops the car.

Maya: Well. *She laughs.* I was thinking we should put something *under* the car.

Diva: I think Narian would be the person to ask about that. He knows about cars.

Me: I'm frightened, even more than before. *I can't breathe.* I say, listen; let's get out of here. I don't like being here. I don't feel comfortable with this…

Jim: What are you doing now?

Me: I'm walking toward the elevators.

Jim: What are the others doing?

Me: They're talking. I don't want to hear what they're saying. That was the end of the talking for me. I don't want to be here or in this thing *anymore!* I feel like I'm going to black out…

Jim: Samsara, just breathe slowly and deeply. Do you want to rest? Do you want to come out and rest for a while before we continue?

Me: No. I'm upset, agitated, I say, come on you guys, let's go.

Jim: Do the others say anything?

Me: Diva's talking to Eve, saying this is really a crazy idea. Maya's laughing.

I have to get out now.

Jim: OK. For the moment, let's leave the garage. We can come back there, but instead, let's just pause and take a deep breath. Do you want to stop?

Me: No.

Jim: Where do you want to go, now?

Me: Back to the road. Something's unfinished there.

Jim: Where? What's coming up?

Me: When the word silencer was mentioned, I went cold, like something in me disconnected. *God. Guns. I don't want anything to do with guns.*

Jim: Do you say anything about the guns? Do you say anything about being the shooter, yourself?

Me: No. I'm not even trained to shoot, like the others are.

Jim: How do you know the others are trained to shoot?

Me: Because they are all on the security team and I've seen all of them carry weapons.

Jim: So, there's no one saying, either jokingly or seriously that you should be the shooter?

Me: No.

Jim: Did anyone say that Sila *said* that Samsara wants to be the shooter?

Me: No.

Jim: Now, listen very carefully and see if it comes up anywhere... let your fingers relax... see if you get a pull... as if you're watching the whole thing unfold... you're stumbling around out there... if anyone says anything about you being the shooter?

Me: I shake my head.

Jim: No? OK. Go back to the garage and then leave. How do you feel?

Me: Alone. Scared. Cold. Shaking. Sick. There's a new sensation: I'm on the inside of something big. But left out, somehow. And abandoned.

Jim: Who's abandoning you?

Me: God. Bhagwan.

Jim: Let's go a little deeper, now. Is there a part of you that knows if these people are rehearsing or not?

Me: I nod.

Jim: Then let's go deeper into that part of your mind that knows.

Me: They're capable of doing *anything*. They have the kind of power that Bhagwan gives to those in charge, where there are no rules. They can do anything they want for the good of Bhagwan's work, whether it's killing themselves or somebody else who's labeled an enemy, destroying his work.

Jim: And do you want to be one of them?

Me: *Hesitates.* Yes... I really *want* to be a part of them and have that power. That's what Bhagwan has, and what I wanted all along. I *wish* I could be powerful like them. Diva talks about strength; Maya laughs. Eve's matter-of-fact and I'm the only one who's scared. I better not show it, or they'll reject me, put me down for not defending the commune... I can't let them see that I'm not a part of them.

Jim: Why not?

Me: I'm afraid.

Jim: Afraid of what?

Me: Failing. Like I failed Sila when I had anorexia.

Jim: How did you fail this time?

Me: I haven't done what I set out to do. If I had come up with some wonderful piece of information on how to deal with Tork through the courts, this wouldn't be happening.

Jim: Sounds to me like you feel guilty; if you had done your job, they wouldn't be thinking about killing Tork.

Me: That's right. If I'd done my job, I could have changed things.

Jim: So, what happens after the garage?

Me: I go back to the Ranch.

Jim: Did you ever see Tork's house again?

Me: No.

Jim: No? You're sure?

Me: Yes, I'm sure. I didn't want to see that house or the garage again. Never.

Jim: What happens at the Ranch?

Me: I go to my cabin, where I can be alone to think. I have to think this through by myself and come to a decision.

Jim: And what are you thinking?

Me: That these ideas couldn't ever work. We would fail, be caught and achieve nothing. It's too dangerous. I have to separate the scenario from the people. Is there anything to gain whatsoever by killing, even an enemy? To destroy somebody in order to prevent him from destroying something doesn't stop the destruction. It only increases it. What are we becoming? We came to this Ranch to live in peace and harmony and what are we *doing*? *Killing* people? I've investigated so many groups, and nothing good ever comes from destruction. We're becoming just like them. We *can't* go in this direction. They must *see* this!

Jim: Then what do you do?

Me: I go to bed.

Jim: Are you wondering what they might do?

Me: No. I'm too exhausted. But, as soon as I wake up my first thought is: what are they gonna do next?

Jim: And did you try and find out?

Me: Yes. I went to Jesus Grove. A million people are there preparing for the festival. It's clear to me that nothing more can happen now because everybody's busy. But, I can't get it out of my mind. What happened out there on the road *must* have been a dream. I must have been overtired... Diva said the idea wasn't practical, so that must mean that's the end of it. And, if *anybody* would know, she would. She's a big deal around here, way above *me* in command.

Jim: During these next two weeks, up till the 4th or 5th of July, did you speak with Sila about the surveillance?

Me: I tried several times. Each time I went to her room before work at 6:00 AM or after 11:00 PM, but she was never alone. I was exhausted, worried about what was going on that I wasn't being told; as well as the increasing number of fights between Bhagwan and Viviananda. All my ideas about enlightenment were being shattered. How many years do you have to be a disciple before you're free from these mundane jealousies? What about the people running the Ranch, prepared to eliminate those in their way? And where was Bhagwan in all this? Not helping any of us. There was nobody to talk to. I could identify with Viviananda feeling left out and ignored. That was the way I felt, too.

Jim: Let's move ahead to the time when you are finally able to talk to Sila about Tork, and not continuing with the research.

Me: The day that Bhagwan's doctor collapsed in Buddha Hall, I went to Jesus Grove on my break, and I noticed Sila sitting with Diva in her bedroom. I seized the opportunity to talk to her about Tork.

Jim: Why did you wait until she was alone?

Me: Because no one was ever supposed to know what anyone else did, except your immediate co-workers.

Jim: So, what happened?

Me: Sila saw me and told Diva to go and rest. After she left I said: Sila, I've got something I have to tell you.

Sila: What is it?

Me: I'm dropping all the research on Tork. Finished. As far as I'm concerned, it's useless and a waste of time. Look, if you take my advice as I said from the beginning, Tork's under the Justice Department, so we should research them instead. Please put an end to this, and concentrate...

Sila: Samsara, don't bother me with this now. I have enough to think about. All right, fine, that's the end to it, OK. OK?

Jim: What did you feel once you told her?

Me: Relieved. It's finished. I even took his yearbook picture, tore it up and threw it away.

Jim: Was that the end of it?

Me: Yes. Sila was obviously overwhelmed with other things,

so her attention was diverted. I convinced myself nothing further was going to happen.

Jim: OK, Samsara, I want to ask you, now that you've answered all the questions I have here, is there anything that still puzzles you? Any unanswered questions that your unconscious feels the need to answer? Let your fingers answer...No? OK. Are you ready to come back? Fully present? OK. 1-2-3-4-knowing that we're really done, 99%... 100%. Back. How're you feeling?

"Empty. Not bad. Just empty. Light."

"We've been here for eight and a half hours."

"It feels like a few, long minutes."

"And, do you remember what you just saw?"

"Oh, yes. Clearly."

"Does this change how you feel about what you did?"

"Completely. One thing I never saw before is that the others may have been carrying out instructions from Sila to get information on Tork in order to develop plans I wasn't told about. Also, I didn't realize how afraid I was of the power structure and how much I was drawn to it, trying to please everybody, going along with everyone, trying to fit in."

"Your fear may have been the blocking force that resulted in this fog you've been feeling. Sometimes we don't want to see what's too horrible to look at."

"I definitely didn't want to see violence in a 'peaceful' commune that I had dedicated my life to. Deep down I was also afraid that if I spoke against killing openly, they might kill me too!"

"I think you should rest, now. You've been through a lot today!"

"All right, Jim. I'll lie down a bit before I talk to Trish."

"Good idea."

I told Jim I wanted to be alone for a while.

Trish's gonna tell me that it's of no use to consider trial now, and there's nothing to make a deal with, because I'd be in the position of having to answer questions about others under oath, which means I'd have to expose everyone's involvement. I won't do that.

I can't plead guilty to conspiring to murder because I didn't conspire to murder Tork. I conspired to consider *it, as a good sannyasin, and came up with the decision not to murder him... I am both guilty and not guilty.*

I need to find a solution to this... I've got to pray.

Finally, something exploded in my head. I suddenly remembered when I was in Germany in 1986. Sarah and I were researching Sila's legal options for her murder case and we came upon the "Alford Plea."

In 1963, Mr. Alford was indicted for first-degree murder in North Carolina. Witnesses didn't support Alford's story, giving statements instead that strongly indicated his guilt. Faced with this, and no substantial evidentiary support for his claim of innocence, Alford's attorney recommended that he plead guilty but left the ultimate decision to Alford himself. Alford denied he committed the murder, but pled guilty to avoid a possible death sentence. By pleading guilty he would save the state from having to pay for a trial; but he could state his account for the record. Alford then entered his plea, giving his version of the events stating:

"I pleaded guilty... because they said there's too much evidence, but I ain't shot no man. I take the fault for the other man. We never had an argument in our life and I just pleaded guilty because they said if I didn't they would gas me for it..."

He didn't do what they accused him of, but was in a similar situation to mine, damned by hearsay. He wanted however to tell the court exactly what he did do. If I use this plea, I'm responsible for myself. I can tell the Feds that I'll plead guilty to what I did and only that. And, everybody will be spared the suffering of a trial and the media circus along with it. If the court accepts it, they will sentence me.

It's the solution.

It's the miracle I've been searching for.

Chapter 14
Direct From London and New York:
Miss Theodora Duncan

You were once wild here. Don't let them tame you. – Isadora Duncan

After the hypnosis I returned home.

Dad greeted me somberly shaking his head after I announced that Trish said I could get five years. He then asked the identical question he had raised four times previously.

"You still haven't answered me: did you kill somebody?"

I looked him the eye and said what I had every other time.

"No dad, I told you, I didn't kill anybody. Nobody's dead."

"Well if nobody's dead, why is the government making such a big deal and spending all this money on prosecuting you?"

I looked at him and shrugged my shoulders. Mom retreated to the kitchen.

From that point on, there was nothing further I could say because I saw how bewildering the whole situation must have appeared to them. I was also very tired. I was running out of energy and I still had to write this Alford Plea.

By mid-August 1991 I had written four single-spaced pages explaining to the Court that I was taking responsibility for being part of discussions to kill George Tork. I also described how I came to my own decision not to harm him and to persuade Sila to end surveillance of him.

I sent the finished plea to Trish and she called me as soon as she received it.

"Samsara, Fronten's never going to accept this."

"Make him. Do what ever you have to do."

"It's a waste of time. He - they - won't."

"Make them, Trish. You have to. I won't do this any other way."

On August 29th, right in the middle of dinner, Trish called me again.

"Samsara, are you sitting down? They are going to accept your plea. They want five years. I told them, that's too long, that's more than any of the others had received. But they won't budge. They don't like it, so this is their way to deal with it."

The revenge. "At least they are accepting it Trish. Maybe the Judge will recommend camp or give me probation."

"We can try."

I put the phone down, returning to eating dinner. They looked up at me, worried.

"The government will take the plea I wrote. In exchange they want five years."

"Five years where?" Dad asked angrily.

"I don't know yet. Maybe I'll get probation. Maybe camp here in Phoenix."

That was the end of the conversation.

My sentencing hearing was set for November 16th, 1991.

That morning in Portland was gray and steely cold.

I walked into Court with Trish and immediately saw Fronten. His face was an opaque mask.

Ten minutes later Judge Wallace entered solemnly and sat down.

My body was a suit of armor, presenting a composed unbreakable facade. Inside I was shaking and full of grief, alternating between feeling icy cold and burning hot. It was hard to breathe. I had to keep telling myself, breathe... breathe, I didn't want to convey any of this to the Court, otherwise I knew I would break down and sob from the overwhelming pressure. My clothes were saturated with sweat and my skin was clammy despite the coldness in the air.

Trish opened with a statement from Jim Cordon.

"I am going to read the following statement from Dr. James Cordon, the Court appointed psychiatrist, from his evaluation of my client, which confirms our position."

As Trish was reading the long ten-page statement, I felt a pleasant warmth take the chill out of my bones. Jim had understood.

"'...It is my firm conviction that at no time did this lifelong pacifist expect to participate in the conspiracy... in her own confused, dependent, defensive, self-defensive and fear-deluded way, she was indeed trying to forestall any harm befalling George Tork.'"

Trish finished by stating Dr. Cordon's opinion that prison would be detrimental to my health.

I hoped this would make a difference to my sentencing.

It didn't.

The government countered with their own statement, and accepted the plea, agreeing to drop the second count of weapons trafficking, which was a moot point. The German Court had found no basis for the weapons trafficking whatsoever and demanded it be dropped as a condition of extradition.

They then recommended five years for wiretapping and five years for conspiracy, both to run concurrently.

Trish interjected vehemently. She stood up.

"Your Honor, I strongly object to the verdict on wire tapping. None of the others ever received any prison time at all."

Judge Wallace interrupted. "I reluctantly accept this Alford Plea and I must admit that I waited a long time for the defendant to withdraw it. But she didn't. I find this document to be very transparent. There are holes in it."

My thoughts stopped. I couldn't listen to him. My breath stuck in my chest, choking me.

How could he not believe me? How could he not believe Jim Cordon?

I came back to reality forcefully. The Judge looked directly at me and addressed his next question.

"Samsara Drake, are you submitting this Plea to the Court?"

"Yes, I am, your Honor."

"Is there anything you wish to change in this Plea?"

"No your Honor."

The Judge looked at me, narrowing his eyes. Without skipping a beat, he said, "The Court hereby sentences you to five years in Federal prison for conspiracy to murder George Tork and five years for wiretapping. Both sentences to run concurrently."

Trish jumped to her feet. "Your Honor, would the Court please recommend the defendant be remanded to Phoenix camp so that she can at least be close to her sick and elderly parents as they are unable to travel to see her?"

"No, Miss Peterson. The gravity of the situation, and high security risk surrounding a dangerous felon with such a crime as this, demands the defendant be housed in Federal administrative prison."

I felt faint, but I was relieved it was over at last. Like a soldier at the end of a long battle, where there was no win, I was simply left with not having given in, even though the cost was extreme.

Trish turned to me, eyes full of hurt and sadness, snarling under her breath, "They gave you more time than anybody else!"

My self-commit entrance date to Dublin Federal Prison in California was December 16ᵗʰ, 1991. I was designated self-commit, meaning they trusted me, a "dangerous felon," to get myself there. I was told that this counted as extra points toward my 'good time,' which meant the time came off the back of my sentence so I could be released earlier, saving the government money in transport fees.

The morning I left for prison was pure hell.

"Can I send you vitamins?" Mom asked me, as she set down the bowls of food on the table, afraid to say too much.

"No, Ma. They will think the vitamins are drugs and probably throw me in the hole if you send them."

"What's a hole?" Dad had to say something. I could see the pain in his eyes and hear the heaviness in his voice.

"That's solitary confinement where they put you if you mess up."

"You won't *mess up*," Mom said quickly. She looked down at her feet and quickly turned to walk out of the kitchen.

That left Dad and me sitting there over a cold breakfast.

"I'll call you when I get to Dublin," I said, barely able to get the words out.

There was so much more I wanted to share... so much I knew they wanted to say... it was like we were all about to die and didn't know how to talk about it.

The drive to the station was long and suffocating.

I hugged them and started crying, which embarrassed Mom and agitated Dad.

Neither of them spoke as I got on the bus.

"Goodbye, I'll miss you," spilled out of my mouth.

They were both standing on the platform as the bus pulled away. Dad had tears but he wouldn't let them come. Mom was like a smokestack about to explode.

I was bawling. Hot stinging tears poured out of my eyes. I didn't care who saw me. There was no one else on that bus as far as I was concerned. There was only me, Mom and Dad caught in that moment, still frozen and forever carved in my soul.

Will I see them alive, again? Will they survive the shock? They are both so frail and can't travel to see me.

I closed my eyes on that smelly bus, longing for some escape, going back in time to 1986 and that world of the bar and the girls.

That whole world would have remained unknown - if I hadn't gone behind that curtain....

Chapter 15
Seduction and Conquest

I confess I find more ecstasy in passion than in prayer. Such passion is prayer. Such surrender has been mine. I hunger still to be filled and inflamed, to melt into the dream of us, beyond this troubled place to where we are not even ourselves. To know that always, always, this is mine.

-Dangerous Beauty (a film based on the book Honest Courtesan)

In 1986 I met my first real live call girls. Known in Germany as *bar damen*, they were "high-class" prostitutes. I'd always thought New York prostitutes looked sleazy, because I'd only seen streetwalkers. In Baden-Baden, however, the German *bar damen* looked elegant, like *geishas*.

I was surprised, fascinated... *and* instantly hooked.

I *did* need money. My first experience of earning fifty marks for twenty minutes of conversation, reminded me of college when my power to attract a man was first awakened. The same force was in me that night. Hunger to be set on fire and desire to be wanted became what I lived for and craved. That fire sustained my life. Sex was my food, and hooking men became my fix.

Each experience was different. Each man longed for a connection, kindness, warmth and friendship. Bhagwan taught me to regard sex as a door to enlightenment, giving me the name "Prem Samsara." *Prem* meant love in Hindi and Samsara, eternal cycle of death and rebirth. All I had to do was *love* them and they would be reborn, bringing me more money.

Perfect arrangement.

Plus, I was in good company, for I had entered the world of the *courtesan:* highly educated, well versed in the arts of pleasure, good taste and expert devotion to be sought by statesmen, or at least wealthy businessmen.

There were younger *damen* with their teenage looks and too eager, too perfumed, too made-up aggressive approach. Then there were a few of us "older ladies" offering subtle seduction and perhaps something more. An odd sense of fulfillment settled inside the hollow space, emptied when I left Bhagwan and the commune. I finally belonged somewhere. I walked into a dazzling world, full of dark mystery.

However, my newly found fulfillment was in jeopardy.

My attempt to marry and earn European citizenship had failed. My American passport was about to expire.

Hearing of my plight one evening, a British acquaintance casually offered a solution.

"Why not get a British passport, luv?"

"How would I do *that*?"

"Oh, I've read about it in several spy books! Quite common knowledge, really! All you have to do is go to a cemetery and look at all the headstones until you find a child. The odds are that a child wouldn't have registered for a passport yet. Then, go to the Hall of Records and look up her name and the date she died. That'll give you where she died and where she was born. Then you just go to the birth registry and request a birth certificate. Anybody can request one. You just have to pay a small fee.

"Once you have the birth certificate, you can apply for a

travel pass on the underground with your picture on it. That's your second ID. Then go to the Post Office and they will issue you a temporary passport, which will allow you to travel. It's that easy. That'll even let you work in England, if you want."

Thirteen days left.

I had to try it.

I left for England the next day on a flight to London. To my amazement, it was unbelievably easy to get the papers of Margaret Camilla Bonham, a young child who died at four. Two days later I had a temporary passport.

Back in Germany - where residents have to "register" with authorities - I had to go back to the same city where I had previously registered in my name, Samsara. There I learned that I needed a *permanent* British passport in order to work in Germany.

I had to go back to London again and apply at the passport office.

That was not so easy.

Five days left only and still no permanent passport.

Her Majesty's Passport Office required an interview.

They might want to know why I had waited 54 years (Margaret's age had she lived) to apply.

Many Britons apply for their passports as soon as they start work. In London, I went straight to the Passport Office, filled out the paperwork and sat down to wait for the interview. I was scared, uncertain and still speaking like a New Yorker. I kept going over the story I had come up with, which was that I had devoted my life to caring for my aging parents. Since they died, I now wanted to travel. In addition to making the story believable, I had to learn to control my facial expressions, like a good dour Brit, and not display any emotion – like fear or uncertainty. I tried to sound like an ordinary small-town English woman, whatever that was, and appear completely confident.

As I was waiting, the man sitting in front of me started to chat.

"Where're ya from, luv-y? What ya doin' 'ere?"

"Chelsea, actually. I'm applying for a new passport."

"Don't sound like ya're from Chelsea."

Damn! My accent's not good enough. How am I going to get through this interview? Will they believe me?

"Well, luv" I said in my best Cockney accent. "Not all 'o us sound like ya, ya know!"

Unsure as I thought I was, my matronly British interviewer mercifully believed me.

Still, the passport had to be processed and approved. They might discover the fraud and send me to a British jail. I had to wait seventy-two hours.

On the morning of the third day, nervous and unsteady, not knowing if I would be arrested or collect a passport, I went back to the government office. They handed me Margaret's new passport.

Then I went to the loo, broke down and cried, right there in the grimy passport office lavatory. This passport meant I could continue my life.

In Germany, Samsara Drakke had to de-register in the same office as I now had to re-register as Margaret Bonham. Fortunately "D" was in a different room to "B"

Hairy, nonetheless.

Afterwards when I saw someone in the street who had known me as Samsara, I turned and walked quickly away to avoid them.

I wonder if this is how Jews felt in 1940's Europe.

By November, the tension of trying to juggle two identities and work in bars in two different cities ten kilometers apart, began to show. I lost so much weight that my clothes began to hang on me. My ribs stuck out. I really was a Jew in hiding.

It was time to move to a different city and away from the apartment I was sharing with Sarah and Narian.

That meant separating from the only people here who knew of my true situation. Although I didn't spend much time with them, as our schedules were opposite, it was a comfort to me to know that they were there, silently supporting me.

One Saturday morning in our kitchen, I broke down sobbing. Sarah and I were having breakfast.

"Sarah, I have to move! I can't stay here any longer trying to be two different people. And, it's not good for either you or Narian. I don't want to leave you! You're the only ones here who have any idea of what I'm going through. But, if I have to move, I don't know how I can continue this horrible struggle alone."

"Why, Samsara! I didn't know that it was weighing so heavily on you! I wish you'd told me sooner. We'll look for a place for all of us in Baden-Baden."

Her words lifted my burden right off my shoulders.

A couple of weeks later the three of us moved to Baden-Baden, a magical city that had once been the summer retreat of the wealthy. In the Roman days, the Emperor Caracalla had built a large outdoor spa, which still bears his name. There is a famous casino, which gives the city the air of Monte Carlo and the French Riviera. The cobblestone streets contain quaint shops designed at the turn of the century. Baden-Baden was one of the few German cities not destroyed in World War II. The central square was always buzzing with languages from all over Europe, as the city was a favored vacation and convention spot, with its mild climate and many amenities. There was also a French army base on the outskirts, as well as Canadian and American bases nearby. This made my bar work very lucrative, because men from every walk of life came here in abundance.

For the first time in many, many years, I felt at home. In Baden-Baden, no one questioned me. None of the Germans, except Hans Georg (whom we called HG), a former employer, business acquaintance and now friend, knew the Samsara of before. HG had known us since 1986 when he hired Ruby to be his housekeeper. She liked him so much that she brought him to meet our little band of outcasts. From that time he helped all of us find odd jobs. He also helped me move apartments, while I "taught" him English in exchange. We practiced speaking English and he became another one of my big brothers.

It was HG I called upon to negotiate with landlords, dentists and doctors as well as hang the lights in our new apartment. We talked about my not knowing the sexual quirks of the German males and his not knowing what to do with his jealous girlfriends. He was an expert in everything except women. He liked the attention and knowing that he was so desirable. Which he was.

I was safe with HG. He related to me like a sister, calling me by my nickname Theodora. He never minded that I worked in the bars, and was very sympathetic to my wailings over Marianne, the very greedy bar owner. He helped mop up my broken spirits when the men made demands I couldn't fulfill like asking me to meet them in private or do bondage positions. Nothing shocked HG and I didn't probe why. I was just Theodora, a simple misplaced ex-cultie who landed in his Germany.

Meanwhile, while Sarah, Narian and I were in Baden-Baden, the rest of our little "gang" had scattered.

Sila, Diva and Kiku were still in prison in the U.S. following the raid in Haüsern. Belle went to live in South Africa with her mother who was dying, while Ruby, Diana and Maya went to England. Ruby went so she could find a decent job. Diana went because she was an Irish citizen by marriage and could work and be close to Ruby. Maya, who had British citizenship from a former marriage, fell in love with Charlize, a wealthy businesswoman, who lived in London. Puneet was in Berlin, with a new lover who was helping him to get treatment for his AIDS.

Though I came to work in Club Diana before I became Margaret, I never used the name Samsara or Margaret in the bar. From the start, the girls advised me to adopt a "bar name" so the clientele would not try to track me down outside. Our private lives remained protected. Even we didn't know each other's real names.

'Theodora' was my nickname from my former days of political research in the U.S. Working steadfastly, night after night, my course of action became clearer. Once I had earned enough money and it was safe to go back to the U.S., my Margaret identity would be dropped. I yearned to be simple again: one name, one life. No more being torn between two identities, neither of which seemed quite real.

I've changed so much, I hardly know who I really am. Am I Samsara, the researcher, who elbowed her way into federal offices to please her bosses? Or am I the confused, disoriented Samsara who left one world and landed in another? Am I proper Margaret, the 54 year old? Or Theodora, the bar courtesan? A woman who wanted money, sex and power? Or a helping minister? Did I want only to control? Or to be thrilled and dominated?.

One night in the summer of 1987, the owner of Club Diana approached me.

"Theodora, why don't you start dancing?"

"I have varicose veins, Marianne, how could I possibly striptease? You *are* kidding!"

"That's not a problem, Theodora, wear black stockings and a garter belt, and just take everything else off. If you think you can make it work and earn me money, just do what you want."

That was all the invitation I needed.

When I began working at the bar, a simple black dress, stockings and garters were my standard. I was ashamed of my varicose veins.

The next night, somewhat hesitantly, somewhat eagerly, I walked slowly onto the stage. Then I closed my eyes waiting for the music. I stood, motionless, feeling only the lights beating on my skin as the rhythm started.

Leisurely my hands moved to my hair, my fingers spreading through the strands. My head undulated back and forth, turning and turning. My shoulders, ignorant of my hands and arms, moved in opposite directions, as the beat carried my body to a space my mind didn't know about. Twirling and swaying, I became a conduit for the sound, speaking a separate language. The hands playing me were somebody else's from another time, like the goddess Kali with a thousand arms and legs in every direction.

Slowly, slowly the dress came down over my waist, over my legs moving by itself. My body bending forward with it, crumpled as though the dress was guiding it to the floor into a kneeling position. It was prayer...Thick air and perfume pulled me into a swoon toward somewhere luminous.

I could hear thumping sounds around me. It was as if watchers were breathing me on. Then my pelvis moved all by itself down onto the floor of the stage; I was a snake slithering out of its skin. I took this skin, my dress, and tossed it towards the bar, as the stage took my nakedness and my legs pressed flat against the floor, thrust my body upwards. Raising my breasts, like an electric cobra, to the eyes in front of me, my mouth opened with a long "uh-h-h".

Everyone in the bar was staring at me.

The music finished and I, flushed with warmth, stood up. The lights blotted out people's faces. I couldn't see what the audience was doing, so I had no idea what they thought.

There was silence.

Oh, my God, it freaked them out! Marianne will fire me!

Then, all of a sudden, there was a thunderous applause and shouting: "Bravo!" "Wow!" "I want her!"

Looking up hesitantly at the faces, I saw a hunger in the eyes that looked back at me. It was a longing for something to be satisfied. Two men walked over to me as I was gathering my clothes, asking me to join them.

Nobody has seen this kind of dancing in a strip bar before. If Isadora Duncan were still alive, she'd be so proud of me.

In her spirit, my stage presence, "Miss Theodora Duncan" was born.

Isadora Duncan never cared what people thought of her. She simply got on the stage and let her creative spirit speak through her movements, revolutionizing the traditional ballet form into expressionism. I wanted to be a revolutionary like her. I found myself doing the unthinkable: exposing a body that I had always thought of as ugly to a crowd of strange men because it thrilled me.

I was also embarrassed. I didn't have the unblemished, model-figure that many of the dancers in the bar had. But I could dance. The lines of my body melted into the music, like twittering pulses supported by every beat.

The bar guests adored all this. The other dancers didn't. Otto was one of my regulars, an intelligent self-made industrialist from Stuttgart, who, when he saw me said, "Theodora I feel like you are making love to me on that stage!"

"My dear Otto, you are with me there."

And so he was.

When I walked on stage I looked right at the man I had just been sitting with and worshipped him. It was a message of pure gratitude to each guest for being with me, paying attention to me, appreciating me and paying me.

Club Diana was just the beginning.

I gradually discovered this sleeping talent and had to explore it, before time and my body's aging, took it away from me. I had a limited number of months, perhaps a year or two, before leaving Germany, and this was possibly the only country where my imperfect body would be accepted and admired. I certainly could never compete with the American Barbie-doll. European men were much more forgiving, not all of them turned on by the plastic silicone image.

"You know, Theodora," Otto continued, "I hate those aluminum tits that the other dancers have. I don't know a man alive who likes them, except to gawk at them, once in a while. But you can't touch them! You can't squeeze them, like real tits... like yours. You touch those fake things and you feel like you are touching rocks! Phew!!" Otto and several of the others told me this more than once.

I always thought the pumped up tits were every man's

dream. But perhaps women really wanted them to impress other women.

When men confided in me I felt needed.

Wilhelm, another regular who had a local construction business, whispered, "I can't talk to my wife ze way I talk to you, my Theodora. You understand me so vell. I zink I don't know how to speak wiz women too vell, and wiz you I am not afraid to zay exactly ze ting on my mindt!"

Ah! German-English accents are so delightful.

"Ze others make fun of my aczent, but not yew... it is so spezial to be wiz such a woman!"

It was impossible for me not to be in a constant state of fascination. The more I worked, the more I wanted to work. More and more men kept coming.

My work became a drug that tantalized and enraptured me. Not only did I have a mission to introduce these men to the divine energy in sex; but it was to lead them into a holy tantric temple. I wove a mystique around them, transporting them into another dimension. My passion was my prayer: virginal and ecstatic.

I blossomed in the power to tease and enchant them, psychoanalyze and restore them, bringing them to new heights of their own sexual prowess, which lay dormant inside of them.

And, of course, there was the money.

I received a percentage on the sale of all drinks. My first piccolo drink netted me fifty marks; for each drink thereafter I made about ten or fifteen marks, depending on Marianne's mood. If I talked the man into "buying me a bottle" of German Sekt or Champagne, the prices ranged from 250 marks for the cheapest bottle of Sekt to 900 marks for Dom Peringnon. At times it was 100 marks on a 250-mark bottle and up to 650 marks on the 900-mark bottle.

By February of that year, after I started dancing, I had earned 5,400 marks and by August I had earned 23,000 marks or in American dollars, approximately $20,000. This was more than I made the entire two years I had been a psychotherapist in New York. Since I lived very simply, I was able to save most of what I earned and my legal defense fund grew. I even put aside some money to buy costumes for my acts. Hats, scarves, leather tunics, romantic garters, gloves and matching stockings, enabled men to picture me as the women of their dreams: as femme fatales, Mata Haris, Salomes, or whoever they wanted me to be.

I created a mood, a vision, where they could be kings, heroes, even legends. I penetrated to the core of what these men so deeply and desperately craved: to be gods in the eyes of a woman. Since this was exactly how I saw them, they kept coming back to me. And they paid me royally.

I found a way to use my psychoanalytic skills in my conversations so they could drop their guard, lay their worries at my feet and for a little while become Titans. In this way I persuaded the "guests" to buy the bottles and remain in the bar, without always going with them into the private separee.

But not all guests were willing to be enchanted in the public area of the bar. The noise, distraction and constant intrusions from various bartenders forced the guests to drink more, order more, pay more.

Luise, Marianne's bartender was famous for these annoyances.

"Otto, why don't you order Theodora a BIG bottle of champagne, now, um? You know how thirsty she is!"

Otto, who was shrewd and loved to show off his English as well as his wallet, knew quite well after seeing me for months that I was not thirsty, that in fact I disliked drinking. He hated the continuous interruptions into his private world with me.

"You know, Luise, I only come here to be with Theodora because she won't see me anywhere else. And I damn well do not want to be pushed around like these other oafs! But, I know she has to earn her money, so Theodora, let's go into the separee and continue our conversation there. That way Luise and that dragon, Marianne, won't bother us for an hour. Bring us the Veuve Cliquot."

That particular brand cost him 600 marks and gave us about forty-five minutes of intimacy behind a curtain.

We never got a full hour unless the guest bought two bottles up front. Then I tried to stretch the time to an hour and a half, after which Marianne or Luise came and stood outside the curtain calling our names over and over again, signaling that the time was up or the guest should order another bottle.

In Club Diana, the separee was a large room divided into six cubicles along two walls. Each cubicle had a loveseat and a thick green velvet curtain, which was supposed to be for privacy. But you could always hear what was going on in the next cubicle, as the curtains were not soundproofed. The sounds were often garish, loud and hilarious, depending on how drunk the girls and their guests were. Sometimes, there were groups of guests and girls together, and the curtains would remain open, so the antics could spill out into the center of the room. When I was with a group, I would often be asked to dance in the center, so the girls could then encourage their guests to drink more.

The girls' objective was to earn the most for the least. The guest, depending on how astute he was, tried to get the most for paying the least.

I saw myself as a modern-day courtesan, learning an art form, so natural and vital to living that all my other aims to survive became secondary, like a butterfly emerging from an old, ugly, fat, unisexual cocoon.

Each man was a discovery, awakening new longing, such that the tone of my voice changed for him. Inside me were dormant impulses so seductive, so intoxicating and so extravagant that they started to burn through my skin, as soon as I stepped inside the club. Each evening walking up the steps, overwhelmed with the sense of being on the brink of a new world, I fell in love again. It was this feeling that seduced me. It was the need to fall in love that was at the core of my addiction to this intoxicating world. It was a world that proved there was some intimacy left in the midst of so much insanity.

I never could imagine who would walk through the door, yet I would be lured into every pit of human emotion from anger to ecstasy. The atmosphere of the club, like a primal initiation chamber, invited those who crossed its threshold to strip off the crust of propriety, emerging open, bare, and molten.

I was the dancer/whore with varicose veins and an ordinary body. But I was also a moth drawn to the flame. In Isadora Duncan's words: "you were once wild here. Don't let them tame you."

Tame? Never! I loved playing with the fire and the passion, thinking that in a few months I could walk away, unscathed.

I was wrong.

Voltaire was reported to have said that it was not enough to conquer, but that one had to know how to seduce. I took his words literally, caught in the trap of wanting to be wanted after so much unbearable rejection. Being held and cherished was more important than all my degrees, life experiences and the search for God. I easily switched my addiction from religious quests to power-control-lust-ecstasy. The money was the glue that held it all together, and kept my act focused in the midst of the brutality. An essential part of every conquest was learning how to seduce the prey. Whether being a theologian seducing my believers with brilliant schemas or a businesswoman with clients, there was always the deal, the contract, the win.

My goal became earning a lot of money in as short a time as possible. I was 39 years old, and the gods were not favoring my shape. Plastic surgery became my next course of action.

I chose a small private clinic in London. Two days later I left swathed with bandages on my nose and across my chest. The small bulb on the end of my nose, the mark of the Italian stallions that had always made me feel like a horse, was removed. My small breasts that formerly looked like wet socks were lifted. I felt as if I finally "fit in" with my shapely coworkers. I began to sense that my body was beautiful, in tune with the sexual woman inside me.

Apart from my dancing I still felt quite ordinary. But the men came, always to my surprise. By 1988, my "regular" guests included Axel, an auto VP from Hamburg, who was wiry and drank too much. He said he fell for me because I'd told him his Porsches were ugly.

It was probably because nobody told him the truth before. Besides, nobody else could stand his drivel, poor soul. I don't mind it.

I could bend this very powerful man to my will. That was the way it worked.

Then there was French-Swiss Alain from Basel, who owned his own jewelry line. Overweight with a small mustache, I treated him like royalty.

Poor fellow is so embarrassed about the way he thinks he looks . The first time I talked to him, he wet his pants.

Then there was Wilhelm, who had a lucrative construction business.

He had influence in local politics and law enforcement. A squat plain man, he spoke halting English and knew exactly what he wanted. Our conversations were peppered with German and chopped up English thrown in. He thought I was some kind of goddess, probably because I was tall. He always bought me a 250-mark bottle of Sekt just to have me hold his hand, so frightened was he of rejection that he was unable to say or do anything else.

And there was Helmut, a young German boy in his 20's, who habitually fell instantly in love with bar girls. After talking to him for more than five minutes, I became one of his *girls.* He spoke no English, so we talked in the simplest German possible. Helmut was not what you would call handsome and had trouble meeting girls, which started him coming to bars in the first place. He could usually find some girl willing to sit with him for the price of a Piccolo. He would hang around, sometimes till the bar closed. All the bars in the town came to know him, and he would often spend his last *pfenig* on a Piccolo, just so he could get some attention. Everybody took great pity on poor Helmut, so he was never chased out, but many girls ignored him, because he didn't have much money.

I gave him extra time and attention the first time he was with me, to Marianne's dismay, and he came back the next night.

"Theodora, I want to go to *separee* with you," he said in slow, deliberate German, so that I would understand him clearly.

"Helmut, that costs 250 *marks*, and I know you don't have it. Let's just sit here, drink a Piccolo, and talk."

"No. I have the money. I took my savings."

"Helmut," I said very quietly so that Marianne wouldn't hear, because she would fire me on the spot for refusing a sale. "You can't do that. I won't let you spend your savings on me."

"Theodora, you *have* to let me. This is a business and you have to earn your money. I want you."

"Helmut, be quiet! Marianne will hear you. I can't let you do this."

"Once, Theodora. Let me do this once."

"No."

"Yes! MARIANNE," he said in such a loud voice the whole bar heard him. "Come here! I want to buy a bottle for Theodora in the *separee*!"

Heads turned, as the bar was busy that night, and Marianne instantly came over from across the floor, eager to make a sale. Seeing Helmut, her face fell.

"Helmut," she said in her high-pitched syrupy Austrian accent, "You can't afford Theodora, you know that, my dear."

Her face turned to me in a disapproving stare that said: 'you know better than to sit with him, he has no money!'

"Marianne, here's 250 *marks*, cash, and I want a bottle in the *separee*, now." Helmut could be forceful when he wanted to be. And, Marianne couldn't refuse the cash.

So, off we went. We had forty-five passionate minutes, after which he was my shadow.

There was Tom, a Canadian Air Force Lieutenant, who attached himself to me after our second meeting. He was very tall and slender with no front teeth.

Perhaps that's why he doesn't talk. Intense green eyes, though.

He came in alone. I was with another guest, and didn't notice him at first. All the girls, including Katrin, flocked over to him. He politely refused to buy anything for any of them. When I finished with my guest, Marianne came over to me.

"Try the Canadian. He hasn't bought for anyone else, but usually they pay good. He may want only English. Try."

So over I went.

"Hello," I said in my best British.

"Well, hello. Are you British?"

"Yes." I wanted to get this over with fast. If he wasn't going to buy me anything, I would move on to another guest, and then Marianne would stop bugging me.

"What are you drinking this evening?" He asked, his tone so direct that it took me off guard. I was sure he was going to make me beg.

"A piccolo, please."

"Luise, bring this lady a Piccolo."

I'll get a bottle out of him. I'll use my vocabulary to seduce him.

"My name's Theodora, and what's yours?"

"Tom." Silence. He was not a talker.

"What do you do, Tom?"

"I'm an artillery specialist." Silence. I guessed that the military did not encourage long-winded conversationalists.

I was wrong.

After I asked what an artillery specialist was, he proceeded to describe in detail what the inspections, parts and requirements were. That lasted thirty minutes, the length of my piccolo.

Marianne wanted us to spend ten minutes with a Piccolo guest, gulping down the fifty-mark drink, but I usually spent longer, depending on the guest, because after all, fifty marks was not chicken feed. I saw Luise marching down toward me from the end of the bar. It was time to ask for another drink.

Luise got to Tom first. "Hello, Mr. Canadian," she said in her French-accented halting English, "Theodora is very thirsty. Won't you buy her another drink?"

"I'm afraid not tonight, ma'am. Perhaps tomorrow."

"Then, *I'm* afraid that I must go, Tom."

"I understand, ma'am. Have a good evening, and thanks for talking to me."

"Oh," I was taken aback, as no guest had said that to me before. "Of course, Tom! I do hope you'll return." I gave him a big smile and hugged him warmly, disengaging as soon as I caught Marianne scowling at me from the end of the bar.

"Oh, I will, ma'am."

I didn't believe him at first, but when I saw him come back the next night, I was intrigued.

"Tom, you came back," I said. I spotted him over the head of a very dull guest from Stuttgart. Since he hadn't ordered me a third Piccolo, I left promptly and joined Tom.

"Of course, ma'am. I said I would."

"Tom, you must stop calling me ma'am. It makes me feel like your mother. Call me Theodora, so we can get to know each other, better."

"OK, ma- um, Theodora. Would you like a drink?"

I smiled, "Of course. And, thank you very much for offering." I knew my greeting would captivate him; and I wanted him to be captivated.

"How did you learn to speak German fluently?" he asked as Luise poured the Piccolo and took his money.

I laughed out loud as I took the first sip, almost spraying him with the drink. "I don't speak fluently at all! I barely get along with my German, since I learned it here in the bar. It's much easier for me to speak English. Now, tell me more about yourself."

"Not much to tell, really." Then he went on for another thirty minutes describing his hometown in New Foundland his parents' farm. At the end of his discourse, I either had to ask for another Piccolo, or leave him.

"Tom, I must ask you for another drink, or I will have to leave."

"Why?"

"That's the policy of the bar. We can only stay with a guest as long as we have a drink in front of us."

"So, I have to buy another one of those?" He asked pointing to the Piccolo.

"Yes. Or, we can sit at one of the tables around the dance floor, for a bottle of Sekt, if you want."

"And how much are *they*?"

"150 marks."

"Boy, that's expensive. What does it cost to go in *there*?" He pointed to the *separee*. His question told me that he had been to *separee* before. But, I had no idea what his expectations were.

"The *separee*," I said gesturing to where he indicated, "costs 250 marks for a small bottle."

"And, how much time do we have in there for that?" I liked his direct questions, but I was a little nervous about what he expected for his time. Normally I liked to negotiate a bit more at the bar before going into *separee*, as that gave me time to know the guest better, and assess his sexual preferences.

"Usually thirty to forty minutes." I said softly. "What do you like, my love?" I was forced to ask him directly, although I disliked that approach because it lacked subtlety, diminishing the atmosphere of foreplay. I used the bar-sitting time to build up a mood of desire, enchantment and longing.

"Being with you," was all he would say.

"Well, then, come with me. Luise," I called to her, taking his hand. "Bring us a bottle of Sekt in *separee*."

All eyes were on us, as it was a quiet night in the bar and I had made the first "sale" of the evening. Marianne brought the bottle in herself, fawning all over Tom.

"Oh, my Canadian general! How wonderful you come to take our Theodora to *separee*! Now, if you should need anything at all, just let us know. I'm sure you will have marvelous time!"

She was loud and gushing – exactly what I felt Tom did *not* need.

"Thank you, Marianne," I said ushering her out. We were then alone.

"Please excuse Marianne, Tom, she's a bit overbearing," I said coming over to his side. I sat down and tossed my leg lightly over his, indicating that he could make the first move.

"I guess I'm sort of a shy guy, so we can talk a bit if you want."

"Tom, my dear," I said, taking his hands in mine and looking straight into his eyes. "I want you to feel completely comfortable and do whatever you like. I could tell he was hesitant. Taking him into my arms, much like a mother would take a child, I held him close. His heartbeat increased and I noticed the erection prodding against his shorts. Time to end the mother role.

Go lightly, or he'll come in his pants, and that'll embarrass him. Men have to prove to themselves they can penetrate the woman successfully. It's essential, like some primitive conquest mechanism that makes them feel secure. And it also guarantees their return to the same bed that made them feel that way in the first place.

As soon as I released my hold he came in his pants.

"Tom, you have so much passion," I whispered. "I'm afraid I rushed you, please forgive me!"

"Theodora," he said, breathing hard, when he found his voice. "You turned me on …I was… I was too fast… next time will be better for you, I promise."

He's apologizing to me?

Tom's love affair with me was launched in that moment.

'Tommy' as he became known to the bar folk, followed me from Club Diana to Exotique, a club in the neighboring city, where I had started working during the week.

That started after Jurgen, Exotique's owner, appeared one night in Club Diana, and became my guest.

On this particular Tuesday night the bar was dead.

Thank God Marianne's not here. She'd only get royally drunk.

She hates it when there's no business. The only guest is that blond, muscular, guy, who doesn't want anybody so far. Guess I should try him.

"*Guten Abend*," I said in my funny German.

"You're English, aren't you?" He said without much of an accent.

"Yes. And where did you learn such good English?" I generally asked them this question when they responded in English after I had addressed them in German.

"We must learn this English language in the schools, so I try to practice it whenever I can. You can speak English to me, if you want... Luise, a piccolo for this lady... what is your name?"

Surprised that he ordered for me so fast, I sensed immediately that he was familiar with the bar scene.

"Theodora, and thank you for the drink. So, you are familiar with the bars?" I asked straightforwardly.

He's a businessman because of the suit, but probably has his own, since he wears a black turtleneck. Doesn't follow convention of white shirt and tie like most German businessmen.

"I like your approach, Theodora," he said with a slight smile, amusement in his shocking blue eyes, "and, yes, I am familiar. What are you doing in a place like this?"

"Working. I also love to dance."

"Really?" He sounded surprised, and looked me up and down. Every night I wore the same black dress, and looked rather plain

I hope he doesn't notice how frayed it is.

Under my dress was a garter belt and stockings. I never wore underwear, as it only got in the way and was an extra expense.

"Really. Would you like to see me dance?"

If I thought the guest would take me to separee, Marianne might agree to let me dance. If he paid for more than two bottles, she would pay me the fee in addition to the twenty percent on the bottles. If we didn't go to separee, but she thought he was a good guest, she might give me the fee. If he didn't go to separee, and she didn't know him, I lost the fee.

I took the chance because this man intrigued me, and Marianne was not there that night.

After changing, I walked onto the stage. The music took me over, my body melting like a liquid wand into the raw pulsating sound, guiding my movements.

At the end I walked off the stage right up to him.

"And your name?" I breathed into his mouth.

"Jurgen." There was a very hot pause. "And there is no need to get dressed." Taking my hand he then turned to Luise.

"Get me a bottle of champagne," he said throatily, "and make it Veuve."

My heart was beating so fast I thought everybody could hear it.

He knew exactly which bottle to order for an hour!

I also knew that I would not drink that champagne.

And I knew he didn't care.

It cost 750 marks.

Taking my right hand gently, he grasped the bottle and walked straight into the *separee*. I liked this forceful leading, as if I were both his possession and his challenge. He would have to conquer me.

As soon as we entered *separee*, he carefully removed his clothes. He was practiced in this art. This suddenly dampened my desire because he was too polished, as if he'd done this a thousand times.

But then, he did something unexpected. He sat down slowly and looked at his hands.

"Theodora, this may surprise you, but I have never been in a separee as a guest before."

I looked at him, wondering what he meant.

"I have my own bar. And this was so fast. I'm not sure I should be here with you. I will pay for your bottle, but I'm a little unsure of what we do next."

His honesty was the key that opened my desire.

"Then," I said slowly, "I will show you how a guest should be treated in separee. It will be good for you to participate for once, so you can learn for your business!" I laughed quietly, and stood up as he was still sitting on the couch. He started to open his mouth to say something, and I put my fingers on his lips.

"Don't talk. Just close your eyes and lie down. Only good and soothing things will happen, now. You are in *my* care."

I slowly opened the bottle, knowing all guests wanted to hear the sound of the cork popping, signaling the start. Jurgen's eyes were half-closed. He was observing me, and not quite sure of what I would do next.

Neither was I.

But I knew then that I had him and could guide him in any direction.

That night I never touched his shorts. I touched every other place, and as I did so I felt some part of myself burst alive that had been sleeping. Like knowing there's something deep down inside, and you wonder what it would feel like if it were stirred. It may have been the moment; it may have been the way he looked at me, or the longing I saw in his eyes... I don't know.

This moment was so alive, so different, that I could not be the same person afterward. Nothing was worth more than that feeling.

I went to work for Jurgen from that night on.

At Exotique I was always uncomfortable around Jurgen after our time in *separee* because there was so much electricity between us. I used that feeling to make myself more alluring to the guests, since there was nothing else I could do with it. Jurgen and I *had* to maintain a professional relationship for his bar and my income.

Tom and Otto followed me there, as did Alain –but -for a different reason.

I first met Alain at Diana on a Thursday night when he was in the area finishing business, on his way back to Basel. He sat quietly by himself not buying drinks for any of the girls. I saw him and decided to try seducing him.

"*Guten abend*," I said in my English/German.

"Ah! A British girl," he said in German, which signaled that he wanted to speak German.

"Yes," I continued, "and where come you from?" I tried to think of the proper German sentence construction.

"From where come you" he corrected my German, "and I can see we should speak English or we get not far tonight!" He finished in English, to my delight.

"You speak perfect English!" I said wanting him to keep going so I could gently correct him. That way, he might buy me a piccolo.

"I do not speak perfect English, but I know you want your piccolo, so..." he signaled Luise, "bring this lady her piccolo."

I smiled demurely.

"Thank you." I sensed he had to be handled with kid gloves. Once the guest and I were speaking English, he was in my territory, and I set the rules.

"Perhaps I could help you with your English," I said in my most seductive voice.

Having taught business English to Germans I understood how desperate the businessmen were to perfect their communication. It was vital to their economic growth in the competitive markets. This was my advantage in the bar: I could improve their English (and their business), which the German girls couldn't. The guests got double for their money.

"I think you can help me in several ways," Alain said, directly. He was used to getting to the point. "You seem different from the other girls, here. Do you understand what I mean?"

"In what way?" Simple words would work better with him.

"You seem more intelligent. Why are you working here? Why not in London?"

"It's too cold, there. Too damp and boring."

"And this small Baden-Baden, is interesting?" he chuckled with merriment in his eyes.

"Many businessmen, like yourself, come to the bar; and they like to improve their language skills, along with being entertained. Speaking of which, shall I dance for you?"

"You dance, too?" He was astonished.

"Yes. Wait here. I will return."

I went over to Marianne and asked her if I could dance for this man, who hadn't even told me his name.

"Did he buy you a bottle?" she asked right away.

"No, Marianne, but he bought a Piccolo immediately, and I know I can get a bottle from him after I dance.

She looked at me skeptically. "If you don't get the bottle, I don't pay you for the dance."

"OK." She was used to this response from me, as she knew I loved to dance. But this strategy did not go over well with the other dancers, who were more desperate to get their fees out of her. There were grumbles from two of them who were sitting next to Marianne.

"You better make it good, or you will have to pay *their* fees too!" Marianne called after me.

I dressed in silver, feeling both very feminine and elegant. The sultry beat of the music started.

It was over quickly and I saw his expression of amazement. I walked from the stage around the room to the other guests as his eyes followed me with questions.

I didn't want Alain to feel self-conscious, a mood that would ruin the atmosphere I was trying to create, so I held his eyes, walking from guest to guest, keeping my gaze on him. His eyes burned with desire. Off came the thong, and I put it right in his lap.

He laughed, and shook his head, smiling.

I went back to change.

"That was some dance, Theodora."

So, he listened to the voice announcing my act, and got my name straight. Wonder how much else he noticed.

"Call me Theodora. And, what may I call you?"

"Alain… I know you don't want to, how you say, 'chit-chat?' out here, so what does it cost to go in separee with you?"

Once a man asked me this question, and added the "with you" part, I got bold and quoted a higher price than the Sekt.

He can afford it.

"750 marks for a bottle of Veuve."

"And what is the most expensive bottle… which buys us a little longer, no?"

I paused for a moment.

This is new territory for me.

"900 marks for Dom Peringnon." I said, a bit tremulously, as no one had ever ordered this for me before, and I wasn't sure what I would have to *do* for it. When a man ordered champagne (not the cheaper Sekt) it meant they wanted sex.

"Then that is what we shall have."

"I shall order it, then. Come, Alain". I wanted to get my order in, quickly, before he changed his mind. Once the bottle was opened, the guest had to pay for it.

Inside, and seated, Alain ignored the bottle.

"If you want to drink, go ahead. I do not want any," he said simply, "and I need to be on my way, soon. I wanted to get you alone to ask you to see me, privately."

Shit. The dreaded question, which came up so often…

"The money would be all yours, Theodora. I do not feel comfortable in these places."

"Alain, I can't see you outside. I would lose my job here, and that I can't afford. Let us just have a nice evening. A moment later I heard myself saying "here." Perhaps, though, if you want to improve your English I could teach you in a different setting."

"You are an English teacher?"

"Yes, I taught advanced English before I came to work at the bar."

"So you have other skills, too?" He was amused.

"I have many skills, my dear Alain." In order to continue, I had to demonstrate some sexual skill before he left separee, so he knew what he was buying. I had to be swift; for he already told me he had to go.

I kissed his cheek, gently brushing his pants with the back of my hand.

"You don't have to do anything, Theodora. My idea was only to talk to you... but if you insist..." he was a little resistant, but I interpreted it as the usual game men play to show they could command the situation.

"I insist, Alain. Come let me hold you. You deserve some relaxation after such a long day," I said sincerely, holding out my arms, as he seemed tense.

Then I understood why.

His penis was only an inch long.

He was nervous with embarrassment and must have been so rejected in his life. It might be nearly impossible for him to find an accepting woman. I immediately wanted to take him gently into my arms, showing him that nothing mattered except easing his concern.

He closed his eyes and came before I could do anything.

"Theodora! Ah... that was so good..." he sighed then opened his eyes and stood up.

"Theodora, thank you." I saw the relief in his eyes, and even a small sparkle. He reached in his pocket and took out something, which he handed to me. "This is for you, only. Not for that boss of yours." He smiled. I took it and looked down at what he handed me.

A five hundred-mark note.

"Alain, I can't take this," I whispered astonished.

"Why not?" he looked genuinely puzzled. "Is it not enough?"

"It's too much!"

"Good. Then use it well. When can I see you for the English lesson?"

"Um..." I was in shock, and had to gather my wits.

"Here is my card, Theodora. Call me with the details. My secretary will answer the phone and you can say you are the new English teacher. I will tell her to expect your call. It is not unusual. I have had English *teachers* before! Now, I must go. It is a long drive to Basel, and it is late."

It was 2:00 AM.

Promising to call and not knowing what to do, I left separee. Alain had paid, leaving a fresh bottle of Dom Peringnon sitting on the bar counter for me.

"What's this?" I asked Luise and a grinning Marianne.

"He paid for *another* bottle for you after he left! He will make a very good guest... that is, *if* he returns!" Marianne looked at me with skeptical eyes over the grin.

After visiting Diana and Exotique several times, Alain pushed me to see him privately. Eventually I couldn't refuse him any longer. I arranged for him to come to my room in the flat.

The first time, he gave me 1000 marks.

I had never before received so much money for what came to me so naturally. And Alain blossomed with confidence.

"Theodora, I feel like a new man. It is as if I have finally found something I had been looking for."

I made the mistake in thinking this could continue indefinitely. He wanted me to move closer to where he lived, promising me a flat and offering me work in his business.

"You can represent us on trips to London! I need to improve my English, as well. Just think of all the many ways you can be involved! You can begin a new life, here, near me."

"My dear Alain, I'm so sorry, I can't do this."

"Why not?" He was not used to having people refuse him.

"I just can't."

"You have other lovers, I know." He said sadly.

"It's not that at all," this time *I* was sad. "I have a commitment..."

"It's that damn bar. You think it's more important than me." He said this with such force that the truth was made clear between us without further words. I couldn't risk losing my connections through my work at the bar because I was so dependent on that income which even Alain couldn't guarantee. He left without even looking at me, and I let him go.

That was the last night.

I refused to accept he'd gone. I called him several times, leaving messages that he didn't return. I would not let myself believe that he cut me off. It was not a love affair, but I felt abandoned by my protector. I was no longer "worth" the value of being at the top of the pedestal. I had fallen.

The power has slipped out of my hands.

I wouldn't admit I felt like a failure, losing the best single source of my support. If only I had been wiser, more cunning, more careful not to mention the bar, more feminine, more...

By August 1988, I had increased my clientele to several new men per night in both bars. I tried harder to be more "professional." I forced myself to forget Alain. In addition to the groups of businessmen, a Frenchman, named Roger came, first to Diana, then also to Exotique on every third Wednesday when his bistro closed early. His devotion was a salve to my wounded heart. Alain had left a scar.

I felt alone and longed to pour my heart out to someone. The only person with whom I had shared deeply about bar issues was my dear friend and co-worker, Katrin. She was away in the Greek islands on holiday.

I called Greece.

"You stinker!" I hollered into the phone, "You sent me all that Greek music, which I adore, and now I'm weeping and wailing all over this place! I haven't received a drop of a letter from you since you left!"

"Well," she laughed over the crackling connection, "you know how it is here! The days just dissolve. But, it isn't as if I've forgotten you, my darling! I just can't seem to make the pen get to the paper... too much Ouzo...Now, tell me, honestly, how things are going!"

"Pretty much the same as usual... or maybe a little worse! Last night, Olga the fat dancer hit Julia, that shy one, while Marianne was in her usual drunken state. Of course, secretly everybody was overjoyed that somebody socked that woman, but what a mess... And Alain hasn't called ..."

The connection was fading so I was shouting louder into the phone, "I love you! And write something, for God's sake, or send another picture of Kalos or... something so I know you are alive!"

I still felt abandoned. Talking to Katrin, though, made me feel better, not so alone.

Fights were becoming more frequent in the Club, but that didn't stop the guests from coming. Olga got so drunk one night she hit Marianne and was thrown out. Julia was obnoxious to a good guest, yelling obscenities at him after her third bottle. He left without paying and Marianne took it out on all of us, holding back fifty marks from each of us that night.

One guest from Cologne arrived with six of his partners. In separee they each demanded bondage with the restraints they brought with them, besides wanting to swap us around. After the fourth round of champagne, they got so noisy and rough that I went out to the bar to get Luise to help us. I knew Marianne was too drunk by that time to be of any use, but little Luise was a tiger when things got violent. Besides, Marianne would not want to risk losing any part of a 12,000-mark sale, as each bottle of champagne was five hundred marks.

Luise handled things well, using her motherly voice and calming them all down. I excused myself, as my guest was too drunk to even stand up.

I went to the kitchen behind the bar to make coffee, which is how we sobered up the overly drunk guests and got them out. Espresso and lemon.

All this reminds me how gentle Alain was and what a fool I've been to lose him...

Swallowing my hurt night after night, I had to drink and

smile and pretend to like everyone. My real feelings were buried in the single pillow on my bed, long after I left the bar in the early morning hours when all the drunks went home.

When Katrin returned I talked to her about Alain.

"Katrin, I' m upset that Alain hasn't called in over a month. I called him twice and he hasn't returned my calls."

"Well, Theodora, in a way, you created the situation and now you must live with it. But, what else *could* you have done? You certainly couldn't live there in that village with him! Come on now; be practical, *this* is your place. Right *here* with all of us. *You* know that!"

"But, Katrin, I think part of me loved the guy. I feel like such a failure…"

"Oh, Theodora, I warned you not to get too close to him. You have to ask yourself if it was really *him* you got attracted to, and not his money."

"I can't separate the two, Katrin. So much of his attraction *was* his wealth, and the kind of power and assurance that comes from being in that position. He was a self-made man. I think I grew to care for him…"

"Well, now you made your decision, stop pining for him. There'll be plenty more like him, don't you worry. Come on now, we have to attend to the guests who just walked in, so Marianne doesn't fire us *tonight*."

But she did.

Not that night, but four days later, Marianne went into one of her alcoholic paranoid fits, where she was convinced we were all taking 'her' clients and seeing them privately.

"You're all FIRED!!!" she screamed in her high-pitched shrill. There was only one new guest that night and none the two previous nights.

"Madeleine - or Mady, as we called her, the newest addition to our crew - spoke up, "Marianne, why?"

"…YOU should talk! You probably have taken them all! They stopped coming when you arrived here! You must have instigated this!" Marianne was sweating now, her face red and her eyes bulging, as she looked closely into Mady's emerald green eyes and at her golden hair.

Since July we all had been talking about whether to leave the Club.

"Theodora," Katrin whispered, "I think we should make our move, now."

Katrin and I went to Norbert's Napoleon, a big step... into another dimension.

That very week, August 1989, the city had decided that it had too many bars and lacked a brothel. Norbert, the owner, was told his bar would be shut down and either he would have to advertise it as a bordello, losing its liquor license, or close. Alcohol could not be served in a bordello.

If it became a bordello, we would have to register with the health department as prostitutes, and report weekly for an examination for HIV and STD. The *polizei,* who scoured the bars and brothels on a bi-weekly basis, would check our ID's. In the brothels, sex was legal.

Almost overnight, Napoleon became the largest and most discreet bordello in the area. The atmosphere was relaxed, unhurried, and devoid of paranoia, which enticed the guests to open their wallets. They paid Norbert for the girl's services beforehand.

"Services" meant more sex and less conversation, and no dancing. But Norbert was fair and had a good sense of humor.

Although in many ways it was a good move for me, I began to voice my concerns.

"Katrin, I feel like I'm crossing a line. Up till now I was simply an escort at a bar, where the sex was like a brief flirt, a by-product... I liked to *think* that I used sex for medicinal reasons: to soothe away pain and loneliness. "

"Yes, Theodora, I know and now right from the beginning you can give them those wounded deer eyes, and they'll melt immediately. They'll be like putty in your hands!" She was chuckling.

"But now I'm publicly stating that my registered profession in Germany is prostitution, and be a card-carrying 'mortal-sin-maker.' Nobody would ever understand. This would brand me forever."

"You always did have a way of putting things in those church-ey categories. Why does it bother you so much, my love?"

"I'm having trouble justifying this to myself. On the one hand, I have no other options if I want to continue working and earn this kind of money. But, I don't know how I'm going to handle *being* a prostitute."

I had only met a real, live prostitute once. And that was when I was a Probation Officer in the New York Criminal Courts. They looked scared, undernourished, poor, grimy and young.

"Theodora, Theodora, you always think in these absolutes, and what will happen in the future. Look, you don't know how you'll feel until you *do* it. Try it! If you don't like it, you can always quit. Me, too… you don't think I'm going to have to be extra careful that my family doesn't find out? This is a hard thing for me, too. But, don't you think we should at least *try* it."

She was right. I couldn't judge it because I knew nothing about what it was like to be a registered prostitute in Germany

"And, Theodora, if you *don't* do it, you will always be wondering what it would have been like!"

She was right again. I *liked* the sex too much.

Sex had become the power source: my new guru, replacing Bhagwan, Sila, the church – even god. I believed I could control this source of power by my successful seductions. But with every seduction came this prickly feeling that rubbed against my Old Catholic conditioning: what I was doing was wrong and sinful. "God will punish you," it said.

About this same time, Diva and Sila were released from prison in the USA and flew back to Germany. They moved in. I couldn't afford to have Sila's press photographing the new Margaret Bonham and making the link with Ma Prem Samsara. I had to move. But where?

As I was leaving Club Diana for the last time, Nina, one of the contract dancers, provided me with a solution. She was married to a German named Johann, and was worried about his being so alone all the time. She started talking to me about him.

"It wouldn't be so hard on him, I think, if we had somebody else living with us. Then he wouldn't feel so lonely. He would have somebody else to talk to..."

Here was my invitation.

"Nina, it so happens that *I* need a place to live."

"Theodora! Then come and live with us. That would be perfect!"

I settled into the storage room in Nina and Johann's flat, started work at Napoleon, and began a friendship with a man who was to become another one of my "big brothers".

The bordello world had different rules from the bar. In the bar I used alcohol to my advantage: a drunken guest could be manipulated into seeing whichever illusion I chose to project. If he wanted a Greek Goddess that's who I became.

At Napoleon none of these tricks worked. I was exposed for who I was, an imperfect body with a pitiful knowledge of German and an aging face. The three girls I was competing with were younger, flawless, and fluent in German, French *and* English. Three only spoke German, but were seasoned sex workers. Then there was me, Katrin and Mady.

Fluent in English, Mady was 31, a sultry and bewitching woman from Heidelberg. She came to Diana just as I was leaving and followed us to Napoleon, along with her friend, Tina, petite and raven-haired. Tina did not speak English, had a limited mental repertoire and concentrated on the local townsfolk. Mady, Katrin and I slowly began to build our clientele.

The three of us had intense conversations, and slowly

collected the English speaking guests, as well as the German conference visitors who preferred more "mature" women. "Mature" meant that we had some brain and softer bodies.

A group of Belgians came in one evening. After a short time (and fifty-five hundred marks later) all six of us went to the big room on the second floor. There the Scotch came out and Katrin took the lead.

"Ok, everybody, take off what you don't need!" Peter the "chief" announced laughing. And we began…

Sometime later after I had taken care of my gentleman, I was called over to Katrin and Peter. I could see that Peter wanted me. He was actually turning me on by desiring me, and when the wanting started I lost control. As if a switch in my *brain* had been "turned on," I was being transformed into another personality: the princess, the wanton, the *adored*.

It was not easy for me to collect myself after taking care of a man, and simply move on, as many of the girls could. When he was the least bit tender, there were feelings of attachment, of wanting to stay curled in his protecting arms that welled up in me, and lingered. I couldn't just pull away, the way some men did; or abruptly withdraw the way many of the girls did. I thought of this problem as an asset. I used to tell myself: look at how much I'm *feeling*. Only later on did I see how damaging those *feelings* were.

Gradually everybody joined together, coming over to that bed in stages and we metamorphed into a pile of legs, arms and faces. The visual was too vaudevillian to take seriously or erotically for that matter. We looked like a choo-choo train, chugging along a very bumpy track… I couldn't stop my laughter from spilling out; and soon, Katrin started laughing, then Mady, Peter, and the rest of the crowd. The laughter was a release greater than all the sex combined.

Belgians were usually great fun.

Brits, however, were casual, stiff and afraid of having sex in a group, often self-conscious about their bodies. Swiss Germans were short and serious, with no frills. Swiss French paid a lot, talked a lot and came quickly. Swiss Italians, on the other hand, tried to pay as little as possible for as long as possible, and would invariably slobber all over themselves and us.

The Dutch were generally dull but predictable, often in groups of six or more with a lot of money to throw around. They wanted to be entertained and I had the chance to dance spontaneously. The Scandinavians visited us once a month, on the same date. Sometimes they all came together Danes, Swedes and Finns, other times it was just the Finns, or the Swedes. I found them consistently boring with no sexual imagination. Short conversation, then up to the room, in and out, boom, boom and out the door.

One man who made a habit of 'boom, boom and out' was Hans Peter, the mayor of a nearby village. He went through all the girls at least once.

When he got to me, he simply asked, "How much do you cost?"

I didn't like that approach and immediately said, "Nine hundred marks," figuring he'd back off and leave.

He didn't.

Turned out he liked that kind of attitude.

I decided to do as little as possible. I didn't want to get hurt like I was with Alain, so I turned off every ounce of feeling toward him. He was tiny, no more than 4 foot ten, and spoke with a thick dialect, which I could hardly understand. Normally, I would have tried harder to connect, sure that he was ashamed of his small height, and intent on his keeping me on his "list." A nine hundred-mark catch was nothing to sneeze at.

But I just couldn't connect with him. We went to the room and I lay on the bed in the classic prostitute-pose. He would "do" me and I would lie there and let him. I figured he wouldn't be rough, or I'd have heard about him ahead of time from the other girls. So I thought, I'll just endure it for the money and close my eyes. Perhaps there would be an opportunity to "connect" after.

That was all Hans Peter needed: my compliance. He hopped on the bed and started massaging me. The more I enjoyed it, the more he continued. When I relaxed, he just stopped. I sat up right away ready to do what he wanted but he thanked me, opened the door and left.

I thought I did it all wrong, convinced I'd lost the sale, threw my clothes on and ran down the stairs. I found Norbert in the kitchen counting his money.

"What happened with Hans Peter?" I asked quietly, afraid of the consequences.

"Oh, Theodora, he left this for you. It's probably a tip, and said he'll see you next time."

I thought he was kidding. I opened the envelope and there was a five hundred-mark note inside.

Norbert looked at my face and laughed.

"You must have done well," was all he said.

I was learning a lot about men. Most of the time, my ideas were turned upside down.

One thing I found without fail: no matter what the nationality, the men needed to talk about their relationship difficulties. Often their problems boiled down to one main cause stemming from the way they touched – or did *not* touch - their women.

"Bruno," I cut in when he grabbed my breast roughly, "you have to learn *how* to touch a woman, um?" I removed his hand, gently and playfully. "Let me teach you, umm? Why not, yes?" I coaxed him into relaxing his hand, and placing the fingertips lightly on my cheek.

"Why doesn't my girlfriend show me how to do zis?" he looked at me with hard eyes. *Because if you look at her like that, I wanted to say, she will turn into a pillar of stone.*

"No matter, my dear Bruno, now you will learn, and you can *show* her!"

Rolf, from Berlin, wondered why he was having trouble keeping his girlfriends.

"So, show me how you are making love to them. Go on, show me," I said with authority.

When he pulled me to him and kissed me hard, almost biting my lip, I yanked myself away. He had paid four hundred marks for my "services." I was going to give him a "service" that would last him a while.

"Rolf, stop right there. You have to learn how to approach a woman, if you want to get *anywhere* with them. So, now you're here with me. You've paid for this time to be here with me, let me teach you something." He was shaking his head. "Why not? No one else will do it. No one else will show you, and obviously no one else *has* shown you..."

He slowly agreed. Then, he became a regular.

When I could get the guest to start talking about his relationships – or lack of them - it was the beginning of something real entering into all this fakery. If the man was able to let down his pretense of the 'all-knowing male' for just a little while, I could show him a few things about how to reach a woman, with tenderness. They just didn't know: nobody had *taught* them.

When I asked where they had learned to make love they said: TV. Some source. I got bolder the longer he kept coming back. If he became a regular (more than five times, or at least once or twice a month), I told him *exactly* what to do, how to touch me, kiss me, hold me, and when he was being too rough. I also asked him what he liked every time, as if it were the first time.

There were so many impotent men, cripples who were paralyzed; men who had lost arms or legs in the war; men who thought themselves ugly and frigid. I loved them all, because I knew they had been deeply hurt and rejected. I accepted them all, for it didn't matter to me what they looked like. I remembered how ugly I had thought of myself.

They thought *I* was beautiful. Each one was memorable. All of us were rejects from society, in one way or other.

Although by being an official prostitute I was "labeled" an outcast of society, I never really *felt* that way. Quite the contrary. I felt like I was living every woman's fantasy. I *did* feel separate from the women who were walking down the street with their baby strollers, or who were rushing to some business meeting or shopping in the market with their families. I wasn't one of them: the "normal" ones. And sometimes knowing that I probably never would be like them made me very sad, like I was denied a place in normal life. It wasn't by economics or race or any demographic category that I was cast into this spiritual-seeker-fugitive-sex-worker role. I was a victim of being addicted to wanting more than society would allow me: hooked into a world that offered me every male fantasy I could imagine and more money than I could envision.

I must have been a courtesan in a former life because it suited me perfectly. I read the heroic lives of Aspasia and Veronica Franco. The learning, passion and understanding they suffered to acquire influenced their societies through the philosophers and statesmen they "serviced." I was one of them, and that association gave me comfort in my loneliness, sadness, and fear of always being hunted. In this 'call girl' world there was almost no sympathy or softness unless the woman herself created it.

Once a week I could entertain the feeling of being just another working girl when I went to the clinic for my pelvic exam, HIV and STD tests. The personnel treated us with respect, concern and dignity. Once when I had my period, I apologized for the mess during the exam, and the nurse replied with sincere warmth and sympathy, "this must make things difficult for your work. How hard for you to manage."

Overall my life in Germany was going well. However, my co-defendants who had moved to England were causing me concern.

Ruby called me in March to tell me that Diana had gone back to the US, after being contacted by the FBI. "She was closeted with them in a tiny room for three days and nights," Ruby told me, "in the end Diana said, 'I'm going back home with them. They're really such nice people!' Nice people, my ass! I tell you, Samsara, Diana looked like absolute shit!

If I were kept awake and deprogrammed for three days and nights, I might go off with Hitler thinking he's Saint Peter." Ruby was prone to be direct.

"My God, Ruby! I just spoke to her last month and she asked me when I was coming for a visit. She didn't mention anything."

"Well, she has been so homesick lately, and her parents got this lawyer from the States who suggested that she talk to the Feds. She listened to the guy and her family, and before we knew it, she was gone. I don't know what it will mean for us, but I'll let you know when I hear anything."

I thought of poor Diana, and what a state she must have been in; she was desperate and unhappy in London, and often mentioned how much she missed the States. What would *I* have done in her place? What if *I* hadn't had the opportunities I did? Or such incredible friends like Katrin and Johann?

It was shortly after Diana left that Maya called me from London for the first time. She was "wondering how I was, and if I'd like to come and visit her for a little holiday." After that first call and brief weekend with her and Charlize, where I was wined, dined and treated to the world of the wealthy, I didn't hear from her for several months. But I came away with the desire to live in a world where I did not have to think about money at all, except to use it - freely. I wanted Maya and Charlize to like me. I wanted to be part of their world.

By the end of August, Norbert had enough of the bordello life and left. His replacement promptly fired all of us and replaced us with "his" girls from Dusseldorf.

I was devastated.

Katrin was in Rhodes, where she went every summer, and Mady was away on holiday in the south of France with a Frenchman she had "fallen in love" with.

"What'll I do?" I asked Nina, at the flat, the morning after my last night at Napoleon.

"Come and work with me at 'Cherie!' I'll tell the boss you're a dancer."

'Cherie!' was the cabaret in the center of town, well known for its elaborate stage, two bars, three bartenders and a dance-host, who was supposed to be the bouncer, but was really a sixty-year-old, closet queen. The owner, Rudi, was such a penny pincher that he made Marianne look like Santa Claus. Although he gave his dancers a hundred marks a night for a minimum of three dances, he didn't pay if *he* thought the dance wasn't done well. I heard of his reputation and wasn't sure I liked the idea of having to dance under those circumstances.

But once again, my choices were few.

There were two other small bordellos in town but they had few guests. Working for Rudi I would no longer have to register as a prostitute, but the safeguards of having legal sex with guests were no longer in place.

On the other hand, this was the domain of liquor, where I could manipulate the drunken guest more easily. The drawback was that I would be *required* to start drinking again, which I hated.

But, here was an opportunity to continue working falling into my lap. The one condition, Nina told me was that Rudi would have to "preview" my dancing before he would hire me. So I had to mentally prepare myself to dance in front of a possibly hostile audience. He spoke slowly after the dance.

"All right, we'll try you. Where did you learn how to dance like that?"

I could see his double chin shaking as he talked. A tiny man, he had very small black eyes, a large head of massive black hair, never smiled and spoke excellent English in a monotone. "We need more British girls here. Work with Nina."

I was hired.

Katrin joined me, and shortly after that, Mady.

Katrin, Mady and I shared our thoughts about men, the world, sex and alcohol, where we had common experiences. The only differences were in that my attitude toward the work was therapeutic and sacred, which they didn't feel; and that alcohol was my crucifixion. They both drank easily.

Growing up in a house, saturated with alcohol, every other minute was spent hunting down Mom's hidden bottles. At night my dreams would be full of fear that the stuff would drown me.

I still couldn't tolerate alcohol at all. Two drinks of Sekt made me very tipsy. Champagne made me nauseous often to the point of vomiting frequently in the bathroom. It also gave me a horrible headache, so I tried to get rid of the champagne by pouring it into the flowerpots, or spilling it on the floors, or in the trashcans.

"That plant is going to grow little champagne bottles, Theodora, if you keep emptying those bottles in there!" Otto chuckled in my ear. Many guests knew that we all did this, from time to time, and thought it was amusing.

Much of the bar world was neither amusing nor honorable.

There were the crazy guests, like Stefan, who dressed up in women's clothes and noisily bought every girl a piccolo before choosing whom he would take to *separee*. I tried to hide from him several times because he would ask me to do uncomfortable things, like pee on him. I knew he was nuts, and would counsel him to get a therapist, but he didn't like my advice and started shouting that I was a monster who was taking away his soul. That did not go over very well with Rudi.

"Theodora, we don't want to upset Stefan. After all, he pays bottles!"

"But, Rudi, the poor man needs a psychiatrist!"

"That's NOT your business," Rudi shouted. "Stick to the work!"

Then, there was Waldo, who hit me.

That time, I shouted *and* threw him out of the *separee*.

"Rudi, he HIT me! I NEVER want to see his face in this bar again."

"Theodora, I can't guarantee that. *You* watch out for him. That's *your* business."

"You should have him arrested!"

"Theodora, you're not in England. This is Germany. Men do that."

"Not to *me* they don't!"

There was Manfred who started calling me names after several glasses of Vodka, putting his arm around my neck while attempting to drag me into the *separee*. I struggled against him. When that didn't work, I took his glasses off and threw them against the wall trying to distract him so he would loosen his grip. We were at a table in the corner, and Danny, the "bouncer," was nowhere in sight.

I started shouting, "GET YOUR HANDS OFF ME!"

Then Manfred started shouting, "YOU PIG! YOU BROKE MY GLASSES! I WILL SUE YOU AND THIS DAMN PLACE!"

Brigitte, the robust, and usually jolly bartender, came over at once, since Rudi was not on the premises.

"What's going on, here? Theodora, what happened? Now, Manfred, there's nothing to get upset about!"

"Nothing to get upset about! What do you mean? She broke my glasses!"

"Brigitte," I said indignantly, "he insulted me and grabbed my neck. He could have choked me to death! I should sue him!"

"Now, now, nobody's going to sue anybody," Brigitte said sternly, looking at me with hooded eyes. "We'll settle this amiably." I didn't understand the word 'amiably' in German, but luckily Tina and Mady were also at the same table with two of Manfred's associates, and filled me in. They also saw what happened. There was a brief dialogue between Manfred and his friends, after which Brigitte offered to repay Manfred for his drinks, and took me aside.

"You have to pay for his broken glasses, Theodora, or he will come after you with a lawsuit."

This made me go cold with fear inside. The last thing I needed was a lawsuit in Germany!

"All right, Brigitte, but I don't like it!"

I had to say something brave so that Brigitte would not see how frightened I was. Normally, I would have been declaring my rights and refusing to pay.

That same week there was a disturbing phone call.

It was September 20. I called Maya thinking we would make plans for a holiday she had mentioned. I was unprepared for her reaction. She suddenly announced that she was hiring a lawyer and going back to the States. She advised me to do the same. She abruptly said good-bye and the phone turned to ice in my hands. First Diana then Maya. I couldn't afford any more incidents like Manfred. I had to *increase* my earnings, not diminish them. My life was so fragile and much was still unresolved.

I threw caution to the wind and started to get more involved with the guests, feeling more, giving more, trying harder to reach my soul.

That was when Roger declared that he wanted to divorce his wife and marry me.

"Roger, you know that I don't want to come between you and your family. Maybe it's better you stop seeing me. You know that all I am to you, really, is just a dream, a wish…"

"But I can't *talk* to my wife the way I can talk to you!"

"Sure you can. Try. Every woman is receptive. Just give her the chance, Roger. You may have misjudged her ability to hear what you have to say. Take her away on a holiday, and pamper her. Then, talk to her. Open your heart to her, and you will be surprised what you find. I guarantee it."

"Theodora-*lein*, you cannot be so nice to all these guests," Henreitte, the tall good-looking bartender admonished me when she overheard my conversation

"Why not?" I whispered. "He pays bottles!" She walked away looking unconvinced.

People's unhappiness increased my own sadness about life;

yet seeing how trapped people were helped me appreciate what I had all the more. I was doing the best I could under the circumstances, following my conscience, making my own decisions; not selling myself to a man who made them for me. If I chose to sell sex for money, it was still *my* choice, so I believed then.

What happened to Alexandra however, brought me to a new awareness about the danger in this "pretty" escort world. An exquisite blond dancer, she was a quiet, gentle girl performing whatever act the guest wanted. At 19 there wasn't a single blemish on her body.

I had no idea she was a slave, for sale to the highest bidder.

I didn't even know about the slave trade till Katrin filled me in one night.

"Theodora," Katrin said in hushed tones, "Heinrich is purchasing Alexandra tonight. He is making the negotiation with Rudi right now."

"So?" I asked assuming she meant separee.

"Once he buys her, he owns her and rents her out like a pimp, if he wants; or, he keeps her with him and trots her around like a circus clown. He can do anything he wants with her." I still didn't understand. "Until she decides she's had enough of the Vegas life and leaves him, you mean?" Heinrich was an internationally successful gambler who moved from casinos in Monte Carlo, Vegas and Baden-Baden with a lot of money – and bodyguards. We'd all been with him, briefly.

"Oh, no," she said shaking her head. "She can't leave him. He'll have her killed if she does that. He *owns* her. Sh-h-h. We shouldn't even be talking about it. It's too dangerous. Close your mouth! And don't *look* at them, for God's sake!"

I discovered that the slave trade in white Western women was flourishing.

Alexandra disappeared. Sometime later an Arab guest, who had been educated in the West, confirmed "the trade" giving me details that made me sick.

Desperate people who paid thousands for a "moment" of love surrounded me nightly. It was a miracle that I could still feel anything at *all*.

Treasuring my feelings, allowing myself to cry when I felt the pain of another, helped me to listen to my intuition, which was the only true messenger, telling me what and whom to trust.

Up till now my habit had been to outwardly accept what men told me to do, how to think, what ideology to believe in, all the while deceiving myself into believing that *I* was making my own decisions. They were really and subliminally based on somebody else's rules. But I saw that later.

Bhagwan died in January 1990.

Puneet phoned me at the bar to tell me that he heard the news.

"Wow, Puneet... how did it happen? Who told you?"

"Supposedly he died of a heart attack. That is what the sannyasins here at the center in Cologne are being told."

"Did you hear any news about Diana and Maya? They're both in the States, right now."

"No, and I asked Sarah to ask the lawyers, too. No one's heard a word. I think that if anything were going to happen it would have come by now, so I wouldn't worry. How're you doing with your savings?"

"I'm almost there, Puneet. I'll have enough by November. Can you find me a good lawyer? The prejudice against sannyasins in Oregon should be less, now, especially since Bhagwan's dead."

"OK, I'll do that. You know I think the whole thing will even die down, now. There can't be *that* much interest in arresting a bunch of misguided disciples of a dead guru because they wiretapped their own property."

"Let's hope so. There must be more important things they can spend the taxpayers money on."

I wrote my parents with optimism for the first time. I'd almost forgotten what hope felt like.

In September 1990, after much needed surgery on my varicose veins, I made plans to go to Greece for recuperation. I had to renew my strength to make the final push, the last efforts to earn as much as I could before returning to the States, resolve the wiretap case and leave this lifestyle.

But on the first of October, when I got back from my vacation, I had run out of time.

Chapter 16
The Hollywood Joint

Oh, if only I could have the courage of a hero, I would conquer the fear of death. Instead, I cry.
– Eleanor Ramrath Garner, Eleanor's Story, An American Girl in Hitler's Germany

The bus jolted me out of my thoughts as we came to a screeching halt. In a few hours I'd be entering Federal prison.

God, I'd give anything in the world to be back in Europe, in that world I once knew. That life has truly disappeared, and I've changed so much. I wonder what federal prison will be like? Will I be able to stand it? Will the dykes beat me up? I heard there's no hair dye, which means my gray will come in. They'll probably force me to eat meat, which I've not had for 15 years. Will I even be allowed to keep my contacts? Can't just go to a doctor when I want. In fact, can't go anywhere without chains and leg irons. I'm now a dangerous criminal.

Well, I hope being a self-commit gets me some good time credit. 'This'll count for points toward your release,' Trish said. They trust me to travel, then lock me up and then transport me in chains. Makes no sense.

Designated to Dublin, a Federal all levels security prison in California, the Court refused to recommend me to prison camp in Phoenix, just a few miles from my parents' home, because I hadn't cooperated with the government.

I arrived in the City of Dublin that afternoon. The sun was hazy with clouds, looking troubled, like me. Even the air seemed depressed.

The taxi station was tiny and deserted. I expected it to be like Greyhound, large and bustling, with neon lights flashing, 'Dublin Prison-Express.' My mind was exaggerating every small detail. Looking around for a person or an office, there was only a rusty sign, 'TAXI.'

Eventually, a man walked over from across the street.

"Where're you goin', ma'm?"

I turned around and saw he was looking right at me.

Do I have a sign on my forehead?

"Dublin... prison," I whispered.

"Sure. I drive lots of folks there. Get in, when you're ready," he said with a worn- out look.

Once in the cab, the driver said, "how long for?"

"Five years uh, maybe, three," I said hopefully.

"It's not a bad place," he said slowly. "I've even brought some celebrities there."

I didn't really want to talk to him, but he was being kind so I felt I owed him. I wanted to show him *I* was not a criminal. *I* was normal.

"I'm not, you know..."

"I don't know much, ma'am, but I do know that we're almost there. It's just a ways outside of town. They tell me that time flies when you're in there, so much to do'n all. I wouldn't worry if I waz you."

I couldn't answer but instead concentrated on looking ahead at a winding highway, with some tiny buildings in the distance.

After that there was silence.

He drove me right to the door. I got out, took my small bag and paid him.

"Thanks."

"Good luck to you."

And, he was gone.

A large black rubber mat with 'Bureau of Prisons' inscribed on it was in front of the entrance. I walked up to the glass doors that opened electronically.

"Who are you?" said a matron in a plain gray dress, behind a large wooden desk. There were two oversized steel doors, one behind her and one to the left. Two other people, both in gray, were chatting to each other to the right. They didn't even look up when I entered.

I'm just like a tiny insect.

I'd been expecting a welcoming committee, as if they were all waiting for me.

"Cecilia Edwards," I said, which was the name they told me I had to use, "self-commit."

"Wait outside." Her tone was indifferent.

Wait outside? I'm supposed to be locked up and chained, and they tell me to go back outside? Must be the casual incarceration approach. I've had every other kind.

I sat down on the bench and waited.

This place gives me the willies. It looks like a façade of a hotel. Like it's supposed to be something it's not. Maybe I'm just being paranoid. That I have to say my name is 'Cecilia Edwards' pisses me off.

For one thing, it wasn't my name.

The Bureau of Prisons (BOP) had decided that my legal name, Samsara Drakke, was not the name they were going to use. So they took my original birth name, Cecilia, which was no longer my *legal* first name and put it together with my second husband's last name, Edwards.

So the BOP has more power than churches or gurus. With the gurus you get a new name only if you want it.

I'm not going to let them see who I really am. If they won't call me by my real name, they're not going to get the real me. I'll just pretend to be whoever they want me to be. I'll be Pollyanna. They'll never see me get angry, or hurt, or resistant. I'll always be compliant, doing whatever they ask, being the model prisoner, always positive, smiling and helpful. I won't survive if they see my true feelings.

The gray lady who I'd just spoken to poked her head out. "Come on in."

This time I tripped over the front door mat and followed her back into the foyer.

After the induction, she said, "I'll have Mr. Donovan escort you to your building that'll be your residence for the duration. Good luck!"

One hurdle finished.

Guards were called Miss, Mrs. or Mr. No first names allowed.

Mr. Donovan arrived and was buzzed into the room.

Buzz land again.

"Is this Edwards?" he asked.

Now I'd be known by somebody else's last name.

"She's number 67380-095".

That's gonna be my other name. A number.

The last three digits stood for the location of my case, Oregon.

"You'll have to memorize that number, because you'll be asked for it while you're in here," he looked stern but pleasant, "but don't worry about that today. Come with me."

I'll act sweet, no matter what happens next. I'm gonna be the model prisoner. The Parole board'll have to cut my sentence...

We met up with a sleepy-eyed, statuesque blond.

"Meet Jeanne, our resident French professor," he said her name like 'Jon' with a chuckle. Surprised, I stared back at a model, with enormous boobs, tiny waist and long legs. Her pageboy blond hair was combed to the side, and she wore make-up, with bright red lipstick.

"Oh, Donovan, stop eet! I'm no more a professeur zen you're De Gaulle," she said with a thick Parisian accent.

Donovan smirked and before leaving to go said to me, "Stay with her while I arrange your paperwork and room."

"And zanks for waking me up from my beauty sleep. Zat's most unkind of you," she added with a flirty laugh. Turning her deep blue eyes on me, she looked me over and grabbed my hands.

"Well, cherie! Welcome to ze palace! What do you zink of your new 'ome?" Her accent, warm and gentle like a silky pillow comforted me.

"It's not at all what I imagined."

"Zeldom is. But it's a trap. Looks zo classy on ze outside, but inside it's a pile of sheet!" Even the way she said 'shit' was elegant.

"But you don't need to know all zis information right now. My name is Jeanne and yours?"

"Samsara, but the guards call me 'Cecilia'. I'll get it corrected tomorrow."

"Ha!" she laughed heartily, "Good luck getting anyzing changed! Ze BOP still has my last name spelled wrong for four *years*, now! Imagine!"

"You've been here that long?" Seeing how good she looked, I thought it might be possible to go through this ordeal and still look like a human being.

"...Not here ze whole time. I was first in Brighton, Massachusetts. Zen I was transferred 'ere when my sentence was finalized. What are you 'ere for?"

"A political charge. Conspiracy."

"Sure you are. Ninety percent of ze people here are in for conspiracy. And, what, did you conspire to do?"

What the hell, I have to tell people eventually. Plunge in.

"Murder a federal official."

She didn't flinch. "Well, zat's original. Wait till you meet SJ. She tried to bump off one of your presidents. She'll love you! I'm just an ordinary junkie. Zey tried to hang me for selling dope. Too bad I got caught. It was such good stuff, too! Boy, do I miss eet!" Her candor was infectious.

"How do you manage? I badly need a cigarette. Do you smoke?"

"Absolutely, darling! I'll give you some, and zen you can get zem on commissary. Have zey assigned you yet?"

Donovan was walking back to us, when a shrill bell sounded.

"It's 4 o'clock count. Come on, Edwards, I'll bring you to your room."

"I have a zousand questions, cherie! See you after count. Zere's mail call, zen we'll do dinner togezher!"

After count and mail call, we walked to dinner. The walk was a blur. Dinner was a blur, as was most of the conversation with Jeanne. "Come, cherie, let me introduce you! Zere are several people I want you to meet. Over zere is SJ, your twin for political murder."

She pointed to a Martha Washington look-alike with a long pure-white braid, busy stuffing food in her mouth, uninterested in anything else.

Looks about as likely to be assassin material as I am.

"Normally SJ plops down right at our table and talks till ze cows come 'ome. Once she knows you're 'ere, she'll not leave us alone."

"Sounds like she's not very popular around here."

"She isn't. We all try to avoid 'er. Zen zere's Nia over zere."

"Jeanne, I'm afraid I'm in a kind of fog. Perhaps, it's just overwhelm. So many people… "

"Yes, of course. I understand. Why don't you go back to ze unit and rest a little. I come and see you when I'm done - yes?"

"Yes. Thank you!"

"Here, hav a cigarette. You're going to need eet!"

I got up from the table and walked to the door of the cafeteria, hesitating slightly because I didn't know if it was locked or not. It was open, and I went outside, which felt odd. Walking for the first time by myself, on this compound.

It's like a frontier. Maybe it's the last one. Like an explorer feels coming into uncharted territory for the first time. But no explorer can just hike into this *territory. You have to do something wicked, or be in the wrong place at the wrong time to land on this planet...*

I was beginning to understand why inmates got institutionalized. It was a very well put together planet.

What are the rules? Can I smoke? I need this cigarette so badly my joints are yelling.

I lit up and walked straight to the building I thought I came from.

It wasn't.

Different lobby on the inside...

Now what do I do? Lost on your own prison compound! Boy, that's rich.

I puffed hurriedly and put the cigarette out. There was a guard nearby. I felt so stupid having to ask directions.

"Excuse me?" I approached. She looked at me cautiously and narrowed her gray-green eyes.

"This is my first day, and I'm a little lost. Can you direct me to building C?"

Relieved, her stern expression slowly became a half-smile.

"Sure. Right this way." She walked to the left and slightly ahead of me. I learned that the guards tried not to turn their backs on inmates.

She was my height with short red hair. When we arrived at building C, I asked another question.

"Ma'am, is it possible to make a phone call? I told my family I would call to let them know I arrived. I was a self-commit." I figured telling her that would give me a little status.

"You can only make collect calls. The phones are turned on after dinner, around 6:30 P.M and again in the morning from 6:00 A.M." She saw my hesitant look. "It's OK. You *can* go there." She laughed a little. "By the way, what are *you* in here for? Some white collar gig?"

"Political. Conspiracy to murder a federal official." I didn't know the 'murder' word automatically put me into another category.

Her eyebrows went up and she stiffened slightly. "Oh, boy. We got another one of you over in A. You'll meet her. Good luck! You seem so nice, though. " She was about to say more, then, shaking her head, she walked away.

At the top of the stairs I found the phone booth. Already there was a line. It was almost 6:30 P.M.

When my turn came I was keenly aware of the people waiting behind me, I got into the booth and dialed slowly.

Br-r-ing. "Hello?" Then the line cut off while the operator asked if they would accept a collect call. "Cecilia?" it was my mother's thick voice.

"I'm here. I'm OK. How are you?"

She was drunk.

"OK," was all she could say.

"You wanted me to call you, remember? To let you know that I arrived. Remember?" No response. "I have to make collect calls from here. That's the only way they let us call. OK?"

Mumble.

"What did you say?"

"I said alright!" She sounded irritated. "How're you?"

"OK. Feels strange, but not as bad as I thought. I'll call you tomorrow with more news."

"Don't call too often. Once a week is fine." She was annoyed. I resolved not to call late in the day anymore.

"OK, goodbye. Oh, give my love to Daddy. Please?" I said, not knowing what else to add.

"OK." We both hung up.

Disappointed, I put the phone down.

Is this was how it'll be for the next few years? Don't think about it now. Get out of the way for the next inmate to use the phone. Tomorrow call Trish. Start the appeal... God, how could you do this to me?

Three hours later, I awoke with a bright light shining right in my eyes. I sat up in the dark, petrified.

What are they doing now?

Nothing happened.

My three roommates were asleep. I lay back down. Maybe they were just checking on me to see if I was still there. A long while later, I closed my eyes.

Bang. The lights again.

This time it was 3:30 A.M. No one else stirred.

Must be some weird prison rule: shine lights on us in our sleep.

I closed my eyes again.

5:30 A.M. my alarm went off and I squashed it, not wanting to wake up my cellmates, who would certainly be angry if I did.

Marci moved.

"Forgot to tell you," she said sleepily, "they count us by flashlight during the night. I heard you sit up through the first one. You'll get used to it."

I didn't.

After breakfast, Donovan told me to report for a physical screening to qualify for work. Everybody had to go through one when they came in.

"You vant to get any ozer job but ze kitchen," Jeanne said. "'Orible place! I was zere for too long! Try to get into ze prison industries. Ver-ry big business, wiz an enormous salary of one dollar per hour. I'll introduce you to Nia who will tell you ze ropes on how to get in zere."

Nia was a tiny slip of a girl, who had come to America from Cuba, and unknowingly married a drug dealer. She was also a born-again Christian, so I didn't know how she would take to me. Her husband was on the run – or 'lam', as they called it. His wife was imprisoned in his place.

"They couldn't find my husband, so they got me," Nia began after we met. "It's like that for many of the women here. You'll see," she laughed as if we were talking about husbands being away on business trips. Then she became quiet.

"Jeanne told me you were here on a political charge, like SJ, and that you want to work in ADP, right?"

"I'm not sure what ADP is?"

Thank God she's not asking about my case... in 48 hours I've been asked 17 times.

"Automated Data Processing. We sit at computers and key stuff into them all day long."

"What do I have to do to get in there?"

"Take a typing test."

I only typed with two fingers. "I'm not very good."

"Don't worry. If I passed it, you will."

"And I also passed zis test," Jeanne, who was sitting next to us added, "zo just do eet and don't think about eet."

Two days later I took the test, memorizing the text and typing with my two fingers like my life depended on it. That night at dinner Jeanne met up with me as I walked to the cafeteria after count.

"Hey, cherie! How was the test?"

"Not hard at all. I think I made the cut off."

Jeanne and I went through the chow line together, and sat down. For the first part of the meal she talked about her past and her battle with heroin.

"You know, I used to always start a meal *stoned*, wiz ze best heroin. Made ze food taste so much better."

"Were you on it for a long time?"

"Oh no. I just started taking eet towards ze end, after I had been selling for shree years. Before zat, I never touched ze stuff. Pity. Eet was zo good. Maybe if I had started earlier, I would 'ave been dead before zey arrested me."

"How did they get you?"

"I became too big. I sold too much and got too greedy. If I had stayed small I probably wouldn't 'ave gotten caught. Someone I trusted got arrested and tried to avoid being sent away for a long time, so he turned me in. " She looked down at her food and winced. "I don't 'ate him. He had to take care of himself."

Mm. He had to take care of himself... I wonder if I ever really learned how to do that. Something I need to learn. Maybe here I'll have the chance. Otherwise I'll be carrying out my resentment month after month, year after year, and in the end it'll be me that suffers more than them. And that just might push me over the edge.

Chapter 17
The Last Frontier

America is the only nation in history, which miraculously has gone directly from barbarism to degeneration without the usual interval of civilization.
— *Georges Clemenceau*

The atmosphere in Dublin prison punctured my fear. Although it took a while for me to learn *how* to listen to Jeanne and Nia, when I did, my cranky old self-centeredness began to melt into something I liked a whole lot better. People started to like me because I was less abrasive and demanding.

Nia taught me a lot, even though my superior attitude got in the way.

What can a born again Christian teach me?

Nia was so tiny the wind could have blown her away. But nothing and nobody knocked Nia down. Three days after I came to Dublin she came over to where Jeanne and I were sitting.

"There's an opening in ADP and I'll speak to the supervisor about you. I'm sure there won't be any problem. And after that I'll show you the ropes in case I'm freed tomorrow."

"Nia, you will *not* be free tomorrow! Ze Feds don't work zat fast." Turning to me, Jeanne said, "Nia zinks zat God will work a miracle and she will walk out any day."

"Oh, he will, Jeanne," Nia said with no irritation at Jeanne and a lot of conviction.

"I hope for you, he will," I said without any conviction. "Miracles *do* happen," I added feeling guilty.

"They most certainly do, I have no doubts whatsoever. And, you would too... do you believe in Jesus?" she asked with holy sincerity.

"Not exactly... but I was in a religious commune where the teacher talked about Jesus."

"That was a cult, right? And cults, you know are governed by Satan himself. Are you still in it?"

"No, I..."

"Good! Then there's always hope! But, we'll talk more tomorrow. I don't want to overwhelm you. Today, the most important thing is to get you settled and working. Do you need anything? Toothbrush, toothpaste, comb – anything? I can get anything you need."

"Nia is ze resident caregivea, Samsara. Just tell 'er what you need and she can get eet for you. Nasing illegal of course!" Jeanne smirked.

Thus began my relationship with Nia, which was to last a year and a half. She didn't just talk. She delivered on her promises. She showed me that I had prejudices against people I judged "unenlightened" and "simple minded," no different from the intolerance that had branded me in Oregon. Funny. I was beginning to see that my opinions about others appeared to be coming back to me.

Before I could reply a very tall man I'd never seen before, came over to the table. He looked exactly like Narian, which made me choke a bit.

"Ms. Edwards, I'm your Case Manger, Eric Roberts. Your lawyer called and wanted to discuss some things with me.

Stop by my office behind the officer's station in the unit after dinner, will you?" He turned and walked out.

I stared in amazement as I watched him go: he had carrot red hair and freckles. Exactly like Narian.

"Who was *that*?" I looked at Jeanne and Nia.

"Eric Roberts is *our* Case Manager. He's probably the only truly good staff member here whose heart is in the right place," Nia said. Jeanne was frowning.

Hmm. We'll see.

After dinner I went to his office, knocked on the door and went in.

"Sit down, Ms. Edwards," he said without looking up, "You don't have to be afraid. I don't scream and yell," he said, faintly smiling.

Same as Narian.

Then he looked up.

"Sorry for staring, Mr. Roberts... it's just that you look so much like one of my co-defendants." I said apologetically.

"Mmm," was all he said, looking down at his papers and reminding me of Hanna, who would bury herself in her papers to avoid looking at me.

"Your lawyer, Ms. Peterson, wants to file a request for reduction of sentence. It's not standard, but it's often done... I'm just letting you know. The way she spoke of you seems to indicate you have a good relationship?"

"Oh yes, we do. She's an amazing woman. I'm glad to have her."

"Really? Not many inmates feel that way about their lawyers!"

"Well, I'm sorry for them, then."

"How're you doing here? So far so good?" He looked at me with a hopeful pleading in his eyes, as if he wanted things to be going well and not have to deal with any further problems.

"So far..."

No complaining. Super inmate, remember? He'll have to put in a good report to the Parole Board and that will get me an early release.

That idea was shot to hell in the next forty-five seconds.

"You know, I've reviewed your file and I know you're due to meet with the parole board. As a matter of policy, Ms. Edwards, you should know the parole board has not granted early release to anybody in a long, long time. The Board's being phased out as fewer and fewer inmates come in under the old law. Unfortunately they seem to be stricter than ever. With your status I would not count on them doing anything for you."

No! I don't want to hear that.

"But, there are always exceptions, Mr. Roberts, and I intend to be one," I said, irritated that he was destroying my carefully constructed fantasy.

"I hope for your sake you are, Ms. Edwards," he said gently and sincerely.

"But," he continued, "I'm afraid there's not very much we can do for you with the Board. They respond much better to letters of support from family and influential friends."

At least he's being up front with me.

"I'm supposed to meet with the Board in May, so I'd better get started."

"Yes. I would do that... is there anything else you want to discuss?

"No. Thank you, Mr. Roberts. Except that I want to start work as soon as possible."

That'll give him the idea that I'm a model prisoner.

"Yes, I was told you applied for ADP," which showed me he didn't miss much.

"Yes. ADP has an evening shift, so I'd have time to prepare my case during the day. I intend to take a refresher-typing course in the computer department and tutor English and..."

"Wow, will you have time to sleep?" He said along with that Narian look-alike-smile again. I suddenly decided I'd had enough and wanted to leave.

"I hope so. Goodbye and thank you," I said on the way to the door, glad to get out of his office.

Phew! That went OK. I am still so nervous around authority,

like I have to jump through hoops. Still giving over my sense of self worth to someone else, trying to please. Again...

My first official meeting with the prison administrators was on January 17. It was supposed to be a great day. This first meeting would kick-off my well-rehearsed strategy. I told Nia about my plans just before I went in.

"Samsara," she said hesitantly, "maybe you ought to just listen to what they have to say and not expect too much."

"OK," I said but not really listening.

She understated things.

I was out in seventeen minutes and that was overtime. Roberts and Ms. Beck, the Unit Manager, were courteous and cautious. Beck read my charges and emphasized that they were "v-e-r-y serious," wishing me luck with the Parole Board. *Not* very reassuring.

As I left I could hear their whispers through the door.

"Poor brainwashed kid... "

I'm 42! Some kid.

"She doesn't have a chance... "

I almost ran to Jeanne's room, knocked and burst in.

"Jeez, what a stupid group. Jeanne, what do *you* think? Am I just another brainwashed kid? What do people around here think of SJ? Do they think she's some kind of demon because she was part of that conspiracy to kill the President?"

"Huh? Mmm... you must have been at ze stupid team meeting, eh? Zey didn't like you? Too much murder and not enough conspiracy, mmm?" she chortled.

"I just want to know what I'm up against. I have to prepare for this damn Parole Board, and if I don't get a recommendation from the team it's going to be much harder. It's bad enough dealing with everybody else's ideas about who I am and what I did."

"Listen, cherie, you are nozing special We are all in here for somzing we didn't do, anyway, so it makes no difference what ze title is. Only how you are wiz ze ozers. And you cannot trust many of zem. I waz ze zame as you when I came en. I learned ze hard way! So don't worry about eet.

"Listen to me. Ze team won't do anyzing for you. Look at SJ. She's been trying to get parole for seventeen years. Esmeralda for seven and she has pull wiz some politicos in D.C. because of her Columbian connections. Marietta, ze Mafia blond in A, has been in 'ere on ze murder charge for twenty-two years, already, and no parole. And you zink zey will parole *you*? I don't want to destroy your hopes but maybe zis helps you to be a little more realistic, no?" She looked at my fallen face and softened.

"Besides, cherie, eet's not so bad, zis tree years you 'ave, it will go zo fast, you'll see. Mine went very, very fast. My next seven will go faster!"

It was time to return to work, so I thanked her, and left.

Nothing special? There's that "special" label again. And boy do I still want it. My blood surges each time I think I'm being given attention. But in fact it isolates me. Jeanne pities me; I heard it in her voice. Maybe every time I think I'm hot shit, I actually come across as snooty. But that's not really me. I just want to be accepted. Wow, all those years of chasing importance only made me self-absorbed and I'm only just now seeing it.

Just then Nia came in. She'd been looking for me.

"Hi Samsara," she said in a low voice so as not to disturb the others. "How was the team meeting?" Her large brown eyes looked at me with concern. She knew ahead of time I'd put too much hope in this single event.

"Terrible. They hated me." I said dejectedly.

"Samsara, they don't hate you. But they sure can't do very much. Don't even think about them. Just work on getting those letters of recommendation from your doctor friends. That'll help. Don't forget to get copies sent to you, so you can see what they wrote." She smiled at me sweetly. Nia had lots of faith and a positive outlook. As if I had an injection, I instantly felt hopeful.

She's teaching me how to be patient, forget my whining self-absorption and focus on the work ahead.

Thanking her, I couldn't wait until I had some time to draft some letters.

Two days later, in the middle of my ADP shift, I was called into the Unit Manager's office.

"Ms. Edwards," Ms. Beck began briskly, "there is a Peter James Edwards III, who says he is your former husband. He's making a request to see you. This is highly irregular. Normally, the inmate makes a visitor's list, which is then submitted and approved – or not. Didn't Mr. Roberts inform you of the procedure?" She was a clipped-toned person.

"Yes, but…"

"Then why didn't you submit his name?"

"Ms. Beck, I lost contact with him in 1985 and I didn't know how to locate him. I'm surprised that he found me!"

"So I am to presume that you *don't* want to see him?"

"Oh, no! I would *love* to see him! How do I make that possible?" I started to cry from fear she might actually prevent me from seeing him.

Sam found me! I thought every sannyasin had been brainwashed into believing that the group I went to Germany with were all horrible criminals and any association meant condemnation to hell.

"Well," Ms. Beck continued, "He told me he had just arrived in San Francisco from Australia, would only be in the area for three days, and wants to make a special request to see you. This is all highly irregular," she repeated.

"Ms. Beck, I would be so grateful if there is *anything* you could…"

"I wanted to verify if he was, indeed, your husband." She enjoyed cutting people off.

"Oh, yes. He was my second husband."

"Your *second* husband?" She said with very arched eyebrows, and acid in her voice.

Oops, faux pas there… say something fast.

"Yes, and we remained good friends. Unfortunately we lost contact. You know, Ms. Beck, apart from my elderly parents in Arizona, who can't travel, I don't know if I'll have *any* visitors, as I was living in Europe before I came to prison, and it will be almost impossible for my European friends to come. How I would appreciate the opportunity to see Peter, if there is any way that it could possibly..."

"I will approve it for this weekend, which is the only time he said he could come. But I will do this once only. Good day, Ms. Edwards."

I thanked her gushingly and left quickly, in case she should change her mind.

"Yipee!!!" I squealed, though not as loudly as I wanted.

Wow! He found me! How'd he do it? From Australia no less. Maybe he'd read The Oregonian and their outrageous reports on the Rajneeshees?

I was so excited I wet my pants.

I didn't think anyone would want to come to a prison.

Sam did.

On the day of his visit, January 26, I dressed in my one good outfit that I'd worn when I came in. My wardrobe now consisted of left over clothes from the laundry, including two sets of oxford shoes which didn't quite fit; two combat green army pants that were too big and too long; plain, oversized bras, required wearing by all female inmates; large underpants that kept bunching up as I walked and four green army shirts. Since the Bay area was damp-cold, I was granted an army jacket, which made me look butch. My hair was multi-toned: an inch of gray, then an inch of black roots, which was replacing the blond. There was so much white in my hair that my head looked like a Christmas decoration.

And, I didn't care. Sam had seen it all.

I'm afraid they'll do something to keep me from seeing him. Again, torturing myself with the worst possible scenarios.

Finally I heard the announcement I'd been waiting for.

"Cecilia Edwards to the visiting room," boomed across the compound. I galloped to the visiting area where a guard patted me down, looked in my ears, and handed me a form to list all my jewelry, brand and color of my shoes, laces, socks, and description of my clothing.

"Your number?" I was supposed to have it memorized.

"67390-065?" I said in a wobbly voice.

"That's not right. Don't you know it by now? You'd better get it right when they ask you after this visit. 67380-095," Ms. Davenport, the guard said.

"Thank you, I'm sorry."

"I know you're new, but we have to make sure everybody's who they say they are. Sometimes people try and switch."

"Switch?" I wasn't sure I was hearing right, "You mean the visitor tries to take the prisoner's *place?*" I asked in disbelief.

"Yup. Strange, I know, but we've had it happen."

"Well, I'm seeing a man, and besides the last time I saw him he had a beard," I tried to sound funny.

She looked at me and grinned.

"That would be strange." Then she laughed and I liked her even more.

I learned later that they put the "nice" guards in the visiting room to present a good *face* to the public, following an incident where a guard threatened a visitor and the visitor sued.

"Approved for wear," the guard yelled and the door to the visiting room clanged open.

"Sam!" He sat at a table in the middle of the room, nervously twisting his shoulder length hair.

"Sizzy! He used the old familiar tone and name.

"Wow! I can't believe it's finally you." He stood up and took me in his arms, giving me a long body hug that brought Ms. Davenport rushing back.

"You can't hug that way in here," she said trying to be stern. "Only a brief hug and one tasteful kiss allowed. Not a lot of hand holding, either."

"OK," Sam said releasing me immediately, turning red as if he'd been caught with his pants down. I couldn't help smiling at him.

"Sorry, Sam," I said gently taking his hand.

"These damn bureaucrats," he said in a whisper, "they

want to run every part of our lives. Oh, well, here we are at least." He looked at me. I wanted to see delight on his face but there was only tension, and curiosity.

"Let's sit down, Sam. I have a million questions to ask you. First, though, I'm so happy that you found me and you're here. Thank you so much for making the journey and filling out all that paperwork. But how *did* you find me?"

"My brother. He read in the news that a Cecilia Edwards had been sentenced, and called me in Australia, asking me if that was you. He remembers you real well. You always made such an impression on him. But, it took me ages to track down which prison they sent you to. Nobody wanted to give me the time of day."

"God, Sam. After all these years... Well, at least the BOP did something right when they gave me your last name." I laughed. "How are you? Are you going back to Australia? Are you with anybody, now? I have so many questions. It's been six *years* since we've talked."

"That long? Gosh so much has happened. I was in Europe for a while..."

"So was I! When? Where?"

"Italy, mostly. A group of us left the Ranch. It really fell apart after you guys left. Bhagwan was arrested and nobody could hold it together. I traveled to Italy with a small group, who soon after declared themselves enlightened. After a few months, I'd had enough and split to Australia where I set up a healing center. I met Dara there. Actually, she's out in the car. She wanted to come and show her support."

"She's in the car?"

"They wouldn't let her in because she didn't *apply*, and couldn't say she knew you. She's sitting in the car because she thought she'd be able to see both of us through the barbed wire, if we sat outside."

"Let's go to the patio then," I said immediately, touched that she should want to do this for me, and eager to please Sam.

I owe him for dealing with all the bureaucracy and coming all this way.

Outside Sam pointed out the car. I told him not to be conspicuous or else they'd have her arrested for sitting there. I looked toward the car and smiled. A tiny hand went up behind the window. Then I looked away.

"Please tell her how grateful I am that she came, and that I only looked away so as not to draw the guards' attention to her."

"I will, Sizzy... this must be so hard for you. Do you need anything? Money?"

"Thank you, sweetheart... letters. I would love to have letters."

We chatted for the rest of the hour and a half. I greedily drank in every word.

After he left I realized we'd spoken more to each other in those ninety minutes than in years. My eyes followed him through the doors till he disappeared. It was hard to let him go.

Will I see him again? Will he write? He has a girlfriend, so why should he write to me? Damn. I'm doing it again. Not letting myself relish this visit. Damn...

"I'm confused about my feelings for him," I said afterwards to Nia and Jeanne. "There are too many unresolved things that went down between us. I still care for that knucklehead."

"Knookelhead?" Jeanne's eyes rounded.

"Dad used to call him that mockingly. I liked the term, however. To me it signaled that he wanted to take care of the whole world."

"Oh no, not anozer one of yur do-goodies." Jeanne was cynical about my "do-good" past.

"Yup he was in the commune too."

"Well, his soul is definitely worth saving, Samsara. I would encourage you to pray for him, no matter what else you feel. Will he write a parole letter for you?" Nia asked.

"I haven't asked him yet, but I will."

I didn't want to talk any more because so much of his visit had already been dissected. I wanted to savor something, to take him back to my bunk and remember...

The next day, Sunday morning, I called Mom and Dad. When I told Dad that I had a visit from Sam, he was pissed off right away. Dad blamed Sam for 'taking me away to Bhagwan and destroying my life,' no matter how often I tried to explain that it was *I* who took Sam. Dad disliked talking on the phone, and immediately handed it over to Mom.

She was her delightful morning self.

"Hi, how are you, Mom?" I tried to sound casual while standing in the smelly phone booth on the second floor, removing the stale cans of soda that had been left there the night before.

"Oh *Cecilia*, how *are* you?" she said surprised. Each Sunday, she always had this tone, like she hadn't heard from me in a century.

"I'm fine, Ma, how're you?" we continued on with the next forty questions on how the entire clan of cousins, uncles, aunts and next-door neighbors were.

Then I got to current events.

"Did you ask Reuben if he would write that letter to the Parole Board for me?" Dr. Reuben Rosenblatt was a retired Interstate Commerce Federal Administrative Judge, who'd been on the Nuremberg war trials panel. He'd met me when I was under house arrest, indicating he was eager to help, as he liked me and had become a friend of my parents.

"Oh yes," Mom continued. "He already wrote a draft and will give it to me after his family leaves. They came for Christmas. By the way, did you get the Christmas gift I sent you?"

"What Christmas gift?" I asked a little apprehensively since I had given instructions before I left *not* to send me anything, lest the prison confiscate it.

"Oh, it was just a few of your calcium pills, which I put inside a Christmas card. I figured that you needed your vitamins! I don't know why you left them here."

I dropped the phone panic stricken.

How could she do that? I told her not to send me anything because I was afraid she'd do something like this, which the prison authorities would consider contraband. They might think the calcium pills are drugs and throw me in the hole.

I picked up the receiver and took a deep calming breath. It didn't help.

"Ma, why did you do that when I told you that the prison regards vitamin pills as illegal? They'll think I got you to mail me drugs!" I shouted.

"Oh no. They wouldn't think *that!*"

"Ma. You don't know these people. They would certainly think I made you send me drugs. Now, I'm in trouble. Ma, I gotta go immediately and see if I can clear this up."

"Oh, Cecilia, I thought I was sending you something you could use! I just wanted to send you a Christmas present, I'm sorry." her voice trailed off, and I instantly felt ashamed that I had yelled at her.

I'm so mean to the people who care for me. She had no idea how suspicious they are here and was just trying to help me.

"It's OK, Ma. I'll take care of it. Don't worry. I love you. Bye."

I went straight to the officer's station. Donovan was there.

"Mr. Donovan, I have a problem."

"And what else is new?" he said with a smirk.

"My Mom innocently put some calcium pills in her Christmas card, thinking I could use them. She's 76 and doesn't understand what she can and can't send me. What can I do about it?"

"Probably nothing. But I'll send a message to R&D to look for the *package.*"

"Will they send me to the hole?"

"Depends if it's drugs."

"They're *vitamins!*"

"We'll see."

By the end of February I hadn't been sent to the hole, so I figured it was OK. I also never received the card, so who knows where Mom sent it.

Poor Mom, she tries so hard. Now, stay focused. No self-pity. Just collect the parole letters and keep doing the best you can with ADP. What a struggle, all that three finger typing. Gotta keep my keystrokes up or they'll throw me out. Everybody else is typing like they know what they're doing. I need the cash, if cigarettes go up once more, quit. Can't afford cigs and the phone, especially since we'll have to pay for calls soon. The prisons have to make more money with people increasingly being put away.

At work, Carolyn Jons, my supervisor, who preferred to be called Carolyn, came over to me and said, "Ms. Edwards, you need to look at the manuscript, not at your fingers."

"Carolyn, I'm uncoordinated because of my bad eye and have to look at my fingers," I lied, smiling engagingly.

She's gotta believe me. If I can stay in ADP and move up to a Grade 1, I'll make $1.15 an hour instead of the paltry 33 cents I'm making now.

The other jobs on the compound only paid ten cents an hour without any possibility of a raise. ADP was one of the highest paid and as a Grade 5 industrial worker I was much better off.

I never learned to touch type. Instead I got by, memorizing the words. During the day, I tried to retrain my fingers by taking a computer-typing course, but each time I attempted to put my newly learned finger patterns to the keyboard, my keystrokes slowed down. Keystrokes were recorded automatically and I got in trouble. I abandoned the course.

"We'll get you a colored screen to enlarge the print. That'll be easier on your eyes and help you type properly," Carolyn offered, eager to help the handicapped.

Damn. Now, what'll I do?

Three days later the batcher, who first organized the work into piles, then distributed it before collecting it for transport, was transferred.

I applied for the job and got it. God had arranged a miracle.

Relieved, I threw myself into being the best damn organizer ADP had ever seen.

On February 27, my Rule 35 motion for a reduction of sentence was filed and promptly denied. I wouldn't allow myself to feel the setback, as I had to keep on going for the Parole Board meeting.

By April, I had many letters of recommendation to the Board. People's support was so tangible it helped to increase my own intention, forcing me to concentrate on freeing myself. I could feel that energy radiating such intense heat that my thoughts burned like glowing embers in a fireplace.

Trish was unable to visit but sent me a letter. The details were not so glowing and dampened my fervor. She wrote that Maya had been released after serving sixteen months in camp (a minimum restrictions facility). If I still wished to be transferred to a camp, I should request that the BOP recommend me. She reminded me that since I was not a state witness, Fronten would certainly not recommend me. She finished by saying that if she were me, she would concentrate on preparing for the parole hearing.

Being inside, and thinking of Maya being released, was a bitter pill to swallow.

The morning of July 27, 1992, finally arrived and I learned the Parole Board had gathered in the conference room. In my best prison green outfit, I waited with an anxious dread to be called to see them.

Don't get shaky. Keep your mind sharp. Be clear like a warrior going into battle.

"Cecilia Edwards to the Team room" came over the loudspeaker.

I walked down the hall and opened the door. Two men I'd never seen before sat at the conference table. I nervously fingered my pile of papers, trying to ease my tension.

"Good mornin'. Are you Cecilia Edwards?"

"Good morning! Yes."

"Ah'm Gorden Barry an' this is Robert Norse. Ah believe you were notified of this hearin'?" Barry, who was clearly in charge, began. He was a heavy-set African-American who, even sitting down, dwarfed Norse.

"Yes."

"What we'll do is interview you this mornin', then ask you to step out. Then we'll call ya back in and give ya our recommendation. That's all it is: a recommendation. You'll get the final decision back in about three weeks. It can be appealed and the instructions on how to appeal will be on the letter you receive. You have a five year sentence and ya served about eleven and a half months, now, correct?"

"Yes."

"Why did you commit such a serious offense? You had no prior record?"

"My involvement with a spiritual community."

"That's one thing bein' involved in a community 'n all," he interrupted me too quickly, "but look at what occurred! I know people may have influenced you in the organization, but given your education, and never been in trouble, how could you let those people talk you into and get you involved in such a serious offense?"

"Er," I began, clearing my throat. "What happened was, seven years later, I now understand how I was brainwashed. I joined the community initially because of my doctoral research and the ideals the community espoused, trying to live a harmonious life and... "

"No doubt 'bout it. But when it started to be a campaign against innocent people, it went way beyond... poison put in the food, conspiracy to murder an official... there must have been *some* point where you said, hey I have to extract myself from this."

Norse was nodding in agreement and staring smugly at me, like he'd just caught a big fish.

"I did do that in 1985."

"Yeah, but it'd gone so far. You *did* read the pre-sentence report? Then you *did* participate against the U.S. Attorney, right?"

"Yes."

"Did you surveil him?"

"Yes I did."

"What was the purpose of the surveillance?"

Not again!

I explained and Barry listened to how and when I had watched Tork at his house.

"Then..." I continued, explaining my procedures for getting interviews and profiles like any reporter. Barry punctuated my statements with "mm-mns".

"After all this occurred, did ya go to Europe with the rest of 'em or did you stay here?"

"In September 1985, I finally left the commune, which I had been trying to do for a year. Since I had no money, a friend of mine who had been living in the community... "

"Sila?" Norse asked.

"No, not Sila, someone else, offered to pay my way to Europe. I also felt that I needed some time to recover from some of the awful events which occurred prior to leaving the community, and then I would come back to the States and see my parents."

"Good. What we'll do is weigh what you've had to say this mornin', compared with what the pre-sentence report says and determine if there should be any changes in the severity ratin'." He turned to Norse. "Do you have any other questions?"

Right on cue, Norse began feverishly throwing questions at me

"You sayin' that you were not actually involved in the plannin' of the murder of the U.S. Attorney?" He asked in a loud strident tone.

"What happened was I had a meeting with Sila..." and then I explained the details in exactly the same way as I had to the German Judges.

Why were they asking me again? To see if I would change my story?

"Let me tell you what the pre-sentence report says: 'Samsara spoke of a great desire to be the actual assassin'."

"I never said that. In fact there's an affidavit, submitted to the court, that says that's not true."

"Let's talk a little bit about what's been happenin' to you. Where were you before this institution?"

Then I told them of the litany of prisons, jails and house arrest. While I was speaking, Barry leafed through my progress evaluation and my teaching English ESL evaluation. I knew they had favorable reports from the case manager, along with the medical reports on my eye condition, noting the court order needed to obtain the saline solutions. They acted very impressed that I had Hospice training and my statement to resume it upon release, as well as take care of my parents.

"Now, you realize," Barry solemnly intoned, "that with a five year sentence, you're goin' to serve *considerably* beneath the guidelines, right?"

"Yes."

"So that's what we have to look at today. Now, I know you've waited eleven months, and this thing has been draggin' on for a long time. Now, is there anything else you want to say?"

"Only one thing: did you receive the letters?"

"We sure did. An' they're very good letters. Anythin' else?"

"No, thank you."

"Why don't you step out an' we'll call ya back in."

It took fifteen seconds. I walked in the room, glanced at Barry's face and knew nothing I'd said made any difference.

"At the beginning I indicated this would be a recommendation. If you believe an error's been made, or you've been treated unfairly, you can exercise your appeal rights. We've considered what you said this mornin', and the report; an', at this point we're not goin' to make any changes. Your guidelines remain the same. You're goin' to serve *considerably beneath* the guidelines. We're goin' to recommend you serve forty months, with a review hearin' in eighteen months..."

A total of seventeen minutes from beginning to end, and it was all over.

Numbly I walked down the hall and into my cell.

Even when you expect bad news, it still burns when you get it. I was hurt, tired, angry and something else...

Powerless.

There was not a single thing I could do to change things.

Nia, who'd now become my cellmate, was waiting for me.

"Samsara! I've been praying so hard for you!"

"They refused my early parole release, Nia... all those letters... all that effort..." Tears began to choke my words. Nia came over and put her arms around me.

"I'm so sorry... so sorry. I know how much you wanted this. And for your parents to be able to see you... maybe you can get a transfer to the Phoenix camp. We'll work on that."

Nia meant her entire prayer warrior team would "work on that." But I was still struggling with being useless.

If I couldn't do anything to change this situation, what good am I? Have I ever been any good to anybody?

By August Trish wrote me that our request for an evidentiary hearing had been denied.

I wrote back.

Dear Trish,

Let's appeal. What have we got to lose, since nothing worse can happen? But I never intend to see those Board people again, nor appear at any further parole hearing. They were obviously hostile to me, as you can hear on the tape recording they gave me. Everything was decided before they even saw me. So, why should I waste any more time on them?

She wrote back with news that she'd been appointed an

advisor to the Attorney General, and would have to relinquish her work with me.

This can't happen. Trish is my rock. She's kept me believing that there still is some good in a society that hunts people down solely because of what other people say about them. How can I go on without her?

Prison was dosing me with lots of reality, smashing my illusions. Bitterness crept in like a wet blanket sucking me down. My attempts to be the sweet, uncomplaining inmate were getting me nowhere. I felt like hell, angry, restless and betrayed. I was taught if you abide by the rules and are good, you get something for it. I was getting nothing but the increasing burden of trying to be positive. Inmates who broke the rules got nothing worse than time alone in the hole, sometimes a welcome relief in this overcrowded nightmare.

My brief phone calls to my friend Puneet were moments spent in Europe, where my mind could retreat to the Black Forest hills or the cobbled square in Baden-Baden, where laughter was the language I remembered. Puneet was the conduit to that world, mixed in with the turmoil of his relationship.

"Samsara, I feel so jealous around Georg every time he sees other people. He's so damn handsome. And I know that I have to let him be free, but it's so *hard*."

"Yes," I said. "I know. I've suffered so much from jealousy too: it's a bitch all right. Maybe when he comes here you'll get some relief from worrying."

"Are you kidding? He'll be thousands of miles away, wandering in the sin capital of America."

"I'll keep tabs on him."

"From prison?"

"I'll grill him every time he comes to visit me so he *has* to behave," I said sternly.

"Very funny... and by the way, Thomas Burger called me to ask if we're still speaking. He sends you his regards."

"Is he still Diva's attorney?"

"Yeah. The Americans are still trying to get her back in prison to serve more time."

"Even after the Germans refused to extradite her, and sent that stinging letter to Fronten?"

"Yup. They're not giving up."

"God that must be awful for Diva. I thought it was finished and she was free."

"Well, she is, technically, though she can't leave Germany."

"Why would she *want* to? Anyway, please give my regards to both of them. He did so much for me, especially when he came over to Portland for my sentencing. He was a great support for Trish."

"Well, Samsara, I'll let you know next week when Georg's flight is…"

He stayed a month and visited me each weekend. I kept my promise to Puneet; probing Georg for the details of his "adventures."

The day after he left, Nia was notified that she was being transferred. That tipped me over the edge.

Nia and I had become buddies since the first "born again" discussion, in which she tried to convert me and I told her my cult story. I always resisted being converted, and she never stopped trying, but in the middle we met and became devoted to caring for each other. Her attention nourished me, which I craved. Being scared to death of the big bad prison that first year made me latch onto Nia like a life raft.

She kept me going when Region denied my petition for camp transfer after the warden had signed the request; and got me back on my feet after I collapsed at the news of my favorite aunt dying from colon cancer. I held her hand the day she got the news that her husband had been captured in the Bahamas and thrown into isolation. And we cried together when she found out that the feds had harassed her two children in an effort to pressure her and her husband 'for information.'

Her departure was a big blow. She was my substitute mom. I refused to believe she was going away and the hurt went way down inside. Each shock and disappointment chipped away at my stamina.

"Don't think about it, Samsara," Nia said in our last conversation. "You know how it is around here. They tell you you're being transferred and then you wait months. *You* could be out of here by the time they move me! Anyway, it'll be at least a month before they do all the paperwork. Marelli said he's been working on my transfer for twenty-six months!"

"Yeah, but that was before your husband was caught. They may want you for questioning, or to be on hand to pressurize him."

"Er, to release you as a car-rot for yor 'ubbie to tak," Jeanne said.

"Oh, you two are just being paranoid!" Nia said. "The Feds know they can't get anything out of me! I didn't talk when he was gone. Why should I talk now? No. There's no reason to panic. I probably won't be going anywhere for a long time."

They shipped her out the next day.

That afternoon, I sobbed while distributing my batches.

Carolyn came over to me, touching my shoulder gently.

"I know you miss her. I miss her too." She smiled kindly. Nia was loved by every single person who knew her, which was at least half the compound.

I realized Nia's leaving affected me so profoundly because it touched a deep place I had shut down years ago in order to go on with my life.

I got too attached and it hurts like hell to be separated. I don't want to feel this bad. How cruel life is to keep stealing people away from me. I miss sharing my thoughts and reflections with Nia. And I'll never be able to talk to Aunt Becky any more. Why does the sweetest feeling of caring get taken away again and again and again? And I'm so busy wanting to be taken care of, that I never really got to know them.

Four days later, receiving a letter from HG in Germany, I wondered the same thing again.

How much did I know him? Was I just using him, too?

The simplicity of prison life eliminated lots of distractions, so I could look at myself. I didn't like what I saw, and found myself yearning to escape. The Bookmobile provided me with another fantasy world for a little while.

This traveling library was like having a visiting fairy godmother, who waving her wand produced the perfect book for a journey to a magical kingdom far away from the wicked BOP witches. I was heavily addicted to fairy tales, daydreams and anything that took me away from this wretched reality.

None of the women around me were guilty of anything other than trying to survive the malevolent deck life dealt them. They're just like everybody else on the outside who wheels and deals. Only we're the ones who got caught. The others with money, who were 'successful' on the outside, manage to pay off the catchers. That's all.

I was becoming a hardened, bitter old woman.

Then HG came for a visit and something changed. There were still people who cared about me and I had two arms, two feet, and a body, which mostly functioned pretty well. I saw that my bitterness was disguised self-pity, a convenient distraction to avoid responsibility. And I had to try to find some humor or I wasn't going to survive.

The night before visits was like a pre-prom (or wedding) event with hair rollers, creams, manicures and lots of tossing and turning, wondering how attractive Prince Charming would find you. Husbands, lovers and friends were all treated like kings, riding up on a majestic white charger to grace the lowly inmate-damsel with their divine presence. The "morning of" often dawned with bright promise and often too much heat from the curling iron, leaving some part of the hair burnt.

I used tiny rollers to curl my stubborn sheet-metal hair, and it got stuck constantly in the curler prongs. My then cellmate, Zoe, painstakingly pried each section loose, so I only lost about eight per cent of each clump of hair. I had some resemblance to a tall, gray-haired version of Lucille Ball with a large nest of pepper and salt on my head. HG had only seen the blond call girl version, so he was in for a surprise.

Hold in your belly and pretend he's your brother, not some good-looking German male, full of testosterone, who traveled across Europe and the U.S. to see you.

After the pre-visit search, I walked into the visiting room intending to walk slowly and calm down. Instead I almost ran to where he was sitting, knocking over two chairs, which the guards did not appreciate.

Me, the crimson-faced klutz!

"Hello, HG. God, it's great to see you!" I reached out, wanting to hide my face in his chest, for thirty seconds of the "allowed" hug.

"Theodora! So good to see you!" he said enthusiastically, his brown eyes full of amusement.

I may have looked like Lucy, but HG looked like my counterpart. His wiry brown hair stuck out more than usual, as if he'd had an electric shock, and his tiny brown eyes were buried inside deep crevices that hadn't been there before. The freckles were still there, but now his pale complexion was red and blotchy. He looked very thin and fragile.

"HG! You lost a ton of weight!"

"No, I've been gaining. Look at my paunch. But, what's about you, Theodora? You are much, much thinner. Don't they feed you here?"

"Listen, don't get me started on the food, or we'll spend the whole visit on it. Actually, it's not bad. We even have a salad bar for lunch. But tell me everything. How are you? Is your work still hounding you? And what about your friends? Didn't they all want to know who you were visiting over here?"

"Theodora," he said amused, "you haven't changed a bit. Still asking four questions before we even sit down! I'm fine. And yes work's the same. And my girlfriend and I just split up, again. So, no, she wasn't there to ask who I was visiting. Now, can we talk about the interesting stuff?" He was chuckling to himself as he talked, just like the old HG, but there was an underlying weariness in his voice.

"HG, what's really going on? I've not heard you sound so tired before."

"Ah, Theodora," there was a long sigh, "I'm a broken man. I used to fight off every battle with the people stealing from my company, with the workers who are on my back for more money, with the clients who nag me daily. Those days are over. I have no fight left in me any longer. I think I'll just quit and move to America. What do you think?"

"I think you're off your rocker."

"Off my rocket?" He looked at me puzzled. When I used English expressions that he hadn't heard before, he would try for the closest sounding word.

"Oh, HG, I should have taught you better English, including the best slang. I was a poor, poor English teacher."

"No, Theodora. It was *I* who was the poor student. And I have nobody to practice my English with. That's why I think I should move to America."

"Let's talk about something less depressing. Have you been in touch with Johann? I wrote him he should hang out with you, especially since he split up with Nina. I think you'd be a great friend for him. You'd cheer him up, introduce him to some nice *German* girls."

"He phones me from time to time, but we don't see each other. Our schedules are too opposite. He works days. I work *all* the time! What's the news from your lawyer?"

"She's not my lawyer any longer. She took a position with the government, so she couldn't continue working on my case. I'll have to find someone else."

"That's sad, Theodora. But I know you will find a person you want, no matter what anyone says. I do the same as you, even though I keep getting squashed on my head."

"Hit on the head, HG not squashed!" I smiled as I corrected him. We always had this funny, delightful relationship, in which we tried to teach the other something new. The rest of the visit was filled with his questions about my life in the prison, asking me many times if I needed anything.

"My dear friend, I need you to be there when I get out. You *will* keep writing to me, promise? No matter what! And I *will* come to see you in Germany as soon as my parole allows me to travel," I said taking his hands in mine as the guard signaled that visiting hours were over.

"Yes, Theodora, I will. But you know how slow I am. Don't give up on me. " His words and his plea strengthened me.

"You know, HG, I'll have the words "convicted felon" tacked onto my forehead when I come out. Are you sure you still want to associate with me?"

"That doesn't bother me a bit. Besides, my clients might tack similar ones on me if they get the chance. So we go around with matching letters on our foreheads! Good."

The bell rang, and the guard came to escort him out.

"HG, I love you! Take good care of your wonderful self. Travel safely. Till we meet again."

"I love you too, Theodora, and I'll be there for you. I do promise." For the first time I saw tears in his eyes.

He left and then I started crying.

There was little time for emotion because of the after visit strip search and random urine test. I hardly had a moment to reflect on how I felt and what had happened during our visit. Instead I forced myself to make my sphincter muscles perform; otherwise fear would stop me peeing. Once when one of the guards pounded on my door, as I was trying to poop, my body locked up and I couldn't. Since nothing was in the bowl, I couldn't "prove" I was "in the process of" so she threatened to write me up if I didn't produce in the next ten minutes. I strained so badly that I pulled a muscle. From that moment on, I began to have trouble peeing and eliminating. Fortunately, however, I peed this time and was dismissed.

I began to see my days in prison as an opportunity to review my life and the circumstances that had brought me to this place rather than a curse. So when a church group asked me to write a letter to young people who were in "compromised situations", on the edge of being pulled into criminal behavior, I leapt at the chance to help, and wrote:

I am a political prisoner.

I am in prison because I followed a man's ideals.

I wanted to feel as powerful as he was, to be in control and spread the message to others.

In the process I started to manipulate people and let myself be manipulated.

And manipulation brought me more power, which felt good.

In following his orders, I got arrested.

The prosecutors pressurized me to make a deal and give them information.

My other co-defendants did this and got reduced sentences.

I couldn't do it. I didn't want to hurt anybody else

I am changing the cycle of using people; I am trying to stop it for good.

If you want true power don't let them take it from you That is honor.

Your power is who you are.

If someone makes you mad, who has the power?

He does.

You sold it.

While I've been here I've learned about myself. Power is a struggle. Each day, each moment you have to struggle to remember who you are.

I've seen my anger, frustrations, and resentments.

I've observed them instead of unleashing them.

By this I gained back my power.

Think before you act, and how it might hurt yourself and others

In prison, I have been separated from the people I love.

You have a choice: years of misery, or an instant of reflection before you take a step you cannot take back.

Cecilia Edwards #67380-095

About 18 months into my sentence I filed a request to transfer to Phoenix camp, following all the BOP requirements. My request was referred to The Region, which "governs" the area of prisons where I was housed. A month later it was denied.

Following procedure I then submitted the same request to Washington.

They denied it.

I tried to focus on the next thing, one step at a time. It was a struggle not to give into despair.

I wrote to Hilary Clinton.

What the hell.

A short time after, a letter from the Assistant Director of Correctional Programs arrived.

August 25, 1993

Dear Ms. Edwards,

Your letter to Mrs. Clinton has been referred to my office for response. You believe the Bureau's security and custody classification system needs re-evaluation. Additionally, you cite a document, which recommends program alternatives to incarceration.

You are not eligible for camp placement because application of the threat to government official public safety factor precludes your placement in a minimum-security facility. Although you may disagree with this system, we believe it places inmates in facilities that provide adequate security, balances the inmate population, and limits transfers...

Even though the warden had recommended me as a reduced risk, citing my good conduct, *and* George Tork signed a statement declaring that he was "never physically injured as a result of the crime... and the defendant does not continue to be a threat to him, his family or the community," I was *still* categorized as a "threat to the community."

Here I was: following procedure; being a good inmate, doing all the things I was told to do and clearly non violent. *I'm not giving up. I'll try something else.*

By the end of November 1993 I filed a motion in the U.S. District Court requesting that they approve my four months of house arrest, prior to entering prison, as "time served", enabling me to at least get jail credit for it.

On January 11, 1994 Judge Wallace denied this motion stating I had "failed to exhaust administrative remedies."

On February 16, I filed another motion indicating that since one of my co-defendants with the same "public safety classification " was assigned to a camp; this decision should be considered as a precedent in *my* case. I also cited the fact of hardship on my aging parents who were unable to visit me.

The Judge replied:

"Defendant contends that she has now exhausted administrative remedies and the Bureau of Prisons has denied her requests. Based upon this representation, I am treating her motion as a petition for relief."

The Government immediately opposed the motion stating that

"Even if the Court were to find the defendant's pleading was properly filed, credit for time served... should not be awarded."

I rebutted on March 11:

"...According to the plea agreement, the Government conceded not to oppose any motion of the defendant for jail credit... the Government further states that 'the BOP retains discretion to determine the type of facility' an inmate is assigned. If this were the case in every instance, then court orders, which I myself have seen, assigning inmates to camp facilities, would not exist."

August came, and three things happened.

My old friend Pia (who had saved me from being beaten

up in the Dalles) requested a visit. She was dying of breast cancer.

The visit was denied.

The day after that, I received the Judge's denial of my motion. He declared that I wasn't in the same "category" as my co-defendants because they cooperated with the Government, thus demonstrating a change of attitude.

Two days later, Mr. Roberts approved a "good time consideration request" I had filed for my work in developing the Suicide Watch/Inmate Observer Program. This was my first real victory in the battle with "the system" but it was a hollow one.

When they refused to let Pia see me, I felt there was little hope of getting the rules waived.

A flame went out in my heart. I felt like Pia, whose life shortly after extinguished.

Why should I bother to do anything? For what? For whom? Why should I even try to go back into a world that locks up grandmothers or young female drug mules for 25 years?

Mr. Roberts called me into his office the day after his approval. He asked me why serving a month less was so important.

I told him that even one day less in this system was a gift from God. I did not say that the system was insane.

By April my release date was finally set for November 17, 1994.

Surprisingly after all the time I had thought of being let out, there was little joy. I felt badly that I was leaving and the others were staying.

I spent the following months packing my papers, arranging for someone to pick me up, finding out the details of my parole, teaching someone else how to do my prison job, searching out leads for jobs that would accept me with "convicted felon" written on my job applications. I avoided speaking about my release to those around me. I became more isolated and felt depressed.

I dreaded going back to Mom and Dad, the alcohol and the retirement desert compound in Arizona, where I would spend my parole and possibly many years to come in my new 'prison.' I was maxed out on self-pity.

By November 14, at the beginning of my last week, the prison booked a flight for me from Oakland to Phoenix, changing planes in Salt Lake City. But I had to get to Oakland airport. Fortunately a former sannyasin in the Bay Area, who I vaguely knew from The Ranch, had contacted me in February, and agreed to pick me up. At least I would not be walking out alone.

In those last days I couldn't think of anything beyond the prison gate, without guards and chains and police escorts. I had been "escorted" for longer than I could remember, though it was only four years ago that the nightmare began. It was not over. There were two years of parole, which began as soon as I returned to Sun City West.

But, still, I would be out... exchanging one external prison for another.

Inside, though, I'm a little freer, starting to glimpse why and how I got hooked on god and cults and sex. At least that gives me more trust in myself and an unwillingness to just depend on some one else for answers.

But I dreaded the goodbyes: I'll avoid it for as long as I can. How can I leave them? In over nine hundred women, there are only two really "violent" ones, and they're just crazy. They belong in treatment.

SJ and I had the same "violent" custody level, and she was demonstrating signs of senility, recently diagnosed with Alzheimer's. How could she possibly do anybody any harm anymore?

One inmate had stomach cancer (which she had developed in prison). She thought her years of addiction and stress had probably caused it. She was dying and would not be released to her family. Another was an eighteen year old Columbian who was pressured into being a drug mule by her starving parents so they could feed their family of ten. Alone in a strange country and barely speaking English, she was handed a thirty-two year sentence, with no foreseeable parole.

I can hardly look at them, these days my heart is so heavy.

Nia was still serving her sentence. Jeanne had bad teeth, an ulcer and only wanted to go back to France, having no love for America. Unfortunately because she had a green card, she was not automatically deportable. She had to finish her ten-year sentence, and then it was uncertain whether or not she could go back.

Why not just deport her and save the taxpayers' money?

"Ah, cherie, eet's hopeless. I keep asking myself ze same zing," she said in my last conversation with her.

Then there was Zoe. My precious, big-hearted, loving Zoe. She was sentenced to twenty-five years because they couldn't catch her husband. She was fighting all the way. She encouraged me to be my own lawyer, as she was hers. She was preparing her appeal, and never stopped thinking positively. I was hurt and angry that she'd gotten such a severe sentence.

Short and shitty, lots of little things irritated me, as if I had PMS. I knew it was because I was sad to leave my friends, terrified of what it would be like outside, yet longing to be "free". Free was a concept that kept each of us going in this place. It continually amazed me that the "lifers" didn't commit suicide.

But, there was one valuable thing I carried with me: the newfound ability to believe in myself regardless of what "authority" thought of me. It took knocks, trauma and rejection plus the determination to see what had happened to me as an opportunity to learn something new about myself that finally changed me. I would be tested again and again. Almost nothing remained of my fantasy world outside. And I knew that as long as I breathed, I could meet the next challenge.

The day of release came. Tears came quickly as I hugged

Zoe and Jeanne. Snot was dripping from my nose and I looked at them bound by walls on all sides. I didn't want them to walk me across the compound. Zoe came anyway.

"It's going to be great for you, you'll see. And I'll be out there real soon. My appeal's going to work! I know it. Think of me. I'm counting on you to add your positive thoughts to mine!" she smiled at me with that strong, vibrant look in her eye.

I didn't know how to respond because I had a sinking feeling that I wouldn't see her for a long time. I smiled back with as much conviction as I could muster anyway.

"Zoe, I can't stand it! You shouldn't even *be* in here. I don't want to leave you here..." My voice trailed off.

Yet, I had to break away from her and go.

When your time is up, you can't just say you decided to stay.

I turned my back and walked hurriedly into the discharge area. I had to concentrate on just changing my clothes. They kept your 'discharge clothes' there, so you wouldn't smuggle anything out for anybody. I had 'packed out' the night before; delivered my bag with my legal papers, contact lens solution, one pair of prison issue glasses, the watch Georg had given to me that no longer worked because the battery had gone dead, a comb and tube of lipstick. My bag had already been searched thoroughly, and was waiting for me next to my clothes.

The scene of the nun leaving her convent, from *The Nun's Story* flashed briefly through my mind, burning into my memory.

First my jeans, new socks with my tennis shoes, a new shirt and black vest. Then, with my warm camel coat over one arm, the guard handed me my bag and walked ahead of me to my surprise for the first time in four years. Guards *always* walked behind prisoners.

At the guard booth they handed me my ticket and the remainder of my money, $53.47, which they made me sign a receipt for, and a paper with my picture and Cecilia Edwards on it to match my ticket name. Looking up I saw my friend waiting for me on the other side of the doors.

The same doors I walked in through, three years ago. I wonder if she thinks it looks like a hotel lobby.

I collected the papers and looked back toward the compound. There they were: Zoe and Jeanne, waving. Pain stabbed my heart as I waved with a weak smile.

God, how I love them...

Turning away, I started walking. My legs took over and my hands pushed the doors open.

I'm out.

The sunlight hit my face.

I had no idea on earth that the best was yet to come.

Chapter 18
Cool Water After the Burning: Now

You are born in pain, you live in fear, you die alone. Merry Christmas.
— *Old Scottish Christmas Greeting*

Saying goodbye to my friends and walking out through the prison gates with a small bag, I was still the "poor-me-model prisoner" boiling with rage, believing the world owed me a living after everything I'd suffered. Prison failed to rehabilitate my anger, and the pain that fueled it, which was hidden behind the dazzling sensation of surviving. My senses were overloaded, my body moving through the motions of getting into the car, riding to the airport. Sadness and despair, which was thick in the prison air, accompanied me. I tried to smile and look happy for the kind folks who'd come to pick me up, feeling I owed it to them for their generosity. I was confused. What was I supposed to do? How could I make a new life in a retirement community?

In those last days, getting up, going to work, exercising, having lunch, being in lock down. It was all clockwork, a ruthless efficiency of motion.

Prison *had* changed me. It stimulated my despondency and uselessness. Prison life was stamped on my body. Despite working out regularly, I stooped, and was more nearsighted and arthritic. I also believed that people would see "FELON" written all over me. I was harder, colder, more calculating if I thought I could get away with it. And still blaming somebody else.

As we rode to the airport, I was extremely uncomfortable. My thoughts were still being *extreme*. Prison didn't change that in anyone from what I observed. Punishment never does. It just forces the anger and rage underground. Some of the inmates were so full of anger, adopting bitter attitudes as easily as putting on clothes. Distorted thinking produces ideas that breed darkness, like tiny magnets full of negative electrical charges.

I judged people for what they'd done *to* me. I couldn't see the person, only the label. My hope of having a new life was shattered. Yet, the very events and traumas, which over time wore me down, started to break me wide open.

The inmates, many who had much longer sentences than I, showed me miracles did exist. Zoe and I had discussed this the night before I left. She sensed that in spite of my euphoria of being released, post prison life would be another long hard road, full of pitfalls.

"When I get out," she said, "I'll get a bomber jacket with my prison number stamped on my back, with the words, 'survivor' underneath. All of us can make it. This society forces us women to survive, one way or another."

"Yes," I said slowly. "You've given me so much hope and strength, Zoe, and I'll miss you."

She had worked bravely and tirelessly for her appeal, demonstrating it was possible to keep one's dignity, still be a lady and never give up.

Nia inspired me to believe in myself showing me how she took a horrible situation like her 20-year sentence, transforming her despair into serenity by channeling her worry into taking care of herself and others.

Jeanne gave me the gift of humor. She taught me that it's useless to mope as anxiety simply creates wrinkles; and that we are all in the same boat. This helped me let go of my "political prisoner" identity, which merely camouflaged my sanctimonious martyr routine. In my last year in prison, I finally stopped walking around thinking I was better than the drug mules or bank robbers or the grandmother in the cell next to me who allowed her son to use her house for drug deals. We were all prisoners to authority who did things for others so they would love us, regardless of the consequences.

Arriving at the San Francisco airport, I numbly said goodbye to my friends. The flight to Phoenix stopped over in Salt Lake City to change planes, and I blinked from the glare of the snow-covered tarmac. Like a sleepwalker in a dream, it felt very strange to be in a departure lounge and not in lock down in the middle of the day. Sitting in an uncomfortable chair, I waited for the connecting flight, which was delayed by a storm. Looking around, my eyes were filled with a glittering impression of lights and faces. I watched everyone with a heightened alertness I'd developed in prison. A woman in a tailored suit sat down next to me and smiled. I smiled back.

I bet that lady has no idea she's sitting next to a hardened criminal.

The announcer called for boarding.

Several hours later, arriving in Phoenix, Rachel was there to meet me. She'd visited me once briefly in prison and I was impressed then as now by her quiet confidence. She was a member of the group I had contacted when I was looking for someone on a spiritual path with whom I could correspond from prison. The group emphasized individual development and freedom, and I convinced myself it was different from Bhagwan's teachings. I imagined this connection would lessen the scariness of feeling so alone, providing me with like-minded folks when I got out.

Rachel had generously offered to pick me up, but instead of taking me home to my parents who were anticipating my arrival with dread and anticipation, she drove me to a group meeting. The pressure of trying to please and wanting to belong was stronger than the anxiety about my parents. I started acting out of my old habits, as if nothing had changed: terrified to say no because I'd look ungrateful.

Finally, Rachel took me home. Mom and Dad's appearance shocked me. Dad was bent over and had a lost look in his eyes I'd not seen before, while Mom was puffy-eyed and grossly drunk. Guilt and sadness filled me instantly: it was my fault that they had aged so much.

They were stunned that I hadn't called them since three days before leaving. Rachel left quickly.

"Hi," was all I said, hugging them.

Dad was silent for a second." We were waiting for you the whole day." His anger cut me.

"I couldn't call on the plane," I shot back irritated.

"Are you hungry?" was all Mom said. My anger blocked out her relief and joy of seeing me. Freed from prison, I was chained to the belief that I was to blame for *everything*. Overwhelmed, I went to bed.

The next day I was scheduled to meet my parole officer, Robert Johnston, for the first time. It took three hours by bus to get to Phoenix from Sun City West. I arrived in a sweat.

He was flawlessly dressed in a black suit, about half my age and very formal. Over the next two hours he reviewed my case, outlined my parole conditions, which included random urine tests for drugs, and told me I should try to find a job as quickly as possible.

How do I find a job when I have to put 'felony' on the applications? Because I intend to... No matter what anyone says. I can't lie about it.

"Let me know if you find work before I see you again next month because I plan to show up unannounced to check on you. I'll be visiting your home for the same reason. Have a good day."

I expected him to judge or yell at me, but all he did was

give me some simple commands: be good, don't do drugs and get a job.

I could not handle simple. This realization came to me one morning, as I prepared to leave for work at the local community center, which agreed to hire me. Dad asked me to pick up some mortadella at the Italian deli. He reminded me that last time I got confused and brought home baloney instead. Right away I felt he was putting me down for getting the two items mixed up.

"Why don't you do it yourself since you're the only one who knows which one's which?" I said nastily. He threw me a sideways glance, unabashed hurt in his eyes. Then he looked down and away, his shoulders shrunk and rounded.

"Ba-ba" was all he said. Translated it meant, 'I wish I could still do it and not have to rely on you to do things for me.'

Because I didn't want to see his humiliation, I assumed he was being critical. I went off in a huff, feeling persecuted, shaken up, trembling, righteous and downtrodden as usual.

I needed drama to feel alive.

There wasn't much drama in Sun City so I made up for it with suffering instead. Prison had been bad, but I couldn't have imagined this place to be so lifeless and sterile. The local community center offered me a receptionist job with low pay, which actually compensated for the fact that they did not seem to notice my felon status.

Work was my escape along with the weekly meetings of Rachel's group. This made Dad mad. Grumbling even when I went to the community center because he didn't want me to leave the house. He was losing his memory and falling down frequently. My guilt increased as my parents' health deteriorated. I feared something bad was going to happen to us, like being burnt alive by Mom's lit cigarette that often fell on the floor after she dozed off. Having to watch her more carefully, I discovered ashtrays under the bed along with half-empty bottles of liquor.

In the years that followed, I served my time on parole, was

a devoted member of the group and bitched at my parents for still treating me as their little girl. I cried for my lost youth and dreamt of returning to Europe as a call girl.

My job was merely a charade to pass the time. I was really waiting for death to save me. It was just around the corner, in the boredom and the futility of life in this walled-in-concrete-120-degree compound. The desolateness forced me to see the stark reality of an aging ex-prostitute felon with two masters' degrees earning $8.75 an hour, still trying to look like a girl in blond braids, which Mom blonded within days of coming home.

By 1997, I felt doomed. Even my spiritual group had become as regimented as everything else. Dad's health was worse. I had to make a move.

Through a friend I'd heard of a new spiritual community on the California coast and thought being near the ocean might help Dad. By that time I'd resigned to a life of caregiver, having completely given up searching for a relationship with a man.

I'm too old, too used up and who would want an ex-prostitute-felon anyway? After twenty years of anonymous sex and inconsequential liaisons, I probably couldn't have a real intimate relationship.

It was then that I met a man.

This time, it will be different. Finally, this relationship will save me from my depression.

He was very willing to help us all move, in spite of Dad's personality change, raging at everyone. Meanwhile, Mom and Dad continued to live for me and through me, loving me with a selfish, desperate love. Being the center of their universe made me think I was the center of everybody else's, and I was repeatedly surprised when other people didn't do what I wanted.

It was the startling impact of Dad's death in 1998 that forced me to see something about rejection. The only way he knew how to love me was to take care of me financially. As a kid I thought his absences were because I wasn't good enough, so I tried to ignore him (a pattern I repeated in all my relationships). Yet in the white-hot unbearable grieving, I saw clearly that he was *never coming back to me,* would never again be there to support me. He was perhaps the only man who had always loved me in spite of all the awful things I did. My reaction to his enormous love had been to shut him out. I became crazed with shame.

My mother died six years later.

By then I had joined and left the last spiritual group. I say left, but it was the severest of all rejections. I thought I had finally found a spiritual path in which I could be truly myself and accepted for who I was. No one told me why I couldn't be part of the inner circle. I could only suppose it was because of my prison record, which for once made all the difference.

I thought I was ready for Mom's death having finally accepted that she couldn't help her behavior. But no matter how much you think you're prepared for the death of a person who loves you so completely, you never really are. The loss of all that love is an immense hole that can't be imagined.

What happened next was a nasty surprise.

For years, I had been the complaining but dutiful daughter, trying to put my parents' needs before my own. A few months after Mom's death, I started to regain my equilibrium, ready to return to my work as an event manager, which I loved. Expecting to feel free from the demands of nursing the sick and finally ready to resume my life vigorously, my hip began to grind in pain. I found myself barely able to walk.

My old feelings of uselessness returned.

After all this time, who was I?

Depressed, again, I was still craving my old life.

I lived in this twilight world for a year after Mom's death. On the surface, I pretended to be brave. Inside I was drowning and I didn't care. Told I was too young for a hip replacement, I couldn't have sex because of the pain, and couldn't tolerate the pain medications. Nothing worked.

I would have to take responsibility for who I was and stop waiting for a saviour.

My dreams faded like sepia photos in my brain. Fantasies, not reality, had given my life meaning. They were merely painkillers, buffering me against the horrors of what I saw. The pretend identities were a large part of who I thought I was. My "stage names" of undercover agent, reporter, exotic dancer, courtesan and political prisoner made me feel like an actor. However, I got lost in all the roles I was playing.

But, my pretend world contained a dangerous element: denial. Experts say that extremism is both gender and race blind with denial as a common thread. Extremists are often very simple people, trying very hard to succeed. They have daydreams of glory, knowing that they will be punished if they don't measure up to society's demands. They are impressionable, often outcast, longing for approval.

I had all these attributes.

Groomed in the commune, I was ripe for the legalized sex industry. But what I saw as sacred and therapeutic blinded me from seeing the brutality and lies.

Pretending to be their dream girl I was really lying when I said I 'loved' the clients. I wanted their support, interest and money. My co-hookers and I were extremists, deceiving wives and girlfriends, which often fueled domestic violence and devastated families. Sometimes we read about the men we'd been with in the newspapers the day after. In Dublin prison, I met some of the wives who had committed acts of violence toward unfaithful partners, occasionally resulting in their husbands' death.

I conveniently translated my sex trade actions into liberation from my old, unenlightened, monogamous sexual conditioning. The more sex I had, the more I desired. Believing I was leading johns into sexual transformation, I used them, plying them with aphrodisiacs and wisdom, turning my interest on and off. Or I threw them away as convenient, if another guest came along. Or, I allowed *them* to throw me away.

Among my co-hookers were rich college kids, poor and

middle class teens, bored housewives, grandmothers, men and boys. We bartered sex believing deep inside us that god would rebuke us. But all we had to do was confess and be saved. And start all over again, not knowing how to stop the cycle.

Although we never labeled ourselves as martyrs, we endured continual damage on all levels. Physically there was persistent, demanding sex. Emotionally there was overwhelm: I had to be "on" all the time, I had to perform, watch what I said and did, remember who was who and what turned them on, and never betray any emotion other than utter ecstatic delight at their banalities. The better I acted, the more they believed me and paid me. Although they had different names, they were essentially the same to me. Their personalities didn't matter. I lusted only after their souls. I was going to make them holy. My bosses (pimps/madams) replaced my old gurus. But that loyalty was based on the same fear and need for approval. I was good at carrying out orders.

In this way, the client is dehumanized: he or she no longer exists as a person but is used just as she or he is being used. And using is what addicts (and extremists) do.

Sex, power and money are powerful addictions.

They are also the core motivators in people's lives.

Addiction is the force and the base motivation of extremism.

In prostitution, sex plus power and money equals the most deadly of addictions because it is such an unbeatable combination. I added religious conviction to the mix as a zealot prostitute whose aim was to appear as a pure virgin to the john.

Prostitution spilled out into my life and soaked away the boundaries removing the distinction that separated my work inside the bars, bordellos and the outside. I had to manipulate my bosses and clients while managing the priests, lawyers, police, government officials and God in my private life. I lived my life tiptoeing on their frustrations, resentments or rage, which if awakened would put me in danger. I was their commodity they could smash in an instant. They in turn had to perform their roles perfectly or I would punish them, withdrawing my favors.

I lived in insanity thinking that I was doing what every other modern woman did: barter sex for security, approval or nice things.

I had become like any other addict needing medication to handle the difficulty of living. But the drugs of sex, and religion didn't make things easier. They were crutches I chased because I believed both would give me ultimate clarity so I'd never have to seek anything again. At some promised juncture I would miraculously be transformed into the "ultimately-sexually-satisfied-spiritually-fulfilled-once-and-for-all-complete" human being.

This belief never happened, so it was time to stand-alone.

Scared and shaky, I gave up looking for someone or something to save me and started to slowly accept myself.

I didn't die or collapse.

A quiet change was taking place.

I was not special. Each day was just what it was: simple without labels. Sex was just sex: profound and good without having to act out a role on TV. The craving dimmed along with the belief that *next* time sex would be better, more intimate or more anything other than what it was. I stopped trying to be sexy, alluring and flirtatious, setting boundaries of what I could and would do. It was hard to be real and say what I meant instead of what others wanted to hear. But being indirect had been an avoidance of being responsible and accepting the consequences of my own actions.

It didn't matter what work I actually did as long as I was honest with myself. If one thing didn't suit me, I could leave graciously and find something else. I didn't have to be married to my job, nor be a prisoner to it.

My partner also changed. He had been a man's man and a ladies man. He wanted me, but he also wanted other women and cyber sex. For the first time in my life I refused to accept that. I said if you want to be with me, be committed to me. If you have trouble with that, find a program of recovery and work it. He did.

From that time on, I never stopped looking for what I felt was authentic. Each moment without judgments and expectations is a new adventure. I call this divine or god. It is an extension of myself connecting to everything and everyone around me, ever changing, reminding me that the only real fact in life is death when I will be utterly alone. I want to do it right because I won't get to do it over again.

The former basis of my life fell away, replacing that first set of beliefs when I was seven. I now see that:

#1. Suffering is victimhood. There is no heaven to get to. I can transform my pain, even physical pain, by understanding its message and doing what I need to do. I can meet it with the full force of my willingness NOT to be a victim.

#2. Bowing to authority is ignorance. No one has any real dominance over me unless I allow them.

#3 I am complete as I am. There is nothing "wrong" with me and nothing I can't do. It only takes belief to go beyond my limits.

#4. Nobody else's ideas are any better than mine. Some people may have more knowledge but I can learn whatever is necessary. The real discovery is what *I* think and feel about a situation.

#5. I live my life according to my inner guidance: what gives me deep joy and creates harmony, non-violently.

#6. Safety is what I give myself and not my imagined fear. Comfort means doing exactly what I want to do. It may feel a little risky because the outcome isn't known. Known outcomes are generally boring.

#7. Rich is how I live, not what I acquire.

#8. What's good for me is pretty much what's good for everybody. Goodness is goodness. When I'm full it overflows.

#9. When I'm giving to myself and act from what I know, not what I'm told to believe, there is no longer any desire for reward. The moment is so complete and plentiful.

#10. If something doesn't meet my expectations, it has *nothing* to do with the other person or thing. It has *entirely* to do with my seeing clearly what's in front of me and not what I'd like to be there. Living each day, revealing myself, talking plainly from my heart and experience, willing to learn from others - there is nothing left to hide.

So, here's this book written to share those things we were all taught to hide (like our fantasies); to be ashamed of (like our desires); to think of as sinful (like our lusts); to judge as a crime (like our addictions); and to believe is evil (like our murderous thoughts).

Gradually I knew that I could no longer keep these realizations hidden. We are all searching. There are no experts. All we have is someone's hand reaching out to us as we swim in this sea of uncertainty. Seeing my denial as the root of my addiction to prostitution and extremism, it became clear that the most practical way to navigate is for each of us to recognize our own extremist behaviors, owning them, educating and changing ourselves. One person at a time.

Discover it yourself.

It's a journey for all of us.

After her father's death, Samsara finally became a doctor, finishing her Ph.D. She created her own business and is still married to a wonderful man, in a relationship she describes as beyond her wildest dreams. She and her husband work on themselves with humor and sincerity.

Zoe was granted a Presidential pardon.

Nia received early release she was certain was due to her prayers.

Samsara's co-defendants are all involved in resourceful businesses, living in different countries around the world.

Puneet died in 2005, after being one of the longest living AIDs survivors.

Everyone else, as far as we know, is basically doing the same thing.

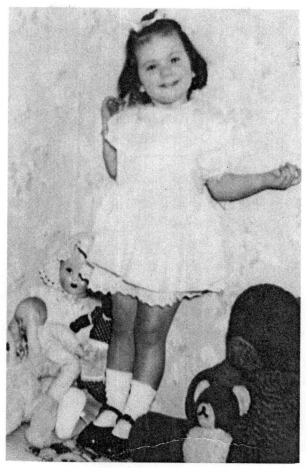

Samsara unconflicted

"Yes, I think that I have never looked for anything but truth...And I do not regret having given myself to Love." St. Therese, The Little Flower, September 30, 1897 moments before her death.

433865

Made in the USA